S0-AHE-334

Family Politics

Family Politics

The Idea of Marriage in Modern Political Thought

Scott Yenor

BAYLOR UNIVERSITY PRESS

Waco, Texas 76798

Jacket Design by Nita Ybarra, Nita Ybarra Design

Library of Congress Cataloging-in-Publication Data

Yenor, Scott, 1970-
Family politics : the idea of marriage in modern political thought / Scott Yenor.
p. cm.
Includes bibliographical references and index.
ISBN 978-1-60258-305-4 (hardback : alk. paper)
1. Marriage--History--19th century. 2. Marriage--History--20th century. 3. Families--History--19th century. 4. Families--History--20th century. 5. Political science--History--19th century. 6. Political science--History--20th century. I. Title.
HQ518.Y46 2011
306.809--dc22
2010020207

Printed in the United States of America on acid-free paper with a minimum of 30% pcw recycled content.

To Sarah, a survivor.

Table of Contents

Part IV

The Old Family and a New Nature

Preface

This book arises from my effort to understand the ambiguous place of the family in the modern liberal order. Marriage and family life seem to make up an institution—a tie that binds people and experiences together. It connects, among other things, spouses to one another, parents to children, sex to procreation, and procreation to parenthood. Modern democratic peoples, however, show a certain scorn for institutions or formalities, which means that the family is always subject to criticisms in keeping with the democratic spirit of our time. The family appears as an unsettled institution, leading many to question society's need for it.

We all know about the virtues and vices of families through our experiences with particular families, but our perceptions are not pure in and of themselves. Intruding between our experiences and reality are unstated assumptions and thoughts that help us to identify problems or happiness or virtues or excellences. This, I believe, is Plato's wisdom from *The Republic*'s book VII. We live in a cave, shrouded by opinions—and those opinions are the poetry of liberalism. I conclude in what follows that the language and categories of liberalism do not do justice to the experience of marriage and family life; we must move beyond liberalism's language and categories in order to understand and appreciate marriage and family life. *Family Politics* seeks to lay bare the poetry of liberalism as it relates to the family so we can move from opinions about the family to the reality of it.

Acknowledgments

It is customary to begin acknowledgments pages by crediting one's scholarly influences, but in my case a more powerful, personal experience deserves preeminence. As I was ready to begin a sabbatical at Boise State to begin work on this book, my daughter, Sarah, then five years old, was diagnosed with advanced stages of cancer. Her two-year battle, through cancer treatments and their baleful side effects, ended successfully and quite possibly (as I think) miraculously, thanks in part to the dedicated and gifted staff of doctors and nurses at St. Luke's Hospital in Boise.

As I stared at Sarah's face as she lay helpless and almost breathless, encouraging her to "take one more deep breath for Daddy"; or as my wife, Amy, spent countless hours harnessing Sarah's strength for her own good; or as we told this five-year-old girl that she had cancer and was going to be very sick, and perhaps die, the often hidden reality and responsibility of parenthood became the urgent stuff of everyday life. In the midst of all this sickness, the wonderful news of the arrival of Mark, our fifth child, into the world forced us to look simultaneously at each of life's gates and marvel at our smallness. It is impossible that my views on the family were not affected by, and, I think, reinforced by, these experiences. The central ideas of this work were formulated before Sarah took ill, though I think I understand what it means to love another human being better than I did before I undertook this enterprise. Countless friends and family helped out in large and small ways during Sarah's illness. I hesitate to mention any by name, but special thanks goes out to Adrian and Ramona Johnson, Amy's parents, for putting their lives on hold to serve, in effect, as parents for our other boys during many critical days and nights. Though those days haunt Amy and me, we remember all your kindnesses in those darkest times. This explains why my first book is dedicated to my only daughter.

A word, perhaps, about surviving such an experience can capture the importance of the professional help I am about to gladly acknowledge. After Sarah was officially in remission, I read, for the first time, Whittaker Chambers' classic *Witness*. In the book's conclusion, Chambers described his attitude toward life after his famous confrontation with Alger Hiss.

> The Hiss Case has turned my wife and me into old people—not a disagreeable condition. . . . Repeatedly, in the last autumn of unseasonable warmth, my wife has drawn me out to stand with her among our gardens, once so pleasant, now overgrown with weeds, because, as we say, neither of us really fooling the other, we no longer can find time to tend them. It is not time we can find. Repeatedly, my wife has planned what we must do to bring them back to life. We do not do it. I do not think we shall unless time itself can lift from us the sense that we have lived our lives and the rest is a malingering.

That, in many ways, is the most insightful description of the prospects Amy and I faced after Sarah confronted cancer.

We do not share *all* of that malingering sense of having already passed through the only trial that matters or of living a life whose energy has been spent. This is partly because time and others have lifted us from that sense of just malingering. It is also, for me, because at the end of the trial was an ambition provided by this book. My career and my life would have been very different had I not received timely support to complete this book after Sarah's treatments. I may never have recommenced the work that led to this book without the generous jumpstart provided by Fred Miller, Ellen Paul, and Jeff Paul at the Social Philosophy and Policy Center at Bowling Green University. When Sarah contracted West Nile virus, they graciously accommodated my unique personal situation and allowed me to postpone my fellowship. When I arrived, I benefited from the outstanding environment, which allows for concentrated work, that they have set up for visiting scholars. I consider those days and nights at the SPPC to be among the most productive and happiest of my professional career, in part because I benefited from the prodding of persistent colleagues, including Alan Gibson, Fernando Teson, and Doug Rassumussen, who encouraged me to take the book beyond the history of ideas into the realm of philosophy. Upon my return to Boise State, I used my long-delayed sabbatical and a generous and timely grant from the Earhart Foundation to complete the manuscript and to do my best to get the family right. Many thanks to Boise State President Robert Kustra, Provost Sona Andrews, and my chairman, Ross Burkhart, for their willingness to leave my sabbatical floating during my daughter's illness, and to my colleagues generally, for their support as I helped nurse Sarah. Mike Andrews and his colleagues at the Jack Miller Center have also helped immensely as I undertook to convert my manuscript into a book and fill a huge gap in professional development. Professor Bradley Watson's invitation to give a lecture on the family in a liberal society at St. Vincent's College's Center for Political and Economic Thought proved to be a godsend, because it forced me to clarify my argument.

My career and life would also have been very different had I not been blessed with wonderful teachers and mentors. Professor Peter C. Myers introduced me to the world of political philosophy when I was an undergraduate at the University of Wisconsin–Eau Claire. To this day, I think of Peter as a model of a scholar—sober, moderate, taking account of the wisdom in widely held opinions. I continue to count on his judgment in many important questions facing my life. Following Peter's advice, I attended his alma mater at Loyola University Chicago. Discussions among graduate students and with the articulate and attentive teachers at Loyola provided an invigorating environment to advance my education. Among my teachers there, Professor John W. Danford taught me invaluable lessons in how to be a serious teacher, a scholar, a gentleman, and a good family man. John's model has been central to my career and my life and for that I am grateful beyond measure, and my wife also learned more than a little from his wife, Dr. Karen Danford. I am grateful to Professor Tom Engeman for his great insight about philosophic texts and about the American experience, and to Professor Ray Tatalovich for his support throughout my graduate career and beyond.

My special thanks, on this project specifically, to Pete Myers, Michael Zuckert, Fernando Teson, Doug Rassmussen, R. J. Pestritto, Stewart Gardner, Greg Hill, John Freemuth, Jeffrey Church, John Danford, Karen Danford, Christopher Kelly, Ralph Hancock, Nick Lantinga, Will Jordan, John Whittaker, Wesley Jessup, Travis Cook, Grayson Gilmore, Baylor's readers, and others for reading and providing critical insights into portions of the book. Thanks to all for saving me from errors, infelicities, and future embarrassments. I do not know that any of the aforementioned agrees with the book's overarching argument, but all helped me improve it. Carey Newman's faith in this project helped me bring it to a relatively swift and painless conclusion, and his staff at Baylor University Press proved helpful at every turn.

My greatest and most unpayable debt is to my parents, Bruce and Jackie Yenor. Please know that I take the family seriously in part because you did. To my five children—Jackson, Travis, Sarah, Paul, and Mark—please know that I never can fully put into practice what I teach in this book, but hopefully you, someday, will do a better job than I have. Finally, my wife lived with me through all of these trials and served as a model of wifely and motherly love, and then, after the trial, she provided me the necessary space to complete this book. We have been lifted from the trial, and have much work to do, and we will walk down that path, to a garden, together.

Chapter 1

Nature, Marital Unity, and Contract in Modern Political Thought

The Western world is experiencing unprecedented changes in how families act and in how they think of themselves. Well-documented declines in birth and marriage rates along with increases in divorce rates, illegitimacy rates, the incidence of couples living together outside marriage, and the number of people living alone bespeak a remarkable change in attitudes about children, procreation, sex, love, marriage, parenthood, and life itself. What Francis Fukuyama describes as the "great disruption" has brought us a new world—attempts to resurrect the old world seem doomed to failure and fraught with selective nostalgia.

There is broad agreement that marriage and family life are being transformed, yet there are widely different evaluations of what that transformation means for marriage and family life. Some see the new family as a victory for genuine love, equality, affection, intimacy, and a freedom from predetermined family roles.[1] Others see it undermining genuine love, fostering inequality, resting on unstable emotional ties, depriving children of the stable family life that fosters responsible liberty, and contributing to various adult pathologies.[2] Our failure to reach consensus about the meaning of family life, magnified as we face controversies over abortion, same-sex marriage, a decline in birth rates, and new fertility technologies, is cause for deep concern. At stake in these controversies is the future of marriage and the family,[3] or, to be precise, the end of the family—end in the sense of its meaning or purpose and end in the sense of its continued existence.

Changes in laws and social expectations surrounding the family are part of a trend known, for brevity's sake, as *modernity*.[4] Modern individuals see themselves as persons independent of unchosen duties such as many of those associated with family life; history seems to be on the side of emancipating individuals progressively from impositions of society and nature. We seem to be working out the logic of consent, equality, and freedom—ever reconstituting the family to match modern ideas better. The conjugal or nuclear family, for instance, centered around monogamous marriage, represents an advance in individual liberty beyond the cramping extended family, and today's family seems to be moving beyond conjugality, beyond monogamy, and beyond heterosexuality by securing greater individual choice in and out of marriage.[5] Modern marriage's emphasis on consent provides more space for personal choice than arranged marriages, and now marriage is being redefined as any close personal relationship of one's own choosing.[6] Yesterday's emphasis on consent in marriage acknowledges female equality, and today's aspirations to build a gender-neutral society and to encourage mothers to work outside the home seem to take that equality another step. Today's freedom to divorce offers more options than the past's indissoluble marriage, and barriers to exit have been removed as society moves from fault-based conceptions of separation and as governments offer greater public support for divorcees and erode the distinction between married and unmarried couples.[7] As modernity progresses, marriage seems less a social institution centered on raising children or fulfilling a communal purpose than a personal relationship between consenting adults. Aspirations for independence and self-sufficiency have led us to see marriage's mutual dependence, childhood dependence, and human interdependence as somehow degrading.

The reconstitution of family life is not confined to precincts of family law. Public policies often encapsulate a view of marriage and family life—its strengths and weaknesses, its capacities and limits. Responsibilities and functions long central to family life and marriage have, in modern times, been exported to other institutions so family life and marriage better reflect the image of personal independence. Government-run school systems are built, in part, on the assumption that parents should not educate their own children or are ill equipped to choose schools for their children.[8] Social welfare support for the aged, a staple public policy in Western societies, implies that children are freed from the burden of providing assistance for their elderly parents and that elderly parents desire to be free from dependence on their unreliable children. Government aid for dependent children in most Western countries is dispensed in a way that undercuts the need for mothers and fathers to provide joint care for children.[9]

The best public account of where the transformation in marriage and family life seems to be heading appears in "Beyond Conjugality" (2001), the recommendations for legal reform offered in the wake of Canada's national debate about same-sex marriage.[10] The authors of the report claim to see through the heterosexual, two-person *form* of conjugality to its *substance*: sharing a shelter, conducting sexual or personal interactions, providing mutual access to services, sharing social activities, and receiving public sanction for the validity of one's relationship. If this is what marriage is, laws have unjustly limited access to it.[11] More troubling for the authors is the way Canada's under-inclusive conception of marriage has limited autonomy and equality. The report defines autonomy as the "freedom to choose whether and with whom to form close personal relationships." Equality has two aspects: "relational equality" or the same treatment between different kinds of relationships and "equality within relationships."[12] The state's role in close personal relationships is twofold: providing adequate "legal mechanisms for people to be able to achieve . . . private understandings" in forming and dissolving relationships; and respecting "the values . . . [of] equality, autonomy and choice" among and within relationships. Replacing restrictive marital conjugality, domestic partnerships—whether a husband and wife sharing an abode, a mother living with a needy son, a same-sex couple, two sisters living together, or even a group of roommates—can be registered with the state to enjoy the benefits of "voluntariness, stability, certainty, and publicity."[13]

This report and the policies and attitudes that go with it signal a change in the ends of marriage, if not the end of marriage. No longer concerned principally with the status of children, preparing men and women for lives of self-control and lifelong love, structuring a mutual aid community between husbands and wives, or, generally, intense communal goals, the goals of marriage are sharing affections, supporting individual fulfillment, providing mutual support, accessing public services, and expressing compatibility. While this revolution remains controversial, a survey of law and opinion suggests that the view of marriage as an egalitarian, private relationship created by and for a couple (or group) is taking hold in Western societies.[14] "Beyond Conjugality" works out the ineluctable logic of modern marriage.

John Witte's *From Sacrament to Contract* treats another aspect of the long-term trend in modernity. Marriage has changed from a sacrament formed under the authority of the church to being a "voluntary bargain struck between two parties who wanted to come together into an intimate association."[15] When the contract model displaced the sacramental tradition, most societies maintained the power to shape the contract to secure the ends of marriage concerning the procreation and nurturing of children, and they even, for a time at least, borrowed the attributes of marriage (such as indissolubility and monogamy) from canon law. Today we are moving from a socially determined contract to a more limited joint venture for ends determined by the individuals themselves. Early Enlightenment ideas of marriage as a contract for the purposes of procreation, mutual support, and protection are giving way to a new understanding of "open marriage" wherein "the meaning of marriage . . . must be independently forged by a man and a woman who have the freedom to find their own reasons for being and being together. . . . Only by writing their own open contract can couples achieve the flexibility they need to grow."[16] Though marriage was once defined by forces such as the church, state, or society, today's couples choose the ends and depth of their marriage. Marriage and family life provide individual satisfaction, and the capacity to achieve goals beyond those chosen by the individual diminishes. This trend marks the disenchanting of the family and its goals and the triumph of our effort to define the nature of our intimate relationships for ourselves.

Both narratives—one emphasizing the emergence of independence and the other the disenchantment of marriage—lead to the displacement of a sacramental or socially defined understanding of marriage and family life by a secular conception emphasizing individual choice, autonomy, self-sufficiency, and equality.

Voices of retrenchment have dogged advocates of personal independence at nearly every step of the way.[17] Early returns from today's revolution in marriage and family life suggest that, when marriage is designed mostly for adult autonomy, children do not do as well and society experiences higher crime rates, lower levels of educational achievement, lower birth rates, and other social ills.[18] Today's voices of retrenchment, worried about inflated claims on behalf of adult autonomy, defend marriage and family life in the name of the older contractual ideal, in which the core public purpose of marriage is the good of children.[19] Marriage is a social construct, according to these voices, but the construct requires a relatively long-lasting, monogamous, and perhaps heterosexual form to accomplish its child-centered goals. While these voices favor modifying the traditional nuclear family to make greater room for female equality, diversity of family form, and the modern acceptance of divorce, the new nuclear family would hold the attention of adults long enough to give kids a healthy head start.[20] The long-term, adverse social effects of family dissolution—effects felt predominantly by innocent children—suggest that the state should promote quality family life, marriage formation, and familial stability.

We seem left with two incompatible approaches. Either domestic partnerships are venues for the exercise of equality and autonomy in close personal relationships or marriage and family life are social institutions designed for the procreation and nurturing of children. The more social goals such as the procreation and education of children define family life, the more advocates of autonomy see inequality and limits on human choice. The more advocates of autonomy emphasize individual choice, the more marriage and family life are disabled from achieving serious public purposes. We seem to have another insoluble iteration of the conflict between the individual and society.

I do not think that either side in this debate fully captures the *communal* character of marriage and family life, and this book attempts to prepare the way for a richer treatment of marriage as a union and of family as a community. Modern advocates of autonomy and personal independence distort the satisfactions of marriage into personal satisfactions. They underestimate how genuinely satisfying marital love creates mutual dependence that limits human autonomy and fail to see how marriage and family life are satisfying because they involve this love and dependence. Modern voices of retrenchment treat marriage and family life as social institutions; they do not appreciate or articulate the glue that holds marriages and families together. Those emphasizing marriage as a social institution must recognize how marriage brings personal satisfaction and is connected to the good of love. Those emphasizing autonomy in marriage must recognize how satisfaction is tied up with the indispensable social goods produced by marriage and family life and the dependency-making experience of love. The *communal* understanding of marriage combines the two conceptions by showing how the personal satisfaction in marriage is bound up with the social goods that marriage produces.

Marital Community, Contract, and the Dialogue of Autonomy and Retrenchment

Today's "war over the family" is a war of visions,[21] a battle of ideas in a longer war among greater, deeper thinkers—the "generals" in the conflict—

that shapes how we view the world. These "generals"—thinkers as diverse as John Locke, Jean-Jacques Rousseau, G. W. F. Hegel, John Stuart Mill, Emile Durkheim, Sigmund Freud, and Simone de Beauvoir—bring conflicting theoretical perspectives to their teachings on the family; they treat today's contested concepts of consent, equality, liberty, and love in deeper frameworks because they find it necessary to define and defend their arguments against the serious alternative presented by communal marriage and family life. We cannot see how much today's family "wars" take for granted until we canvass the deeper modern debate over how to reconcile family with an order dedicated to individual liberty and human equality.

Revisiting these modern philosophers reveals the contours of the communal marriage and family life that modern peoples have slowly displaced. Participants in today's controversy characterize the traditional vision of family life as "patriarchal" and "rigid" or child centered, concerned with property, or connected to an agricultural mode of production.[22] Examination of these deeper thinkers reveals that these are secondary or ancillary attributes cohering around a communal vision of marriage and family life. The "sexual division of labor," restrictions on divorce, an emphasis on children, and a family's communal property arrangements are intelligible elements of a unified marriage and family life. At their deepest, today's family wars are debates over whether we should maintain elements such as monogamy, conjugality, permanence, sex differences in marriage, heterosexuality, and the privileged place of children as elements of unified marriage. The problem is that participants in today's controversies criticize or defend attributes that are elements of marital unity without linking them to marital unity; the parts are abstracted from the whole. The result is that these attributes are not understood in the proper context or they are detached from their *raison d'etre*. Detached from the vision that lends them meaning, these attributes appear as low-hanging fruit to be plucked by advocates for autonomy. The deepest modern thinkers do not share this blind spot, though they are, often and for good reasons, critics of marital unity.

Let us ascend to first principles. Debates about the status of marital unity reflect a deep disagreement about the nature of human society. In the classical conception, the household is the fundamental unit of society—the temporally prior unit from which political life grows. In the modern conception, the individual appears to be the fundamental unit of society—the unit that contributes and consents to the building of all other units. Let us investigate these competing fundamental ideas.

The idea that the family is the fundamental unit of society suggests that the family is a unit or unity and that its members, in a significant sense, subsume their identities in the marriage or family as they form a community. Marriage unites individuals, satisfying their needs for belonging and love and reflecting an aspiration to serve something higher than self. The union of two in marriage creates a third thing, the married couple.[23] The quintessential expression of marital union is seen in the Christian idea that "two shall become one flesh."[24] This view consists with the fact that a man and a woman unite in the sexual act to create a child, so that the two literally become one flesh in the person of the child. No knife in the world is sharp enough to separate what in a child belongs to a father from what belongs to a mother; children are living testimonies to the unity and love shared by a husband and wife.[25] The idea of two becoming one also expresses an understanding of marital love containing two distinct moments that are reconciled in a third. The first moment of love is a thirst, a sense of inadequacy and longing reflecting the reality that one finds individual existence insufficient. The second moment is the discovery of someone with whom one feels contented and satisfied. The third moment, the moment of genuine love, involves the giving of oneself to another in order to forge a deep, long-lasting common destiny with the other. What comes of this third moment is a heightened discovery of self that accompanies the donation of one self to another. That two become one in love is a profound mystery. This form of love, different from though encompassing affection, mutual support, care, and erotic desire, is the experience representing the beauty and perils of marital unity; this understanding of love captures the experience of a happy, satisfying marriage. We must not get bogged down, as many of today's voices of retrenchment tend to, identifying which socially desirable goods marriage promotes. The love experienced in a marriage union is a human good.[26] It reflects the idea that marriage and family life are competitors for a person's allegiance, competitors that do not simply serve other goods such as the political community, philosophy, religious devotion, or anything else. The mutual love and heightening of self experienced in the marital union give human beings deep, untold joys. Any attempt to understand such love as a means to other desirable ends fails to do justice to the experience.[27]

As a matter of law, marital unity means that the identity of each individual is melded into a new being, so the interests and destinies of the married couple are difficult to disentangle. David Hume, arguing against divorce, defends this idea of marital union. "Nothing," writes Hume,

> is more dangerous than to unite two persons so closely in all their interests and concerns, as man and wife, without rendering the union entire and total. The least possibility of a separate interest must be the source of endless quarrels and suspicions. The wife, not secure of her establishment, will

> still be driving some separate end or project; and the husband's selfishness, being accompanied with more power, may be still more dangerous.[28]

Marital union implies the mutual dependence of spouses. Mutual dependence involves the sharing or pooling of resources, a sense that one's own time is also the family's time or a spouse's time, and a mutual dedication to a deeply held common good. The idea that marriage establishes a single unit persists in law and opinion in various ways. The vast majority of married women assume their husband's surname as an expression of marital unity, though there is no legal requirement to do so.[29] Many things pass between husbands and wives—property, information—without government recognizing it as a transaction. Husbands and wives acquire assets together, give gifts to one another, and use assets in common—"all in serene disregard of such notions as title and without keeping track of the precise contributions each has made."[30] Spousal privilege protects confidential communications between a husband and wife, for the purpose of maintaining harmony and trust and because husbands and wives are much more likely to lie for one another, rendering their testimonies unreliable. The thinking behind these legal recognitions and cultural norms of mutual dependence and unity is that marriage melds a couple's interests and lives so tightly that neither is simply an individual any longer. Perhaps Hegel characterizes this vision best: "The precise nature of marriage is to begin from the point of view of contract . . . *in order to supersede it*."[31] Much contemporary social science supports Hegel's view, seeing in marriage a transformative event.[32]

While the idea of marriage as a union persists in law and opinion and in the lived experience of married couples, it is waning as an ideal and as a way of understanding marital experience.[33] Modern thinkers offer a trenchant critique of marital and familial unity. Families that are too unified are problematic for the establishment of rational self-government because they do not prepare children well for the exercise of independence and liberty. Such families may also cultivate in children a politically dangerous spirit of obedience too easily associated with arbitrary patriarchal government. Unified families could be established by arranged marriages, which promise that the flighty young are subjected to a father's rule of reason, but which can form in opposition to love, affection, and fidelity. Marital unity creates risky dependencies and dangerous inequalities. Dependence is sown in the idea of marital unity and love, where one's identity and interests are joined to another's. Inequalities come about because when families and a married couple become one, someone must represent the family unit and that has, historically, been the husband.

The dependence and, perhaps, the inequality characteristic of a unified family are problematic in light of our emphasis on natural independence and equality. Unified families bind individuals together and encourage them to forget themselves while serving others, seem suited to environments in which people accept authority from outside themselves, and seem linked to the idea that human beings are born to the unchosen dependencies and inequalities of the household. In contrast, modern thinkers emphasize that families and legitimate acts generally arise from consensual acts of free individuals, and that independence should remain accessible after consent has formed the relationship. According to such principles, people no longer forget themselves while giving themselves to others; they only lend themselves to others as they establish an alliance for specified goals. Devotion to others declines as the people realize the importance of human individuality.[34] The idea of contract captures the modern sense of marriage and family life. Contracts are agreements entered into by individuals to serve their mutual interests. Parties to a contract expect to be better off as a result of what the contract requires them to do and what it requires others to do for them.[35] Parties are not transformed in contractual relationships, and marriage as contract seems to maintain the ideal of personal independence. When the marriage bargain is determined by society, it seems men give protection and support to women in return for regular sexual access. Today's contractual ideal allows individuals to design a contract's terms. In any event, contractual families are associations structured around individual needs and desires, apart from models handed down from tradition, and they last as long as the needs and desires they serve. When individuals are the fundamental units of society, the family's form is a product of human choice, its goals determined by the individuals, and its future subject to changes in how individuals perceive their needs.

The range of devotion and unity narrows over the course of modern life, as law and opinion adopt ideas implied in marriage as a contract. The predominance of ideas such as independence, freedom, equality, and consent obscure the experience of unity, and modern peoples tend to shoehorn dependency-making relationships into a liberal framework. At their least revolutionary, modern people (such as the contemporary voices of retrenchment mentioned above) think of marriage and family life as means to important biological ends, though our actions often betray these thoughts about the centrality of biology; it is not biology alone but love that draws us to the family. Modern people tend to justify marriage in terms of self-interest rightly understood,[36] though again it seems that this does not do justice to our self-giving and continuing experiences of marital unity. Marital unity has not disappeared from human experience—it may be a "dream that refuses to die."[37] The wide acceptance of ideas of contract, independence, and equality has made it difficult to conceive of and appreciate intrinsic goods associated with marital unity. We characterize remaining experiences of marital unity with anachronistic terms such as "self-sacrifice" and "traditional marriage," or we say that marriage serves "collective interests" (as opposed to selfish interests), or that it promotes our subjective preferences, or we justify marriages as promoting economies of scale. We seem to lack, if not the experience of marital unity, a viable language with which to articulate it.

Neither the language of unity nor the ideology of contract is sufficient to explain the place of marriage and family in human life. Unified marriage and family life terminates at some point, for family life is not an all-sufficient human good. Children are freed from family control to become independent people. Identities of husbands and wives are complex mixtures of elements, including, but not limited to, marriage and family. Family life depends, to different degrees, on outside agencies for economic goods, wage and labor, religious life, police protection, and other goods, which shows that family life must be situated in political life. Ideas of contract, on the other hand, fail to account for the inevitable dependence and limits on consent entailed in marriage and family life and how marriage transforms the couple. Relations between parents and children cannot easily or entirely be conceived in terms of consent, contract, or individual rights. Children are born to an unchosen web of dependencies or at least an unchosen condition. Children do not choose particular parents, nor parents particular children; and children are, for a time, dependent on parents for their care and nurturance. Parental care of children calls for (what may appear to be) uncompensated sacrifices. Consent withdrawn from marriage (i.e., divorce) leaves adults whole, in theory, as they return to the *status quo ante*, but removal of consent from parenthood is a crime and there is no *status quo ante* to which children return.

The dialogue between today's advocates of autonomy and retrenchment forces us to recognize this clash between different conceptions of society, nature, and marriage.[38] This deeper dialogue between emphases on human dependence and independence is sown in the nature of things; neither experience can be blotted out and neither can or should emerge completely victorious. Modern societies long maintained a flexible, prudent balance among these different views of nature and marriage. Today's intellectual trend is away from the idea of marital unity and toward the idea of marriage as a contract and away from the idea of nature as implicating dependencies and toward the idea of marriage made in the image of natural independence and equality. This book aims to reorient contemporary debate about marriage and family life by placing it within the dialogue between contract and autonomy on one hand and unity and salutary dependencies on the other. Marriage and family life exist on a continuum with the communal family and marital unity on one side and the personally independent family (aided by the state) on the other. Marriage and family life existing only at either pole will cause political, social, and personal problems. The question is not whether marriage should conform either to the model of marital unity or marriage contract; it is, rather, how can married individuals blend their independence and contract thinking with the continuing experience of dependence and unity. By putting forward this analytical framework, I hope to show voices of retrenchment the web of meaning in which to understand their arguments and findings. Defenders of the family must take a higher road and move beyond biological or social defenses of the family, and this involves the risky move of articulating the human goods, especially the good of love, served by marital unity. Advocates of autonomy and independence must also understand and respect the limits within which their principles operate so that they can appreciate the unique goods served by family life.

I aspire to provide an account of the modern family in the spirit of Tocqueville's treatment of modern democracy. The "art of the legislator," Tocqueville writes, consists in discerning the tendencies of human societies in order to counteract them and slow them down so that we can maintain democratic society over the long haul.[39] If I had been born in an age when human beings saw only the goods associated with family life (such as the moment in preclassical Greece, perhaps), I might be tempted to insinuate ideas about the goodness of independence, human equality, philosophy, or devotion to God to temper their ardor and limit the power of the family. We live in a time taken with ideas of natural equality, independence, and human power and one in which the alternatives to those principles are difficult to appreciate. In such a time, it is necessary to locate the goodness that lies in dependence and the human goods to which it is connected.

Recognizing the endurance of unified marriage and family life would force us to restructure debates about marriage and family life. Consider a contemporary example, the debate about same-sex marriage. Advocates of same-sex marriage often justify their arguments by showing how same-sex marriage is consistent with the thinnest conception of marriage as a contract maintaining personal independence and equality or with the subversive attempt to bring about the end of marriage.[40] Even the "conservative case for same-sex marriage," which promises to reinvigorate marriage institutions by bringing serious gay couples into the fold, adopts a thin conception of marriage.[41] Opponents of same-sex marriage generally offer two kinds of arguments. One emphasizes the centrality of child-bearing to marriage as a social institution, suggesting that efforts to further separate marriage from procreation implicit in the case for same-sex marriage will have further detrimental effects on an already troubled institution.[42] Others emphasize the communal character of marriage and argue that only the heterosexual, procreative form represents the communion of purpose that is marriage.[43] If my framework is correct, marriage serves serious, time-intensive, resource-intensive, emotionally intense communal ends. Among these communal ends is child-rearing, but there may be no reason to limit marriage to only that communal end. Advocates of same-sex marriage must show that same-sex marriage is consistent with a standard emphasizing the communal character of marriage. Marriage is more than a social institution for child-rearing, and its ends may go beyond, or be other than, procreative love. Opponents of same-sex marriage must show that the communal goals that could be asserted by same-sex marriage advocates are either illusory or outside of marriage's ends.

The debate goes well beyond same-sex marriage toward often ignored, more difficult questions. To what extent do modern peoples desire the unified family and communal marriage? What arrangements are likely to be consistent with this time- and resource-intensive community? What communal ends does the family serve in modernity?

The Book's Plan

Times of confusion and revolution, while disruptive to social life and often harmful to individuals, are invitations to return to first principles and reassess the costs and virtues of shaken institutions. We live in such a time of confusion and revolution with respect to marriage and family life. Few generations have needed to answer the following questions more than ours: Why does marriage exist? Why do families exist? Is the family a valuable human end to be served by other institutions? Is it a means necessary for us to secure other valuable human ends? What is the character of the love and responsibility supporting family life? Is the family still necessary in the modern world? If so, for what goods is it indispensable and for what goods is it a dispensable means? Is family life an essential ingredient of human happiness? For whom is family life most suited and for whom is it least suited?

Concerns about the health of the family hearken back (at least) to the 1600s and the birth of the modern nuclear family. Sympathetic concern about the bourgeois, nuclear, contractual family is present at the creation of the modern family in the thought of Locke. Critics of the nuclear, bourgeois family emerge initially from the Right in the name of traditional, more unified family and character development and later also from the Left in the name of greater equality and personal liberation. Many contemporary advocates and scholars pay little heed to this past and hence underestimate the inherent costs in the different ways of structuring family life, not understanding how the qualities we promote through marriage and family life undermine other, often equally valuable qualities we seek. The effects of this regrettable historical amnesia are that we lack perspective on contemporary problems and we attempt to adhere to ideological principles without an appreciation for the tension-filled and complex reality to which these principles must correspond. The modern family, like the modern world, seems to be entering what might be called the postnuclear era. What this future holds can be anticipated only if we remember the ends served by the nuclear family and the residual experience of marital and familial unity.

One of the difficulties in providing an account of the family in modern thought involves determining which thinkers to treat. In any treatment of this sort many great thinkers must be excluded, and I have chosen not to treat the thought of Mary Wollstonecraft, Tocqueville, or Charles Darwin. My criteria involve a compromise between significance or influence, excellence or philosophic seriousness, and representation. Take my choice to consider Hegel's treatment of the family. Hegel is not famous for reflections on family life, yet his profundity of insight and his out-of-season meditations on marital unity and on the prerequisites for marital and familial unity are unparalleled in modern thought. It is necessary to understand why he thought what he thought and why his thoughts are rejected if we are to understand the trajectory of modern thinking on the family. I treat Comte and Durkheim, two French sociologists, because they are representative of social science positivism, a prominent approach to understanding the family and its relation to the society, yet these thinkers remain influential today for their method as much as for the content of their thought. Freud, whose writings partake of social science positivism and whose historical research appears so derivative, is included because of the immense influence he wielded on how we think about the family, though some aspects of his thought may not pass the laugh test.[44]

I treat the major modern thinkers chronologically, for the most part.[45] A mostly chronological treatment is the best way to bring out the reasons for the eclipse of marital and familial unity. Modern thinking turns on themes such as nature, our ability to discern nature, the ends of marriage, the meaning and extent of consent, the promise and perils of divorce, the obstacles to sound family life, and the characteristics of marriage and family life. Let me discuss the trajectory of modern thought on the family by tracing two of these themes, starting with the modern approach to nature. Modern thinkers on the family depend on an understanding of nature generally and human nature in particular. Over time, they become ever more skeptical of our ability to found teachings of the family on an understanding of nature. Further, the modern conception of nature proves too unstable to ground family life and this forces us to reassess what we mean by nature. Beginning with Locke (chapter 2), the family is seen as a social institution designed to meet the challenges of nature's givens (the long dependence of children and a woman's longish, debilitating period of pregnancy). Nature, for Locke, appears as a set of constraints of which family life takes account. Rousseau (chapter 3), one of Locke's greatest critics, argues that the "givens" Locke identifies are characteristic of social man, not natural man, and hence family life, for Rousseau, need not be built around Locke's specific understanding of nature's givens but around what he sees as the real aspects of nature relating to sex differences between men and women. Hegel (chapter 4), building on the insights of Rousseau, draws a more radical conclusion, namely that most things of value are the product of human history. History is the venue through which man acquires rationality, recognition, freedom, and self-consciousness, and all of these desiderata arise from man's confronting and overcoming nature through labor; nature seems to be left behind. Yet, when it comes to the family, Hegel suggests that History's accomplishment of a genuine marital love depends on the continuation of nature in the form of sex differences (among other things) that make marital love possible and just. The French sociologists Comte and Durkheim (chapter 5) dwell in Hegel's shadow as they enunciate a dynamic account of sociological change built on a static conception of natural sex differences. Beauvoir (chapter 9) finishes what Rousseau, Hegel, and others, in a sense, start, in that her feminism is based on a dismissal of nature as mere immanence and an embrace of human creativity and transcendence as the genuine goods toward which human beings aspire. Beauvoir seeks to extricate human freedom from the immanence of nature, and this leads to a thicket of problems, not the least of which is a contempt for the human body and the wishing away of human limits.

This is the dynamic of nature that rocks modern thinking throughout. On the one hand, whenever modern thinkers identify nature, they do so in an effort to lend stability, form, and goals for family life. On the other hand, the modern conception of nature and modern thinkers' penchant to emancipate human creativity in the redefinition and conquest of nature lead to continual reconstructions of marriage and family life.

Another theme in modern thinking is the analysis of the threats to sound marriage and family life. Generally, thinkers that define the family in terms of community and ethical love see it as threatened by the intrusion of calculating reason or the object-for-use mentality (Rousseau, John Paul II as discussed in chapter 11), the spirit of individualism or subjective freedom (Hegel, Comte, Durkheim, John Paul II), or an inhuman desire to establish gender neutrality (contemporary sociobiologists as discussed in chapter 10). Other thinkers see excessive unity as the problem to be combated because it gets in the way of developing other human desiderata such as the development of self or sexual equality. Locke, for instance, aims to bring down the partisanship inseparable from too much family unity and to limit and channel the family's formative influence by freeing children from the control of parents. Mill (chapter 6) sees excessive familial unity as connected to the subordination of women, and he is willing to sacrifice one in order to end the other. Karl Marx and Frederick Engels (chapter 7) take Mill's insights further in their search for substantive liberty and equality. Like Mill they criticize the merely formal freedom offered by traditional liberalism as a mask for the oppression of women and children because women will still "choose" to participate in unified families. They see the need to end the regime of private property and the private family if we are ever going to establish "individual sex love" as the ideal governing human relationships. Freud (chapter 8) finds that the tools that keep families together are so many masks for unhealthy repressed desires that lead to the great discontents of modern civilization, and he recommends an indulgence of sexual passion as a way to satisfy human desires. Beauvoir builds on the insights of Marx and Freud and questions whether human beings need one another at all and whether marriage and family life can ever really be free. Her teaching leads to the family's end.

Much of the following story lies at the intersection of nature and the threats to family life because at this intersection lies each thinker's vision of human thriving and its relationship to marriage and family life. Connected with these visions are reflections on the nature of human thought and our ability to prophesy and shape the future. I confront these deeper questions in a chronological treatment of these thinkers. Chronology is an indispensable first step, though chronology must give way to a philosophic treatment of the family. This book culminates in such a sketch, titled "What Is to Be Thought?" (chapter 12). I apply a philosophic orientation that recognizes our middling condition and the incommensurability of human goods to our thinking about the family and try to show what that means for our understanding of family life. Love and freedom, two great human desires, seem to be in conflict with one another, and we cannot define that conflict out of existence. It is best to acknowledge that incompatibility and to understand the place of family within it. What follows may not be satisfactory to any or all, but that is the unique consolation and anguish of philosophy.

Part I

The Ballast of Nature and the Ends of the Family

Chapter 2

Locke and the Invention of the Modern Family

John Locke (1632–1704) is the founder of modern liberal society and inventor of the modern, nuclear family. For this latter he is praised and blamed. Locke-blamers think he destabilizes the family, in part because he does not place the family on a Christian basis and in part because his account is rife with tensions that, eventually, loosen family bonds. Locke is the greatest exponent of modern natural rights teaching, whose political principles have done so much to introduce liberal democracy into the world. In pre-natural rights political arrangements, rulers ruled because of birth, strength, age, wealth, tradition, or religious faith. Under natural rights teaching, legitimate governments rule by the consent of the governed. What is true of government is also true of other civil institutions—labor relations, churches, and marriage. Yet Locke-blamers sense that it is difficult to remold the relationship between parents and children on the basis of consent. Contracts are open to negotiation; if families are based on contracts, individuals are free to make relations as they please. Family life, on the other hand, requires reference to ends and a framework to achieve them. The principles of Locke's marriage—marriage by consent, the child-centered goals of marriage—work well in an atmosphere informed by Christian faith. Faith prevents marriages formed by consent from devolving into a divorce culture; love supported by faith sustains parents to dedicate time and energy to their children. Locke's family unravels without these props.[1]

Yet some think Locke's teaching on the family could solve today's confusion about what the family is. The case against the Locke-blamers makes sense at first blush. It is strange to blame a man whose writings appeared in the late 1600s for *today's* problems or to hold the inventor of the modern family—one of the most enduring family forms in history—for its demise. Would the Locke-blamers prefer the sexual libertinism of post-Restoration England or patriarchal politics and family life to Locke's prescription for family stability?[2] With religion weakening in England and divine notions of marital right dissolving, Locke's contractual marriage binds personal interests in rational liberty to the future of marriage. To what other place could he turn amidst the universal disturbance of moral standards?[3] It is also reasonable to ask what political system, and what family system, can hold up in the very long run, as the seeds for the destruction of all or most human arrangements are often sown in their founding principles. Those praising Locke think his principles lend stability, order, and sanity to family life. He faced some of the problems associated with today's family decline (poor marriage formation, incompetent parenting, divorce) and may have anticipated others (associated with feminism). Those praising Locke (especially today's voices of retrenchment) are impressed with his declaration that marriage accomplishes important ends, namely procreation and the education of children, and that some family forms accomplish these ends better than others.[4]

Both these views require that we ask how stable the stable things in Locke's thought are and how unstable the unstable things are. This demands that we can identify the stable and unstable things and understand why they are what they are.

Patriarchy and Partisanship

Locke's *Two Treatises of Government* contain his writings on the family, though *Some Thoughts Concerning Education* and *Essay Concerning Human Understanding* shed light on his thinking too. Locke seeks to remove confusion between paternal and political rule. This confusion arises at the "beginning of political societies,"[5] but the problem of patriarchy is a case of the permanent problem concerning the origin of partisanship. This problem demonstrates the difficulty of reconciling the family with justice.

Patriarchal politics grow from an unlimited, tightly knit family. "In the beginning of things" children found that where a father's authority is "exercised with Care and Skill, with Affection and Love to those under it, it was sufficient to procure and preserve to Men all the Political Happiness they sought for in society." Such "nursing Fathers" resolved conflicts among their children, protected their families from outsiders, passed down property to their heirs, and, generally, served as lawmakers and governors for the family and for the little nation the family formed. The father was "fittest to be trusted" and the "Custom of obeying him, in their Childhood, [made] it easier to submit to him rather than to any other" when children reached maturity.[6] How was a father's authority established in the family initially? How did his paternal affection translate into political rule? These questions force us to see the connection between patriarchy and partisanship.

Families are rooted in biological facts, and marriage is a contrivance arising to deal with those facts. As with animals, man and woman come together for "Procreation" and the "continuation of the Species."[7] Unlike many other newborn animals, children are dependent on parents for continued care, which explains why men and women need to be "tied to a longer conjunction than other creatures." Marriages and families are artificial institutions designed to answer the natural needs of children. A man is "bound to take care of those he hath begot" and in the interest of their "common Issue" a man and woman will stay together so "their Industry might be encouraged" and they can store up sufficient goods for their family.[8]

Mothers, it seems, feel attached to children, inducing them to provide affectionate care for their offspring, yet men do not by nature seem interested in being husbands or fathers or in having other long-term commitments. "What Father of a Thousand," Locke asks, "when he begets a Child, thinks farther than satisfying his present Appetite?" So little are men interested in family life that God found it necessary to place "strong desires of Copulation" in men to confound them into perpetuating the race. Sexual desire leads men to beget children "without the intention, and often against the Consent and the Will of the Begetter."[9] As men pursue fleeting desires, "the Husband and Wife part"—that is, in the words of one scholar, the "husband *de*parts"[10]—and the "Children are left to the Mother, follow her, and are whole under her Care and Provision." Easy and "frequent Solutions of Conjugal society . . . mightily disturb" the provision of children, as does an "uncertain mixture" leading to conception,[11] and such events are common in primitive America and other locales. Far from beginning his analysis by identifying the problem of patriarchy and partisanship, Locke begins with the primitive problem of "Fatherless America" or "Life without Father."[12] Nor is it necessarily best if primitive men stick around. Locke catalogues the "sports of men"—including incidents of cannibalism, child sacrifice, exposure, feeding children to wild beasts, and burying children alive—when they are freed from law and censure.[13] Neither the meandering nor malevolent man constitutes a civilized and civilizing family.

Locke does not take the establishment of the patriarchal family for granted, nor does he presume the sufficiency of natural or innate sentiments to build families. The family responds to natural needs, though nature has not instituted the family to meet those needs. Are parents and fathers in particular obliged to care for their children though they must "neglect their own private good" to do so?[14]

Patriarchy is an accomplishment that meets natural needs and purports to solve the problem of the wandering, uncivilized man. Women seem to consent to patriarchy as a survival strategy, receiving protection, help, and support from men in return for granting men access to sex and control over the family and its property. Political society emerges after stable families form. "Without such nursing Fathers tender and carefull of the publick weale, all governments would have sunk under the Weakness and Infirmities of their Infancy."[15] As a matter of right, the power of a husband and father is limited by his wife's consent; his power cannot extend to political power over life and death or over property labored for by his children.[16]

As a matter of fact, paternal power exceeds these limits; paternal rule is taken as proof that God intends fathers to be kings. This cultural apparatus of patriarchy is formed by a complex of opinions, many of which are central to the Christian, ancient, and medieval traditions.[17] The central goal of this tradition is for children to learn obedience to something greater than, and outside, themselves. Parents are charged with training a child's will, so that the honor children should show to parents is a preparation for the honor all owe to God and all citizens owe to established governments. Just as fearing the Lord is the beginning of wisdom, so also is fearing one's parents essential to a Christian education. The patriarchal tradition links filial obedience to social order: "Honour thy father and thy mother: that thy days may be long upon the land which the Lord thy God giveth thee."[18]

The fact that patriarchy is sustained by closely supervised opinions about obedience reveals much about human nature and the character of patriarchy. Locke is often associated with the view that human beings are acquisitive, possessive, or antisocial because he envisions man alone and hungry in the state of nature. Yet it is best to see Locke's emphasis on the individual as a counterpoise to man's predominantly and anxiously *social* nature. One would have to be, Locke writes, "little skilled in nature or history of mankind" to miss the fact that the greatest part of mankind "govern themselves chiefly, if not solely, by this *law of fashion.*" The desire for esteem being natural to man, it is also "natural for [him], and almost unavoidable, to take up with some borrowed principles . . . from his education and from the fashions of his country." Thinking through the way people borrow principles reveals that the family is the agent that gives them to children. Children come into the world anxious, desiring to please others, and ready to be impressed with a character; parents get the first stab at molding character while children are at their most pliable. Children recognize an inequality between themselves and their fathers and this inequality has great political importance—it fosters obedience. It also has great importance for the family. Children are taught to prefer their family to outsiders, and they are indoctrinated to the family's religious opinions, which can reinforce opinions about kingship, obedience, and a suspicion about the other. Children lose their independence of judgment before they are allowed to cultivate it, and this "giving up our assent to the common received opinions, either of our friends or party, neighbourhood or country" is the chief source of all intellectual errors and also of great injustices.[19]

Locke reforms the family by stripping away layers of custom that reinforce patriarchal rule while asking men and women to revisit the survival strategy underlying the patriarchal family. Will ending the culture of patriarchy return us to a more natural time of the wandering male and the abandoned woman and child? Not out of an attempt to escape nature, but rather from a hope to satisfy its demands, Locke seeks to defang patriarchy and reconstitute the family. Can the givens of nature—the facts that children are long dependent on mothers and that mothers have long, somewhat debilitating gestation periods—be satisfied without resorting to patriarchy, its partisanship, and its tendency to political absolutism?

From Eve to the Epidural: The Nature of Nature in Locke

The old survival strategy leads to a distorting partisanship, but it interested men in a version of responsible family life. We must know more about human nature to grasp the new strategy. For Locke, "the first and strongest desire God Planted in Men, and wrought into the very Principles of their Nature [is] that of self-preservation." Self-preservation can point away from family duties. The priority of self-preservation suggests that we would put our survival above others' survival. With little food to eat, for instance, a mother governed by the first passion might be tempted to eat the food herself instead of sharing it with her young. Not all natural desires point so profoundly inward. Next to the desire for self-preservation, "God Planted in Men a strong desire of propagating their Kind, and continuing themselves in their Posterity."[20] But can this be, especially since not one father in a thousand thinks of begetting children when satisfying his "strong desires of Copulation"? Is this "strong desire" to propagate another phrase for the "strong desire of Copulation"? The fact that God confounds men into propagating through their sexual appetites suggests that their desire to propagate does not easily point to the family. The desire to copulate and the desire to propagate *can* point to family life, but in different ways. Sexual desire emphasizes a man's access to a woman, while the desire to propagate can point to an enduring relationship with a wife and child. Both point to a man's neediness and to how self-preservation alone does not satisfy. Man hungers, and that points him outside himself.

Natural passions point ambiguously to family life. The "first and strongest" desire for self-preservation and the "strong desires for Copulation" seem to have pride of place in men. These desires seem to be the almost useless materials out of which family life must be built. The trick is to transform the desires for self-preservation and copulation into the more stable desires to propagate and to continue oneself in one's children, and then to expand the desires to propagate and continue oneself into a desire to educate; the trick is to expand and enlighten the self. Patriarchy accomplished these tricks, but it was too great a temptation to the patriarchs, who continued themselves in their progeny by *enslaving* or *mis-educating* them to an intense partisanship.

The problem of ordering desires gets more complicated when we compare married life to life within the family. For Locke, human beings possess a "perfect Freedom" wherein to "order their Actions and dispose of their Possessions, and Persons as they think fit" and they live in a "State . . . of Equality, wherein all the Power and Jurisdiction is reciprocal, no one having more than another."[21] No person holds a power over another due to natural inequality, and legitimate power is exercised only by consent. What is true of political society is also true of conjugal society, which "is made by a voluntary compact between Man and Woman" consisting in "such Communion and right in one another's bodies, as is necessary to its chief End, Procreation."[22] On these terms, it is difficult to see how parental rule or family life itself could be legitimate, since children do not consent to the rule of parents and parents do not choose their children.[23] Families cannot be baptized by consent the way marriages can: marriages can emphasize freedom and choice to an extent, while family life cannot avoid incorporating limits on freedom. In reproduction and individual maturation, there are moments of un-freedom, when parents accept what nature or nature's

God provides, and when one's actions cannot easily be conceived in terms of self-preservation, choice, or mastering nature.

Patriarchal thinkers think these moments constitute a pattern for political and familial life. Such moments, when nature's facts assert themselves, pose a serious challenge to Locke's account of the family. Everything in his thinking on the family hinges on how he defines nature's facts or "givens" and on what he thinks our attitude toward them should be.[24] Nature has brought children into the world in a prolonged state of dependence, where their need for individual attention seems great and enduring. Nature seems to demand that a male and a female are needed for procreation and, perhaps, that both are needed for educating youth to rational liberty. Nature seems to have given women the job of bearing children, often with great pain, and to have prepared their bodies to feed and care for children. Nature seems to lend support to the patriarchal tradition because of these facts. These natural "givens" limit human power, creativity, and freedom, insofar as they are "givens." These facts are natural, or, as Locke characterizes the patriarchal tradition, "almost natural,"[25] but this tells us nothing about whether we should submit to nature or try to overcome it.

Locke's orientation toward the pains women experience in childbirth is a test case for his attitude toward nature's "givens."[26] Through an unorthodox reading of Eve's curse, Locke suggests that women need not endure the burdens nature and nature's God placed on them for partaking first of the fruits from the tree. There is no "Law to oblige a Woman . . . that she should bring forth her Children in sorrow and Pain, if there could be a Remedy for it." It is a woman's duty to "endeavour to avoid" such pains—through advances in medical technology or in ceasing to give birth altogether. Similarly, when God laid Eve under the curse of desiring her husband and being ruled by him, he did not establish an immutable order of nature, but only foretold "what should be a Womans Lot." There is "no more Law to oblige a Woman to such a Subjection, if the Circumstances either of her condition or Contract with her Husband should exempt her from it."[27] Similarly, people have been mistaken to think "by Nature government was Monarchical, and belong'd to the Father."[28] These and other aspects of human experience *seemed* natural, but their force is limited to the "negligent and unforeseeing Innocence of the first ages" when human beings did not try to provide for themselves.[29]

These *seemingly* natural features of human life may be removable, and Locke directs people to seek their removal. It seemed impossible to get rid of the patriarchal tradition, yet we did. The same may be true of male rule of the family, women's pains in childbirth, and other seemingly natural "givens" of family life. If these aspects of "nature" can be reconstructed or mitigated, what other aspects of nature survive only because we have been too lazy to assert our power over them? Locke exhorts people to free themselves from the stupidities and scarcities to which nature *seems* to have consigned them. Locke not only resists the move from the "hath been" to the "ought to be."[30] He distinguishes the "hath been" and the "can be" and does not think we can draw a definite line between what can and cannot be done.

Locke's much-criticized claim that rule in the family "naturally falls to the Man's share, as the abler and stronger"[31] should be seen against his unstable account of nature. Let us begin with a strict constructionist view of his understanding of marriage, to show how it can be deconstructed and reconstructed. The "chief, if not the only reason" that conjugal society arises is to deal with the natural facts that children are born to a prolonged state of dependence, more children often arrive before the first ones fly the coop, and two complementary parents are better equipped to raise children. The nuclear family is the human institution that best satisfies natural necessities, yet it is also not provided for by nature, so human beings have come up with an understandable variety of artifices for meeting natural needs.[32] Men and women combine resources, unite interests, and "make Provision" to sustain and educate their "common Issue."[33] Marriage serves the family and must maintain a suitable form to do so. Even as he admires people's foresight in constructing marriage to provide for natural needs, he is critical of patriarchal constructions. Locke seems nevertheless to maintain a softer, privatized patriarchy as he gives headship of families to the "abler and stronger" man, to the consternation of many.[34]

At the same time, softer patriarchal arrangements are open to revision. Consider the living principles in Locke that qualify his defense of man's superiority in the family. First, men rule as abler and stronger persons, not as men. Locke's family is open to claims from superior women since he justifies rule on the basis of merit. He adds a second, deeper qualification reflecting his openness on the terms of the marital contract:

> Community of goods, and the power over them, mutual assistance and maintenance, and other things belonging to conjugal society, might be varied and regulated by that contract which unites man and wife in that society, as far as may consist with procreation and the bringing up of children till they could shift for themselves; nothing being necessary to any society, that is not necessary to the ends for which it is made.[35]

If and so long as the husband's rule is necessary to procreation and the education of the young, husbandly rule in the family stands. If not, rule in the family may be negotiated between rational, independent, and equal parties entering the contract. If previously it was necessary to give men rule of the family as part of a strategy to keep them around, another strategy could be devised so long as the end is still met. Third, in contrast to parent-child relationships, where parents do not seem to be subject to "Magistrates power," controversies between husbands and wives can be appealed to "the Civil Magistrate."[36] This ambiguous entrée of the magistrate in marital controversies qualifies the rule of the husband, as does the fact that Locke allows for divorce after the marriage's terms are fulfilled and, perhaps, when one does not keep up one's end of the bargain. Locke is open to women owning property, bequeathing inheritance, receiving an education similar to a man's, and possessing the rationality necessary for citizenship.[37] The principles Locke plants in the family can reform it again, depending on the circumstances. Family form follows function; more than one form may fulfill that function.

That Locke is *open* to alternative family forms does not mean that any form will do.[38] Locke soberly submits to stubborn facts (i.e., the neediness of children and the differences between men and women). The stability of Locke's family derives from his ability to identify enduring natural facts and his willingness to grasp their implications. Locke debunks institutions that were mistakenly thought to be natural or unavoidable responses to stubborn facts (i.e., patriarchal government, patriarchal family governance, the necessity of painful childbearing, etc.). Locke's family, designed in light of human equality and liberty, encourages critical distance from parental authority and is suited for the political and economic independence suitable to a liberal order.

Family Life and the Ends of Political Society

When Locke defends a form of the family, he puts forward an institution, a complex of rules, expectations, and mores that makes a law of fashion to structure how people think and act. An institution emphasizes *connections* between various things, such as form and function, or education and parenthood, or marriage and parenthood. The question about institutions is whether the connections connect what they purport to connect. For example, a single mother who rears a child into responsible adulthood reflects an experience, which, if generalized, would undermine a connection in Locke's nuclear family. Evidence that the connections are not *really* necessary shows that the essential thing is not what the institution thought, but rather another, less formal thing that gets us what we want.[39] Locke separates church from state, legislative from executive power, and copulation from fatherhood. In light of his willingness to separate, it is interesting to see why he connects what he connects in family life.

Perhaps I have pitched this at too general a level. The value of the family's "chief End" cannot be taken for granted. Let us assume that the family form Locke describes fulfills the function he sets for it. The general tenor of Locke's thought—his refusal to equate what "hath been" with what "ought to be"—requires that we understand the need for the functions centered on procreation and education that Locke gives the family. We must know what education is before we can say why families are necessary for education. Patriarchal government was, after all, an "almost natural," not unreasonable response to natural facts, and it worked moderately well; patriarchy posed an *educational* problem.

Under patriarchal arrangements, sons revered fathers as rulers of the household. This reverence translated into obedience from sons. In such families, a hierarchy of succession and a rooted sense of belonging to a tradition stretched backwards and forwards in time. Patriarchal families present a cold, unfamiliar, and unfriendly environment. Patriarchs convey a "constant stiffness" and a "mien of authority and distance" to their children. This "reservedness and distance" deprives sons of a sure friend in times of trouble and poisons the domestic hearth with suspicion and jealousy.[40] The aristocratic coldness of family relations also serves a dangerous political ethic of obedience and absolutism. Subject to absolute rule in the family, all are prepared to expect it elsewhere and to swallow the opinions necessary to sustain that partisanship.

Locke's is an education for liberty, rationality, and civility. He avoids patriarchal mis-education by separating the family from politics and by giving marriage and family life different ends than politics. The goal of political society is "to secure [men] in the Possession and the Use of their Properties." People contract to establish a commonwealth whose magistrates have the "power to make Laws for the regulating of Property between Subjects one amongst another."[41] In contrast, parents aim to "*preserve, nourish, and educate the Children*" and exercise such power over them "to supply their want of Ability, and understanding how to manage their property" and control themselves.[42] Conjugal society is formed for the purpose of "Procreation and mutual Support and Assistance" in educating their "common Off-spring."[43] Locke's argument has two steps: (1) conjugal society is necessary, or at least important to and convenient for, the education of children; and (2) the family's goal of educating children is necessary for a child's independent entry into adulthood and political society. Let us take these steps in reverse order, first to highlight the character of Lockean education and then to see the institutional support necessary to accomplish these goals.

The Origin, Extent, and End of Family Life

Political society aims to secure men in the possession and use of property, while families seek to teach children how to acquire and manage property. By property Locke means material possessions and estate and also one's life and liberty.[44] Property arises when human beings mix their labor with what is in nature, and human beings make themselves freely in much the same way that they make a house from a collection of trees. Human beings do not initially possess the rationality or freedom to make themselves consistent with reason. Parents direct their children so their necessities are met, their health maintained, their mind formed, and their character prepared to exercise rational liberty.[45] Liberty involves deliberating and acting on the basis of one's own reason.

> To turn [a child] loose to an unrestrained Liberty, before he has Reason to guide him, is not allowing him the privilege of his Nature to be free; but to thrust him out amongst Brutes, and abandon him to a state as wretched, and as much beneath that of a Man as theirs. This is that which puts the *Authority* into the *Parents* hands to govern the *Minority* of their children.[46]

Children are not capable of knowing the natural and civil laws or of acting within the bounds of those laws without the training of the will. The educative goals of the family precede the goals of political society, for the family cultivates the rationality, civility, character, and, perhaps, technical skills that allow children to become members of a civil government.[47] Parents lead in education to virtue and breeding by their example and because the close supervision necessary for these goals is best provided by those most observant of a child's distinctiveness and most concerned about a child's success. Locke proposes a slew of techniques for parents to teach their children the value of labor, liberality, and reasonableness. He recommends, for instance, that parents have children construct their own toys, to teach the children "to see for what they want, in themselves, and in their own endeavours: whereby they will be taught Moderation in their Desires, Application, Industry, Thought, Contrivance, and Good Husbandry."[48] Closely related to this advice is Locke's reaction to children who demand, whine, or carp: such a child should not have what he "*cries for . . . or so much as he speaks for.*"[49] By example parents model the virtues attendant to labor and acquisition for their children. Household matters, the security of which are now the end of the political society, are best taught in the household, while the laws and institutions outside the household reinforce this teaching.

Most crucial to the promotion of a child's ability to labor and his freedom is the cultivation of self-control or the ability to resist impulses and examine them soberly:

> The mind [has] in most cases . . . a power to suspend the execution and satisfaction of any of its desires; and so all, one after another, is at liberty to consider the objects of them, examine them on all sides, and weigh them with others. In this lies the liberty man has; and from the not using of it right comes all that variety of mistakes, errors, and faults which we run into in the conduct of our lives, and our endeavours after happiness.[50]

Locke's account of childhood education begins with the importance of self-control, "the great Principle and foundation of all Vertue and Worth."[51] If children were born in possession of self-control, if they gained self-control spontaneously, or if another institution could more effectively cultivate self-control and its attendant traits, the family might not be needed. The "weakness and imperfection of their Nonage," however, makes "Discipline" provided by parents "necessary to their Education."[52]

How is this accomplished? First, paternal rule must be limited, in the sense that the father's exercise of unlimited and arbitrary power must be transferred to the newly constituted political authority.[53] Second, families must be temporary so they prepare children for independence and the attainment of equality with the parents.[54] These aspects of family organization shape expectations and acts of parents and children: parents prepare for the time when their authority comes to an end and when their relations with their children will not be based on the command-obedience dynamic of old family, and children prepare for when they must shift for themselves.

The self-control that makes reasonableness, the capacity for labor, and the desire to labor possible does not arise spontaneously once institutions of patriarchy are removed; parents must be interested to cultivate their children's liberty. The culture of liberty is threatened from above by a too-patriarchal education. It is also threatened by too indifferent and too one-sided an education. In this context, Locke appears to accept a traditional sexual division of labor in the household or the view that men and women bring complementary qualities to child-raising. Men and women have characteristic vices, each corrected by the other. Mothers seem to be possessed of a "Natural Love and Tenderness" that induces them to spoil their children, as does the mother who indulges every whim of her little darling.[55] On the other hand, there are extreme examples of parental indifference and even cruelty, inflicted, it seems, mostly by men. This adventuresomeness, if tamed more than a little, can liberate children from necessary, though often excessive, maternal affection. The child's world is more likely to mix the welcoming and the disruptive, the secure and the unsettling, when parents of each sex are around.[56] This balance secures children while preparing them for independence and citizenship in Locke's civil polity.

There must be some reason for men to stick around. Locke rejects the strategy of patriarchy but seems to insist that men are necessary to child-rearing, so he recommends another way to keep men interested in the family. The key to this is friendship mixed with interest, as seen in Locke's account of inheritance and its limits. Some have, not without reason, seen Locke's account of the parent-child relationship as calculating and crudely materialistic.[57] Parents provide children education, nourishment, support, and kindness, while children owe parents honor, support, and respect based on the gratitude they feel for the benefits their parents have bestowed on them.[58] An obvious problem arises in this bargain: parents give what they have and get something in exchange for their time and trouble at a much later date. There is no guarantee that kids will deliver, and there is reason to suspect that children raised to independence will see themselves as self-made instead of parent-made and not pay up. Since there is no natural way to glue parents to children, Locke tinkers with conventions surrounding inheritance to keep the family together after its formal dissolution.

> There is another power ordinarily in the father, whereby he has a tie on the obedience of his children. . . . And this is the power men generally have to bestow their estates on those who please them best; the possession of the father being the expectation and inheritance of the children, ordinarily in certain proportions, according to the law and custom of each country; yet it is commonly in the father's power to bestow it with a more sparing or liberal hand, according as the behaviour of this or that child hath comported with his will and humour.[59]

This is "no small Tye on the Obedience of Children" through which parents obtain "voluntary Submission" from their older children.[60] Parents may also have greater incentives to accumulate property and use it to tie children to their homeland and person.[61] Locke, who makes one of the earliest and most persuasive cases against laws of primogeniture and entail,[62] in contrast to later thinkers who seek to abolish the right to bestow inheritances altogether, maintains heritable property to solidify parent-child relations. He sacrifices some equality of opportunity resulting from the different abilities of parents to earn in order to use inheritance as scaffolding for continuing the parent-child relation beyond a child's nonage.

Locke knows that such an interest-based bond is subject to objections. Relying on inheritance to secure the allegiance of children will lead them to raise an unpleasant question, "*When will you die, father*?"[63] Understanding Locke's modern family as the home of modern friendship is the key to seeing the limits to Locke's emphasis on inheritance and to understanding why fathers are interested in their children. Locke equates the goals of education, from a father's perspective, with rearing reliable friends. Locke suggests that a father should consider a son to be an "obedient subject (as is fit) whilst he is a child, and [an] affectionate friend when he is a man." The theme of friendship is present when Locke discusses the relaxation of parental authority. A father "will obtain . . . *his friendship*" by treating a son properly.[64] Lockean education aims to prepare children for self-governing adulthood and for a lifetime of familial friendship. The "lure" of trusting friendship is no small lure for fathers; the prospect of having a more experienced, dependable friend may be attractive to reasonable sons as well.[65]

Locke is not recommending that fathers be the friends of their sons while they are still children. A father and son can be friends only when they can be thought equals; that is, when sons reach the age of maturity. Efforts to treat a son as a man before manhood may benefit children by hastening their maturation. On the other hand, fathers who dumb down their own behavior to the level of children will create perpetual children unworthy of friendship. Fathers must act as equals of their sons when sons arrive at an age of maturity. Mindful that a grown child's sense of equality is respected, Locke warns fathers to offer advice to sons "only as a friend of more experience but with your advice mingle nothing of command or authority, no more than you would to your equal or a stranger."[66]

There are a number of ways to establish friendly relations with one's son. "Nothing cements and establishes friendship and good will so much as *confident communication* of concernments and affairs."[67] A father should initiate this by discussing a variety of affairs with a son "familiarly, and ask his advice." This encourages sons to reciprocate. Anticipating an objection to what might be called familiar fatherhood, Locke tells fathers that this mode of conduct "will not at all lessen your authority, but increase his love and esteem of you." Patriarchal leadership depends on unsentimental distance; the Lockean family will be characterized by sentimental closeness and equality. Clever fathers, cultivating this sense, have power over their "equal" sons. Locke justifies the new arrangements, ambiguously, in terms of parental power. "For you have not that power you ought to have over him till he comes to be more afraid of offending so good a friend than of losing some part of his future expectation."[68]

Are fathers akin to Machiavellian princes who find ruling through fear to be the way of gaining outward forms of allegiance?[69] Or ought fathers shift the grounds of sonly allegiance from holding out the promise of inheritance to love and affection for the father? Locke provides answers in his discussion of parental authority.

> When . . . you have reconciled him to your company and made him sensible of your care and love of him by indulgence and tenderness . . . when, I say, by these ways of tenderness and affection, which parents never want for their children, you have also planted in him a particular affection for you, he is then in the state you desire, and you have formed in his mind that true *reverence* which is always afterwards carefully to be continued and maintained in both parts of it, *love* and *fear*, as the great principle whereby you will always have hold upon him to turn his mind to the ways of virtue and honor.[70]

It is not clear, however, that Locke would tell fathers, as Machiavelli tells princes, that "it is much safer to be feared than loved."[71] The emphasis on parental friendship illustrates the limits of Machiavellianism. The love of a man who may be unequal, but who poses as an equal, may be the means whereby fathers secure their children's friendship. The qualities of character that lead to the accumulation of an estate may gain the confidence and affection of children more than the estate itself.

The Goal, Origin, and Dissolution of Conjugal Society

We have canvassed the goals of conjugal society in the procreation and education of children and the fact that conjugal society originates in contract for Locke, but we have not considered these points in all of their depth and complexity. Basing marriage in a negotiable contract allows the institution to adapt to individual differences and to different cultural circumstances so long as the terms are consistent with the ends of marriage. What limits and liberates the contract is that "nothing [is] necessary to any Society, that is not necessary to the ends for which it is made." Not only does Locke think that the "ends of Matrimony require no such Power [to rule the family] in the Husband," he also suggests that the sharing of goods and the mutual assistance offered by husband and wife can be "varied and regulated by that Contract" and that the relationship between husband and wife can cease upon the maturation of the children.[72] Through this port Locke's egalitarian defenders ship Locke's openness to a woman's right to own property, labor, bequeath inheritance, and to women receiving an education equal to men's.[73] These rights can be safely granted if they are consistent with the ends of conjugal society. What form is *necessary* to the procreation and education of children?

Marriage begets obligations, and only freely chosen obligations are consistent with an individual's freedom and equality. Consensual marriage implies a distinct way of knowing. Under previous marriage regimes at their best, arranged marriages were a norm, and, insofar as arranged marriages reflected their origin in patriarchal societies, they reflected a view that others (i.e., fathers) were better judges of what was best and suitable for those seeking to marry. Youth are clouded by ardent desires and romantic fancies, while those interested and outside are capable of taking a longer, broader view of what it takes to maintain a marriage. The idea of choosing a marriage partner implies an unrealistic stability in human character and creates unrealistic expectations of our ability to tell what lies in a couple's future. Marriage "made by a voluntary Compact between a Man and a Woman," in contrast, depends on evaluating a prospective marriage from inside of the relation and reflects the view that people are the best judges of their own interest. Above all, consent acts as a guarantor of the sentiments necessary for a conjugal society to perform its tasks of procreation and education. Consent to marry is evidence of a willingness to provide "mutual Support, and Assistance" and signifies a "Communion of Interest too, as necessary . . . to unite their Care, and Affection."[74] Consensual marriage *recognizes* sentiments and passions as essential, if not the essential, traits of married and private life.

It also demands that future spouses think about their impending marriage before entering it. Such forethought can have the effect of taking sentiment and illusion out of the marriage or of stabilizing them. Thinking about the terms of a marriage contract beforehand may also encourage the betrothed to understand the true nature of the marital bond. Passion, romantic flights, excitement, and even *eros* may lead each to desire another; they do not lead a couple to stay together for the fulfillment of marriage's purposes. Locke eschews the language of love in his discussion of marriage; he uses softer terms such as "Care and Affection" and "mutual Support" to characterize spousal relations. This bespeaks Locke's recognition that less elevated, more habitual bonds cement a long-term relationship better than sexual attraction or romantic dreams. Inward and sober, sentimental and calculating, Locke's marriage contract places the burden on individuals to make the right choice in light of marriage's end.

There is something sweet and tender about this shift, and something unstable in it. Locke deals with the topic of divorce since he recognizes sentiment at the heart of marriage and limits the ends of conjugal society to begetting and raising children. Consistent with his account of marriage's ends, Locke allows that marriages can be terminated once their child-centered goals are accomplished.[75] Locke implies that divorce is permissible when minor children are still at home and that the contract could determine if the "Children upon such Separation fall to the Father or Mother's Lot." "Natural Right, or their Contract" determines when such a separation can occur.[76] The "natural Right" implicated in divorce is likely the preservation of the wife and children, which overrides one's duty to remain in a marriage when threatened by an abusive husband. Though Locke does not expand on this point, he suggests that the civil magistrate can dissolve marriages for nonperformance of contract, perhaps if one fails to allow access to "one anothers Bodies," or to provide the "mutual Support, and Assistance whilst they are together," or to guard, nourish, educate, and support one's children. The civil magistrate decides "any Controversie that may arise between Man and Wife" about the terms of their marital contract.[77] Neither whim nor subjective will apart from evidence of a breach of contract nor one party pure and simple can dissolve a marriage. [78] The fashion Locke cultivates is that marriages should endure, except where they should not (because of a breach or abuse) or need not (for the sake of the children).

The prospect that a marriage could end may tend to change how spouses approach it. The logic by which Locke defends the right to revolution and the dissolution of government as a means of making citizens more vigilant and rulers more responsive applies to the right to divorce and the dissolution of marriage.[79] Spouses must fulfill their part of the bargain for a marriage to work. Care and affection are the ways to ensure a marriage's smooth functioning, but living under the threat that nonperformance of contract may be grounds for dissolving the marriage may induce partners to respectful, accommodating ways. Locke's openness to separation can point in the other direction. The expectation that the marriage can end when the children are gone may shape how each approaches it. Uneasiness about its temporary character may encourage spouses to secure the resources needed for survival and prosperity after marriage.[80] The freedom to divorce underlies the view that women should enter marriage contracts without impairing their ability to accumulate property independent of the family, and, despite what critics think,[81] Locke allows for such a possibility and for the education of girls that may be necessary to support it.[82] Since marriage can be dissolved, every mother should prepare to be single again and may design a marriage sensitive to this fact. In any event, the possibility of a future divorce may encourage individuals to hold something back from the "Community of Goods" or "Communion of Interest" important to achieving the ends of marriage.[83] Far from encouraging couples to be accommodating to one another, the dissolution of marriage suggests that spouses may act less like a unity and more like a temporary alliance.

Notice the uneasy dynamic. The chief end of marriage is the procreation and education of children. This calls forth from parents the commitment of time and energy to prepare children for the exercise of their faculties. Sacrificing time and energy in the rearing of children may mean that one is not shoring up for when the marriage may end (i.e., when the children are mature). The more one shores up one's own future, the more one neglects the chief end of marriage. The more one invests in one's marriage and family, the more precarious one's future. Locke articulates a modern dilemma without suggesting that there is an easy way out of it.

There is another factor in Locke's approach to divorce that may serve to loosen or tighten the family, depending on the situation. Municipal laws and the laws of fashion themselves shape marriage in particular settings. Examples, drawn from his private writings, suggest that Locke is open to institutions of polygamy, polyandry, and a more or less open marriage. The acceptability of such institutions depends on where one lives. Polyandry may be acceptable when it occurs "separate from the rest of mankind . . . but it is a vice of deep dye when the same thing is done in a society wherein modesty, the great virtue of the weaker sex, has often other rules and bounds set by custom and reputation, than what it has by direct instance of the law of nature in a solitude or an estate separate from the opinion of this or that society."[84] Opinions held by society affect the effectiveness of parenting—in some Native American societies, unmarried motherhood is not a blemish to a woman's reputation nor is it a hindrance to carrying out the educational responsibilities of parenthood, yet in the England of Locke's time it was a hindering blemish. Local opinions affect one's judgment about what conjugal arrangements are suitable to childrearing.[85] Nowhere in these writings does Locke suggest that such institutions would be sufficient to the demands of educating toward a civil government and rational liberty. People should consider the law of fashion specific to each locale as they act, but many fashions (e.g., patriarchy) are inadequate to the demands of liberty; perhaps these more permissive fashions are inadequate as well.

Locke's teaching about marriage is shot through with the need for prudence in achieving marriage's ends. While procreation is easy, the education of children to rational liberty requires attention, effort, and care structured in a limited, potentially temporary family founded by consent and promising mutual support and care for parents. Education depends on parents putting in the time and resources that married parents have to a greater degree than other child-rearing institutions. Marriages cannot ignore the natural needs of children, the educational demands of self-control and rational liberty, and the differences between the sexes with respect to procreation and child-rearing, though people can make prudential accommodations in how these needs are met. Locke connects the establishment of a civil, liberal polity with the ascension of this nuclear, limited, consensual family. Children from such families are more likely to have the ability and inclination to govern themselves, to pursue and protect property, and to pave the way for a vigilant independence.

There is an inherent instability in Locke's teaching on the family, derived from several of Locke's notions. Locke's account of nature's "givens" is prone to shift as we become more able and willing to transform nature's "givens." Institutional connections grounding Locke's sobriety depend on the persistence of several of these "givens"—a man and a woman are necessary for procreation; it is necessary and convenient for fathers and mothers to educate their own children; women need a husband's support during and after pregnancy; and the education provided by families is the most effective way to cultivate self-control and effective citizenship in a liberal polity. Locke makes arguments for several of these more controversial connections, but he is open to revising them. There may be other ways of connecting these things—though it is often not so easy to refute the connections Locke makes. As we will see in chapter 10, much contemporary social science on the family confirms many of Locke's conclusions. Locke's limited defense of divorce is another place that instability creeps into his teaching. The availability of divorce may encourage people to hedge their bets in marriage and may make them less willing to fulfill marriage's primary goals. Men, always difficult to tie to the family, may be less attached to it, and women less committed to it; parents generally may be more willing to abandon their children or to leave the job of rearing them to others.

Then again, these instabilities seem, to put a fine point on this, true reflections of the world, bespeaking the diverse range of human goods involved in family life. They seem unavoidable given the desiring, and unstable, and anxious, and opinionated nature of human beings. Given these obstacles, perhaps we should marvel at how much stability and order Locke's teaching on the family often yields. There is a lingering sense that we can build a better family by taking Locke's principles more seriously than Locke had, by tinkering with them, or by suffusing them in a different cultural milieu. There is also a lingering sense that Locke's teaching, in its effort to ground the family on reasonably defensible connections, has avoided the most delicious and alluring element of the family—conjugal or romantic Love.

Chapter 3

Rousseau and the Romance of Family Life

Anticipating later arguments of Marxists and feminists and continuing the argument of Locke, Jean-Jacques Rousseau (1712–1778), the unforgettable French philosopher, sees the family as a salutary product of human artifice. Rousseau's contention is made more radical and interesting by his notion of what is natural and hence what is artificial. All hands, it seems, agree that the family is, in some sense, conventional or artificial or a cultural institution. Crucial questions remain. Is the making of the family consistent with nature or against nature? In what ways is nature subsumed in the making of the family? In what ways is it transformed? What goods do we seek in the making of families? For Locke, the family begins as an ingenious response to the natural facts that children have longer periods of nonage than the young of other species and women have long, debilitating gestation periods. Locke's family—a modern nuclear family—is a reasonable response to those natural facts consistent with the achievement of civil government.

Rousseau raises radical questions about Locke's approach. Are the facts to which Locke points *natural* facts? Has Locke properly understood the moral implications of these "facts"? One of Rousseau's great insights is to see that only a civilized man looking at civilized people could embrace Locke's conclusions. Rousseau's critique of Locke's teaching on the family is an instance of his rather devastating argument against Locke's account of the state of nature and of human nature. "Philosophers who have examined the foundations of society," Rousseau writes in his *Second Discourse*, "have all felt the necessity of going back to the state of nature, but none of them has reached it." Earlier thinkers (such as Locke) spoke "of need, avarice, oppression, desires, and pride" in describing human nature, little thinking that they were describing traits that people only acquire in society.[1] Rousseau aims to strip man of his social attributes; what is left is natural man. This puts the family in an ambiguous position. Are the needs that give rise to the family natural? Rousseau's answer is an emphatic "no." Locke thought the family more natural than it is, and he invented "natural" problems for the family to manage.

The Family and the History of Human Needs

According to Rousseau, civilized people are not as tough as they once were and their desires are altogether different than natural man's. Our idleness, our dependence on others, our refinements, our artificial pleasures and desires, our active imagination, our boredom—in short, our civilization—all make us more helpless and more driven for status than natural man is. In the beginning, human beings were more like the animals, especially as they related to these supposedly natural facts.

> In the primitive state, having neither houses, nor huts, nor property of any kind, everyone took up his lodging by chance and often for only one night. Males and females united fortuitously, depending on encounter, occasion, and desire. . . . They left each other with the same ease. The mother nursed her children at first for her own need; then, habit having endeared them to her she nourished them afterward for their need. As soon as they had the strength to seek their food, they did not delay in leaving the mother herself.[2]

Mothers were tough enough to forgo the protection of males since differences in physical strength between men and women were not so great or relevant. The fact that human beings are bipeds allowed women to forage or run while holding and breastfeeding their infants. Once children could walk and find their food—something easier to accomplish without our civilized coddling—they did so without their mothers.[3] Rousseau does not divulge how long it takes for children to cultivate such survival skills, but primitive helplessness bears no resemblance to the civilized helplessness of Locke's children. The mother-child bond in the savage state is temporary, physical, and not emotional.

In fact, Rousseau's great insight into the state of nature is that human beings are much more independent of one another and more defined by physical or "natural" things than people in civilization. Savage man's desires, Rousseau writes, "do not exceed his physical needs, the only goods he knows in the universe are nourishment, a female, and repose."[4] Hunger moves the savage to eat, exhaustion moves him to sleep, and sexual need moves him to copulate. The savage's dependence on food, drink, and a sexual partner does not compromise his freedom or independence. Yet these physical needs are not on the same level. As Joel Schwartz tartly asks, "one can starve to death or be worked to death; but can one die of celibacy?"[5] Sexual desire is an uneasy mix of natural and social passions in Rousseau's taxonomy. Like a savage's desire for rest and food, sexual passion is physical and need not involve psychological dependence on others; at the same time, like the passions of a civilized man, a savage's sexual passion exceeds the desire for mere physical survival and requires the intervention of another human being. Engaging in sex is not as important or as connected to one's survival as the need to eat or sleep.

Sexual desire is naturally indiscriminate and weak.[6] Savages meet only as strangers in the night. Sexual relationships in the natural state are ephemeral, nonexclusive, unenergetic, and present-oriented. With no imagination and no understanding of beauty or merit, any woman satisfies the savage. "Men must feel the ardors of their temperament less frequently and less vividly. . . . Everyone peaceably waits for the impulsion of nature, yields to it without choice with more pleasure than frenzy and the need satisfied, all desire is extinguished."[7]

Extended childhood neediness, a more disruptive and disturbing sexual passion, and the vulnerability of pregnant mothers result from a momentous change in human nature when civil society is established. A syndrome of concerns—including the invention of language, private property, the family and its abode, a moral element of love, and the differentiation between the sexes—arise together. Through hunting expeditions or some such thing, savage man recognizes differences in talent as individuals compare themselves to others. Human imagination, dormant in the purely sensual savage, transforms man's understanding of his needs. No longer will any woman do. Products of imagination, ideas of beauty and merit especially, lead human beings to desire exclusive and reciprocal affairs with members of the opposite sex.[8] Relations between man and woman cannot be, and, in any event, are not, purely physical anymore. The creation of the family home enflames the passions of men, and they invest their pride in what they have made. What is physical in love is no big deal, but what proceeds from investing pride in a beautiful, meritorious woman, and the future a man imagines spending with that woman, make him expend "a greater degree of energy for [his] preferred object." Investing male pride in a "conquest," this element of love eventually gives rise to the "impetuous ardor" and jealousy typical of love in civil society.[9]

Love is an invention, a product of human imagination and pride. It takes two forms: conjugal love and romantic love.[10] Conjugal love is experienced in a relatively isolated family, while romantic love arises with the birth of government and the mingling of families typical of civilized society. Primitive civil society forms when family and private property arise. "The first revolution . . . produced the establishment and differentiation of families, and . . . introduced a sort of property" that resembles the family home.[11] It is difficult to disentangle cause and effect.

> The first developments of the heart were the effect of a new situation, which united husbands and wives, fathers and children in a common habitation. The habit of living together gave rise to the sweetest sentiments known to men: conjugal love and paternal love. Each family became a little society all the better united because reciprocal affection and freedom were its only bonds; and it was then that the first difference was established in the way of life of the two sexes, which until this time had had but one.[12]

Women *become* accustomed to tend to the children and the household and they *become* more helpless and dependent on men for their subsistence. No longer will they forage for food and hunt while holding a baby. Coddled children are accustomed to the attentions of their mother and *become* needy and dependent on her for a longer time. Men are taken with the satisfaction of new passions and *become* more ardent, proud, responsible, and avaricious. This first family ends the epoch of human history where human sexuality was consistent with human independence. Yet even with such dependencies, Rousseau sees this time as "the best for man" and "the happiest and most durable epoch" in human history. It is preferable to the "indolence of the primitive state," presumably because its dependence is a genuinely free, reciprocal, somewhat spontaneous or less fully self-conscious, mutually regarding relation.[13]

The web of dependencies at the heart of this happy epoch is, *ceteris paribus*, what Rousseau hopes, in the best case, from marriage in civil society. In contrast to Locke, Rousseau would draw the family into a tighter unity based on love with the ultimate hope that such a family may foster a deeper political unity than Locke envisioned. Rousseau is more concerned than Locke that the family approximate nature. In fact, Rousseau tries to protect the more or less natural features of this first family from being undermined by excessively "civilized" principles. What I mean by natural here requires clarification.[14] By nature (in the sense of being first or even innate) human beings do not live together in families and even the web of dependence in that happiest and most virtuous epoch is unnatural. The marriage that Rousseau depicts is natural in two different senses. It is closer to nature, in the sense that it is rooted in biological needs and in what are close to original human needs of this happy and durable epoch.[15] Examples of things natural in this way are maternal breastfeeding, the needs all children have for extra attention during their infancy and beyond, and sex differences between men and women more generally. The family also appears natural, in that it creates a *relatively* self-sufficient unit approximating man's savage unity. Family life is based on the idea of mutual attraction, something brought under an individual's control and hence more likely to be genuinely free.[16] (Political life, in contrast, depends much more on accidents of birth and circumstance and cannot be brought under individual control.) Conjugal love, properly understood, can help cure divisions that debilitate modern peoples and can lead to happiness on the level of civil society.

Is conjugal love satisfying? In his *Essay on the Origin of Languages*, Rousseau argues that early barbarous families spoke a domestic language defined by "their own immediate milieu": "They had the concept of a father, a son, a brother, but not that of a man. . . . Apart from themselves and their family, the whole universe would count as nothing to them." Life in this narrow span is defined by an intense, sweet love of their own and an equivalent suspicion of outsiders.[17] Conjugal love in these first families counters the more primitive belief in individual sufficiency and counters a generalized sympathy with humanity by reflecting the sufficiency of the family. Rousseau follows this thought to its logical conclusion, contending that barbarous families reproduce themselves by inbreeding. Here we find a paradox: Rousseau tells us in the *Essay on the Origin of Languages* that these earliest families had "marriages but there was no love at all," while in the *Second Discourse* he waxes that the first families experienced "the sweetest sentiments known to men: conjugal love and paternal love."[18] Is there sweet love or no love at all?

From the intense perspective of romantic love, conjugal love may appear to be nothing at all; conjugal love itself is based on a reading of human families that sees them as too self-sufficient. Rousseau connects happiness to desiring and desiring to trans-familial love: "I do not conceive how someone who needs nothing can love anything. I do not conceive how someone who loves nothing can be happy."[19] In the same manner, Rousseau sees that "genuine love" is connected to enthusiasm and enthusiasm with "an object of perfection, either real or chimerical, but always existing in the imagination."[20] Romantic love arises with felt insufficiency or restlessness, a feeling, born of the imagination, that what we have falls short of what we should have. Romantic love and language arise when man no longer wants to be alone or alone with his immediate family. Rousseau paints a bucolic picture of this transition in the *Essay on the Origin of Languages*.

> Girls would come to seek water for the household, young men would come to water their herds. There eyes, accustomed to the same sights since infancy, began to see with increased pleasure. The heart was moved by these novel objects; an unknown attraction renders it less savage; it feels pleasure at not being alone. . . . There at last was the true cradle of nations: from the pure crystal of the fountains flow the first fires of love.[21]

Rousseau depicts the same phenomena in the *Second Discourse*, but sees it as the first fateful step toward inequality, dependence, and baleful pride. As contacts between families spread, young people see each other more often, and "by dint of seeing one another, they can no longer do without seeing one another again." In each account, the youth lose their ferocity, they mingle more openly with one another, and eventually they dance and sing in something akin to festivals. In each case trans-familial political communities arise from this new birth of love, as do desires for individual distinction and attachments among individuals. No longer will the first available woman do (as it had for the savage and, in a sense, for those in the first families whose men had sex with their sisters): our notions of handsome and beautiful, virtuous and vicious, strong and adroit, ugly and eloquent arise when we start to desire a particular human being. Love outside the family brings with it an idealized picture of the beloved, along with a proud desire for distinction and esteem, feelings of jealousy, and our ability to be two-faced or divided. Whereas savages "peaceably wait[ed] for the impulsion of nature," now people seek out attachments and "at the least obstacle" their passion "becomes an impetuous fury."[22] Conjugal love is a "sweet habit which makes a man affectionate toward his companion," while romantic love is an "unbridled ardor which intoxicates him with the chimerical attractions of an object which he no longer sees as it really is."[23] The sweet habits of earlier love give way to the self-consciousness and illusion of romantic love. Disputes arise over sexual partners; men and women exploit one another. Beautiful sentiments of romantic love are connected with the origins of politics, the loss of personal independence, inequality, and vice.

Does Rousseau prefer the self-absorbed savage, the family-absorbed experience of conjugal love, or the intense desiring of romantic love? Mutual dependence is now a fact of human life, as is the civilized desiring associated with romantic love. Rousseau defends a sedate, natural dependence in the family. This means that his family embodies conjugal love more than romantic love, but without the baggage associated with conjugal love in its earlier forms (i.e., inbreeding). Whatever the label, Rousseau seeks, through the family, to inspire sentiments to combat the vain selfishness characteristic of modern life.

The Family of Natural Dependence

There is no avoiding dependence in the family, but not all dependencies are conducive to equality and human thriving. Rousseau seeks a family based on natural dependencies, one in which the essential man relies on a woman for the things that are essentially womanly and the essential woman relies on a man for things that essentially manly. This leads him to his controversial claims about the centrality of natural sex differences.[24] Men and women are not looking to strike a marriage bargain (as in Locke), for that involves all of the crude selfishness of a corrupt society. The impermanence and unease involved in striking a bargain leads to mutual use and sexual exploitation. Instead, marital and familial bonds are drawn tighter so the lens of individualism finds little place in these bonded relations. Heightened sexual desire, for both men and women, leads to marriage. This is part of the *new* nature. "Men depend on women because of their desires; women depend on men because of both their desires and their needs."[25] These dependencies are expressions of spiritual or moral life *and* they have a foundation in nature or bodies. "Observe," Rousseau suggests, "how the physical leads us unawares to the moral, and how the sweetest laws of love are born little by little from the coarse [*grossiere*] union of the sexes."[26] The law of love or this mutual dependence between the sexes sits on top of the law of nature, where the man's merit and rule in the household is based on his superior power: "This is not the law of love . . . but it is that of nature, prior to love itself."[27] How do we get from the coarse act of sex and from man's power to the law of love?

Rousseau draws the moral portrait of men and women from two biological tendencies implicated in the coarse sex act. Let me take the least controversial part of Rousseau's argument first. Only women bear children. From this fact Rousseau adduces many duties of mothers and wives and from their status as mothers and wives he accounts for the character appropriate to combine these two stations. "There is no parity between the two sexes in regard to the consequences of sex." Women have needs due to the fact that they bear children—a need for rest during the pregnancy, for peace so a woman can suckle her child, and for patience and gentleness to raise a child.[28] A mother also links a child to a father, and this part of her station leads me to suspect that the "laws of love" arise from the "coarse union" in another way. The coarse union also refers to the way in which men and women tend to participate in the physical act of love. "In *everything* connected with sex, woman and man are in every respect related and in every respect different." It is not from observing childbirth that we, with Rousseau, might conclude that men are "active and strong" and women "passive and weak"; nor does childbirth explain why men "must necessarily will and be able" while women "put up little resistance."[29] These are references to how sex is usually conducted among human beings (with man as the more active and controlling partner) and to man's unique physical contribution to sex (i.e., his erection). In sex as well as in bringing home the bacon, men's potency pleases women. If the woman does not please the man (and this requires that she be appealing to him), he cannot engage in sex. Woman is "made to please man and to be subjugated,"[30] two things that can be done at the same time when a man "takes" a woman during sex. Sexual encounters also depend on a woman's consent—she consents "to let him be stronger" and constrains "him to find his strength and make use of it."[31] Women use consent and constraint to establish *their* empire over men. Men and women have a republican arrangement—they rule and are ruled in turn[32]—though men may be unaware of how or even that they are ruled.

Let us move, with Rousseau, from making love to conjugal love, or from the differences in childbirth and sex to a more or less natural sexual division of labor. Women have a tougher time without men than men do without women, for women depend on men to give them what they need and to deem them worthy of it. Because women understand this, they see the need to move their men to a higher level of commitment, from the sexual to the moral. Women use their wiles to make themselves agreeable because they cannot rely on their physical power to get men to meet their needs; it is no small task to make men into faithful lovers and interested fathers. "Her own violence is in her charms," and in her willingness to resist sexual advances through her modesty and self-control. It is best for her to be esteemed sexually modest, and the best way to be so esteemed is to be sexually restrained. Sexual restraint among women not only reassures the father that the children are his, but also assures the husband that he has exclusive sexual control over his wife. Women play hard to get to ensure that they get what they need and desire from their men.[33] She is not taming the man's sexual passion pure and simple; she first must heighten it and then tame it. This is the woman's art. Since she depends on how she is viewed by her man, a woman depends, more than a man, on another's opinion. Society's opinions may *enslave* women to control their sexual desires and they do so to protect women from breaking "all the bonds of nature."[34] Though women are subject to public opinion and men rule them, they maintain an empire, a government, and a control over public opinion and over men through the cultivation of their womanly virtues. It is not unimportant for women to know how to make themselves attractive enough to men so men will stay interested. "Woman's empire is an empire of gentleness, skill and obligingness; her orders are caresses, her threats are tears. She ought to reign in the home as a minister does in the state—by getting herself commanded to do what she wants to do."[35] Women educate their husbands to responsibility, industry, care, and attention as willing providers and to their job as reasoning, patriotic citizens.

A woman rules the home by educating men and future citizens from this elevated perch as domestic empress. Bringing children into the world leads women to educate those children to their stations. The relation between mother and child has a physical basis in pregnancy and delivery and in the sustenance mothers provide by breastfeeding. Long-lasting maternal bonds arise out of these natural facts. Just as nursing a child requires a soft touch, women acquire the trait of gentleness with children. Just as a child is somewhat unpredictable, women learn to accept a certain level of suffering or deprivation and learn to defer to and accept (to an extent) others' ways. Attentions lavished on children by mothers are part of an effort to cultivate self-control, strength, judgment, modesty, and respect in their children. Mothers have time and attention to give and they give part of themselves in raising their children. Women swing between the poles of mother and wife, civilizing here and there with great attention to particulars. Rousseau's woman is a miracle, combining the ideal of republican motherhood with a modest and a bit of an austere public persona, yet she is a promising, ardent lover when she gets behind closed doors.[36]

The character of social men also derives from their active role in sex. Their role as father, not their rule, is mediated through the mother, and they support their children mostly by supporting their mother. Men bring what the family needs from the outside. By gathering the products of the field or hunting animals or, more generally, providing for the family, men give support and sanctuary to women so they can attend to their children. Mothers seek to instill this desire for physical labor in the service of the family in their sons, and wives should seek and cultivate this ability in their husbands. Even as women make men obey in the household, "it is part of the order of nature that the woman obey the man."[37] The relations men build with the outside world and their laboring power suit them to be the public presentation of the family. In his *Discourse on Political Economy*, we find Rousseau's most systematic discussion of why men rule the family and hence what the character of men is. Rule must be lodged somewhere, and, even if women are incapacitated for a short time, this "straw is enough to tip" rule to the man. Also, since a husband can never be as sure about the paternity of his children as his wife is, it may be necessary for him to oversee his wife's conduct because it is so important for him, in fulfilling his husbandly and fatherly duties, to be certain of paternity.[38]

The character of men and women, not that different by nature in one sense, becomes different through family life and later civil society. Their different destinies demand different educations.[39] Generally, women must learn to submit to the reasonable demands of, and even to love, the public opinion that constrains them; a woman's education is designed with her relation to man in mind.[40] In that context, Rousseau, the most disaffected intellectual ever to step foot on earth, insists that "what is, is good,"[41] for women appear subject to public opinion. Her natural practical reasoning and her discernment of individual differences should be made effective through daily practice in household management, and this task fits her native predilection for "getting to a known end." A herculean task lies in her future, and she needs all the practical wisdom she can muster. Men will gain a degree of independence from public opinion as befits their future station, and their education prepares them for hardihood in labor and fierceness in battle. Their reasoning skills are directed more to ascertaining general rules and "finding that end itself."[42] These different educations prepare them not only for the sexual division of labor, but for the separate spheres that they will occupy in married life.

Willing Partners and Separate Spheres

I have not discussed the legal regime (i.e., inheritance and divorce law) of Rousseau's family because that is not where the action is. What concerns Rousseau are the mores that interpret the demands of nature and foster expectations and actions. The law of fashion is the fundamental law. The war over mores centers on the family, and the most significant battles concern the status and role of female modesty and the separate but equal spheres occupied by the sexes that Rousseau thinks is most beneficial to, and most beautiful in, men and women. On this battlefield Rousseau meets his enemies in his day and ours. Rousseau's enemies are love's enemies, for they would have men and women share the same character and the same spheres, or they would so separate the spheres that they would sap the joy out of conjugal love and family. Paris is the locus of this cosmopolitan vice; Calvinist Geneva the locus of an opposite, restrictive vice.[43] Rousseau's marriage mores weave between Paris and Geneva, so it is necessary to look at these two inadequate models of marital relations to get our bearings for his discussion of love.

The Problem with Geneva

Geneva's premier political institutions are the *circles* or clubs, which bring men together in their societies and women to theirs for common amusements. Relaxing from their business, men gather to "gamble, chat, read, drink and smoke"; women chat and engage in "inexhaustible gossip."[44] There is nothing necessarily harmful in this picture, but it seems men are apt to stay out all night as often as they can get away with it because their severe and censorious wives are joyless shrews. Modesty and self-control have become repression and antipathy to sex among women. Feminine virtue without feminine charms is not feminine virtue. Men shirk their political and familial responsibilities because there is no joy in their homes. The men of Geneva are interested in commerce and business, in which their "austere parsimony," industriousness, and sound business sense displace the loving and tending virtues related to fatherhood and citizenship. Geneva is filled with cheapskates and gossips, laborers and busybodies. Rousseau seems to describe Geneva when, in *Emile*, he complains that "so much has been done to prevent women from being lovable that husbands have become indifferent," and "by enslaving decent women only to gloomy duties, we have banished from marriage everything which could make it attractive to men."[45] So concerned with coquettishness and flirtatiousness, women become sexless and austere. Rousseau traces the root of this problem back to what he sees as Christianity's world-denying asceticism and to the arrangements of marriages for the purposes of maintaining or establishing rank.[46]

Geneva's marriages are not based on consent, which signifies a political problem. Arranged marriages or marriages based on rank or property perpetuate society's castes and factions. Women do not marry men for their character. Suitableness and preference take a back seat to pecuniary, political, or class interests. As such marriages multiply over the generations, factions based on family name reinforce divisions based on class and economic inequality, to the detriment of civic unity. Geneva was rent by faction in the 1700s, as Rousseau knew but rarely mentioned.[47] Cities that unite men and women in this way undermine civic unity, denude the public square, and dampen the domestic hearth. "The more the gap between noble and commoner widens, the more the conjugal bond is relaxed," Rousseau writes, "and the more there are rich and poor, the less there are fathers and mothers."[48] Geneva's unhappy marriages are as much a cause as an effect of its civic corruption.

Rousseau offers specific remedies for the problem of faction in the *Letter to d'Alembert*. The general principle underlying his recommendations is found in *Emile*:

> Do you wish to prevent such abuses and to promote happy marriages? Stifle prejudices, forget human institutions, and consult nature. Do not unite people who suit each other only in a given condition and who will no longer suit one another if this condition happens to change; instead, unite people who will suit one another in whatever situation they find themselves. . . . I do not say that compatibilities based on convention are immaterial in marriage, but I do say that the influence of natural compatibilities is so much more important that it alone is decisive for the fate of married life.[49]

Geneva needs nothing short of a revolution in its approach to marriage and hence nothing short of a political revolution will do. Couples must be taught that marriage originates in consent reflecting a judgment about suitableness, and that consent is the result and proof of love. Consent buckles love to marriage through an analysis of character.

How is this to be accomplished? After lambasting d'Alembert's proposal to introduce theatre into the city, Rousseau recommends the introduction of public dances and beauty contests in the hope that men and women develop "a taste for one another."[50] Girls will doll themselves up and, modestly, demonstrate that they can, like their Parisian sisters, glitter and be gay. Rousseau depicts the dances under the dour supervision of Puritan zealots, so such dances will not corrupt the youngsters, but he intends their introduction to have profound, long-term personal and political implications.

> These occasions for gathering in order to form unions and for arranging the establishment of families would be frequent means for reconciling divided families and bolstering the peace so necessary in our state. Without altering the authority of fathers, the inclinations of children would be somewhat freer; the first choice would depend somewhat more on their hearts; the agreements of age, temperament, taste, and character would be

> consulted somewhat more; and less attention would be paid to those of station and fortune which make bad matches when they are satisfied at the expense of others. The relations becoming easier, the marriages would be more frequent; these marriages, less circumscribed by rank, would prevent the emergence of parties, temper excessive inequality, and maintain the body of the people better in the spirit of its constitution.[51]

Rousseau seeks to insinuate conjugal love into Geneva's marriages so there will be genuine reciprocity and mutual dependence between husband and wife. Reciprocity would require that one loves the other for that other's own sake and that there is a sense of equality and freedom in making the marriage. Spouses relish the complementary stations of husband/father and wife/mother. "Mutual dependence ought to be their first bond. Their eyes and their hearts ought to be their first guides. Their first duty once they are united is to love each other; since loving or not loving is not within our control, this duty necessarily involves another, which is to begin by loving each other before being united."[52] The coarse sexual union is present as raw material for a deeper sentimental attachment symbolized in children. What begins in consent becomes, ideally, a union of two different creatures into a single one—the union of hearts, in which each invests pride and their most beautiful and meritorious self into what they create. The reform of Geneva opens this cold and cranky people to the charms of civilized love.

The reform has a political tincture as well.[53] A more complete intermarriage scheme will tend to introduce a greater degree of civic unity, corroding the city's factionalism. Founding families on consent and genuine love will tend to populate the city with concerned, responsible citizens instead of disengaged husbands. Dullards incapable of being stirred, the men of Geneva have not been men in the strict sense. Love of family leads to a manly demand to protect it from all forms of despotism. Perhaps the greatest political reform, however, lies in the elevation of choice and individual right over external authority in marriage. We take this for granted, but it is a revolution. When marriage begins with an agreement proceeding from the desires and will of men and women, politics more likely will be thought of in the same fashion. Republican Geneva will become more republican if it accepts Rousseau's proposal.

The Problem of Paris

So offended were Parisians at Geneva's Calvinist and Christian repressions that they threw the baby out with the bathwater and made love more difficult while trying to make it easier. If the people of Geneva had ignored love based in attraction, the more sophisticated Parisians questioned all differences between men and women in establishing a way of life in which each sex would be treated equally and the same. Rousseau knows that his views on this matter will not be popular among Parisian advocates of a more gender-neutral society and he anticipates their arguments at nearly every turn. He knows that chastity will be denigrated and the complex of feminine virtues will be lampooned as part of a plot to preserve the power of men; that modesty will be exposed as a social construction denying women access to primordial, sexual pleasures; that his opponents, desiring to establish the equality of the sexes, will try to find ways of making the consequences of sex equal; that the sexual double standard violates modern sensibilities of liberty and equality; that modesty and shame, self-restraint and patience, gentleness and courtship will be characterized as popular prejudices reflecting yesterday's morality; and even that those seeking to free women from dependence on both men and public opinion will question the importance of fathers for children.[54]

The Parisian vision of sexual relationships and marriage involves a critique of modesty, a defense of human equality and freedom, and an idea about nature. Modesty is an unnecessary refinement that inhibits sexual pleasure. It is, above all, an *inauthentic* virtue, in that it forces women to sublimate their otherwise strong sexual passions in the service of a vague social good (the attachment of fathers to their children) that may be served by offering easier access to sex and the lure of more agreeable company. Since men do not feel shame about their sex lives, there seems to be no need for women to feel any about theirs. Women can win men's acceptance by making themselves agreeable and risqué company for men—by becoming a bit more like men. Such a relationship also seems to be demanded by the modern principles of equality and liberty, which seem to require the commingling of the sexes at the times, in the manner, and in the places of their choosing. It would be a betrayal for women to try to exercise an unjust ascendancy over men, their equals, who just seem to want the same thing; what is good for the gander is, after all, good for the goose. Undergirding this is the modern disposition toward nature as a problem to be solved through ingenuity. Womanly modesty may be one way of handling man's commitment problem and of keeping men interested in sticking around, but other means may be devised. Whatever problems (i.e., children) may result from sexual unions, perhaps a new way will suggest itself and replace modesty. Marriage, in any event, may survive the decline of modesty, and sexual enjoyment combined with marital friendship will be the hallmark of this new, improved, enticing alternative.

The linchpin of Rousseau's argument against this view concerns his understanding of how mores operate. Human nature is malleable, but there is logic to how things change. He spins out that logic to counter sophisticated progressive tendencies. "The two sexes have so strong and so natural a relation to one another that the morals of one always determine those of the other."[55] Removing modesty undermines the basis for mutual respect, enduring love, and sweet and beautiful family life. Men desire women. The decline of modesty means that men will no longer *esteem* them, nor will men need to show, over the long haul, that they will serve their woman's needs. Without the need to demonstrate strength of character and self-restraint, men settle on making themselves agreeable, on flattering women, and on serving women for as long as is necessary to gain satisfaction. When women are immodest, the commitment men are willing to make to them tends to be only skin deep. Love in this circumstance will last only as long as man and woman please one another, so theirs is destined to be a temporary arrangement. This has a terrific long-term effect on the quality of men, for "men's thinking in large measure depends" on what women want.[56] Love dies without the erotic tension provided by sexual modesty. Men cease cultivating the strength of character necessary to prove their seriousness to women, and they lack the strength to be concerned fathers and citizens. What modernity is left with when men and women mingle to trifle with love is, in Tocqueville's haunting phrase, "weak men and disreputable women."[57] Parisian ethics cause women to choose between their self-respect and acceptance by men, most of the time to the detriment of their self-respect.

Rousseau's other reaction to the Parisian visions sounds more conventional. In effect, Rousseau asks: what about the children? Rousseau tries to get women to return to modesty by showing them that it is to their advantage, rightly understood, in helping to keep their men around for their children. In any event, human beings cannot wish away the consequences of sex, and those consequences burden women more than men. The "austere duties of women" are derived from the "single fact that a child ought to have a father."[58] These duties need not be too austere (as Rousseau's hope to introduce love and consent into Geneva shows) nor need they undermine the capacity for love (as his treatment of modesty suggests).

We must not put too much emphasis on modesty here in connecting men to the family. For Rousseau, love depends on acts of imagination surrounding the virtue of modesty. Paternal love depends on a different, and perhaps a greater, act of imagination. Modesty is necessary to connect men to the family, but it is not sufficient. The joys of family life are interpreted as joys (instead of as burdens) by a properly constituted imagination. Rousseau paints a picture of family life that interprets natural duties as fulfilling and beautiful. "Is there a sight in the world so touching," Rousseau asks, "as that of a mother surrounded by her children . . . procuring a happy life for her husband and prudently governing the home?"[59] Not in founding a successful business or in winning a sports competition or in waging successful battle are the truest joys to be found. Politics may not even be as satisfying as family life! What man would not want to love and be loved by the one at the center of a lovely domestic life? What person would disrupt this scene of wondrous love and dedication? Only when men and women embrace such an image is the family complete. There is no scornful treatment of raising children as being too uninteresting to involve the man, nor is there a denigration of it as "woman's work" in Rousseau, nor is family life seen as disconnected from the real purposes of life involved in "man's work."[60] Rousseau paints a picture of happy domestic life so that the family can make itself in the image of warmth, consistency, and repose. Families must spend significant time together in developing the habits of caring. Without numerous points of contact, families consist of polite strangers, without deep mutual concerns or sentimental attachment.[61] When Rousseau discusses parent-child relations, he is worried not so much about the quality of care provided by non-parental custodians such as a governess or a wet nurse (or a day care). He is concerned that when parents leave their duties to others, the child will not be capable of loving as deeply or attaching as unconditionally to another. Quality of life is his concern, not quality of care.[62] Rousseau elevates the status of domestic life and thus the place of women, the domestic governess. The love of a "peaceful and domestic life" is acquired by tasting it in one's paternal home and being loved by a dedicated mother and father; the beauties of this life will die unless the taste for them is acquired.[63]

Where does this taste now exist? Rousseau's novels—especially *Julie* and *Emile*—draw portraits of warm family life, though these portraits are more problematic than they first appear. Rousseau also draws another portrait in his improbable account of England in the *Letter to d'Alembert*.

England's Ideal Solution

Geneva wisely separated the spheres of men and women, but sapped marriage of the love necessary to interest people in it. Paris rightly emphasized love, but misunderstood the resistance and separation necessary to make love last and deepen. Neither city properly laid the groundwork for beautiful domestic life: Geneva was too austere; in Paris, the sexes mingled too easily and kids did not enter the picture overmuch. England's economy of love is more sustainable because it emphasizes the joyful bringing together of two from separate spheres. Could this nation of shopkeepers, as that great lover Napoleon called it, have something to teach Parisians about love?

English couples as Rousseau depicts them enjoy separate lives that heighten the differences between the sexes, and yet have similar tastes. English families have a greater "taste for the true pleasures in life" and "think less of appearing happy than of being so." "English women are gentle and timid,"[64] and they confine themselves to the private realm and its joys. Precisely what this means we can glean from Rousseau's praise of breastfeeding, something English women seem to enjoy.

> Let mothers deign to nurse their children, morals will reform themselves, nature's sentiments will be awakened in every heart, the state will be repeopled. . . . The bother of children, which is believed to be an importunity, becomes pleasant. It makes the father and mother more necessary, dearer to one another; it tightens the conjugal bond between them. When the family is lively and animated, the domestic cares constitute the dearest occupation of the wife and the sweetest enjoyment of the husband. . . . Let women once again become mothers, men will soon become fathers and husbands again.[65]

English men respond to their wives by becoming "hard and haughty" and, in contrast to the French, English citizens "love their country and its laws." Unlike Genevans, English men and women maintain a taste for each other. English men and women, for instance, enjoy the pleasures of the table and enjoy a good drink after the meal; but English women prefer to sip tea while the men like the grape. They both enjoy novels, quiet walks in the park, and amusing games. Love, for the English, is "terrible and tragic; nothing less is at stake . . . than losing reason or life in it."[66]

Sexual differentiation sits with tight marriages, marriages based on consent, and the experience of political liberty, and these connections exist by an inexorable logic. Heterosexual love is the most natural basis for human beings to associate with one another.[67] Marriage ties men to the political community by tying them to their wives and families—men serve the community in part because it is good for their family. This does not mean that service to the community is done for the sake of the family. It means that there must be a "natural base on which to form conventional ties." It is the "good son, the good husband, and the good father who make the good citizen."[68] Rousseau's portrait of the English is relevant here. English men are "hard and hearty" because they recognize how much their women and children are dependent on them; this recognition motivates them to participate in politics (to fight, to vote, to deliberate) because it is part of protecting their more natural relationships. The sexual division of labor—the private woman's dependence on her man—prepares the way for healthy community life. "In a republic, men are needed,"[69] and the English are manly because they practice the sexual division of labor; English women are loving enough to interest their men and dependent enough to prompt their men to citizenship. Without a "natural base" in family life, it is difficult to imagine that the English would "love their country and its laws." The love for a political community is an artificial sentiment prepared by more natural sentiments of family love.

Rousseau's depiction of the English is a fascinating work of imagination that does not sit well with his complaints about the disappearance of citizenship among modern commercial peoples and his criticisms of the bourgeois.[70] It draws attention to the fact that human beings imagine reality to suit the grain of nature. Or should I say the grains of nature? Nature is open enough so that more than one work of imagination may explain and shape our experience for us. Above all, imagination allows us to see the conjugal-romantic love and paternal love among the English for the goods that they are. This emphasis on imagination brings us back to the importance of how we think about nature's stubborn facts. Should we think of those natural facts as obstacles to human freedom and impediments to human happiness that, if possible, we should remove through our ingenuity? Should we relish those natural facts as essential to what it means to be human and resist efforts to remove them? If the latter, what is the underlying reason for respecting nature instead of overcoming her?

The Family's Ground and the Limits of Romantic Love

Rousseau walks a tightrope on these questions, as he must. The whole of Rousseau's *Emile*, for instance, aims at preparing Emile for marriage to Sophie. As Rousseau, Emile's tutor, builds up the taste of Emile for Sophie and Sophie for Emile and brings them to the point of ecstatic anticipation of their joining together, he pulls Emile aside to tell him that this is as good as it gets. "Before tasting the pleasures of life, you have exhausted its happiness. There is nothing beyond what you have felt. . . . You have enjoyed more from hope than you will ever enjoy in reality. Imagination adorns what one desires but abandons it when it is in one's possession. . . . If your present state could have lasted forever, you would have found supreme happiness."[71] Love and marriage may not go together like a horse and carriage after all: human beings seem consigned to a hopeless subjectivity. Rousseau goes even further in this direction before he introduces Sophie to Emile.

> In love everything is only illusion. I admit it. But what is real are the sentiments for the truly beautiful with which love animates us and which makes us love. This beauty is not in the object one loves; it is the work of our errors. So, what of it? Does the lover any less sacrifice all of his low sentiments to this crude imaginary model? . . . Does he detach himself any less from the baseness of the human *I*?[72]

Rousseau's understanding of love contains a profound paradox. On the one hand, the pursuit of love is a standing reproof of those who embrace a selfish system of morals, for it reflects the human desire and need to join together into something larger. Love reflects incompleteness in human beings and a need to detach themselves from themselves in reaching completion. The imagination is central to this: it imputes ideas of beauty and merit to the beloved, so that when a man loves his beautiful and meritorious woman, he also loves the good in the ideas transcending her. On the other hand, ideas of beauty and merit, products of imagination, are *self-consciously* human inventions, errors, and illusions.[73] What transcends the beloved is itself the product of human imagination. Earlier thinkers (and some later thinkers) found it necessary to ground imagination in History (Hegel), in sound science (Comte, Durkheim, and other positivists), or in the transcendent order (John Paul II). Rousseau's imaginary ground for romantic love is more open-ended, and he invites a battle for, by, and of the imagination in subsequent generations. With apologies to Freud, what is the future of this illusion when it is known to be an illusion?

Rousseau's understanding of love is not entirely open-ended. His understanding of romantic love is built on all that is implicated in the coarse union of the sexes. Rousseau's portrait of romantic love is a plausible and powerful product of the imagination. The plausibility and power of that image depend in part on the strength of the cultural apparatus that supports it and in part on how well it matches the experience of romantic love. These two things—the image and the experience—are not unrelated, but they are not the same. Here it is necessary to mention children again and the tensions between conjugal love and paternal love that all are bound to experience. Rousseau, Emile's tutor, prepares him for a life of marriage after the fire has gone, a "marriage for all seasons," in which he is also ready to fulfill rather unromantic duties such as being "a member of the state" and a "head of the family."[74] *Emile* itself has the trajectory of a romantic comedy out of Hollywood: the relationship is sealed and the marriage promised, but the audience does not get to see the spouses feeding slop to the pigs, draining the bacon grease, or squirting ketchup on a shirt. Like Locke, Rousseau sees that romantic love is an unstable basis for enduring family life. "Whatever precautions anyone may take, enjoyment wears out pleasures, and love is worn out before all others. But when love has lasted a long time, a sweet habit fills the void it leaves behind, and the attraction of mutual confidence succeeds the transports of passion."[75] We seem to be back to basing the family on Locke's more mundane "mutual Support, and Assistance" and "Care, and Affection."[76] The sensible English approach shorn of Locke's contractual apparatus—a civilized conjugal love based on "sweet habit" supported by mutual taste, compatibility based on difference, affection, and the raising of children—is more likely to endure. Questions remain. Is such a love satisfying to human beings? If so, has the natural account based on the nature of the sexes sufficed to ground it?

Rousseau knows that mere common affection will not satisfy all. Because parental duties can be uninspiring and unromantic, and because human beings long to be completed, Rousseau is more worried about adultery than divorce. If a couple is invested heavily in romantic love, what happens when its stock falls? The search for another begins when one's beloved no longer satisfies one's ideal of beauty and merit, and experience eventually exposes the falsity in an imagined ideal. Vain searches animate the clueless Parisians, whose mores and institutions only exacerbate the problem, but such vanities are heightened by Rousseau's project. We can gain a deeper appreciation for the English mode, as Rousseau imagines it, in light of this observation. The separation of the sexes separates the mundane from the beautiful. Separate bedrooms, separate toilets, separate spheres of work keep the mundane things out of the marital relation so as to make it easier to imagine and see the beauty in a spouse. The ideal is kept alive as spouses meet to do (some) beautiful things. They walk in the countryside, bounce the kids on their knees, share a passion for contemplative readings and novels, play whist, and enjoy the pleasures of the table, all of which, in one way or another, suggest ideas of beauty or skill connected to the other.

Adultery was not a sustained theme in Locke, that most English of philosophers, because he did not tempt marriage with so elevated an understanding of love. For Locke, marriage is a contract for the procreation and education of children. Drawing the marriage tighter around an imagined spiritual ideal, Rousseau, it seems, prohibits divorce not because of the children but because of the nature and morality of consent.[77] In this there is an analogy between sex and marriage. In consenting to have sex, a woman consents to and identifies with the potential consequences of sex; her willingness to live a mother's life follows from her consenting to sex. Entering into marriage is a free act, wherein human beings bind themselves to another by their own choice. Times will be hard and persons will no doubt change, but respect for the initial choice and an unshakeable commitment bind marriage. Marriage contracts are not based on interest, mutual service, or helping out with the kids. Contracts construct an ideal and make a promise to serve that ideal throughout a lifetime. Freedom seems sufficient to create morality in this case.

The city cannot stand without the family, nor the family without people inside with properly constituted imaginations interpreting sexual and familial experiences in a particular way. The family provides the city with citizens capable of attachments. Mothers are the key to this political project, for they must rule as domestic empresses. Once they leave this perch, no one will be home to ensure that individuals are habituated to serving something outside of themselves. Thus Rousseau is famous for celebrating the role of "republican motherhood," a role in which mothers nurture future citizens.[78] This place for women marks a step up in their political importance, and their lack of direct participation in politics is not overly regretted. The family seems to be the sphere of life in the modern world that is most likely to give rise to happiness and immense satisfaction for both men and women. In fact, it is almost with a sense of doleful duty that men leave the house to participate in the corrupt, corrupting job of politics. Family life is the closest civilized approximation to original wholeness, innocence, and goodness, and it seems to be an end in itself.

At the same time, family life cannot really satisfy human beings. Rousseau's defense of the family requires that people have a properly cultivated imagination, but there are limits to poetic artifice. The attachments that make up family life are, in a decisive sense, artificially or socially constructed because human beings are, for Rousseau, self-centered and malleable. Natural selfishness and human malleability work against each another. Malleability suggests that human beings have tendencies to change, adapt, and expand, and this leads to a corruption of man's original simplistic self-centeredness. Rousseau's portrait of family life is designed to point human beings toward a less corrupting way of life; this way is illusory, a work of Rousseau's philosophically informed poetic imagination. His artistic works are necessary to prevent the worst forms of life from arising, but these constructions remain constructions nonetheless.

The fact that love is self-consciously a construction does not mean it will cease to be alluring. Rousseau's dramatic works—including *Narcissus* and *Pygmalion*—show that the most self-conscious people can fall in love with things they know to be illusions. Yet Rousseau's thought also shows that the self-conscious embrace of an illusion may not be powerful enough to hold the family together. He tries to show that his portrait of the family is more than a work of imagination by drawing a line from the facts of human sexual biology to his understanding of separate spheres occupied by husbands and wives.[79] This is what gives Rousseau's most astringent critics the idea that he traps women (and men) in a cage of biological determinism. Rousseau gives this impression because it serves his purposes of grounding his family and its mores in something relatively constant like human biology and of showing that a return to natural innocence and wholeness has a basis in biology. The beauty of family life is cultivated by imagination, and Rousseau's impression gives rise to sentiments friendly to establishing human happiness and virtue. This remains a product of imagination, and there are progressive elements in human nature that work against securing such happiness and virtue. Imagination alone is not enough to form an aesthetically consistent whole available for human life and defensible by reason. The perfect human whole, of which the family, for Rousseau, is a prime example, must be or become inherently rational and possible instead of illusory. Celebrating a new kind of heroic wholeness is not half as good as showing that this satisfying wholeness is achieved in History. History ceases to be what alienates man from himself; it can be what helps man achieve unity, happiness, and reconciliation.[80]

Few modern thinkers draw the family closer together than Rousseau; few call into question the sufficiency of nature more. Rousseau insists that human beings respect nature, but he provides such a low portrait of nature that he suggests that the most interesting, edifying, and important aspects of human development are acquired through time. If Rousseau manages to embrace each side of this without contradiction, his successors wonder why human beings should and if we could make a better world for ourselves if we left nature behind. This turns Rousseau upside down, and it is the work of G. W. F. Hegel.

Part II

The Moving Ballast of History

Chapter 4

Hegel's Modern Marital Unity
More Than a Contract, Less Than a Sacrament

Hegel's thinking about the family is penetrating and challenging to all sides of today's family debates. He shows the sense in seemingly contradictory opinions about marriage and family life and then shows how the contradictions are only apparent. For instance, many today see marriage as a means to self-fulfillment. Perhaps this means that marriage helps us to become better people or to cultivate our talents and grow. Perhaps it means that we learn how to gain a stable character as we love someone through good times and bad. These views evaluate marriage according to what it provides the *individual.* Today's voices of retrenchment see marriage as an important social institution that makes moral and legal claims on individuals. Married couples have children. They create, use, and save property. This view emphasizes what marriage provides as a *social institution* and how it transforms individuals into parts of something larger than themselves.

This most persistent problem in modern marriage is the conflict between the individual purposes of marriage and its transformative role and communal purposes. A husband is deeply dissatisfied with his marriage, yet he sticks it out for his children. His inner conflict represents a conflict of genuine goods: the desire for individual satisfaction and a desire to assist his children. Women want the satisfaction of work outside the home and the satisfactions of family life too. Men sacrifice their freedom so they can work more hours and the family can prosper. The tragedy of modern marriage and family life is that it makes contradictory claims on human beings.

Hegel tries to show that this tragic conflict is not the deepest rendering of claims on human beings. The contradictions between individual satisfaction and communal demands introduce instability to marriage, but, when we reconcile the contradictions, we see that both individual satisfaction and contentment depend on the importance of the claims made by the marriage.

Hegel reconciles the goods *within* marriage and family life and reconciles family life to the goods pursued *outside* family life (i.e., shows how family life comports with life in civil society and in the state). When the family is reconciled to what is *outside* family life, individuals can be reconciled to life *within* the family. This reconciliation is an accomplishment of History. Family life is essential to the enjoyment of freedom and the support of individual emotional needs. It also prepares people for a rational and free life of citizenship in a fully developed state.[1] Family life is a moment in a free, rational, and happy life, but the virtues associated with family are not the highest virtues: ethical love in the family is lower in dignity to the satisfactions of self-consciousness enjoyed as a member of the rational State. This simultaneous elevation and diminution of family life defines Hegel's treatment of the family.

Much like Rousseau, who thinks man is perfectible and that he acquires most of his interesting attributes in history, Hegel sees freedom as a latent possibility for human beings. He sees that it is mankind's destiny to be free; freedom is revealed and made real through History. History is where human beings make their self-consciousness by differentiating themselves from mere nature.[2] Man's turn against nature outside and inside himself educates him to the creative power of his will. This in turn starts the engine of History toward its goal of Freedom. Spirit [*Geist*] emerges from nature and transforms it into a second nature that makes up the human world.[3] Man labors and creates in part by intending to do so, but the making of freedom happens as the cunning, unintentional result of thousands of such acts in History.

The family is a realm of "immediate" and "natural" spirit; it is "ethical life in its natural form"; it expresses "merely *natural*" feelings.[4] Since the family is a realm of nature and since History involves the overcoming of nature, must not the "natural" family be overcome by the progress of History? Hegel's discussion of the family reveals, to abuse one of his famous phrases, the rational in the natural. This leads to conservative and radical results. As much as any other modern thinker, Hegel draws the family together and accounts for what the family does and does not do, how it should be organized, how it unites form and function, and what principles limit it. He sees families as units or wholes, and he conceives of modern countries as communities of families. All of this is enmeshed with his respect for nature in the case of the family. On the other hand, as much as any other modern thinker, he shows that respecting the family as a *natural* unit is problematic in light of our human propensity to transform the merely natural. Seeing the rational in the natural of the family and in opposing the application of individualistic thinking to the family, Hegel appears as a conservative defender of mores and institutions sustaining the traditional family unity. Opposing nature and embracing the transforming power of History, Hegel appears open to successive remakings of family life and a more complete conquest of nature. Hegel sees a process that points to an end, yet may refuse to stop.

The Place of Family in Ethical Life

The importance of family recedes as the State rises above other aspects of human life. Human beings make social institutions according to the needs of Spirit and freedom. History is the unmaking and remaking of conventions, products of Spirit, by desiring individuals. Individuals seek unity and reconciliation when they dismantle existing conventions and institutions, which aimed to make individuals feel at home. Hegel shows that the perfect reconciliation is a differentiated and mediated unity characteristic of the modern world. The State, with its conventions of liberty, is the apex of this complex mediation. Hegel's philosophy of History, a story of how the rational State arises, is also a story of how the family falls in relation to the State.[5]

Patriarchy as such declines as human beings limit paternal rule and as they grasp for the liberating distinction between public and private. In Hegel's account, true patriarchy dies in the Orient as individual or subjective freedom finds a place in the world. Blood relation and "the simply natural elements" of the family basis are limited and "outside of these limits the members of the community must enter upon the position of independent personality." Families lose self-sufficiency. The gods are no longer family gods, which means that religion leaves the sphere of the family and human beings come to embrace civic religion and then universal religion. Economic production gives way to trade and commerce, which means that the family no longer aspires to be a self-sufficient economic unit. Political rule is no longer dynastic and the power of fathers over sons is limited. Hegel embraces the removal of extraneous fetters that bind individuals to the family and the exclusion of the political principle, religious devotion, and economic production from the familial realm. Families become what families should be after extra-familial functions are forfeited to social institutions better able to accomplish them. A "natural" family—private, small, tightly knit, mutually dependent, affective, emotionally intense, and unified—emerges once History purges it of unnatural elements and transfers those unnatural elements to their proper spheres.

This new family sets mature individuals free from the family, and there is a free space for them in civil society (economic and civil life) and in the modern State to pursue their supra-familial identities. Yet the creation of the civil society, a great achievement of the modern world, poses a distinctively modern threat to the family. Previously, in the Orient, the family was the imperial power; in modernity, civil society is. Civil society is a realm of life where individuals think of themselves as self-subsisting in their effort to satisfy their own needs and pursue their own interests.[6] Individuals tend to maintain the individualist mode of thinking characteristic of civil society when they think about communal institutions such as the family and the state. The idea of subjective freedom spreads to all in the modern world, and it threatens to become ferocious, reckless, and destructive of the family and the state if it is not made more rational and stable through a proper understanding of the modern world's institutions.

Free human beings are situated in a culture that favors the emergence of freedom, properly understood.[7] Ethical life is the "*concept of freedom which has become the existing world*." Human beings would not liberate themselves from merely natural drives and subjective desires without institutions conducive to the development of rational freedom.[8] Freedom is real when we see that we have made the world's institutions consistent with our freedom. Without *seeing* this, self-legislating, free people tend to see institutions as arbitrary, "natural" limits on human freedom and to embrace a willful, arbitrary destructive power to refashion the "natural" world according to subjective will. Modern utopianism, dangerous to settled and reconciled political existence, follows from this failure of understanding. Without the existence of institutions consistent with freedom, individuals are not free. Hegel educates modern people about how freedom exists in institutions; his task is to get those smitten with subjective liberty to see how the modern world's institutions, far from limiting freedom, promote it. Ethical life, for Hegel, is where human beings recognize that an individual attains freedom "only by becoming the citizen of a good state."[9]

Not just any family will do for establishing the idea of freedom. An advanced, bourgeois family supports the idea of freedom, just as advances in the idea of freedom bring human beings to embrace the institution of the bourgeois family.

Ethical Love and the Institutions of the Marital Unity

When subjective freedom is imperial, it shapes the way we see the family, civil society, and the state. As it affects the family, the triumph of subjective freedom encourages people to see love as an arbitrary passion and to see marriage as a contract restraining freedom. Confusion about marriage arises from a failure to see how love relates to marriage. Having surrendered Hegel's conception of ethical love as creating a unity, people seek alternative ideas about love and, finding no common ground, they base relationships on subjective, arbitrary, personal ideas about love. Such ideas point to a deinstitutionalized, *laissez-faire* family—a family without form and without ends.

The most famous example of privileging the standpoint of subjective freedom is social contract thinking. Equally troubling, for Hegel, are efforts to define love and the family from the subjective standpoint. Subjective love leads to three crude notions of marriage. Systems of natural law reduce marriage to its "physical aspect or natural character" or sensuality in making the "sexual relationship" into marriage's essence. Locke, Kant, and others also err in seeing marriage as a civil contract "entitling the parties concerned to use one another." A third error (founded in romanticism and popularized by Mill) equates marriage with love without purging love of its arbitrary, indeterminate, and unstable humor.[10] Errors about the nature of marriage are based on a love feeling that is neither satisfying nor able to be satisfied, because, in them, the individualist stance is never superseded.

Let us examine these errors so as to orient Hegel's idea of the marital and familial unity against its alternatives. First, marriage is not essentially a physical relationship. Sexual drives—quintessential subjective feelings—are "made subordinate in marriage" and are "destined to be extinguished in [their] very satisfaction, while the spiritual bond asserts *its rights* as the substantial factor and thereby starts out as indissoluble *in itself* and exalted above the contingency of the passion and of particular transient caprice." Love does not exist against sensuality, but the ephemeral feelings associated with sex lack the durability and rationality of ethical love. Human sexuality points to a substantial, marital unity.[11] Sexual desire is spiritualized in marriage and leads to a freer, less corporally defined way of unifying with another. Face-to-face sex is about more than sex: sex is an incomplete or temporary act that points toward the human need for a complete and permanent joining with another in deeper, lasting human relationship.[12] Sensuality abounds in marriage because it finds its proper, subordinate place there.

Second, seeing marriage as a contract is "disgraceful." Contractual relationships are temporary alliances to promote mutual interests. The giving up of goods under contract depends on an evaluation of how the other party fulfills its duties, which means that each party stands apart or holds back from the contracting relationship. Contracting parties are not transformed by the contract: contracts are agreements based on "arbitrary will" and not the rational will, and they do not transform the individual into part of a larger unity. Conditions of equality are necessary to establish a contract—a contract is made between two parties "alike in power and thus in one another's eyes living beings from every point of view," yet these conditions do not guarantee the experience of love. As Hegel writes, "The precise nature of marriage is to begin from the point of view of contract—i.e., that of individual personality as a self-sufficient unit—*in order to supersede it.*" Marriage overcomes contractual thinking by uniting man and woman internally as sharers of ethical love, not externally as those who rent each other's equipment. Marriage partners "consent to *constitute a single person* and to give up their natural and individual personalities within this union."[13] This does not mean that women surrender their identities to husbands, as the convention of wives accepting their husband's name suggests. "Marriage arises out of the free surrender by both sexes of their personalities."[14] Marriage changes the way individuals view themselves. Husbands and wives each start to view themselves as members of something larger than themselves and to sense their own dependence on the marriage.

Hegel's critique of the third error—the equation of marriage with love—brings us to the heart of the matter. For Hegel, marriage is a relationship about love, but the fact that something is called love does not make it love; love has a character. Love is a feeling.[15] If it stays on the level of feelings, it is a mutable matter of taste, an infatuation, or a passing fancy. Ethical love is rational so that the marriage can be genuinely human and free, in that the partner is chosen on the basis of rational, self-determined principles; and it is objective, in that it joins the self to a common good shared with another. The reasonableness underlying marriage flows in predictable channels. Couples preparing to marry make judgments about their prospects in marriage—whether a spouse will be a good parent, or will find gainful employment, or will be faithful. Reversing

Rousseau, Hegel sees that the "more ethical course" is when "the decision to marry comes first and is followed by the inclination so that the two come together in the actual marital union."[16] It is more ethical for a decision to precede inclination because marriage involves many unpredictable and unforeseeable eventualities (jobs are lost, kids get sick, people change, etc.) that affect how we feel. It is unreasonable to expect anyone to take in all the data about a prospective spouse, weigh that information, and make judgments about *future* compatibility. Marriage is much less a contract based on fleeting love than it is a partnership held together by a somewhat arbitrary but still rational decision to marry and stick together.[17] People demonstrate an awareness of this unavoidable arbitrariness when they realize that decision precedes inclination; privileging inclination means privileging subjective freedom and a mutable love. Privileging the decision subordinates the arbitrary and the subjective moment and makes love truer, more lasting, and ethical.

Marriage is a communal relationship, consisting in "love, trust, and the sharing of the whole of individual existence."[18] Genuine love "excludes all oppositions," Hegel writes in the early "Fragment on Love," and lovers make up a "living whole." This substantive goal embodies "the most immense contradiction" that illuminates the nature of love and the human need for it.

> The first moment in love is that I do not wish to be an independent person in my own right . . . and that, if I were, I would feel deficient and incomplete. The second moment is that I find myself in another person, that I gain recognition in this person [*daß ich in ihr gelte*], who in turn gains recognition in me. . . . There is nothing more intractable than this punctiliousness of the self-consciousness which is negated and which I ought nevertheless to possess as affirmative.[19]

First wanting to lose one's identity in another's, then sensing that one's identity and self-satisfaction are heightened by a beloved's recognition, the contradiction in love points to a unity based on mutual recognition by rational spirits. The moments in love—the simultaneous losing and the enhancement or enrichment of self—augment each separate feeling and bring feelings together in a unity accomplished by joining with another. These moments resolve the tension in modern life between the need to find individual satisfaction and to belong to something greater than oneself.

Michael Hardimon questions whether this "deeper and more thoroughgoing union" is good for human beings. "We might take exception to this view" of a communal marriage embodying love, he writes, "but it is crucial to recognize that it *is* the view that Hegel holds."[20] Losing one's self-sufficiency in marriage may foster psychological despair, economic vulnerability, or an insufficiently cultivated sense of self-actualization; such seem to be the worries, shared by many of today,[21] informing Hardimon's reservations. How does Hegel talk himself into communal marriage, or does Hardimon talk himself *out* of it? This love is not "natural," and such an appellation would not necessarily commend such love. Hegel reasons in two modes, looking at why unity is important to individuals (what I call anthropological reasoning) and how this understanding of love grows out of the facts and institutions associated with marriage (what I call phenomenological reasoning). These two ways of reasoning lead to the same conclusions in Hegel's judgment.

Let me begin with his anthropological reasoning. We have it on high authority that the greatest of things is love, but what is so great about it? It is crucial that this "living whole" responds to intractable human needs for belonging, acceptance, sharing, and serving. Those in loving unions recognize one another's emotional needs and they find their own life in giving what the other needs. "In love, life is present as a duplicate of itself and as a single and unified self."[22] Nowhere else in the modern world can we find the emotional attention paid to our unique selves. Loving family life presents a refuge. Neither market forces, nor corporations, nor governments take heed of one's emotional particularity. Modern governments treat people objectively (i.e., as numbers) instead of as individuals, and it is good that they do. Love grows from our neediness and our expanded sense of self, which can only be found when it is joined to another self. The space to surrender oneself to love is an accomplishment of civilization brought about in the fullness of time and not natural in the sense of being innate or given. It is our destiny to be able to love, just as we are destined to be free.

Institutions of ethical life nurture and sustain love as such a unity. If laws and customs encourage people to marry without surrendering their selves, those institutions pull the rug out from under marital unity and love. If people *think* the institutions discourage partners from surrendering themselves, the rug is pulled out as well. This medium—how people think about practices and institutions—is crucial. Hegel interprets institutions and facts to show that family life is sustained by a public recognition of unity and how this recognition transforms one's self-understanding. What I call Hegel's phenomenological reasoning emerges from this interpretation of the facts on the ground.

The subjective side of love must be made objective in institutions. Two errors arise in contractual thinking about marriage in this respect. First, as we have seen, critics misunderstand the subjective side as a mere embodiment of natural sexual desire. Hegel corrects this view by seeing the sexual urge as a nascent, immature expression of more profound human longings for recognition by another. The will for recognition appears to be a sublimated and improved form of the sexual drive.[23] The union of man and woman "is a self-limitation, but since they attain their substantial self-consciousness within it, it is in fact their liberation."[24] Hegel refuses to leave it at this still-too-romantic level, however, so he insists that institutions are necessary to sustain this unity. The worry that marital unity will be insufficiently institutionalized leads to Hegel's thoughts on property, children, divorce, and other aspects of bourgeois marriage.

Common Property

Against romantic efforts to see property as something dead or foreign or as material intruding upon the truer spiritual connection, Hegel spiritualizes property by showing that how one thinks about property shapes how one thinks about marriage. "Since possession and property make up such an important part of men's life, cares, and thoughts, even lovers cannot refrain from reflection on this aspect of their relations."[25] Hegel's most serious and pervasive theoretical opponent is Locke, who views the right to property as an *individual* right. Mill's later effort (discussed in chapter 6) to provide a legal basis for wives' owning property is, on this reading, an attempt to perfect Locke's liberal view.

A reform such as Mill's undermines marital unity. Marriages that respect the *individual* right to property do not overcome the standpoint of contract and do not transform one's self-understanding. The disposition that Hegel considers appropriate to the family is "to have self-consciousness of one's individuality within this unity . . . so that one is present not as an independent person [*eine Person fur sich*] but as a member."[26] This means that family members think of themselves in their family roles rather than (or before) thinking of themselves as separate, particular individuals. A husband holds his wife's hand during childbirth not pursuant to a marriage bargain, but because it is what a loving husband does. This idea of membership sustains Hegel's understanding of property. "No member of the family has particular (i.e., individual) property, although each has a right to what is held in common." Family members have a right to draw on the family's resources. Husbands and fathers are "primarily responsible for the external acquisition" and "the control and administration of the family's resources" and they represent the family "as a legal [*rechtliche*] person." Any selfish grasping involved in acquiring resources is transformed "into care and acquisition for a *communal purpose*, i.e., into an *ethical* quality" by the father's attitude of service to the family commune. Not a legal fiction, male headship is also, in Hegel's view, supported by nature, as we shall see.[27]

The father's headship of the family also reflects the fact that the state must recognize the family in accord with marital unity, or corrode that ideal. How the state conceives of the family—for the purposes of property, or taxation, or insurance, etc.—reveals an account of what the family is. Consider taxation. Filing taxes separately encourages family members to think of themselves as individuals and to hold something back from their marriage. Sweden was the first country to do away with joint filing to promote the "economic independence of marriage partners" and to "eradicate the principle of the man as the chief wage earner in the family."[28] Tax systems shape and reflect how we think of marriage. Having fathers file taxes for the family may encourage them to see the family as theirs, but this mild patriarchy serves an ethical, communal purpose.

Children

There are limits to how united husbands and wives can be. "Lovers can be distinct only in so far as they are mortal"; since each will die, they remain distinct. Ethical love demands that the consciousness of a separate self disappear and that "all distinction between the lovers is annulled." This is difficult to accomplish since husbands and wives occupy different bodies. The distinction can be overcome only outside of their bodies, that is, in their children, and what is united in this case never can be divided.[29] In children this unity is present "in a spiritual form in which the parents are loved and which they love"; mothers and fathers "see their love before them"—it is objective, concrete, alive, *and* spiritual. Children are, as evolutionary biologists claim, little pieces of immortality: not individual immortality or an individual's genetic legacy, but a couple's legacy of enduring love and their hope to make a more perfect union, or to make two into one. Love seems to be an invention that aids in the propagation of the species from "the point of view of nature." The result of their unity, from the physical point of view, "runs into the infinite progression of generations." This natural or physical point of view does not account for the human desire for love and recognition: we do not grasp the meaning of children if we simply reduce our love for them to propagating the gene pool. Children embody marital endurance and unity, the substance, essence, and spirit of love.[30]

Children are stubborn facts, and much hangs on how we think about those facts. Hegel, the modern defender of the communal family, is also the first advocate for children's rights, properly understood. Children have "a right to be *brought up*" and supported by their mothers and fathers. The upbringing of children has the aim of forging a person with an independent will that someday will leave the family to form another. There are two moments in the upbringing of children. Children require a "positive determination" in "the form of immediate *feeling* which is still without opposition, so that their early emotional life may be lived in this [context], as the *basis* of ethical life in love, trust, and obedience." During infancy, "the mother's role in the child's upbringing is of primary importance, for [the principles of] ethics must be implanted in the child in the form of feeling." This "natural immediacy" or altruistic service, essential for a child's survival and happiness, does not suffice, for it would lead to a "merely sensuous and natural" existence. Children must also be pulled from the stream of nature toward an ethical existence, wherein a loving discipline breaks their natural "self-will." Hegel does not say that fathers are responsible for this aspect of bringing up children, though there are reasons to suspect that, for Hegel, men are generally better suited for this task. Children must learn that the world does not cater to their caprices and they must transcend childish play. Hegel's advice to parents can be reduced to a simple maxim: act as if childish immaturity should be remedied. This "*negative* determination of raising children from natural immediacy in which they originally exist to self-sufficiency and freedom of personality" enables children "to leave the natural unit of the family."[31]

At this "ethical dissolution of the family," the state recognizes a child as a legal and free person. While children may still love their parents, they also leave parents behind just as they leave the world of mere nature behind. Parents, on the other hand, love their children more than their children love them. Children represent the "objective and concrete form of their union."[32] Without daily reminders of their love, one might expect that Hegel would see marriage losing its luster, if not its purpose (as in Locke[33]). Since Hegel rejects the contractual idea of marriage, he also rejects the contractual idea of marriage's purposes and dissolution. Marriage continues until the death of the parents, which Hegel considers to be the "natural dissolution of the family."[34]

Why do marriages last after the nest is empty? Hegel does not argue, as Hume did, that the freedom to divorce after the children have left will encourage people to think of their union as only partial and temporary and hence undercut the ability to raise children.[35] Hegel seeks, through marriage, to secure the good of ethical love, not just to secure a future for the children. Marriage secures the deep human need to be recognized and loved in an ethical bond. The difference between Locke and Hegel boils down to this: Hegel sees children as a sign of the love that is central to marriage; Locke sees care and affection as helpful to the procreation and education that is the chief end of conjugal society. Children are, in a sense, incidental to marital unity for Hegel, though they are central to making the marital unity a spiritual and concrete reality.

Marriage Ceremony

Let us grant that ethical love reflects a deep need. Can it be secured without marriage? Marriage, for Hegel, is publicly acknowledged and difficult to dissolve; both of these characteristics attend to its ethical, unified, and unifying character. Against the reduction of marriage to love, which tends to deprecate the need for a "dead formality" to solemnize the bond, Hegel defends the need for a public ceremony to signify the subordination of the "sensuous moment which pertains to natural life" (i.e., sex) to the "external existence of an ethical bond."[36] The ceremony embodies the moment when the standpoint of contract is superseded, while seeming to be a contractual moment. Those who equate love with marriage are like seducers, who often argue that physical acts of love are proof of love or the essence of love. Ethical love demands more. Love assumes its ethical shape in marriage and the moments of love attain their "rational relation to each other":[37] our separateness is acknowledged and overcome, fleeting feelings are made subordinate, and men and women are transformed from being individuals to being members of an ethical whole that enhances their sense of satisfaction.

Divorce

Hegel regards marriage as "indissoluble *in itself*." Dissolubility brings the possibility that married individuals will act on a fancy for another. More precisely, the indissolubility of marriage must be upheld, but not absolutely, since feelings are implicated, though subordinated, in marriage. "Since marriage contains a moment of feeling, it is . . . unstable, and it has within it the possibility of dissolution." Ethical love builds on, subordinates, and goes with the grain of affections and feelings held by a married pair, and affections and feelings retain significance and do not disappear. Because marriage involves feelings and affection, "there could be no merely legal or positive bond which could keep them together once their dispositions and actions have become antagonistic or hostile." Antagonisms must be reasonable—that is, comprehensive, unredeemable, and irreconcilable. To testify to this, a "third ethical authority" ensures that partners are "totally estranged" and not separated by "merely transient moods." Divorce must be made "as difficult as possible" to "uphold the rights of ethics against caprice."[38] This third party investigates whether an emotional estrangement exists, something that the parties, caught up in the passions of the moment, would be less able to accomplish.

Hegel follows his noncontractual logic in his qualified defense of divorce. While Locke argues against divorce when children are present, Hegel leaves children out of the discussion when it comes to deciding when a divorce can be granted. Divorce can be granted when a third party determines that a pair is estranged. In this we begin to see the promise and perils of Hegel's conception of marriage. The unity of feeling and its self-giving recognition of others make marriage beautiful, appealing, and somewhat fragile. The concrete unity may make estrangement less likely because the living reality of love is present to the eyes of the couple. Children embody and symbolize the marital unity, but the affective unity can dissolve though the embodiment of that unity survives.

Monogamy

The Catholic case against divorce is linked to the case against polygamy, and even so un-Catholic a thinker as Hume considers these issues under the same head in his *Essays Moral, Political and Literary*. Prohibitions on divorce are enforced when we see marriage as a physical and spiritual union as long as both live. One cannot separate from a union before the ethical third party (i.e., God). If one tries to separate from it and join another, one is part of two unities; this is polygamy. Hegel, who allows divorce in limited circumstances and thus sees marriage as less than a sacrament, maintains that polygamy is inconsistent with marital unity. The unity that constitutes marriage arises out of a "mutual and *undivided* surrender" of individual personality to another recognized individual. Ethical love demands that "I find myself in another person."[39] Polygamy means holding something back from that surrender or dividing one's love so that one can give it to two or more people. Human beings cannot give all of themselves twice *at the same time*. Hegel's is not the typical liberal argument against polygamy emphasizing its historical links to patriarchy; he no longer sees such patriarchy as viable.[40] The modern world must understand its opposition to polygamy differently since the modern world faces new challenges and limits. It is conceivable that there will be a new, modern polygamy consistent with the principles of choice and subjective freedom. Modern polygamy is inconsistent with mutual self-surrendering.

Incest

Hegel understands the prohibition on incest in light of ethical love. If, as liberal theory suggests, marriage is "an arbitrary contract" grounded in "the natural sexual drive," and if the reasons for monogamy are based on the "physical relation between numbers of men and women" and only "obscure feelings are cited . . . for prohibiting marriage between blood relations," such arguments are "based on the common notion of a state of nature and of the naturalness of right, and on the absence of the concept of rationality and freedom."[41] Liberalism's emphasis on consent, and its unwillingness to discuss the rationality of consent or whether the consent leads to ethical love or objective freedom, leaves liberal theory unable to provide a case against incest. Hegel is free from the assumption that marriage is about "immediate natural existence . . . and its drives"; he sees it as "an ethical act of freedom." The obscure feelings of revulsion or shame that human beings experience when they think about incest point to a deeper "concept of the thing." Those feelings are consistent with reason, if not strictly reasonable, in that they reflect a proper understanding of ethical love. Since marriage is the free surrender of one's unique personality to another, it must begin with a separation and a uniqueness; to make one out of what is already one is absurd. Shared habits of brothers and sisters or fathers and daughters tell against separation and hence preclude the lacking that is the first moment in love. Hegel's worries about incest culminate in a defense of traditional courtship that emphasizes decision over inclination. "Familiarity, acquaintance, and the habit of shared activity should not be present before marriage: they should be discovered only within it, and the value of this discovery is all the greater the richer it is, and the more components it has."[42]

The ceremony, property, and children institutionalize marital unity. Marriages are immediate ethical wholes, united in purpose, and loving and supporting particular individuals. They prepare people to transcend immediate wholes of feeling toward the universal whole of reason.

> This unity is in the case of the Family essentially one of *feeling*; not advancing beyond the limits of the merely *natural*. The piety of the Family relation should be respected in the highest degree by the State; by its means the State obtains as its members individuals who are already moral (for as mere *persons* they are not) and who in uniting to form a state bring with them that sound basis of a political edifice—the capacity of feeling one with a Whole.[43]

Not just for the benefit of individuals—their educational achievements or their mental health—does Hegel see the family as important. It is for the kind of human being that the family unit produces. Just as Rousseau's mothers cultivate republican citizens, Hegel's family nurtures the feeling of being a member of a community and encourages its members to live as part of a larger whole in which members are not just independent beings.[44] Family life inculcates communal habits shaping individuals to express dissatisfaction with the individualist, arbitrary world of civil society. The triumph of subjective freedom would compromise the substantive ethical life in the family and the universal ethical life in the state: no communal family, no universal citizenship or State.

Woman, Marital Unity, and the Transformation of Nature

We are investigating what I call Hegel's phenomenological account of institutions surrounding marriage so we can see how marriage contributes to ethical life and how marital unity looks in practice. These institutions reflect ethical love, an idea that Hegel, almost alone among modern thinkers, perceives as a beautiful, real, rewarding, almost necessary human experience.[45] Any defense of the communal family must incorporate at least some aspects of Hegel's argument. I have delayed discussing Hegel's account of natural sex differences so we could first appreciate the ethical love to which sex differences, in Hegel's view, contribute.

Natural differences—between father and mother on one hand and children on the other, and especially between men and women—pervade Hegel's account of ethical love. The family presumes natural sex differences in how the State recognizes the family, in the family's communal resources, and in the way families rear children. Men and women complement each other as they erase the natural differences between adults and children. Mothers provide the "*positive* determination" during infancy by satisfying the child's natural needs and by providing emotional affirmation and ethical principles "in the form of feeling." Aside from providing resources, fathers help with the "*negative* determination" by disciplining children and encouraging them to risk.[46] What is significant and most challenging is that Hegel's account of History, which usually insists on the overcoming of nature, *in this one case* depends on the *persistence* of natural difference. The natural difference, Hegel writes, between "the two sexes acquires an *intellectual* and *ethical* significance by virtue of its rationality."[47] The unique character of women is seen in institutions emphasizing trust, emotional ties, and sacrificial love, while subjective freedom—the unique character of men—is seen in civil society and the economy and emancipates them to pursue their own economic interests. Each sex contributes to the achievement of the State—women's emotional support and men's reflection are necessary to the creation of modern citizens. Hegel's marital unity rests on the difference between husbands and wives being a rational and enduring product of History.

Men and women are "Spirit," which indicates that both are free and rational.[48] Hegel embraces natural differences; abstract rights and moral personhood are not real unless they are grounded in roles. Males, more "powerful and active" than females, are "spirituality which divides itself up into personal self-sufficiency with being *for itself* and the knowledge and volition of free universality." The male is characterized by negation, tearing down, building things, and competition, all of which aim at achieving the capacity to reason in objective or universal terms through life in the state. The abstraction of men suits them to destroy the institutions of the world and to rebuild them. Man "has his actual substantial life in the state, in learning, etc., and otherwise in work and struggle with the external world and with himself, so that it is only through his division that he fights his way to self-sufficient unity with himself." Women, in contrast, are "passive and subjective"; their spirituality "maintains itself in unity as knowledge and volition of the substantial in the form of concrete *individuality* and *feeling*." The psychology of women tends to be more personal, emotional, contextual, unified in feeling, practical, and aimed at the particular—all of which tend to make women best suited to nurture children to rationality and virtue. Woman "has her substantial vocation in the family, and her ethical disposition consists in this piety" (i.e., familial intimacy). Women are "not made for activities which demand a universal faculty such as the more advanced sciences, philosophy, and certain forms of artistic productions." Men are suited to face outward,[49] while women are suited to look inward in caring for the family's emotional needs as they welcome children into homes and provide for them the first glimpse of love.

Can subjective liberty be contained without natural sex differences? Hegel shows the inexorable logic underlying marital unity. For Hegel, to argue against natural sex differences is to argue against the conditions that sustain ethical love. In bowing to sex differences, he makes a virtue of necessity, but it is a necessity that serves virtue.[50]

There seems to be a link between marital unity and ethical love on one side and the naturalness of sex differences on the other. Rousseau, as we have seen, took sex differences at least to Hegelian heights and defined the family by a conjugal-romantic love grounded in the complementary nature of the sexes. So too will other advocates of marital unity such as Comte. Critics of natural sex differences and traditional familial arrangements see the same logic, but they seek to narrow or undermine marital unity in an effort to defend or establish sexual equality; they try to show that the love of the traditional family was not real so that they can reconstruct the family in light of justice (instead of love) and individuality (instead of communal ends).[51] Implicit in both traditions is the idea that the communal family depends on natural sex differences. We must understand this dependence because much modern political thought turns on it.

Marx's definition of communism is a suitable starting point as a description of communal family life: from each according to his abilities; to each according to his needs. Marriage and family life are about something held in common. Each member invests time, treasure, and talent in securing the family's common good. Someone has to earn family resources. Someone has to do housework to make family life run smoothly. Someone will probably administer the finances of the family—pay its taxes, consider its investments, and so on. Someone will bear the children. Someone will discipline them. These duties may be shared in some ways, and they may, at times, seem like distasteful fetters on subjective liberty, but they are the fetters that enrich and ennoble family life when they are part of an ethical love. There are many facets to building ethical family life; no single member brings all that is needed. If the abilities, needs, and contributions of each member were the same or the ends of ethical family life were easily attained, there would be little reason to form families.

There is a corollary to this. The more serious and time- and resource-intensive the goals of communal family life, the more the members are inclined to, and need to, practice the division of labor in the family.[52] Families whose goal is the survival of their children will have less work to do in common than families whose goal is the moral, intellectual, and spiritual thriving of their children. Spouses whose aim is the furtherance of two separate lives have less common work to do than spouses interested in furthering career(s), accumulating a large estate, and raising children. Families interested in eating home-cooked meals together, reading together, and pursuing other common interests have more work to do in common than families uninterested in such ends. The fewer ends, the less work in common; and the more work in common, the more the division of labor is practiced in the family. The institutions of ethical life—the way property is owned and earned, the way children are raised, the relative difficulty of divorce—support the family's attempt to establish a division of labor to serve serious ends.

How is the labor divided? Four options suggest themselves to modern thinkers (though there may be other options): androgynous equality, personal choice, the idea of nature, and a socially constructed idea.

Contemporary feminists suggest that the principle of androgynous equality should guide the division of labor in the household. This principle holds that men and women would divide jobs without regard to gender. "One's sex," to use Okin's words, "would have no more relevance than one's eye color or the length of one's toes" in the division of jobs.[53] What is striking about this approach is that deviations from equality of job distribution—if only 33 percent of parents staying at home with children were men or 75 percent of kindergarten teachers were still women, for instance—would be evidence for a lingering, patriarchal construction of gender and could trigger government action to reallocate "mal-divided" labor. Those advocating this view hold that "government does indeed have an interest in who does the dishes, given that patterns of inequality and inequity in the home may shape both adults' and childrens' capacities for and opportunities for self-government."[54] Okin suggests that preferential treatment be given in hiring for jobs that have traditionally been the domain of one particular sex—men would get preference in hiring for kindergarten jobs, women for school superintendents.[55] Other solutions relating to college admissions might be used to attain androgynous equality. This approach to dividing household and other forms of labor is based on the assumption that *none* of the differences between men and woman are natural or respectable (I survey this view in chapter 10).

Against this view of how labor should be divided is the principle of choice, held, with qualifications, by liberals such as Mill (see chapter 6). Individuals that make up the family choose the roles they want to play. There need not necessarily be great worries about the natural or conventional context for choices spouses make, for *all* choices take place in *some* context. If household jobs are, as per the androgynous equality model, maldistributed, the liberal approach holds that the distribution's legitimacy comes from the fact that it is chosen. This approach frowns on government's efforts to engineer the family's division of labor: freely chosen roles should be freely chosen, not coerced, incentivized, or "shaped" by government action. This liberal approach is, in principle, more or less agnostic on what underlies personal choice and is willing to live with the consequences.

Labor in the family could also be divided according to a preconceived, artificial social ideal. An example of this is the sexual division of labor that feminist critics of the social construction of gender see defining most of human history. Society invents ideas of what it means to be a woman, what it means to be a man, and what it means to love,[56] reinforces these creations through law and opinion, and then pigeonholes people in "proper" roles. These creations may be put forward so important social goals can be accomplished, goals such as raising children or living a communal life. A group (i.e., men) may put them forward to maintain its status and power. Much like the androgynous feminist model, this self-conscious social construction model, in its most extreme form, suggests that human nature is so malleable that men and women can take on whatever form is necessary to accomplish important social goals.

Nature may determine how family members divide labor as well. This explanation may overlap a great deal with the others. Its core idea is that men and women have different characters that guide them to make choices or to construct environments suitable to their respective paths. Political communities may "construct" laws and opinions, but they do so to fit the different natures of the sexes. Men and women may exercise choice in their plans of life, and those plans are shaped in part by their different natures; choice informed by nature leads the sexes to somewhat different paths. Men will choose competitive careers more often than women; women will choose courses of life emphasizing empathy and care more often than men. Nature shapes choices and constructions and nature is normative (up to a point, at least)—trying to fight the course set by nature brings social disharmony and personal unhappiness.[57]

Just as the communal family requires a division of labor, so Hegel thinks that the division of labor is based on sex, that the sexual division of labor is natural,[58] and that nature is, in this case, normative. Locke's apparent flexibility in the arrangement of a family's authority structure is less present in Hegel. Things are not this simple, of course. Institutions of ethical life nurture natural sex differences. Hegel contends that the institutions of ethical life provide necessary support for the sexual division of labor, and that those institutions are just because the sex differences are natural.

Because I developed the idea of marital unity before discussing how it is linked to sex differences, I did not dwell on the gendered character of the institutions of ethical life. Let me return to that idea. The state sees property as owned by the male head of household. Child-rearing requires the attention of women and the intervention of men, as they provide positive and negative determinations for children. Divorce is relatively difficult, for Hegel, so that it is safer for women to participate in the unpaid labor of the household. These institutions protect the family from the corrosive intrusions of subjective liberty. What protects against the corrosive effects of individualism also protects the possibility of the marital and familial unity.[59] When, due to the ideas of subjective liberty, men and women see themselves as individuals instead of as family members, the communal family is undermined. If men and women are different, subjective liberty will manifest itself differently in each. Men, on Hegel's account, more easily detach from the family and are more attracted to a life of "work and struggle";[60] women are more likely to involve themselves in caring for others.

Institutions of ethical life protect the communal family from manifestations of subjective liberty. Men are helped to see property as the family's instead of as their own; by viewing themselves as heads of household, the "selfishness of desire" that they display in the marketplace is transformed into "care and acquisition for a *communal purpose*."[61] Without this communal purpose, men are tempted to work and struggle and serve themselves. This puts the family and especially the wife at risk and may tempt women to acquire their primary identity outside the family. The foundation of private property and the institution of marriage appear together at the beginning of "civilized social life."[62] The emergence of the breadwinner role speaks to the responsibility that follows from the idea of a communal marriage. Given sex differences, a wife does not want to get into an earning competition with her husband, so her contribution to the marriage is different from his. The state does not attempt to relieve women of their child-rearing role. Child-rearing is a communal activity requiring the unique contributions of mothers and fathers; it is not a limit on one's own freedom nor something glorified by men to promote their empire. It is the physical and spiritual manifestation of enduring love. Hegel's divorce regime is safer for women who dedicate themselves to the family than today's no-fault regime of subjective liberty. These quasi-patriarchal institutions are part of Hegel's effort to confine the sphere of subjective liberty, nurture natural sex differences, and build marital unity. Without natural difference grounding the family's sexual division of labor, the marital unity would be an unjust arbitrary human construction.

Hegel's diverse critics have failed to understand how central his theory of sex differences is to his understanding of the communal family. The deeper and more serious the goals of the family, the more the family must consider itself as a communal relationship; the more it is communal, the more it depends on the division of labor in the family (as a practical matter); the more it depends on the division of labor, the more social institutions and the laws of fashion divide the labor along the sexual lines suggested by nature. There is, it seems, in Hegel's view, an intrinsic connection between marital unity, the communal family, and the sexual division of labor. Attempts to eliminate the sexual division of labor will begin, Hegel implicitly predicts, by eliminating, or significantly confining, the communal purposes of the marriage. Attempts to do so also implicate the value of the ethical love at the center of the marital unity.

Problems and Tensions in Hegel's Unified Family

Feminist theorists complain that Hegel's account of sex differences does not do justice to women's capacities, or that history has overcome natural sex differences. The phenomenological context in which we understand love, marriage, and family life is certainly different today. To cite only the obvious examples, most, if not all, modern states allow women to own property in marriage; permit at-will, one-party, no-fault divorce; think it permissible or desirable that women pursue vocations in civil society while leaving children in institutions designed to free women from some burdens of motherhood; consider cohabitation to be a rough legal equivalent to marriage; and pay less heed to the idea of marital unity in their marriage law. The greatest change is the belief in the withering of sex differences and our aspiration to create a gender-neutral society. We have a different present, with different crosses—could and would Hegel find different roses?

We are dealing with how Hegel would handle a situation that his thought did not contain, and in fact that he actively opposed. Some argue, not without reason, that Hegel privileges the phenomenological approach and his belief that History ends in his time over his dynamic, progressively liberating vision of History.[63] This explanation fails because it imputes to Hegel an endorsement of his own constitution that he withheld. Hegel saw various problems or tensions in the modern constitution (the problem of poverty) and even within the family (divorce), showing that he rose above seeing the prejudices of his age as rational. Let me be clear about what problem arises from Hegel's account of women. Sex differences make ethical love consistent with human nature because women find fulfillment in the household and this fulfillment serves familial unity. Yet the evidence is in, and *Hegel overstates the difference between the sexes* and fails to see that reason has force enough in women to allow them to aspire to the universal for the purposes of citizenship in the modern constitution; women too are political animals. Acknowledgment of this does not necessarily open the family to the imperialism of subjective liberty and civil society thinking, though it can do that. It is to acknowledge that Hegel does not do justice to women's nature.

It is not Hegel's style to be bitter about historical change; he would seek the reason in it. It is necessary to consider the implications of Hegel's failure to see the force of rationality in women for ethical love and to adjust his thought accordingly. Can marital unity and ethical love be sustained on a more individualistic or gender-neutral basis? Can the human need for ethical love be maintained by different institutions while still allowing for an emotionally satisfying integration of the individual into the state? Does Hegel understand the place of love in the psychology of modern peoples?

The problem relates to Hegel's elevation of the political. He paints the picture of a purified family, a family that is not concerned fundamentally with economic production, perpetuating political rule, or keeping a grip on adult children as it had in the past. Ethical love makes the family. The family is shaped by how it is viewed in law and culture. Hegel finds the place for the family in his constitutional order by subordinating it to politics and by seeing it as significant insofar as it contributes to making moral citizens. No family thinks of itself as merely producing future citizens, but Hegel finds the cunning of reason at work, producing the rational order despite the intentions of its citizens. Not only women, but marriage and the family as such are, in a sense, turned into means, in Hegel's analysis, so individuals can fulfill their "*highest duty*," which is "to be members of the state."[64] The family is lower in dignity than participation as a citizen in the state; the family's self-understanding is shaped by the state's legal conceptions of the family. The state, for instance, recognizes the man as the head of household for the purposes of taxation or property ownership because acknowledging two owners or earners would introduce a creeping individualism into the household. The same logic leads to the embrace of a family vote instead of an individual vote. The paramount importance of the state as a shaper of individual identity, for Hegel, makes it necessary to acknowledge the family as a union based on sex differences.

What if Hegel overestimates the importance of politics for human life in the modern world? What if genuine unions could be formed in this more gender-neutral legal environment because the acknowledgment of the state mattered less? These questions boil down to several others. Why does Hegel privilege the order of freedom and the right to recognition over the realm of love? Why does he see the human desire for recognition as the motive force of history instead of love? Why is it analytically and dialectically wrong to see the ethical family as the aim toward which History is tending while seeing the State as a subordinate moment in that order leading up to the family?

Let me put forward some speculations about why, perhaps, the desire for recognition by other rational agents in the universal state is not the underlying engine of history. What human beings desire above all is happiness and a worthy self-admiration, not recognition or universal recognition. Philosophers, for instance, long to understand the order of things, not to be honored. Genuine love is among the deepest human desires, not a pale or immature imitation of the right to recognition. Hegel may have it backwards: the right to recognition is a relatively less intense, less meaningful refraction of the deeper human longing for love and happiness. Whether it is the love of wisdom or love as such, human life is an ordering of, or a web of, loves—each stage may be incomplete, but each points to the others. Hegel's subordination of the family to the state is a consequence of his hope to reconcile human beings to their world; but, if such a reconciliation is not possible or if, as Nietzsche had suggested, it is dehumanizing, the analysis of love and its limits promises a truer approach. Hegel's analysis of love is second to no modern thinker, and as a phenomenological account it bears scrutiny. Some elements of Hegel's thought must be a part of any defense of marital union and familial community in the modern world. However, his belief that love and the family are superseded by the realm of politics is an indication that he has given too high of a priority to recognition and the state over love and the family. His account of human perfection is overly politicized.

Yet we may not have gotten to the bottom of things yet. Hegel's priority of recognition presumes the priority of History itself. This brings us back to the issue we have been wrestling with throughout: the relationship between Hegel's phenomenology and his Historicism. These aspects are united in Hegel's mind, which enabled him to give a rational account of the phenomenon as part of the rational unfolding of History. These aspects are separated once later philosophers laid a knife to the belief that History has a rational purpose. Can Hegel's attempt to find the rational in the actual survive without attaching to the deeper, structuring, "metaphysical" stratum of History? Must human beings respect or grasp History (or something akin to it) in order to respect phenomenology? My sense is that Hegel answers these questions with a resounding "yes."

Without a faith in History, most modern thinkers lose interest in the nature of love and marital unity as such. What emerges is an ever greater thinning of the family, accompanied by an ever deeper skepticism about the goodness of love. Only when love is properly grounded can it survive, but proper grounding is not a typically modern concern. The French sociologists attempt to ground love in social science positivism, and this uneasy marriage begins in the work of a famous loser in love, Auguste Comte.

Chapter 5

In Hegel's Shadow
French Sociologists and Positivist Defenses of the Family

What is intriguing about Hegel is his effort to defend traditional institutions of marriage in an age taken with the principles of autonomy, individualism, and human equality. He defends the institutions of marital and familial unity as rational supports for the deep human concerns of ethical love and recognition without recourse to religious traditions. Religion, Hegel suggests, played a historical role in sustaining "conservative" familial institutions, but History has now placed "conservative" institutions on a rational foundation. This is why Hegel, whose respect for the historical role played by religion is deep, is perhaps the most profoundly antireligious thinker the world has known. Finding the rational in the actual, his thought renders religious support for these institutions superfluous.

Hegel's positivist successors also seek to defend such traditionalism without recourse to the prop of religious belief. Positivism is the scientific methodology derived from the understanding of people as historical beings, as beings whose character changes with the times. This view blossomed with Hegel, who also propounded the idea that History culminates in the freedom and rationality of the modern State. Knowledge of where

History is headed provides the loadstar for social science positivism at its inception: History shows where the family fits in with man's destiny.

The shotgun marriage between social science positivism and Hegel's Historicism did not survive when the deepest thinkers of the late nineteenth century raised doubts about the rationality of the Historical process. The divorce between positivism and History left social science positivism without an anchor, so positivism tried to orient itself by attaching its findings to the social needs of man as they revealed themselves in a particular time and place. This is a softer historical knowledge, reflecting goals neither rational nor consistent with a destiny for man. Positivism guided by soft historical knowledge is still based on the idea that human being changes with the times. Softer historical knowledge understands that human needs are mediated by society and that they change with changes in social organization. Social science positivism informed by soft historical knowledge is subject to several decisive objections. There is always the worry that the social needs of man served by the family are changing and that the family form must change as well, despite the dire warnings of social scientists. Positivism guided by softer historical knowledge tries to hit a moving target (the social needs of man), so its findings rarely convince.

"Hard" Historicism and the Birth of Positive Philosophy

The founders of social science were confident Historicists in that they thought they grasped the rational direction of History. Comte (1798–1857), developer of the positive system of knowledge, began with the view that "no idea can be properly understood apart from its history."[1] This view contains a profound conception of human being and human understanding. Human beings are products of their time; phenomena such as climate, laws, religious practice, political institutions, and family norms *shape* individuals, and it is the job of social science to ferret out the causal magnitudes.

Positive science arises as an effort to understand and direct human relations after the waning of traditional religious belief (what Comte calls theological knowledge) and the failure of modern political philosophy (what he calls metaphysical knowledge). Absolute knowledge is the aim of the theological way, in which people seek to answer "the most inaccessible questions" about the causes and ends of things and the purpose and constitution of all that exists.[2] Deep questions proposed mysteries to human understanding that those in the theological era resolved by kicking the mysterious up a level to a single God, who promises to control the external world. Institutions such as the medieval university and the Church grew up around these mysteries to articulate them. These institutions were progressive, insofar as they promised order and were based on the idea of man's unity, but they also created artificial passions, absolutist knowledge, and intolerance that wasted lives and led to religious wars.

The metaphysical polity dissolved the institutions protecting the theological way, but the natural rights thinking and abstraction in early modern thinkers was "a transitional form of philosophy." Metaphysical thinking provided the doctrines and gathered the energy to destroy the old order, but it was "attached to a complete doctrine of methodical destruction" inimical to order.[3] Consider the metaphysical dogmas of liberty of conscience and equality. Liberty of conscience freed people from the old authorities in religion and politics: it gave people a reason to fight and a language with which to challenge the old-time religion of authority, it enabled philosophers to explore new principles of social organization, and it encouraged discussion that popularized principles that brought down the old order. "Indispensable and salutary as it has been," liberty of conscience now "constitutes an obstacle to reorganization," in that it prevents society from deciding along the lines of reason once positive science has spoken, and it assumes that the masses themselves will be able to weigh in on matters of extraordinary delicacy and complexity. Liberty of conscience is fine in times of confusion, but it inhibits order after social science reveals the truth. Modern equality similarly is seen as "absolute" and "permanent," when it is really "relative" and "temporary." Its leveling tendencies helped overthrow feudal hierarchies; now the love of equality is undermining the respect for expertise necessary to establish civilization, progress, and social reorganization. The "alarming and ever-widening . . . intellectual anarchy" born of the metaphysical school has especially affected family life and marriage, for it has let loose "dogmas of independence and isolation" inimical to family spirit.[4]

Europe suffered political upheaval because it was morally confused, and the moral confusion was due to the persistence of these three incompatible ways of knowing: those seeking to restore the monarchy and Church clung to the theological way; revolutionists and anarchists to the metaphysical; and a small avant garde, Comte included, to positivism. Positive science, the "only possible agent in the reorganization of modern society,"[5] would reconcile the forces of order and progress and end the intellectual anarchy of post-Revolutionary, modern society. Abandoning the search for absolute knowledge (knowledge of the why), positive science confines itself to relative or hypothetical knowledge (knowledge of the how).[6]

> If . . . we consider the actual scientific conceptions in positive philosophy, we see that in contradistinction to theologico-metaphysical philosophy, [positive philosophy] has a constant tendency to make all those notions relative which had been considered absolute. This transition from the absolute to the relative constitutes one of the most important philosophic results of each one of the intellectual revolutions that have brought various orders of speculation out of the theological and metaphysical state to the scientific state.[7]

Borrowing methods and aspirations from modern natural science, the most successful part of modern philosophy, positivism is capable of building, guiding, and teaching: "The mind has given over the vain search after Absolute notions, the origin and destination of the universe, and the causes of phenomena, and applies itself to the study of their laws—that is, their invariable relations of succession and resemblance."[8] No longer is science concerned with questions about the way a familial order contributes to happiness. Positive knowledge is *relative* in the sense of being *relational.* It is concerned with the type of family order that fits into a particular social form—for example, how the polygamous family forms a system with Islamic law and the Caliphate.

Positive science incorporates the goals of each earlier way of knowing and puts each on a rational foundation accessible to some and applicable to all. Comte accomplishes this by developing what he calls sciences of statics and dynamics. Social statics concerns the necessary conditions of social order and stability (the effectual truth of what theologians had aimed at), while social dynamics concerns social transitions (appealing to progressive metaphysicians). Like Hegel, Comte fancies that he knows where History is headed so he can distinguish static from dynamic elements in history. Comte goes further than Hegel by insisting that social science positivism helps lead human beings to History's destiny. Comte saw History heading from the dominance of selfish interests to a society of altruism and a respect for Humanity, and away from the conflicts between industry and proletariats and toward a harmony between a ruling class (of capitalists doing the making and of intellectuals providing spiritual authority to ensure that the making redounds to the common good) and lower classes. Relative knowledge learned through sociology leads us to History's goals; definite knowledge of History's course guides sociological findings. Knowledge of History's course allows positive science to be prescriptive and to distinguish what is changing from what is not.

Comte's teaching on the family arises in opposition to metaphysical thinking and serves History's goal of developing mores of humanity. "The serious assaults upon [the family] which we witness in our day must . . . be regarded as the most alarming symptom of our temporary tendency to social disorganization," Comte writes.[9] This assault arises from liberal political theory, which regards "society as composed of individuals," and equal ones at that. Against this liberal tendency, Comte thinks that "human society is composed of families, and not of individuals."[10] Abstract liberal principles of independence and isolation undermine the two pillars of family life: the subordination of the sexes and of children to parents. Comte promises to divorce marriage and the family from the religious tradition out of which they grew. He defends these pillars based on "an exact knowledge of human nature" and "an appreciation of social development."[11] Nothing less than the fulfillment of History's purpose is at stake in his defense of the family.

Marital Unity

In each of his seminal works, Comte's discussion of marriage appears under the rubric of social statics.[12] Marriage is the "complete fusion of two natures into one."[13] It is the "noblest aim of human life," wherein women and men join their interests and form a union based on love, mutual confidence, and "mutual service and perfection." The "true object" of marriage is the "mutual perfecting of the two sexes,"[14] which means that marital unity must be drawn tighter than the contractual conjugal society pictured by Locke in the name of something even more serious than the ethical love that Hegel envisioned.[15]

Comte accepts the logic of marital unity implicit in Hegel's thought. Marital unity depends on the laws and customs within which marriage exists, on nature, and on the attitude of the couple toward nature. Concerning laws, so tight is marital unity, for Comte, that he provides an almost blanket prohibition on divorce to maintain the exclusivity and indissolubility of the marriage. Comte insists on the indissolubility of marriage, not for cultivating habits of staying together for the kids, but to effect the "object of all marriage, the raising and purifying of the heart."[16] Comte goes further than maintaining the indissolubility and exclusivity of marriage, carrying its unity beyond the grave by promulgating a "moral duty" to "perpetuity of widowhood" and suggesting that married couples "be laid in the same grave together" so that they rot together. Previous thinkers lacked the sense to include these last two institutions, though Comte thinks "both were [needed] to make monogamy complete."[17]

Deep love must be "constant in its object." Permanence in marriage protects one's life from degenerating "into a miserable series of experiments ending in failure and degradation." An egoistic sex instinct leads men to conjugal attachments and provides energy for affection; women do not need such "coarse stimulus" to ground affections. Access to a loving woman ennobles man's affections, allows him to "throw off [his] original selfishness," and forms the basis of "a perfect ideal of friendship." The relationship is deeper and more beautiful than friendship, for each "possesses and is possessed by the other." The sex difference and separate spheres of life exclude "the possibility of rivalry" and foster as complete a happiness as any experienced. This conjugal circle is the first, most intense, and most necessary in a sequence of concentric circles tending to "the final object of moral education, namely, universal Love," the destiny of History. "From personal experience of strong love we rise by degrees to sincere affection to all mankind, strong enough to modify conduct."[18]

The extraordinary, durable, tight unity of Comte's marriage is matched by its unparalleled defense of sex differences. In a manner again reminiscent of Hegel, natural sex differences suit men and women to play complementary roles in a unified marriage. Men are superior in "practical energy" and "the mental capacity connected with it," which suits them to be public faces of families, while "woman's strength lies in Feeling" and love and breeding "Social Feeling" from raw "Self-interest," which suits her to provide for the family's emotional needs.[19] "It is indisputable that women are, in general, as superior to men in a spontaneous expansion of sympathy and sociality, as they are inferior to men in understanding and reason." Comte links the psychological differences between men and women to the science of phrenology, of which he is a founder.[20] Bigger brains mean greater intellectual capacity, and men have bigger brains than women. Grounding sex differences in biology, Comte assumes that these differences are enduring, natural features of human life and hence part of social statics. The family could "never be inverted," Comte quips, "without an entire change in our cerebral organism."[21]

Why are natural sex differences central to marital unity? Comte radicalizes Hegel's thinking on this question. Married couples resemble two puzzle pieces that fit perfectly together, in which two separate and incomplete pieces form a larger, different, and transformative picture. Marriage educates the couple and its children to fulfilling History's purpose. Marriage to an affectionate, sympathetic woman tutors a man out of his egoism and his excessive reliance on speculative activity and calculation. "Domestic affections become the only natural medium between Egoism and Altruism; and thereby we obtain the essential basis of a real solution of the great human problem." Social feeling must be guided by intelligence; intelligence by love and social feeling; and intelligence and social feeling must admit in political and familial action—for these reasons men and women perfect each other as they constitute an ever completer union.[22] It is not that the married partners are compatible, though they are. Subsuming one's personal identity in the marriage is indispensable to its being a transformative union—neither women nor men are as they were before marriage. Marriage moves the man toward the woman's altruism and it moves women to follow manly reasonableness (though the woman changes the man more than he changes her).

Please forgive me for sanitizing Comte's vision out of a fear of making his thought seem offensive. He does not really talk of sex *differences* as essential to marital unity, but rather of the *subordination* of the sexes as being essential to it (and I have performed this legerdemain only because I think these ideas are different and that it is possible to stop Comte's vision short of his treatment of subordination). "Between two beings," Comte writes, "no harmony can exist unless one commands and the other obeys." The subordination of women is necessary for two reasons. First, a woman exercising command becomes "deeply degraded" as relating to her true purpose of cultivating feeling, and this would undermine the accomplishment of the family's great social task.[23] Commanding precludes the softer feelings and sympathy that women inculcate. If they commanded the family, no one would effect History's purpose of promoting universal love: men are incapable of leading mankind to it, and women would be otherwise too occupied in the sometimes messy task of commanding to promote it. Second, it seems that command is necessary in marriage generally so that children are reared in an environment in which they accept the authority of intellectual superiors. The command-obedience relationship prepares family members for an enlightened command-obedience relationship in politics: the workers and masses are prepared to accept the spiritual leadership of a secular, intellectual clerisy that will end the intellectual anarchy of the times by applying the findings of positive social science. Authoritarianism in politics requires a patriarchy in the family—and Comte cultivates both.

As the purposes of marriage and family life are conceived of as more and more important and difficult to attain, it is necessary to draw the family closer together. The objects in Comte's case relate to the mutual perfection of the sexes and achievement of a society based on the principles of universal love and altruism; positivism shows which institutions are necessary to achieve these goals. There is a manifest logic to Comte's portrait of the family if one accepts his conclusions about the direction of History and hence the purposes of education, about the need for continuing exercise of command in society, and about the sources and nature of sex differences.

The Problem of History in Comte's Correspondence with Mill

John Stuart Mill (1806–1873), Comte's contemporary and sometime correspondent, was as taken with positivism—especially the sciences of statics and dynamics—as anyone. Within this broad agreement, Mill and Comte argued about the science of social statics and its application to the family and especially to women. It is worth exploring the debate that Mill began with a letter to Comte in November 1841. Comte established his reputation on the strength of his *Positive Philosophy* (1830). Mill's obsequious praise of Comte, with Comte's irrepressible self-importance, pervades the correspondence, as they see themselves as the two agents of scientific progress in a world shrouded with darkness. After several letters, Mill raises the issue of his "heresy" from Comte's views on women and the family.[24] Relevant for our purposes are two of Mill's objections. First, whereas Comte thinks sex differences are permanent and rooted in biology, Mill sees them rooted in environmental factors, which, if changed, could equalize the sexes to an untold extent. Second, Mill contends that the legal subordination of women is not justified, even if sex differences were natural.

Comte responds by acknowledging that the anarchic times in which they live may give one the impression that the emancipation of women from the family and the narrowing of sex differences are waves of the future. Mill rides them, while Comte sees them as passing fads promoted by elites and intellectuals stuck in metaphysical thinking. What is crucial here is that Comte and Mill each supplement their positive social science with a conception of historical progress. Comte sees the subordination of women as effecting History's purpose of cultivating universal love and altruism, while Mill sees the subordination of women as standing in the way of a history of autonomy and equality. Both attach their arguments to History; as a result of their different visions about the ends of History, they disagree about whether the family belongs to social statics or dynamics. Questions persist. Who has properly divined History? How can we know, at any time, what the proper divination of History is? How can we be sure that the family as Comte understands it is central to History's purposes as Comte thought? Positivism loses its explanatory punch without guidance from History or when the concept of History's goal becomes controversial. The correspondence between Mill and Comte shows the difficulty of establishing positivism because it reveals a deep and abiding disagreement about the direction of History and, what was more distressing to Comte and Mill, a scientific disagreement about the *relative* knowledge of what kind of family promotes progress.

I explore Mill's late liberal approach to the family in the next chapter. For now, I concentrate on how Comte responded to Mill with the purpose of fleshing out Comte's thoughts on the family. The almost uniform evidence of history seeing the subordination of women to the family is conclusive and important, for Comte, because history is a mirror for biological or physiological traits. Women's "characteristic ineptitude in abstraction and intellectual argument [and] their almost total inability to eliminate the inspiration of passion from logical reasoning" denies them the "elevated position" earned by men. If this were not the case, women would have entered into politics or great enterprises more often. "The immense experience already behind us here of the whole of humanity" speaks with one voice, and only a fool would ignore it. The tumultuous period of transition seen in the times of Comte and Mill presages a return of women "to their essentially domestic life" so that they can model altruism, live happy lives consistent with their character, and fulfill their destiny as cultivators of morality. Comte even worries that the emancipation of women, if continued, would lead to a dangerous decline in fertility, threatening the survival of the species.[25]

Positivist social science is on a collision course with History. Modeled on natural science and seeking laws akin to the law of gravity, the science of social statics seeks rules that exist in all societies, independent of human will. We discover these laws or characteristics by identifying the characteristics that societies share. History appears as a reservoir of data for discovering the laws of positive social science, and the diversity of history masks (some kind) of underlying unity, which Comte's positivism seeks to find. History is also dynamic. What looks indubitable at one age is doubted later. How is a thinker to think given this? How can we distinguish the accidental from the natural, the historically constant from the mutable? To the extent that Comte raises these questions, he sees a biological and psychological basis for social statics and he projects the past into the future to an extent. Comte understood that the Western world was becoming more humane, yet, if anything, it seems that his positivism was insufficiently sensitive to the strong undercurrents of modernity, in that he did not foresee that marriage itself would be transformed and that what he saw as the temporary blip of metaphysical liberalism would or could continue apace. What could survive of positivism once a knife was put to the ideas that History was rational and that human beings could divine its direction?

Society, Nature, and Family Life in Durkheim's "Softer" Sociology

Immense intellectual changes separate the positivism of Comte from the sociology of Emile Durkheim (1858–1917).[26] Under the influence of Nietzsche and with the exhaustion of faith that History had a discernible, rational destiny (nascent in the Comte-Mill debate), scientists no longer aspired to establish universal sciences to accord with the goals of History. Comte's hopes of removing intellectual, social, and moral anarchy by serving History's ends gave way to the belief that history has no direction or that history is the field of battle between irreconcilable values. Ultimately, this spawned the distinction between facts and values, with social scientists focused on the former.

How was positivistic social thinking to proceed in light of this exhaustion? Among the greatest guides to this question is Emile Durkheim (the other is Max Weber). Durkheim was as concerned as Comte and Weber with establishing the foundations of sociology, and he devoted some of his early writings to laying foundations for his subsequent career. Walking in Comte's footsteps, Durkheim thought this new science constituted a complete break from all previous knowledge. Consider the following from his early work "Montesquieu's Contribution to the Rise of Social Science" (1893):

> The subject matter of social science is social "things," that is, laws, customs, religions, etc. However, if we look into history we find that until quite recent times, no philosopher ever viewed these matters in such a light. They thought that all such phenomena depended upon the human will and hence failed to realize themselves in actual things, like all other things in nature, which have their particular characteristics and consequently call for sciences that can describe and explain them. It seemed to them sufficient to ascertain what the human will should strive for and what it should avoid in constituted societies. Accordingly they sought to know, not the nature and origin of social phenomena, not what they actually are, but what they ought to be; their aim was not to offer us as true an image of nature as possible, but to confront our imagination with the idea of a perfect society, a model to be imitated.[27]

At first blush, Durkheim seems to repeat the modern philosophic objection to ancient philosophy—that ancient thinkers were unrealistic or concentrated on the "imagination" of things instead of the "effectual truth," to use Machiavelli's phrase. Durkheim thinks earlier modern philosophers lacked realism too. Modern thinkers shared what Durkheim regards as the superstition free will or the desire to shape the future. "A discipline that looks to the future lacks a determinate subject matter and should therefore be called not a science but an art."[28]

Durkheim's sociology represents a separation between science and art, resembling the distinction between facts and values.[29] "The subject matter of science can consist only of things that have a stable nature of their own and are able to resist the human will." Social science is modeled on the same deterministic assumptions as natural science. Human acts can suspend neither the laws of gravity nor the laws of social organization. Durkheim writes with great urgency on this.

> If we assume . . . that there is no such causal relationship and that effects can be produced without a cause or by any cause whatsoever, everything becomes arbitrary and fortuitous. But the arbitrary does not admit of interpretation. Hence, a choice must be made: either social phenomena are incompatible with science or they are governed by the same laws as the rest of the universe.

A sociologist in "the peace and quiet of his study" ascertains these intelligible laws.[30] When human beings are (apparently) free agents causing events or changes, there is no telling what they will do. Human beings, in these circumstances, confront a future of their own making and use or ignore practical wisdom at their peril, but also at their choosing. This indeterminism or contingency, for Durkheim, precludes the possibility of sociology, which explains a "determinate order." Human beings are effects of social order or social phenomena; they are acted upon, not actors. The only remaining scientific problems are technical, as scientists try to ascertain how religious, ethical, legal, familial, and other norms contribute to making human beings what they are.

Durkheim's sociology seeks to lay bare the relative knowledge of society in two stages. First, he seeks to show how geographic, religious, ethical, legal, and familial facts come in bundles constituting *systems*. For example, geographically small and somewhat sparsely populated city-states have relatively active citizenries and practice domestic slavery. These constitute a complex of norms that necessarily go together. Montesquieu, whom Durkheim considers the father of sociology, noticed that these practices made a system, but Durkheim complains that he nonetheless condemned slavery as antithetical to the spirit of republics. This condemnation was a vestige of older social science, one that condemned systems on the basis of some abstract ideal instead of merely stating what factors went together.[31] Second, sociologists try to show how human beings *in the aggregate* are passive agents of systematic social forces. Durkheim speaks of the "abnormal" number of people that are maladjusted to social forces around them in his seminal *Suicide*.[32] Durkheim's preoccupation with suicide indicates the field of values in which sociology operates. Suicide is an "abnormal" or "pathological" reaction to the social system of modern life, and it is the job of science to help identify what a socially determined sickness is, to discover what factors contribute to these pathologies, and to recommend changes in the system to militate against them. Durkheim's is a softer historicism—one in which science tries to help society live up to its own systematic demands, but one that does not question those demands. Any discussion of the inherent evil of suicide or its inconsistency with the principles of human nature would be mouthing "the preacher's language, not the scholar's."[33]

This two-stage approach is manifest in Durkheim's treatment of the family. As part of the social system, familial norms change logically with changes in religious, economic, political, and ethical practices. Patriarchal and communal family forms thrive in times of a primitive division of labor when the family is concerned with politics, economic production, land ownership, and religion. The modern conjugal family arises when families shed material concerns and specialize in procreation and social control. Family, to use analytical modes of today's social science, is a dependent variable, varying with changes in other social factors. Yet family is also an independent variable, the changes in which affect society's other institutions and an individual's destiny. Durkheim asks how family life affects individual thriving in the modern social system and how family life should be adjusted to protect against the evils of suicide and modern individualism.

The "conservative" elements in Durkheim's science of the family appear as cures for modern individualism. Individualism or, to use Durkheim's word, *anomie*, arises from an unfulfilled, morbid "desire for the infinite" arising after the disintegration of meaningful common consciousness of feudal societies.[34] Feudal society found ways of satisfying this desire with communal attachments and religious devotion. Ways of registering the "desire for the infinite" dissolved, and very few institutions in the modern world can replace them. Individualism also arises with a pervasive equality of opportunity that opens all vocations to everyone and from the great increase in human power that results from a dedication to modern science. Modern peoples, Durkheim notices, are "more readily stimulated and inflamed beyond all measure to the point of knowing almost no limits." These aspirations are thwarted because man is by nature a limited creature—limited in that he dies, limited in that he must live with others, and limited in that all his aspirations for dominance cannot be fulfilled.[35] That the quasi-religious "desire for the infinite" cannot be satisfied does not stop it from arising. "New hopes constantly awake, only to be deceived, leaving a trail of weariness and disillusionment" and leading human beings to wander the woods of choice without a path and with little hope of finding one. The result is "a state of disturbance, agitation and discontent which inevitably increases the possibilities of suicide" and other deviances.[36]

Modern individualism is tempered when human desires have definite objects and where those in society are subject to the salutary, life-lending discipline by social forces. This account raises questions about the character and status of nature's limits. Nature is not, for Durkheim, natural facts or "givens," such as the longer period for maturation necessary for human children or sex differences between women and men (as in Locke). What used to be seen as nature's givens have so often been transgressed by social contrivances that Durkheim abstracts from the fact that nature seems to manifest givens. Instead, he outlines nature's *formal* traits as they limit and create challenges for social institutions. Men desire, yet our social nature limits how many desires can be satisfied. It is not so much that nature dictates *which* desires cannot be fulfilled; it dictates that they cannot *all* be fulfilled. Men and women are different (these differences are historical for Durkheim, as we will see[37]), yet they are distinct creatures, and this limits human power: we cannot make another wholly ours. Durkheim does not suggest that nature's limits are sown by providence into the human condition: these limits *are*. Promethean rebelliousness (a peculiarly modern problem) against these enduring, formal limits causes despair and melancholy (which is modern anomie).

Durkheim never wrote a book on the family,[38] though his concern about anomie dictates that he would be preoccupied with the family in his major works, in his teaching, in his public career, and in his occasional pieces. Family life is a salutary vestige of feudal communalism that registers our otherwise unlimited desires and reconciles us to the limits on human desire. The centerpiece of his analysis is the conjugal family, "the most perfect form" of family life.[39] Durkheim's conjugal family resembles Locke's liberal family. It is named for the conjugal bond between husband and wife, the only permanent bond in the conjugal family. The conjugal family encompasses the wife, husband, and (temporarily) dependent children. While children are dependent, fathers dispose their property and person, but after children are independent they "separate from the household" and, if they choose, constitute their own families.[40]

From Communism to Conjugality

The conjugal family is a late flower of human civilization. Looking at family life through the lens of the law of contraction or the division of labor, Durkheim sees early families fulfill many functions that they later forfeit to other social institutions. The conjugal family specializes in procreation, showing affection to its members, and lending unconditional support to the total person in an otherwise competitive, impersonal society. To fulfill these tasks, it transfers religious, political, economic, and, to an extent, educational functions to other institutions, especially the state.[41] Has the family's loss of functions improved family and human life? Are there limits to how much the family can transfer functions to other institutions and still sustain itself?

I address these questions through Durkheim's account of inheritance. Familial communism "had been the basis of all domestic societies" until the rise of the conjugal family. Property, especially landed property, was held in trust by an extended family, and all individual claims on familial property were limited by the need to maintain the patrimony. What is for most of human history a close, often sacred relation between family feeling and the land is surpassed in modern times where "links which derived from things [no longer take] precedence over those which derived from persons."[42] Mirroring Tocqueville's treatment of inheritance,[43] Durkheim sees the rise of the conjugal family connected to laws of primogeniture and entail, which sustained familial communism by maintaining family property whole. The sphere of familial communism retracts as the extended family (holding political power as well as property) gives way to the paternal family (which maintains a connection between the family and land). The conjugal family rents all connection between family and property and gives priority to the individual instead of to things or extended family. Each person "increasingly assumes his own character, his personal manner of thinking and feeling." Communism becomes "more and more impossible because it . . . presupposed the identity and fusion of all consciousness within a single common consciousness" embracing all family members; people now rise or fall based on their own merits instead of family connections determining their status.

Durkheim finds it difficult to say whether conjugal society weakens "domestic solidarity." On the one hand, conjugal families are stronger since "bonds of relatedness" and genuinely felt, apparently consensual relationships glue them together. They are more and more based on individual emotions, which can be warm and strong. On the other hand, the number and importance of the obligations in conjugal families decrease and the material expressions of domestic solidarity disappear (property and children are no longer, as in Hegel, expressions of domestic solidarity). As family togetherness loses its material expression, family members have fewer points of contact with one another. The state has been and will be a key player in the "progressive disruption of familial communism"; it tames patriarchal and paternal families as it tightens the personal aspect of the family; Durkheim welcomes the state's goal of promoting individualism. Durkheim even thinks one of the remaining material expressions of familial communism—the right of parents to bestow inheritance to their children—is "destined to disappear" as the individualistic logic of the conjugal bond and modern society plays out.[44] Just as hereditary offices and honors were abolished during the French Revolution, so also does he foresee the abolition of hereditary property.[45] This change is consistent with justice: "as long as riches are transmitted" by way of heredity, there will be some who are rich and others poor based on factors "other than those which derive from the personal worth of each individual." The state must minimize effects from inequalities deriving from "external causes" such as heritable wealth.[46]

The old habits of familial communism die hard. Most important, in Durkheim's view, is the fact that leaving an inheritance is, with children giving assistance to parents in old age, one of the last links between parents and children once children achieve independence. This link stimulates parents to work hard and accumulate property, which increases society's prosperity. Whither this stimulus to work and save with the abolition of inheritance? Matrimonial society is not enough to provide the stimulus, for leaving money to one's spouse means leaving money to one who is, probably, also knocking on death's door. The prospect of bequeathing a legacy to an "occupational group" (say, the American Political Science Association) will, Durkheim hopes, bind people to their work by putting that legacy in the service of occupations that they love. "Professional duty must assume the same role in men's hearts which domestic duty has hitherto played," Durkheim writes,[47] if this stimulus to hard work and accumulation is to survive.

However far-fetched this may seem (I say that with no disrespect to the APSA), with the disappearance of inheritance all that remains of primitive familial communism is the support children may give to their aging parents. Once the welfare state arises to provide for the old and infirm, all expressions of familial communism will be gone. I am not aware that Durkheim envisions this complete exorcizing of the material. The tenor of Durkheim's discussion of family life suggests that ridding the family of material bases after the children leave home purifies it by making it rely more on feelings, affections, and emotions instead of on calculations and cold hard cash. The fact that his general concept of "the State is . . . an individualistic one" and that this conception does not stop the state from securing objects beyond "an entirely prohibitive justice" opens the door to state provision for old age.[48]

Another feature of the old, large, patriarchal and communal families was their enforcement of general, impersonal rules for moral action. "The chief of the group" was "clothed with a higher authority. He was lawmaker and magistrate, and all domestic relationships were subject to a genuine discipline." In the constricted conjugal family, the bonds between parents and children become more personal, indeterminate, sentimental, and affectionate. This creates a problem. As the need to cultivate self-discipline as the effectual foundation for combating anomie increases, the "usefulness" of the family in accomplishing this discipline becomes "quite restricted." Like Locke, who sees self-control as a preparation for the exercise of rational self-government, Durkheim lauds a "wholesome self-control" as essential to social stability and individual happiness and as befitting man's nature as a limited being. With the decline of organized religion and other "conventional restraints," personal, internal checks provide "the necessary regulatory influence."[49] The conjugal family cannot cultivate this desideratum, however.

> The family, especially today, is a very small group of persons who know each other intimately and who are constantly in contact with one another. As a result, their relationships are not subject to any general, impersonal, immutable regulation. Family duties . . . are likely to accommodate themselves to differences in personality and circumstance. It is a matter of temperament, of mutual accommodation, that promotes affection and adjustment. . . . All the members of this small society are too near one another; and, as a result of this proximity, they have too much feeling for their reciprocal needs; they have too much consciousness of one another for it to be necessary, or even useful, to guarantee their co-operation through regulation.

Instilling discipline is the *sine qua non* for controlling the "desire for the infinite" and for resolving the problem of anomie. Increasingly emotional and personal families cannot do it successfully. Schools must accomplish the tasks of regulating passions and preparing individuals for social life by promulgating impersonal rules. As Durkheim writes, "serious life" begins in the school, where children learn "to respect rules" and develop "habits of self-control and restraint."[50]

Is this move a departure from, or a fulfillment of, Locke's thought that the chief reasons for conjugal society were the procreation, nourishment, and education of children? On the one hand, to better fulfill Locke's aim of taming paternal authority and its attendant partisanship, Durkheim would transfer more authority from the family to the state. Families are still necessary to nourish young children, to teach the youngest ones that the world welcomes them, and, at the margins, to instill some sense of moral authority.[51] Children are likely to pick up peculiar opinions in their families—opinions perhaps inimical to social order (I suspect that he is concerned with religious opinions generally and Catholicism in particular); or they may be spoiled by parents in a way that undermines the prospect of instilling self-discipline, so schools must supplement the family's effect on education. On the other hand, we have the plain words of Locke and a principle underlying those words, namely that no one will care as much for a child's education and well-being during that child's nonage as that child's parents, and that the state is ill-suited for the task of moral education. Perhaps a limited partisanship on behalf of one's own children is both more effective for instilling self-control and preparing children for independence.

Durkheim sees the state assumption of a child's education in terms of the division of labor, dividing the tasks of procreation and nourishment, which remain with parents, from the task of education, which is transferred, more or less, to the state. To put Durkheim's teaching in the context of Locke's, Durkheim eliminates two pieces of Locke's family bargain. For Durkheim, parents should not be responsible for educating their children, and they should give up the power "to bestow their Estates on those, who please them best." Eliminating these affects the adult child's assessment of how much honor, respect, and support a parent is owed, for Locke sees children offering "respect, reverence, support, and compliance" to their parents "more or less, as the Father's care, cost and kindness in his Education, has been more or less."[52] Durkheim's critique of the family as an educational institution marks a dramatic thinning of the family's responsibilities, and, according to the logic of marital unity, makes familial communism less and less necessary. Parents will have less need to invest in their children, and they will spend less time with them as the state assumes their duties.

With the loosening of the parent-child tie, marriage comes to be more central to the family. "The family has developed by becoming concentrated and personalized. . . . While the family loses ground, marriage, on the contrary, becomes stronger." There is an ambiguity in this well-known claim by Durkheim: marriage may not, as most suppose,[53] become absolutely stronger in modernity; it may only be stronger compared to the now weaker and narrower family bond. Marriage is purer and more emotional or affectionate as it comes to specialize in relations between the partners instead of being complicated, as it seemed to be in Hegel, by material things such as property or children.

Socialization and the Ends of Conjugal Society

What is conjugal society about if it is not primarily about the education of children, the time-consuming task for which Lockean marriage is designed? I can answer this best in the context of Durkheim's discussion of divorce and the efforts, afoot in his day, to equate cohabitation with marriage. The divorce debate for Durkheim arises from a policy issue vexing France in his time: should society permit divorce by mutual consent or maintain its fault-based system of divorce law?[54] Individualism manifests itself in attempts to legalize divorce by mutual consent, to equate free unions with marriage, and, generally, to apply sexual equality to men and women. As Durkheim combats these innovations, he sees himself combating individualism.

With respect to divorce, and in contrast to Comte, Durkheim does not question the principle of divorce, but asks when and under what legal regime divorce is permissible. Though he seems conservative on the question of divorce (in his own day and today),[55] in keeping with his aim of transferring the task of education to the state, Durkheim does not argue that access to divorce should be limited for the sake of children. He thinks a regime of divorce by mutual consent would undermine the way marriage regulates husbands, and, as a consequence, that it would harm both partners and society.[56]

> Marriage, by subjecting the passions to regulation, gives the man a moral posture which increases his force of resistance. By assigning a definite, determinate, and, in principle, invariable object to his desires, it prevents him from wearing himself out in the pursuit of ends which are always new and always changing, which grow boring as soon as they are achieved and which leave only exhaustion and disenchantment in their wake. It prevents the heart from becoming excited and tormenting itself vainly in the search for impossible happiness; it makes easier that peace of mind, that inner balance, which are the essential conditions of moral health and happiness. But it only produces these effects because it implies a respected form of regulation which creates social bonds among individuals.[57]

Durkheim replaces Comte's cultivation of altruism with a less elevated but presumably more achievable inculcation of social discipline over individual passions. Since *social* discipline is the most important goal of marriage, *society* oversees the making and breaking of marriage bonds.[58] Matrimonial society is a "public act," and civil magistrates preside over the establishment of the contract. The law should allow divorce for cause—"excessive maltreatment and grave harm" or abandonment, for instance—and the law should be applied by judges to prohibit low-conflict marriages from ending in divorce. Wider availability of divorce would undermine marriage's social purpose: "Regulation from which one can withdraw whenever one has a notion is no longer regulation."[59]

Lowering Comte's almost insanely high goals, Durkheim also loosens marital bonds from Comte's remarkably tight union to a usually lasting, not-so-easy-to-break-up conjugal society. He refrains from endorsing Comte's requirement that spouses be buried in the same grave. This does not send Durkheim careening, as Comte would think, into accepting what we call, in the spirit of social science objectivity, non-marital cohabitation or what Durkheim calls "free union." Marriage entails obligations, and fulfillment of these obligations is necessary for marriage to accomplish its social goals. Breaking up is easy to do under free unions, so men especially will be more likely to part after being sexually satisfied. "Free union is a conjugal society in which these obligations do not exist. It is, therefore, an immoral society." Children raised in free unions will not be as well nourished and their moral education will manifest a deficit in the sense of obligation toward others and in its initial acceptance of moral authority.[60] An acceptance of this pattern throughout society would return mankind to a pre-moral, barbaric age before the introduction of social controls, but it would do so with the augmented, Promethean desires characteristic of modern men.

When viewed from the perspective of Hegel, Locke, or Comte, Durkheim's conception of marital unity seems attenuated, for he is not worried about the children, the property, or other elements that make a couple one. Durkheim would restrict autonomy much more than does today's family law, in that he expects marriage to maintain a certain form to secure the good of social control. The passions brought under control arise from sex differences.[61] Durkheim does not see women as inclined to promiscuity; their natures are more easily regulated by "mores and opinions" and they mature without as much inner conflict arising from an unfulfilled desire for the infinite. "To find calm and peace," Durkheim writes, "she needs only to follow her instincts." Never suggesting that women are less than rational, Durkheim argues that "a woman's mental life is less developed" than a man's and that "society is less necessary to her because she is less impregnated with sociability." Man is "more highly socialized than woman."[62] Marriage subdues restless male sexual desire and helps men realize their rational capacity. Because men are by nature more disorderly than women, men benefit more than women from the order brought by marriage.[63] With the conjugal family,

> family life is much more intense and important than in previous types, women's role, which is precisely to preside over that interior life, has taken on a greater importance and the moral position of wife and mother has been enlarged. At the same time and for the same reason, the husband and wife have been brought more directly and more constantly in contact, because the center of masculine life has ceased to be . . . outside the home. The greater the place occupied by the family in man's preoccupations, the more he feels himself to be his wife's associate, the more he loses the habit of seeing in her an inferior.[64]

Women may need marriage less than men, but women's status elevates because the sphere in which they operate elevates even as the taming of male passions characteristic of the conjugal family moves man's character closer to the more self-controlled woman's. If men and women live in progressively different spheres, their differences draw them closer and reduce the difference.[65]

Durkheim, one of the deepest interpreters of the division of labor, sees the sexual division of labor as a progressive and an ever more deeply entrenched feature of modern life. Like Comte, Durkheim was a phrenologist, yet his was not that old crank's phrenology. His was dynamic. Like Comte, Durkheim thought brain size mattered when it came to intelligence, yet, unlike Comte, Durkheim saw brain size as itself determined by social context and historical developments. In the beginning the brain sizes of men and women were not so different and there was little or no sexual division of labor. Marriage under these circumstances was "very weak" since relationships were made and unmade on whims and relationships were established only where men and women always diverge, their sexual organs. With the advent of modern times, brain sizes diverge, perhaps due to the different kinds of work men and women engage in, resulting from and reinforcing that division of labor, and differences between men and women go beyond sexual anatomy, encompassing psychological and intellectual difference. Women withdrew from politics, warfare, and the harshest forms of labor so that "among civilized peoples the woman leads an existence entirely different from the man's." Women specialize in the "affective" and the arts and men in the "intellectual" function and the sciences.[66] Durkheim could have argued that this sexual division of labor serves the interests of educating the whole child, as Locke and Hegel, to different degrees, did, but Durkheim narrows the application of the sexual division of labor by relating it mostly to how women tame and stabilize men.

The sexual division of labor, like the social one, fosters greater interdependence, comity, productivity, and solidarity. In light of the historical record, he sees the emancipation of women, as proposed by some of his esteemed contemporaries, bringing with it a "laxity of the conjugal bond," and a denigration of domestic life.[67] Again, this reflects the modern logic of marital unity. "The matrimonial bond could not tighten and the family concentrate without the result being a juridical subordination of the wife to the husband, for *that subordination is the necessary condition for family unity.*"[68] To be sure, for Durkheim, unity is not an end in itself—it serves social control—so the need for marital unity depends ultimately on the importance of the need it serves and on the extent to which marriage serves that need. It is precisely on these points—on the nature of sexual passions, on the desirability of controlling sexual passions, and on whether those passions should be controlled—that Durkheim's "scientific" successors would call the marital bond itself into question.

The Problems of Reproduction and Social Control

Durkheim favors equality and individualism as they free children from the rule of parents. Sometimes, as in the case of inheritance, he seeks to free children from material bonds in the family and to promote the individualistic moral constitution of modernity. In the case of education, the ineffectiveness of conjugal family leads him to seek another way to instill the self-discipline children need to understand the limits endemic to the human condition. Durkheim does not want to see those liberal principles turn on the conjugal bond, for the loosening of the conjugal bond would promote anomie. This problem manifested itself in the decline of fertility in modern Europe and especially France after its disastrous and ominous defeat in the Franco-Prussian War. Fertility is related to social vision.

> The inadequacy of our fertility is due above all to moral causes and the principle of those causes consists of a certain development of the spirit of individuation. . . . A change was produced in the domestic order . . . which renders it less appealing to us to have large families.

That change is a "weakening of the domestic spirit" that allows "the cold wind of egoism [to] enter, which ices hearts and beats down courage."[69] Durkheim wants to allow the erosion of the communal family up to a point, but he wants to sustain family life in some form. What Henry VIII could say to the Reformation, Durkheim would say to the spirit of individualism, "Thus far shalt thou go and no farther."[70] Durkheim sees lower fertility rates as a sign of a debilitating retreat into self that threatens the existence of society, not by what it does, but by what it leaves undone.

While I do not dispute how Durkheim interprets the decline of natality, there is a sense in which that decline follows from the division of labor. The stability-lending, sexual-passion-concentrating goals of the conjugal bond can be accomplished without leading to procreation. Contraception practices, which Durkheim himself appears to have opposed, have the effect of dividing procreation from sex. Children are material expressions of a man's focused sexual passion. Preventing births is consistent with, perhaps it is even the fulfillment of, the effort to promote the spiritual, affectionate nature of the conjugal relation. Remove children from the equation and the marriage bond is strengthened even more in relation to the family bond, or so the argument goes. To put this differently, if parents are not to leave anything to a child after they die, or if they are not going to see children as part of their legacy, or if they are not going to be charged with educating children, why bother having children at all?

In this problem we reach the limits of Durkheim's positivist science. Much contemporary work on the family, following the lead of this distant kindred spirit, tries to shore the family up by appealing to the principle of self-interest rightly understood, arguing that, in the subtitle of one such study, "married people are happier, healthier, and better off financially."[71] This is all well and good, on the grounds of positivist social science, and I do not challenge the conclusion that marriage fosters a kind of social discipline important to the health of individuals and to the survival of a society.

Myriad studies in contemporary family studies repeat the general pattern set by Durkheim. They identify a social disorder (for example, juvenile delinquency, spousal abuse, declining school achievement, social inequality, obesity, drug abuse, anger mismanagement, teen pregnancy) and show how this disorder is related to the decline of the family (measured as nonmarital cohabitation, increases in divorce rate, use of parental substitutes, the rise of single-parent, female-headed families). David Popenoe's book *Life without Father: Compelling New Evidence That Fatherhood and Marriage Are Indispensable for the Good of Children and Society* follows this sociological pattern, and I discuss this scholarship in chapter 11.[72] This literature establishes that the family is a social institution fulfilling important social needs. My question concerns what these findings *really* prove.

Durkheim, the sociologist, provides a telling mode of argument that cuts against his own approach and the approach of today's pro-family sociologists. Consider Durkheim's argument about the relationship between hard work and savings on one hand and the bestowal of inheritance on the other. The ability to bestow inheritances on children was a substantial goad to work under familial communism and patriarchy, but Durkheim recommends getting rid of inheritances in the name of the greater individualism. The incentive to work and save will not disappear, for professional organizations (or some such thing) will replace the familial organization as the reason why individuals work and save. One social organization arises to meet the needs formerly met by a different social organization. If a need is a genuine need, other social organizations will arise to respond to that need. If a need is not a genuine need, there is less reason to be concerned. What is so uniquely important about the family as an institution that *only it* can meet a particular need? Superseded in so many other respects, it seems stodgy and unrealistic to think that the family cannot be superseded in other and, perhaps, in all respects. At each change, defenders of the family warn about the dire consequences of adopting that change; yet it seems that at each stage new social organizations intervene to protect us. Stripped of its relation to Historical destiny, positivism lacks a metaphysic to demonstrate the durability of its findings. (In chapter 11 I will explore how today's family scholars try to show that the structure of family life is less amenable to change by adopting a variation of nature.)

A similar difficulty arises in Durkheim's treatment of nature. One brand of suicide is caused, as we have seen, by the persistence of a morbid and unfulfilled "desire for the infinite" in modern peoples. Everything depends on the status of this desire. For Durkheim, this desire is the product of a unique historical place and time, and it causes social problems because adequate social institutions have not yet arisen to register or tame it. He propounds his teaching on the family, in part, so that the desire will find a definite, realistic, salutary focal point. Sex differences are historical and acquired as well, for Durkheim. If the very size of male and female brains and craniums changes with social circumstances, other expressions of their seemingly unique circumstances could also change. Men and women were once similar to one another, and they could become so again with changes in the social parameters. Men and women experience sexual passion in different ways and with different intensity, but there is no reason on Durkheim's grounds that this is a permanent feature of human life. Historical analysis holds that the desire for the infinite and sex differences are eradicable, for there are, in principle, no permanent features of the human mind or psyche; if they are eradicable, then it may not be necessary to defend the family in Durkheim's fashion, or it may someday be possible to consign

Durkheim's defense of the family to the dustbin of history. Unable to say anything *definite* about the direction of society or about the character of human nature, positivistic sociology can only discuss what the family *has been* and not what it *may become*.

This is all unfair to Durkheim and to today's pro-family sociologists in at least one respect. Sociologists are still human, and nature—understood as the unchangeable—still often makes its way surreptitiously into their systems. What they know about human nature is that it is caused by social phenomena: the Greeks see human beings as playthings of the gods; sociology portrays them as playthings of social phenomena. If these social phenomena were stable, the findings of sociology would resemble the discovery of nature. Like the Greek gods, however, social phenomena are fickle, and hence sociology is always trying to hit a moving target; absent a belief in History's destiny, it must remain relatively silent on the question of where the target is moving. Durkheim seems to maintain a neutral scientific attitude more than our pro-family sociologists (who are part of a "marriage movement"). This difference is superficial, however, for both Durkheim and today's pro-family sociologists are concerned about what society is making of the family. There are two underlying assumptions within this positivistic perspective. The first concerns whether social control is good for human beings (as such or at a particular time and place). Durkheim eschews the problematic concepts of love and trust when he defends family life on the safer, apparently more definable, less contentious ground of "social control." Subsequent thinkers (including Marx, Engels, and Freud) criticize the social control propounded by modern marriage. Second, Durkheim's positivism is open-ended in suggesting that family life is subject to innumerable social forces and hence innumerable permutations. Today's pro-family sociologists see this open-endedness as a problem and try to remedy it with a revived understanding of human nature to show the limits within which family life operates. This "naturalistic" positivism is the topic of chapter 11.

Both of these issues point to a larger and deeper one. Durkheim's sociology concerns the ability to establish the relationship between one phenomenon and another, and it eschews concern about deeper meanings beyond or behind those phenomena. It begs a question: can we understand any of these institutions and relations without seeking their deeper meaning? Marital sex may have the effect of focusing a man's passions in a salutary way; the presence of children in a conjugal relation may also contribute to that goal, although Durkheim does not insist on it; and the subordination of woman may be necessary to achieving marital unity—all of these things may be true, but that does not shed light on their meaning. In fact, resting secure with an understanding of relations may short-circuit our search for meaning; the theological or metaphysical modes of thinking are necessary, and positivist social science conceals as much as it reveals. It is one thing to ask how children *affect* a marriage, another to ask what children *mean* to a marriage. It is one thing to ask how sex *affects* men and women, another to suggest what sex *means* to a marriage and to a husband and wife. If scientists or, to be more precise, human beings cannot address these questions, can they understand the phenomena they purport to explore? If our science is to be human, some way of discovering and revealing the meaning of human institutions is necessary and salutary. The positivistic project makes it more difficult to unearth the meaning of family life.

Part III

Liberation and the Movement toward the Family's End

Chapter 6

The City and the Soul Mate
Mill's Late Liberal Vision

Mill's liberalism stands between an older and a younger liberalism. An inheritor of a tradition of freedom and contractual thinking, Mill seems more consistent than older liberals in seeing all relationships established and maintained by free and equal consent. In view of Mill's consistency, older liberals like Locke and other modern thinkers like Rousseau and Hegel appear stodgy and patriarchal. Or were they soberly educating against the regime of liberty and equality in order to balance and preserve it? Was it patriarchy or sobriety? Mill sees his modern predecessors as defenders of patriarchy, not as sober balancers, and he sets out to correct their errors. The family and the private realm are new fields of conquest for the empire of equality and choice. In Mill the principles of equality and liberty are made young and vital again as they move from remaking politics to remaking society.

Mill embraces reform because he thinks liberal political life would be incomplete without liberal family practice. This parallel between the city and the hearth, never neglected, takes center stage with Mill, as he sees the need to impress liberal ideas on the hearts of all people as a central imperative of modern life. Mill's central insight is that spontaneous individuality comes under unique assault in modern societies unless those societies hold freedom and equality most dear. The lamentable philistinism of the masses causes most to neglect self-improvement. This problem can be solved if average people participate in their own "moral regeneration," as Mill frames the issue in *On Liberty*,[1] in *The Subjection of Women*, and in other public and private writings.[2] High-minded cultivation of faculties, self-control, and deliberation contribute to overcoming the leveling tendencies of modern democracy. Mill's defense of individuality induces one of his most enthusiastic commentators to conclude that Mill's account of liberalism is the "only one that is both consistent and coherent."[3] Mill's defense of liberty takes the high road by linking liberty with human perfection and the cultivation of virtue.

As we shall see, some critics charge that Mill's dedication to individual freedom stops at the kitchen door and that Mill endorses a "privatized" sexual division of labor.[4] The sexual division of labor persists, if it does, for Mill, on the basis of personal choice and necessity, not by maintaining socially constructed, traditional, or natural sex roles in the family. While there is force in this feminist criticism, it fails to connect Mill's *Subjection of Women* to *On Liberty*. Efforts to understand Mill's new family in *Subjection of Women* apart from his political vision in *On Liberty* present a still photo, and a black and white one at that, instead of a living picture of Mill's vision. His politics requires a new family, one in which husbands and wives share more experiences and resemble each other more; the new "city" needs a family constituted by soul mates. What I mean by a marriage of soul mates is a marriage emphasizing the compatibility of two individuals assisting each other to achieve personal growth and development instead of the complementariness of a marital union where two become one. Mill's vision of family contains a deep rejection of the institutions sustaining unified families seen in Hegel and Comte, though Mill does not seem to reject the idea of freely chosen marital union. Whatever traditionalism appears in Mill's thinking will corrode once his animating vision of autonomy and moral regeneration is invited into the home and its reconstructive work proceeds, and Mill, I believe, is aware of this.

Individuality and the Problem of the Unified Family

Mill holds that "'the end of man . . . is the highest and most harmonious development of his powers to a complete and consistent whole'"; this development presupposes that an individual can and will "use and interpret experience" free from any political or social pressures to conform to others' visions of a proper life. "In our times," Mill observes, "everyone lives as under the eye of a hostile and dreaded censorship." Public opinion is "everywhere become or becoming the dominant power," which means "society has now fairly got the better of individuality."[5]

Mill announces a "simple principle" to determine the scope of government and social pressure that can be brought to bear on individuals: what affects an individual directly and primarily is the individual's own concern, even if it *indirectly* affects others. This principle limits compulsion to the cases where government restrains individuals from hurting others. As the problem of tyranny does not begin or end with government, neither does Mill's solution to the problem of tyrannical public opinion. Mill writes "of the limits to the authority of *society* over the individual," not of *government* over the individual.[6] Mill emphasizes society because the rules of engagement and mores in society percolate to democratic government and because individual freedom is as essential to moral development as to political self-government. When a man's character displeases us, "we may express our distaste, and we may stand aloof from a person . . . but we shall not therefore feel called on to make his life uncomfortable."[7]

Liberty is the policy that allows for the benefits of modern life while mitigating its drawbacks. Spontaneous individuality invigorates action and connects independence to life-lending virtue. If we would embrace liberty, Mill promises we can have it all—freedom is a prerequisite to human excellence, and with one comes the other. The obstacle to the rise of this best of all worlds is the unified family and its seemingly necessary concomitant, the subordination of women through the sexual division of labor. The "legal subordination" of women in the family is "one of the chief hindrances to human improvement."[8] "All the selfish propensities, the self-worship, the unjust self-preference, which exist among mankind, have their source and root in, and derive their principal nourishment from, the present constitution of the relation between men and women."[9] The problem goes beyond the legal status of wives.

> Not only in what concerns others, but in what concerns only themselves, the individual or the family do not ask themselves—what do I prefer? or, what would suit my character and disposition? or, what would allow the best and highest in me to have fair play, and enable it to grow and thrive? . . . I do not mean that they choose what is customary, in preference to what suits their own inclination. It does not occur to them to have any inclination, except for what is customary. Thus the mind itself is bowed to the yoke.[10]

Especially insidious is women's role as "the auxiliary of common public opinion" in maintaining this yoke. Women are enslaved to sex roles, customs, and quasi-feudal feelings by the disapproving looks and nods of other women, who perpetuate patriarchal order. Too often families leave an illiberal stamp on children, as husbands and wives model unequal roles within the family. Sons follow a father's footsteps instead of making their own way.[11] Daughters are prepared for a life of subservience to husbands and children, not to liberate themselves from society's preconceived roles.

The condition of women described in *Subjection of Women* is the intractable manifestation of social tyranny described in *On Liberty*.[12] Mill's defense of vanguards of change, in which individual geniuses elevate mankind as they adopt "different experiments of living," implies greater diversity of family form. "There is no reason that all human existences should be constructed on some one, or some small number of patterns"; "different persons . . . require different conditions for their spiritual development." Mill's strategy in *On Liberty*—to see tradition and custom as antagonistic to individual liberty—grounds his introduction of experimentation into family life in *Subjection of Women*. "The moral training of mankind will never be adapted to the conditions of the life for which all other human progress is a preparation, until they practice in the family the same moral rule which is adapted to the normal constitution of human society."[13] A new, open, thinner conception of the public—less burdened by traditions—requires a new, more flexible, and thinner conception of the family, also less burdened by traditions.

Mill sees marital relations as the "primitive state of slavery lasting on,"[14] and he makes us consider the elements of traditional family life by his extreme dismissal of it. For Mill, the traditional communal family's most sophisticated defender is Comte.[15] What Mill views as an enslaving marriage is Comte's vision of a loving, unified family. Comte exaggerates Hegel's communal family, seeing the unity of the family as even tighter and more long-lasting and seeing the family as vastly more important than Hegel did. For Comte, as we have seen, marriage is the "noblest aim of human life," in which men and women join their interests as they form a union based on love, mutual confidence, and "mutual service and perfection." So tight is this unity that Comte closes the door to the extension of the franchise to women, prohibits women from owning property, and prohibits divorce to maintain the exclusivity and indissolubility of marriage. The individual identity of both men and women are lost to their marital bond. He goes further, carrying marital unity beyond the grave by promulgating a "perpetuity of widowhood" and suggesting that married couples "be laid in the same grave together."[16] Comte accepts the logic of marital unity: the more serious the ends of marriage, the more marriage and family life must be communal and unified; and the more a marriage is communal and unified, the more it practices the division of labor in securing its purposes; and the labor will likely be divided along sexual lines.

The tight unity of Comte's family matches his unparalleled defense of sexual subordination and the sexual division of labor. What Comte defends is in line with Hegel's logic but *exaggerates* Hegel's conclusions. The division of labor servicing marital unity is grounded in sex differences, which advances in civilization only accentuate. Sex differences suit men and women to play complementary roles.[17] To repeat, men are superior in "practical energy" and "the mental capacity connected with it," which suits them to be the public face of the family, while "woman's strength lies in Feeling" and love and breeding "Social Feeling" from raw "Self-interest," which suits them to provide for the family's emotional needs. The woman's role in the family is "closely connected with the grand object of all human effort, the elevation of Social Feeling [i.e., altruism] over Self-love."[18] There is "no greater happiness than to live for another," and women are suited for that in marriage and in their vocations as mothers.

Mill rejects the pillars of Comte's marital unity, and, perhaps, marital unity as such, as inconsistent with the dignity of women and personal growth in marriage. We explore Mill's treatment of property and family finances, of women's suffrage, and of divorce to limn his criticisms of the unified family.

Property and Finances

While a member of Parliament, Mill sponsored a bill to allow married women to own property.[19] The regime of property ownership Mill opposed was based on coverture, the idea that a married couple is "one person in law," and that the male head of household holds property on the family's behalf. The property that a woman brings to marriage becomes, legally, the man's property, and the property the woman earns or inherits after marriage is "*ipso facto* his."[20] What Comte and Hegel uphold as a support for communal marriage Mill takes to be an institution of woman's oppression sustaining patriarchal institutions. Mill's critique of the communal family is based on the belief that marriage transforms women to see themselves as members of the family, but that marriage does not have the same effect on men. Men see themselves as empowered to govern others absolutely and arbitrarily—they are, like Hobbes' Leviathan, master of the domain without being a part of it. "Many people," writes Mill, "seem to think it impossible that two persons can live together in harmony unless one of them has absolute power over the other."[21]

Mill criticizes communal property by applying liberal theory and referring to examples of how communal property *really* works; the examples illuminate the theory. Men own property absolutely under the legal regime of communal property. This absolute power corrupts them into committing all sorts of debauchery, irresponsible spending habits, spousal abuse, marital rape, and thievery. Wives have little or no recourse to this abuse and profligacy. Such are common occurrences,[22] suggesting that a person whose property belongs by law to another is akin to a slave. Like slave masters, husbands and fathers can carouse on the resources of their wives; at the slightest complaint, such husbands dress their thievery and abuse in the pleasant propaganda of marital unity and communal property. Mill has no relish for communal property arrangements based on the principle that "what is mine is yours but what is yours is not mine."[23]

Mill would have marital property arranged by a simple rule: "Whatever would be the husband's or wife's if they were not married, should be under their exclusive control during marriage." This appears to mean that husbands and wives keep separate what they bring into marriage, and they keep separate what they earn in marriage. It is not clear how strictly Mill would apply this simple rule because everything could, in a sense, be under the exclusive control of one spouse during marriage. The rule could be applied to make common life nearly impossible. (Every act would raise questions. Who buys dinner? Who owns the car or house? Who pays the mortgage?) There may be a way of applying the rule enabling the couple to divide the spending and earning power without giving up exclusive ownership of their property. Mill encourages spouses to consider fruits of their labor as their own, and not the family's, property. This movement is designed to free women from the irresponsible, patriarchal enslavement of the "one person in law" idea. Mill continues after announcing the simple rule:

> Some people are sentimentally shocked at the idea of a separate interest in money matters, as inconsistent with the ideal fusion of two lives into one. For my own part, I am one of the strongest supporters of community of goods, when resulting from an entire unity of feeling in the owners, which makes all things common between them.[24]

This ambiguous endorsement of the community of goods leaves unanswered whether the "entire unity of feeling" is possible, or if it is healthy, and what that "entire unity of feeling" is organized around.

Women's Suffrage and Consent

The difficulty of achieving an "entire unity of feeling" also affects Mill's stance toward the question of women's suffrage. Those opposed to extending the franchise to women adopt the Hegelian logic of marital unity. There is in the family such a "community of interest" and such a sharing of mutual "good feeling" that it is safe to have men represent women in the choosing of representatives.[25] The nation is, under Hegel's logic, a community of families, represented in public counsels through fathers as heads of household. Mill again counters the logic of marital unity with examples illustrating the principles of liberal theory. For those who think that marital interests and feelings converge to make head of household suffrage safe and just, Mill brings forward several examples of how a husband will kick his wife "to death's door," and he repeats how men are prone to exploit wifely labor for their own selfish benefit.[26] The message is that the communal family is harmful to a woman's health and to her dignity. The remedy to the problem of arbitrary husbandly rule is the same as the liberal remedy to the problem of absolute despotism in politics. "To have a voice in choosing those by whom one is to be governed, is a means of self-protection due to everyone"; this principle applies to the choosing of husbands as well as the choosing of representatives. The laws passed by the government (property laws, for instance) have a profound effect on a husband's character. What appears as Mill's utopian hopes from the extension of suffrage is, when seen in light of Mill's critique of marital unity, a means of eroding the abusive, dependency-making marriage.[27] Extending the franchise extends a way of thinking that encourages women to see themselves apart from the family. As Mill writes, "the greatest good that can be done for women and the preparation of all others is to recognize them as citizens—as substantive members of the community instead of as mere things belonging to other members of the community."[28]

Key factors in a woman's enslavement are the lack of real consent to marriage and what we now call the social construction of gender. The "whole force of education . . . enslaves [women's] minds" to communal marriage, so the consent that appears to reign is *really* a false consciousness leading women to submit to bourgeois patriarchs; the pedestal on which women sit is really a cage. Not only does public opinion pigeonhole women to wifely roles, but laws and customs deny unmarried women economic and educational opportunities. Women face a "Hobson's choice" of having their needs met by marrying a potential tyrant and not having their needs met at all. Once in marriage there is no chance for women to sustain themselves apart from their masters, and there are no effective legal vehicles to obtain a divorce. "If she leaves her husband, she can take nothing with her, neither her children nor anything which is rightfully her own. If he chooses, he can compel her to return, by law, or by physical force."[29]

Mill concedes that the treatment of women is better than her legal status suggests. Figuring out why women are treated better is central to understanding Mill's thinking, though few commentators pay this concession heed.[30] "Feelings and interests" temper the exercise of male tyranny, and the existence of children and common property tends to strengthen cords of affection. These "mitigations in practice" are proof that something in human nature softens the male's otherwise vile despotism.[31] True marital sweetness, for Mill, occurs between equal and independent persons—only this justifies his view that the sweetness found in unified marriage is *extrinsic to* or *independent of* it. It is plausible to argue, with earlier thinkers, that the sexes occupying separate spheres are bonded through "long acquaintance and mutual obligations," grounding a "calm and sedate affection."[32] It is even likely that the convergence of "feelings and interests" surrounding children and property are, as Hegel suggested, sources of familial pride and ethical love. Why does Mill think the mitigating sentimental sweetness lies outside of marital unity?

Divorce, Human Inequality, and the End of Marriage

An answer to this question must await a description of Mill's better marriage and a treatment of where spousal unity fits into human development. I first consider Mill's "On Marriage" (1832–1833), written for Harriet Taylor and coupled with her shorter essay of the same name, in light of Mill's later *Subjection of Women* (1869).[33] In "On Marriage," Mill posits the existence of an inequality in human nature unrelated to sex that complicates the task of public morality. On one hand are the "highest, impassioned natures," capable of greater happiness through development of "mind and heart" and a mutual joy in contemplating their beautiful natures reciprocally. For such beautiful people "it would be idle to prescribe rules," for their impulses are guided by the best judgment, and their judgments by "an open loving heart."

> To such, marriage is but one continued act of self-sacrifice where strong affection is not; every tie therefore which restrains them from seeking out and uniting themselves with someone whom they perfectly love, is a yoke to which they cannot be subjected without oppression; and to such a person when found, they would naturally, superstition apart, scorn to be united by any other tie than free and voluntary consent.

Mill adopts the romantic view Hegel had criticized in defending marriage ceremonies. External demands for a public ceremony, third-party witness, and church consecration are inconsistent with the depth, inwardness, and purity of soul mates. Such beautiful people point toward the deinstitutionalization of marriage and a conception of marriage in which it is wrong "that there should exist any motives to marriage except the happiness which two persons who love each other feel in associating their existence."[34]

The other class consists of brutish male sensualists, whose idea of happiness consists in the desire to lord themselves over others, and the women who love them. Laws made by and for such sensualists aim "to tie up the sense, in the hope by so doing, of tying up the soul also, or else to tie up the sense because the soul is not cared about at all." For brutes, the indissoluble marriage is an improvement over wandering male detachment from the family, for it fosters restraints founded on habit. They are still not capable of "any real aspiration towards, or sense of, the happiness which such companionship in its best shape is capable of giving to the best natures," but at least they are constrained to behave more responsibly and peaceably.[35]

Can society accommodate beautiful people without undercutting the brutish? Or, as Mill asks, "Will the morality which suits the highest natures, in this matter, be also best for all inferior natures?" Mill answers,

> My conviction is, that it will: but this can only be a happy accident. All the difficulties of morality in any of its branches, grow out of the conflict which continually arises between the highest morality and even the best popular morality which the degree of development yet attained by the average human nature, will allow to exist.[36]

We see what this "happy accident" means in his discussion of divorce. For most of history, the "indissolubility of marriage acted powerfully to elevate the social position of women" by tying men to marriage after the fire was gone. A "community of interest" arose from the indissolubility and the children it produced. Accomplishing these goals sufficed for women with inferior natures, either because lesser women were incapable of greater happiness or because insecure women were afraid of abandoning the gains secured by making men stick around.[37] Inferior, enslaved women enter into corrupt and corrupting bargains, gaining security at the price of freedom.

Mill deepens this historical defense of indissoluble marriage with two thoughts relevant especially to the "great majority." First, offspring are "wholly dependent" for their happiness and character on their parents and "*must* be better cared for in both points if their parents remain together." Even when parents are less than competent, children suffer from the separation. Second, the ability to choose, reevaluate, and rechoose (or not) one's spouse, abetted by the power of divorce, unleashes a paradox of rising expectations from marriage. Love is a restless and unstable passion, capricious in its direction and intensity. Such a passion leads people to imagine that they can find a better spouse. The freedom to divorce frees them to act on that imagination. Frivolous disputes and disgusts, forgotten when a person must live with an irritating spouse, fester into animus and grounds for separation when divorce is easy. Chosen roles are forfeited when one believes greater happiness will be found with another, though this belief is usually unfounded for those with a moderate capacity for happiness; the grass only looks greener. This problem promotes frivolous marriages and despairing restlessness within marriage, both of which undermine unity, fidelity, and happiness.[38]

Despite these misgivings, Mill embraces an approximation of an unlimited right to divorce in "On Marriage" as part of his critique of marital unity.[39] Mill's position on divorce lies at the crossroads of three progressively important arguments. First, the case against divorce assumes a false dichotomy, in which prohibiting divorce lies on one side and divorce at "the most passing feeling of dissatisfaction" lies at the other. Human motivation is a complex set of habits, feelings of duty, choices, social pressure, and shame that would militate against divorcing for light and transient reasons; there would be no pandemic of "low-conflict" divorces because autonomy would be limited by these realities or because legal freedom is separate from moral freedom. He believes that, "in a tolerably moral state of society," parents with children will stay together "unless in case of such uncongeniality of disposition as rendered it positively uncomfortable to one or both of the parties to live together, or in case of a strong passion conceived by one of them for a third person."[40] This argument resolves the paradox of rising expectations because moral responsibility, the presence of children, and habits qualify free choice.

This first argument *for* the legality of divorce merely puts a positive gloss on his previous arguments *against* it. Whereas earlier he worried about the creation of restless passions leading people to switch spouses in the mostly vain hope of finding happiness, here Mill endorses divorce when a spouse has conceived a "strong passion" for another. But, as Mill had earlier argued, the ability to divorce fosters such strong, illusory passions; the power to divorce corrodes habits of staying together. Whereas earlier he was sanguine about parents staying together for the children, here he suggests there may be a way to allow divorce and still take care of the kids. He hopes the day will come when society will "allow of a regulated community of living among persons intimately acquainted, which would prevent the necessity of a total separation between the parents even when they had ceased to be connected by any nearer tie than mutual good will, and a common interest in their children."[41] Mill's reading of when parents would divorce is shot through with tension: they would "almost always" stay together "in a tolerably moral state of society," but would divorce if "uncongeniality of disposition" rendered their union "positively uncomfortable." Presumably the "tolerably moral state of society" would be one adhering to the principles of *On Liberty*. This would be a society in which actions directly affecting one person and only indirectly affecting others are beyond the reach of government and, to a lesser extent, public opinion. The society envisioned in *On Liberty* removes the legal penalty and mitigates the stigma of divorce, suggesting that society would become more tolerant of low-conflict divorce.

We can see why Mill justifies divorce as good for the beautiful as well as the brutes by visiting his other arguments. His second argument, perhaps drawn from his experience with Harriet Taylor, suggests that opposition to divorce impairs the happiness of beautiful people and does not elevate the brutish as much as it once had. The era of indissoluble marriage is over. As Mill writes of the need for the best to compromise with popular morality at the onset of "On Marriage,"

> The greatest, indeed the only real, sufferers by this compromise [are the higher natures]; for they are called upon to give up what would really make them happy; while others are commonly required only to restrain desires the gratification of which would bring no real happiness.[42]

His endorsement of moving law toward at-will divorce, when seen with his observations about the harms divorce causes, implies that allowing divorce may in the short term cause a restless dissatisfaction and harm children, but *in the long run* a new ideal of marriage will improve the lives of all. Considerable suffering and unhappiness may mark the transition from indissoluble marriages to a better family, but such beautiful marriages more than compensate for the costs.[43] This conviction rests on his belief that human beings have attained a "degree of development" where the conflict between the "highest morality" and the "best public morality" is resolved in favor of the "highest morality." Whence this conviction that, again, arises in time from a "happy accident"?

This leads to Mill's third and decisive argument, which links "On Marriage" to *Subjection of Women*. All previous tensions—the optimistic gloss on the paradox of rising expectations, the hope that flexible institutions will rise to care for children of divorce, the hope that divorce will affect "high-conflict" marriages, the conviction that the better marriage founded on the ideals of beautiful people will compensate for the suffering this may cause—all these tensions, I say, are resolved, for Mill, by the prospect of bringing forth a new kind of woman.[44] Mill's critique of the marital unity must be read in light of his writings on female equality. "The question is not what marriage ought to be, but a far wider question, what women ought to be. Settle that first, and the other will settle itself." With this new woman in mind Mill defends divorce in "On Marriage," and he is committed to this vision of the new woman in all his writings. Mill's public writings either suggest a mild, moral opposition to at-will divorce (*On Liberty*) or are silent on divorce (*Subjection of Women*).[45] Mill's tepid pronouncements on divorce reveal his willingness to advocate for female equality without drawing out all the legal and moral implications of that idea.[46] Once the new woman is accepted (and Mill advocates for her vigorously in *Subjection of Women*), laws and social practices (including divorce law) will have to adapt.

Nature and the New Woman

Mill tears down the old unified family and the old woman to build new, more alluring ones. The "best forms" of family were previously schools of "sympathy, tenderness, and loving forgetfulness of self," wherein true unity between man and wife was defined by sacrificial love in the service of a common good. Staying together, through better or worse, was crucial to maintaining marital unity. Often unified families were schools of "willfulness, overbearingness, unbounded self-indulgence and double-dyed and idealized selfishness, of which sacrifice itself is only a particular form." So inseparable is the school of "loving forgetfulness of self" from this "school of willfulness" that Mill matriculates the family in the "school of sympathy in equality" that remembers and serves the self.[47] The tight indissoluble family must be loosened and familial unity and self-sacrificial sympathy must relent to a less communal "sympathy in equality"—with a narrower and less permanent community and greater individual autonomy for husbands and wives—to avoid spousal abuse, manly willfulness, the self-serving tendency of mothers to make themselves indispensable, and womanly dependence. The new family promotes personal moral regeneration in bringing about this new woman. Marriage would not entail a surrender of each to a marital union, and it would not necessarily involve service to a defined end. Each party can hold something back, so that the surrendering would not annihilate the individual and the marriage would come to serve the individual's interests.[48]

Marital unity presupposes that the married couple holds some goal in common. Mill abjures throughout his corpus from telling us *what the com-*

mon ends of marriage are. His silence on the ends of marriage reflects his willingness to allow individuals to define marriage's ends for themselves and suggests that the institution does not serve any socially determined ends. When people define the ends of marriage for themselves, they construct the form of marriage for themselves; freedom on ends requires freedom on means. Rigidity on the question of ends would mean that the number of family forms that might achieve those ends would, in some measure, be limited. In this context, recall Mill's willingness to endorse "different experiments of living" when it comes to family form and his belief that "different persons . . . require different conditions for their spiritual development." Attempts in law that enforce, and attempts in opinion that stigmatize, any particular conception of family form are, for Mill, tyrannical limitations on human choice. Mill even defends the freedom to enter into polygamous marriages on the grounds that people should be able to form the families they choose with whom they choose.

Mill undercuts the basis of marital unity in the name of what he takes to be the higher ideals of spousal friendship, female equality, and personal growth. His teachings on property, suffrage, divorce, and education point in this direction. Mothers and wives should be able to seek an independent means of employment: "The power of earning is essential to the *dignity* of a woman, if she has not independent property."[49] Supporting women's dignity, such a policy also encourages women to be less self-sacrificing, more assertive, and more independent of wifely and maternal roles. Mill's idea of voluntary dependence is founded on prior and always-accessible independence. The "first and indispensable step" in ending a woman's subjection "is that she be so educated, as not to be dependent either on her father or her husband for subsistence." Independent women may need the dignity found in the freedom to work outside the home if they want choice before and in marriage. As feminist writers emphasize, only a fully mature woman—maturity means accessing the creative world of work—can enter into this kind of union, though Mill does not denigrate housewives the way some feminists do.[50]

Leaving marital unity behind, Mill draws marriage in the image of friendship based on a unity of feeling. Earlier in history men and women led separate lives, but we have arrived in a new era where "home and its inhabitants" mean more to men than friends at the club or at work. Husbands and wives are to be companions and friends.[51] Marriage comes to resemble friendship as it was understood in the Western tradition from Aristotle on,[52] with the caveat that, for Mill, husbands and wives can now be best of friends.[53] The key to Mill's twist on this argument is that spousal friendship emerges when separate spheres are eliminated. This means that husbands and wives will share more experiences and have similar characters so they will interpret those experiences in much the same way. The new marriage is founded on "a union of thoughts and inclination" of "two persons of cultivated faculties, identical in opinions and purposes." Such marriages are founded on "the best kind of equality, similarity of powers and capacities with reciprocal superiority in them."[54] Each commits to the other's development or moral regeneration. Just marriages serve each spouse in a manner consistent with the equal independence of the man and woman. The search for a perfect marriage resembles a search for a "second self" or a soul mate, in which each gets something high and elevated and spiritual out of it. Marriage will have no command or obedience, no one-sided sacrifice, and no preconceived roles for men and women. The new marriage reflects the needs and desires of the spouses as they understand them and as long as they understand them to be consistent with the marriage.

Consistent with this vision of marriage as friendship, Mill often denigrates sex as an "animal function."[55] He equates beautiful people to those with "impassioned natures," but these passions do not appear to be exclusive, erotic desires, which, in the view of Montaigne, that skeptic of spousal friendship, serve as a "thousand foreign tangles." The dishes and the kids, the laundry and the bills, familial property and infinite other mundane details distract soul mates; sex is another mundane detail. Far from failing to see the "positive role which sex might play in marriage,"[56] Mill seems to separate sex from spousal friendship. He seems to think that putting sex inside friendship either complicates friendship, diminishes the sexual relationship, or leads to consequences (i.e., children) that stress the understanding of equality at the heart of spousal friendship. Leaving sex and its consequences out of it reflects his judgment on the elevated structure of spousal friendship, not his reputed prudishness or shyness.

Nor is this Mill's only remarkable position on sex. His opposition to prostitution, expressed in a series of letters, is founded on a view that men and women have the same levels of sexual appetite. W. E. H. Lecky, Mill's contemporary, for instance, argues that easy access to prostitutes, those "eternal priestess[es] of humanity," helps to ensure "the unchallenged purity of countless happy homes" because short-term trysts are a less dangerous way of venting male sexual longing than sustained affairs.[57] Mill is appalled at how this defense of prostitution reinforces what he takes as the teaching of the Catholic Church, which exaggerates the force and intractability of "natural passions," or original sin. Mill believes that "this particular passion will become with men as it is already with a large number of women, completely under the control of reason." Men too will feign headaches, once equality and consent define marriage; suppressing prostitution, for Mill, fosters male self-control.

The mutability of sexual desire that Mill anticipates is an instance of his general belief in the mutability of nature. He seems to think that differences between men and women will disappear once the cultural and legal superstructure of patriarchy is dismantled. Many contemporary feminists find Mill's apparent respect for women who choose to occupy separate spheres from men inconsistent at this point.[58] Despite the fact that Mill advocates removing legal and cultural barriers to women working outside the home and the fact that he remains silent about communal purposes of marriage, he seems to accept a traditional sexual division of labor in the family—women as responsible for educating children and beautifying the home and men as the primary breadwinners.[59] Mill's first revision of the traditional position is that the sexual division of labor is legitimate only if it is based on genuine marital choice and an open marketplace in which women and men are equal competitors. The deepest feminist criticism of Mill is that marital friendship would not survive Mill's acceptance of traditional sex roles even in that context. Mill ignores, as Mary Shanley relates, "the potential barrier between husband and wife which such different adult life experiences might create, and the contribution of shared experience to building a common sensibility and strengthening the bonds of friendship."[60] The sexual equality and friendship Mill offers with one hand he withdraws with the other. But even this criticism only heightens the central perplexity in Mill's thought on this matter. Does he think there is a difference between male and female characters? And if so, should this difference be respected or overcome?

Mill's vision encounters one of its deepest obstacles here. History affords few examples of the sexual equality Mill sees grounding marital friendship. The nature of both sexes has been "entirely distorted" by the condition of slavery in which women have lived. External influences have made women feminine and men masculine. Because our ideas of men and women have been so corrupted, Mill rejects "all opinions, customs, and institutions" that favor notions of unified marriage founded on inequality and sex differences as "relics of primitive barbarism." His rejection of marital unity sits uneasily with his repeated claims that we know little about the natures of women or men because society has so distorted each.[61] He claims that the question, "What are the natural differences between the two sexes?" is a "most difficult" one, on which "almost everybody dogmatizes" and nothing more authoritative than "conjectures" can presently be offered,[62] but his advocacy of equality reflects a view more authoritative than mere conjecture. Does Mill know the nature of women (and men) or not?

We must enter the realm of philosophy. The family has a plausible claim to be a natural society because it seems to rely on spontaneous or preexisting biological differences between adults and children and between men and women. To what extent does this spontaneous natural difference affect family structure? The fact that there is variety in family form confirms that spontaneous nature does not determine what human beings do; cultures nurture spontaneous nature, at least to an extent. Mill runs with this thought. Human experience and history have exaggerated such differences to the point of having invented them. Mill thinks we learn *nothing* about male and female natures by studying history,[63] because nature is so easily manipulated by external circumstances. Women and men can be made into what they ought to be. Redesigning the family requires a more complete conquest of nature by extending human choice.

Not claiming to know the nature of men or women, Mill understands the nature of ruling as such. Male rule is "*grounded on force*" and "*has no other source than the law of the strongest.*"[64] Thus Mill debunks paternalism in the family in much the same way that early modern thinkers such as Locke debunked paternalism in politics or the divine right of kings. The domineering man and submissive woman appear as constructed, "almost natural" ideas men build to perpetuate their rule (as kings perpetuated themselves by divine right); men rule because they rule, not because they are men. Knowing that men rule because they rule bespeaks knowledge about what the nature of men, and women, is *not*, which presupposes knowledge of what their natures are (i.e., malleable).

In this context we should consider Mill's two minds on whether women will still want to be wives and mothers after doors to employment are open and the ideal of the new woman and family is accepted, and whether the sexual division of labor is consistent with Mill's view of moral regeneration. On one hand, Mill insists that a "pleasurable enjoyment of life" depends on having a "worthy outlet for the active faculties" and that "women who have cares of a family . . . have this outlet."[65] Mill seems to defend the dignity of mothers dedicated to the moral and intellectual development of children. On the other hand, the "incessant vigilance" involved in the "superintendence of a household" is "extremely onerous" and stunts the development of higher thoughts and ambitions. Mill does not think women play a maternal role because of anything in their nature; he never asserts, as earlier defenders of the sexual division of labor had and later ones would, that women are naturally suited to be mothers. Their role in the family appears to be founded on custom (as if it could just as easily have been the man staying with the kids). In his most elaborate praising of the sexual division of labor, Mill refers to it as a "desirable custom." Working in the home deprives women of the chance to earn an independent income and dignity. Mill also envisions a society in which women are educated like men and employed, at least in "business, public affairs, and the higher matters of speculation," in equal numbers to men.[66] Millian mothers would have fewer family functions to occupy them. Having each mother instruct her children is inefficient, so educational duties will be carried on in schools hired by the families. A mother's educational task involves training the affections by "being with the child," a task Mill never describes. One more consideration is relevant. Mill expects women with a beautiful nature to be occupied outside the home, in the "higher services of humanity."[67] Yet, as feminist critics point out, he seems to leave the brutish lower class women in the home; his gendered expectations have a class tinge. History has reached a point, however, where the compromise in society must no longer be made to protect the brutes: what was true of divorce may also be true of careers for all women. These factors point away from the home toward a less maternal vision of what a woman ought to be.

Mill's embrace of choice solves the riddle of sex differences while taking into account his two minds on motherhood. Mill rebuts observations that women are more self-sacrificing, intuitive, nervous, tender, practical, moral, and relational than are men, and that they are less philosophical, strong, selfish, ambitious, original, inventive, and commanding. While listing these sex differences, Mill again denies knowing "how much of the existing mental differences between men and women [are] natural and how much artificial." If these sex differences are natural, they do not need social and political support; natural differences will thrive in an atmosphere of freedom in which all choose to follow their "natures."[68]

> If nature has established an ineradicable and insuperable difference in the capacities and qualifications of the two sexes, nature can take care of itself. What nature has decided may safely be left to nature. But when we find people making themselves uneasy for fear that nature's purposes should be frustrated unless law comes to her assistance, we may be pretty certain that it is not nature they are so careful about, but law pretending to be nature. To all such pretences the growing improvement of mankind is making them more and more adverse.[69]

A society-wide experiment based on the principle of choice can reveal what differences, if any, separate men from women.[70] Choice appears as a neutral way of respecting individual peculiarities and natural differences (if such there be).

But Mill is not simply an advocate for choice. He endorses this experiment in choice because he thinks patriarchal institutions cause sex differences and an emphasis on choice will corrode those institutions and those differences.[71] A reconstitution of legal standards and cultural expectations affords women the choices their natures demand. Dismantling vestiges of patriarchy will diminish and perhaps erase differences between the sexes. The political structure of choice—a woman's right to own property in marriage, the ability to seek employment, the right to divorce, the extension of the franchise, and so on—supports Mill's effort to assimilate the sexes and to make spouses soul mates. Mill doubts that "if women's nature were left to choose its direction as freely as men's, and if no artificial bent were attempted to be given to it except that required by the conditions of human society, there would be any material difference . . . in the character and capacities that would unfold themselves."[72]

> I believe that equality of rights would abate the exaggerated self-abnegation which is the present artificial ideal of feminine character, and that a good woman would not be more self-sacrificing than the best man: but on the other hand, men would be much more unselfish and self-sacrificing than at present, because they would no longer be taught to worship their own will as such a grand thing that it is actually the law for another rational being.[73]

A "gradual assimilation of the tastes and characters to one another" is Mill's ideal of a marriage of equalizing equals. More women will more selfishly pursue careers, and men will more selflessly help with the housework and the kids. The division of labor will be chosen and labor more equally allocated between the sexes. We again face Mill's more radical argument. Previous patriarchal constructions of gender may point to the need for a reconstruction of it. Just as the logic of his position leads to legitimating divorce for both the beautiful people and the brutes, so also does the logic of the moral regeneration point all women—the beautiful and brutish—away from the choice of committing themselves to family and toward a choice of building a life outside of it both before and after that family forms. The more we take Mill's idea of moral regeneration seriously, the less committed women are to the family and the less marriage and family life are defined by a tightly knit union.

Mill's Progressive Faith

The force of Mill's argument reinforces feelings of universal human likeness, wherein human beings identify and sympathize with their fellows. Mill's achievement presupposes the extension of male sympathy to females and the identification of men with women's suffering due to legal and cultural injustices. Not on sympathy alone does Mill depend. His teaching on the family epitomizes the progressive narrative: human diversity, moral regeneration, and human happiness converge when we dismantle the legal and cultural edifice of the unified family. The time is ripe for the "happy accident," when public morality will be made to serve the interests of all.

The fading significance of sex differences opens avenues for women to achieve a dignified independence in and from the family. It is not clear which comes first, the dignified independence earned through labor outside the home or the fading sex differences. Mill pitches his argument in each direction: the promotion of choice causes sex differences to fade, and fading sex differences open up greater avenues for choice. His belief that male sexual passion can become much like a female's illuminates his hope that choice can develop people and society. What happens if choosers choose incorrectly and society does not progress toward the erosion of sexual differences Mill seems to suppose? What is the goal: choice or regeneration? Let us, with Mill, imagine a scenario in which the patriarchal legal framework and cultural expectations have been dismantled and in which most women choose to dedicate themselves to child-rearing and homemaking, while most men are primary breadwinners.[74] Mill's feminist critics are correct to see that Mill seems to find such a condition acceptable (or even desirable) and to see that what they view as Mill's lamentable traditionalism in this respect contradicts his liberating vision of moral regeneration. The freedom to earn a living is not enough—one must actually *earn* a living in order to experience genuine independence. Mill is the disappointing though promising brother to these critics; he noticed female equality and the need for independence and the dignity of work, but did not add them up correctly to equal a sufficiently loose family critical of the sexual division of labor.

I believe that Mill would be friendly to this criticism, animated as it is by his own principles. This riddle points to the question of what should guide choice. For Mill, "ethical questions" are resolved with reference to "the permanent interests of mankind as a progressive being,"[75] which are revealed by an equalizing mechanism of progress.

> The course of history, and the tendencies of progressive human society, afford not only no presumption in favour of this system of inequality of rights, but a strong one against it; and that, so far as the whole course of human improvement up to the time, the whole stream of modern tendencies, warrants any inference on the subject, it is, that this relic of the past is discordant with the future, and must necessarily disappear.[76]

Mill believes in the progressive wearing away of nurtured inequalities, and he believes sex differences are nurtured. Whenever Mill denies the naturalness of sex differences, he presupposes that they wither with time. Consider his arguments, many of which are still heard today in one form or another. Just as artificial differences between Southern slaveholders and slaves or kings and serfs withered with time, so also will inequalities and differences between men and women.[77] This argument is sound only if sex differences are artificial, but this is what Mill was trying to prove with the argument. Mill also claims, as we saw, that sex roles are based on a form of false consciousness, whereby women have their minds enslaved by patriarchal ways. This diagnosis is true only if true consciousness is the assimilation of the sexes to one another. Faith in progress (understood as the progressive withering of human difference) buckles his experimental, conjectural liberal argument for choice to his more certain, feminist condemnation of traditional sex arrangements and his embrace of sexual assimilation.

What will family life be like when external circumstances no longer have such power? The assimilative marriage Mill favors and expects is connected with a forgetting of children; the parent-child relationship is not easily fashioned in the image of liberal consent and equality, and Mill handles this issue by remaking the family in terms of friendship; he spends little time on the children. His silence coupled with his occasional statements that some flexible institution will arise to meet society's needs indicates, in my view, that Mill embraces a variation on the theme that children are resilient and can be raised equally well in a number of acceptable institutions. Society need not maintain any particular institutions for the benefit of children. Mill's progressivism points toward eliminating rules, patterns, and structures related to bearing and rearing children. As children are outside the purpose of marriage, the institution is not defined for them.

Mill ignores the kids in order to propound an alluring promise of spousal friendship—the idea that husbands and wives will share the same experiences and the hope that they will be soul mates. With this promise in mind, children seem to be distractions from the reflection of the husband in the wife and the wife in the husband. The legal and cultural institutions of the older family must be jettisoned to encourage a new, safer kind of love based on a revocable commitment to personal regeneration and growth. Leaving children outside of the purpose of marriage marks a decisive shift from a family that constitutes a unity where children are an outward, concrete, living expression of ethical love to a marriage defined by sympathetic equality for adults. Marriage is not seen as mutual service of different and complementary sexes, but as the joining of likes that lasts as long as the partners like. An equalized marriage serves the self's moral regeneration, which means that marriage does not seek to join the self to something over and above itself but rather that marriage invigorates the self. Marriage partners sympathize, but they do not form a new whole. They neither join their identities into one nor view their marriage as something that supersedes the standpoint of individual interest, broadly understood. The communal family—with its ideas of membership, unconditional acceptance, and support for emotional needs—leads, in Mill's judgment, to dangerous and debilitating self-sacrifices and mutual surrendering, conditions that are at the heart of what love is. This revolution in what marital and familial love is marks Mill's most significant contribution to modern teachings on the family.

There is the possibility that a "conservative" Mill would survive—that cultural expectations could hem in women's emancipation from the family and most women would choose vocations of motherhood. We could have Mill's public principles, in a word, with Hegelian private lives. Such an expectation presupposes the naturalness of sex differences (something Mill rejects), but it also presupposes the widespread acceptance of the value of the love associated with the idea of two becoming one. Hostility to sex differences, opposition to marital unity, and the embrace of independence in marriage are Mill's principles too. Does acceptance of Mill's critique of marital unity entail a more profound critique of love? Can we conceive of the family without that understanding of love? Mill seems to recognize this logic and to be willing to sacrifice sacrificial love and marital unity for the marriage of soul mates and the promotion of female equality.

Mill's revised family serves public purposes by providing adequate training for children in the values of equality, sympathy, and freedom. The family must become, in Mill's vision, a "school of sympathy in equality . . . without power on one side or obedience on the other," if family life is to serve as a moral training ground for mankind and if a society committed to freedom is to blossom.[78] Family life based on patriarchal principles—whether privately chosen or publicly enforced—is inimical to the maintenance of our democratic political institutions. Our new city is insecure if we do not people it with those who cut their teeth observing a marriage of soul mates.

Chapter 7

Marx, Engels, and the Abolition of the Family

Karl Marx (1818–1883) and Frederick Engels (1820–1895) are known for their view that history is defined by persistent class antagonisms reaching an apex under the conditions of modern capitalism and their hope that classes would be eliminated by a spontaneous revolution of the oppressed. As a result of this revolution, the means of producing goods would be held in common. They are led to these conclusions through their dialectical materialism, their unique contribution to political philosophy. Dialectical materialism holds that developments in society proceed from contradictions that arise in its material basis. Materialism, for Marx and Engels, is the view that the way goods are produced in an epoch determines the character of human life in that epoch. Modes of production force people to adapt to the requirements of life shaped by changes in technology. Nomads, for instance, settle into sedentary habits once agricultural implements allow them to farm for a living. Cultural life, or the "superstructure" of society, adapts to changes in the structure of society. Morality, science, philosophy, family life, politics, religious beliefs, and art are all caused by man adapting to the demands of the mode of production.[1]

The dialectical portion of Marx and Engels' theory is that material conditions or the modes of production develop logically through time. Each era of human life has both a structure (its mode of production) and a superstructure (the cultural apparatus adapted to the mode of production). Changes in the mode of production—stimulated by changes in what human beings regard as needs or by technological developments that make the older mode of production untenable—introduce a contradiction in an era and prepare for a revolution in the mode of production. Under feudalism, for instance, the mode of production was small-scale, somewhat piecemeal work by apprentices and guilds, whose lack of productivity was papered over by a superstructure of those nobly born and pious. Machines and steam power undermined the basis of the feudal mode of production and the French Revolution, spectacularly, brought down the remains of the feudal superstructure.

This dialectic has manifested itself in a history of class struggles. All modes of production have been controlled by a few at the expense of the many, whether it was the patricians in Rome or the nobles in the Middle Ages. Revolutions occur in human history when a portion of the oppressed class breaks off and seizes control of the mode of production characteristic of the next era. Capitalism, or the modern era of manufacturing and commerce, arises when the industrious, active, and unscrupulous among the serfs displace guild masters as the owners of the new mode of production. With this bourgeois comes the proletariat, the class of laborers who subsist on the money-wages earned from selling their labor. Like previous class orders, the capitalist or bourgeois order contains the seeds of its own destruction, or, to use a more poignant phrase, "what the bourgeoisie . . . produces, above all, are its own gravediggers."[2] Industry and commerce expand, as does the use of machines in producing the goods of capitalism; laborers become mere appendages of productive machines; more and more workers compete over fewer and fewer jobs; laborers are reduced to living a pauper's existence. There will come a day when the continued existence of laborers conflicts with the continued existence of the bourgeois state, and that day will be a new dawn for human beings. The revolution that follows will end class antagonism and the oppression that it creates.

The end of class antagonisms puts an end to the need for the state, the coercive power created to protect the few from the depredations of the many and made necessary by the fact that society is broken into hostile classes; the state masks in modern society, as it has in all societies, the reality of class struggle. Modern bourgeois may speak about the protection of private rights as the epitome of justice, but Marx and Engels think that they put the lie to this pretension. Liberal states do not transcend the conflicts of the market economy, nor do they really secure equal protection of the laws. The state exists to protect the interests of the powerful bourgeois, and the laws offer protection for the unjust gains of those who end up on top. Liberal states emerge from Marx's analysis as thinly disguised gangs of robbers that keep the poor and oppressed quiescent by buying them off, by distracting them from their miseries with religion, ideology, and other forms of false consciousness, or by sheer force. The mythical private realm is a distraction used by the bourgeois oppressors to maintain their rule. Oppressors invented the institutions of family life, religious life, cultural attractions, the ideology of property rights, and so on as part of their effort to protect wealth and power.

Marx and Engels, however, are writing at a time when the bourgeois oppressors no longer need to support the family as much as they once had. Marx and Engels seem, at first, to present themselves as defenders of the traditional family.[3] Their early writings suggest that they want to insulate the family from an excessively individualist, corrosive ideology. Early in Marx's career, he seems taken with Hegel's idea of the family unity representing ethical love; he seems worried that the material and spiritual rug is being pulled from under the unified family or that the idea of two becoming one has become a lie that people tell themselves to cover up their own misery. Marx penned a newspaper article against a liberalized divorce bill, arguing that marriage is an ethical relationship that should not be reduced to the standpoint of contract. Marriage, writes Marx, "cannot be subordinated to [a man's] arbitrary wishes; on the contrary, his arbitrary wishes must be subordinated to marriage."[4] Capitalists, with their typically egoistic standpoint, sought to reform the family so that individuals would be influenced more by the money culture than a culture based on love. Capitalists turned against the indissoluble family because it was in their interests to produce more wage-earners and to perpetuate their oppression by dividing society further into powerless individuals. The family, which stood as one form of resistance to the capitalist state, would no longer be such an obstacle. The bourgeois need more workers, so they would find it necessary to tear children away from their parents by employing them cheaply in factories. Capitalists need women to produce more children and workers, so they degrade a beautiful, sacrificial relationship into an exchange and production relationship. Wives have been reduced to being little more than glorified prostitutes.[5] As Marx and Engels write in the *Communist Manifesto*,

> The bourgeois claptrap about the family and education, about the hallowed co-relation of parent and child, becomes all the more disgusting, the more, by the action of modern industry, all family ties among the proletarians are torn asunder, and their children transformed into simple articles of commerce and instruments of labor.[6]

Marx echoes this theme in *Capital*, where he argues that the English have found it necessary to consider laws limiting child labor because "modern industry, in overturning the economic foundation on which was based the traditional family . . . had also unloosened all traditional family ties."[7]

Marx and Engels often present themselves as thinking that the destruction of the bourgeois family is "terrible and disgusting," yet they never really thought the bourgeois family was that great. In fact, the approach to the family they put forward includes a powerful and familiar critique of traditional family life (including the idea of marital unity and the sexual division of labor), echoing, in large measure, the critique put forward by Mill. Much like Mill, Marx and Engels compare the status of women in the bourgeois family to slavery and drudgery.[8] Again, much like Mill, Marx and Engels emphasize that human beings are largely, if not wholly, determined by their environment. They may even embrace a rather Millian understanding of the human liberation that awaits us when human beings achieve progress. In any event, they embrace Mill's hope that things are going to get better and freer, and they put that hope in the context of what they take to be a scientific account of human history defined, in their case, by a commitment to dialectical materialism. More unequivocally than Mill, it seems, they look to the day when women will participate fully in life "outside the domestic sphere" and when young people will create "a new economic foundation for a *higher form of the family* and the relations between the sexes."[9]

Marx and Engels may embrace a vision of the *history* and *direction* of family life similar to Mill's, but they embrace a different account of what factors *move* history and family life. This observation forces us to step back to consider the basis of their thinking on these matters. Engels published *The Origin of the Family, Private Property and the State* (henceforth *Origin*), the key work laying bare the philosophic assumptions of the Marxist approach to family life, in 1884, shortly after Marx's death. Marx was a promising author, often promising to deliver works but not always doing so. We learn from Engel's preface to *Origin* that Marx was preparing to write something on the family based on Lewis H. Morgan's work *Ancient Society*. At the time of his death, Marx had written extensive notes on Morgan's anthropological research on the transition from savagery to barbarism and finally to civilization as it relates to the family. In *Origin*, Engels tried to reproduce the views of Marx, whom he considered, probably with justice, the greater genius of their partnership.

During the time of Engels and Marx, anthropology took on greater importance than before, for it claimed to reveal the historical evolution of peoples and to show the plasticity of familial arrangements. Anthropological studies purport to show that sometimes women are in command in families and societies, sometimes men; sometimes property is held in common, sometimes it is held privately, and sometimes there is no property to speak of; sometimes marriage is monogamous, sometimes polygamous, sometimes polyandrous, and sometimes it is group marriage. What interested Marx in Morgan's work was Morgan's endorsement of a "materialistic conception of history,"[10] in which he shows how family form relates to society's mode of production.

The History of the Family

Engels sees the need to investigate the origins of the family in a manner reminiscent of Rousseau, and, not unlike Rousseau or Hegel, Engels sees a strong relationship between family form and the system of property. For Engels, the mode of production determines family form. What is novel and interesting about *Origin* is that it goes back to an epoch antedating private property and class conflict in an effort to find the range of possible ways to organize sexual relations. It shows how the family *becomes* subordinate to the mode of production. In the beginning, human beings, little different from the animals, subsisted on the spontaneous products of nature (fruit on a tree, roots in the ground), and the "family form" that corresponded to this lower stage of savagery was one of "unrestricted sexual freedom" in which every man belonged to every woman and vice versa. The sense of "belong" is not that characteristic of a property-owning society: human beings did not claim exclusive access to others. Sexual relations in this primitive time are immune from feelings of jealousy, self-control, shame, and pride; primitives resemble animals in that they copulate when feelings urge them with little thought about reproduction, and they have no compunctions against any form of sex. We cannot prove that such a state ever existed from an anthropological investigation of "social fossils." The existence of such a time is an inference from later family forms backward, based on materialist assumptions about evolution.[11]

Primitive times end and savage times begin, though we do not know how or when. With savage times we have a better idea of how human development occurs. Savage times (where man appropriates directly from nature) have two kinds of group marriage: the consanguine family and the punaluan family. The consanguine family prohibited sex along generational lines, so fathers and mothers could not have sex with daughters and sons, but brothers and sisters could have sex with one another. The consanguine family is extinct and we have no direct evidence that it ever existed, but, again, "the whole subsequent development of the family presupposes the existence of the consanguine family as a necessary preparatory stage."[12]

It seems that various societies persist in the world at this time and a variety of family forms are consistent with primitive, savage ways. Group marriage may exist in one tribe; some incest prohibitions in other tribes; other arrangements in others. Sex between brothers and sisters is prohibited in tribes instituting what Engels dubs the punaluan family, which defines brothers and sisters as the common issue of the same mother and, later, the common issue of "collateral brothers and sisters." Such prohibitions beget an evolutionary advantage; inbreeding inhibits advancement, so the earlier forms of family melt before the powerhouse punaluan family. Two elements of this family contribute to subsequent developments. First, sexual access is the default position in societies; prohibitions are exceptions (somehow) foisted on people from the outside. Those who create these prohibitions have power over the individual, presumably, because the collective (however understood) determines access to the necessities of life. Second, given the promiscuousness of savages, children can be certain only of who their mothers are. Brothers and sisters are common issue of a common mother and the incest prohibition, such as it is, develops from this knowledge.

Engels' unique observation pertains to the second, barbaric stage of history. Barbarians (who domesticate animals and seek to increase what nature produces through human activity) begin with pairing marriages (in which men and women come together in weak and unstable pairs). Somewhat reminiscent of Rousseau's discussion of the origin of languages in erotic experiences around drinking wells, several families from the punaluan families coalesce, forming larger tribes or gens. There is a difference. Rousseau emphasizes how communities are born out of *eros*, or a feeling of individual lacking. For Engels, this larger community arises from its evolutionary advantage over preceding family forms, an advantage gained, it seems, because of a superior genetic makeup derived from the extension of the incest prohibition. Pairing marriages, which "brought unrelated persons into the marriage relation, tended to create a more vigorous stock physically and mentally." The mixing of diverse peoples gave them a "new skull and brain," which "widen and lengthen" the capabilities of both.[13]

Pairing marriages are loose, informal arrangements in which mothers have custody of the children. Pairing marriages exist within communist gens and housework is done collectively. This constitution is "wonderful" in its "childlike simplicity." All are "equal and free." Whatever quarrels arise are "settled by the whole of the community affected." There are no "poor or needy—the communal household and the gens know their responsibilities toward the old, the sick, and those disabled in war." Communist barbarians extend shares of the community's production to people who contribute little of their own labor; those that do not or cannot labor appropriate the surplus value. Families loosely fit in a tribal network whose production comes from the labor and abilities of some; the community reallocates products to those in need. Though Engels does not explore the issue, there may be a micro-communism specific to the family in which some members of the pairing family produce the goods necessary to support those members unable to support themselves (e.g., children and the old). Some manner of social control or mores must exist among barbarians at this stage or else the incest prohibition would not arise. The allocation of surplus goods may be provided through these mores.

Engels sees these barbarians, much like Rousseau's savages, developing courage, heart, and endurance that make them superior to their civilized counterparts (but for the weapons developed by the civilized). Especially in their earlier stages, barbarians see themselves as part of nature and they do not seek to subdue it, so they remain in an "almost complete subjection to [nature's] strange incomprehensible power."[14] Pervasive communism at the tribal level has profound implications for relations in the pairing family.

> Communistic housekeeping . . . means the supremacy of women in the house; just as the exclusive recognition of the female parent, owing to the impossibility of recognizing the male parent with certainty, means that the woman—the mothers—are held in high respect. One of the most absurd notions taken over from 18th century enlightenment is that in the beginning of society woman was the slave of man. . . . The position of women is not only free, but honorable.[15]

What Marx elsewhere calls the "natural division of labour"—men as food-gatherers, women as housekeepers—exists at this stage of history.[16] The sexual division of labor derives from the primitive community's "almost complete subjection" to nature. The greater strength and swiftness of men suit them for production, while the debilities and sex organs related to childbirth, and the capacity to breastfeed, presumably suit women more to reproduction.[17] Such primitive communism "cannot serve in any way as a model for fully developed communism that presupposes alienation as well as its abolition."[18]

In fact, it seems that women wear the pants in the pairing family. Engels does not relate the rise of mother right in the gens to the cultural prominence of educating or having children. The importance of mothers seems derived from the incest prohibition and poverty. People in barbaric times were sexually promiscuous, so efforts to enforce and extend the incest prohibition required that they be able to identify brothers and sisters. This could be done only through the mother. Identifying mothers becomes the key to promoting human evolution. The fact that the gens subsists through a time of relative poverty and stupid submission to nature leads to the denigration of the man's food-gathering, hunting function. The sphere of reproduction has priority during times when the sphere of production is "extremely undeveloped." In any event, women were not subordinate to men in the time before private property and the monogamous family, and no antagonism existed between them either.[19]

Subordination and antagonism enter with the rise of private property. Private property promotes the evolution of society by giving greater incentive for attaining wealth, by making the incest prohibition easier to enforce, by encouraging the production of tools and other labor-enhancing devices, and by putting man in a position to conquer or exploit nature for his benefit. The domestication of animals and breeding of herds develops "new, *social* forces" that lead to the overthrow of mother right, "one of the most decisive [revolutions] ever experienced by humanity," and the "*world historic defeat of the female sex*." The sphere of production is valued more than the sphere of reproduction when production finally produces wealth.

> In proportion as wealth increased it made the man's position in the family more important than the woman's, and on the other hand created an impulse to exploit this strengthened position in order to overthrow, in favor of his children, the traditional order of inheritance.[20]

In the private, monogamous, patriarchal family, men take control of the home, turning wives into slaves and objects of lust and making wives into instruments for the production of children. The Roman institution allowing husbands to have power over life and death of the wife and children epitomizes monogamous marriage, though the situation of wives is prettified by the bourgeois claptrap of love, duty, or religious obligation.[21] Men desire the "undisputed paternity" of their children for the purposes of passing inheritance to them. Wifely chastity and the indissolubility of marriage are essential to the reliable transmission of heritable property. This view of marriage persists, Engels insists, until (at least) his day. Monogamous marriage is "not in any way the fruit of individual sex love, with which it had nothing whatever to do." Instead it makes "the man supreme in the family and . . . propagate[s], as the future heirs to his wealth, children indisputably his own." The transmission of property drives love, not the other way around. Monogamous marriage is not based on natural conditions, but "on economic conditions—on the victory of private property over primitive, natural communal property."[22]

With the monogamous family human beings reach the highest stage of human life so far, civilization, a time of industry and art. Monogamous marriage and its corresponding bourgeois family maintain the charming barbaric distinction between laboring and non-laboring members, and they seem to secure the needs of the latter. Thus civilized family life seems to maintain the communal aspirations of precapitalist families. Where Hegel and others saw a communal core, Marx and Engels see the form of a communal family masking serious oppression and class domination. Dating back to the Greeks,

> monogamous marriage was a great historical step forward: nevertheless, together with slavery and private wealth, it opens the period . . . in which every step forward is also relatively a step backward, in which prosperity and development for some is won through the misery and frustration of others.[23]

Men gain at the expense of women, just as the bourgeois gain at the expense of the proletariat. Tremendous scientific and economic advancement accompanies this transition in which human beings no longer submit to the crude dictates of nature nor subsist in the simple, poor "idiocy of rural life."[24] Tremendous exploitation of the workers based on inequalities arises as well. No longer are men and women "free and equal" as they were under the gens, but the inequality between men and women is the basis for a deeper subordination of women as well as great moral advances in family life.

The Promise and Perils of Monogamous Marriage

Monogamous marriage professes to respect the freedom and equality of men and women and thus to be an improvement upon the patriarchal family. Civilized, bourgeois systems of law emphasize that marriage is "a contract freely entered into by both partners" and that men and women have "equal rights and duties" in this pairing. Engels insists that the marriage contract only guarantees formal equality, "equality on *paper*."[25] Consent presupposes options and the freedom to choose among them. A free person's condition must be such that the force of necessity does not impinge too much upon the ability to choose. "Necessitous men are not free men," to borrow a phrase borrowed by Franklin Roosevelt. Women enter a marriage contract without any real freedom to turn down a proposal to marry, just as, for Marx and Engels, workers contract with employers without any real freedom to turn them down.[26] "Equality on *paper*"—a formal request and acceptance of the contract—cloaks an oppressive, unequal relationship; the man coerces the woman to accept the terms of the agreement or else starve or put up with the opprobrium of public opinion or alienate her family. What is at stake is the distinction between the private (or family life) and public. Within obvious limits,[27] modern legislation does not take into account the relative power of men and women when they enter into the marriage contract,[28] that is, whether conditions of *genuine* equality are satisfied. Laws made by modern liberal governments enforce contracts and other public acts (such as a marriage vow) so that people can arrange their affairs as they see fit. Such a minimalist, *laissez-faire* approach is the problem, for Engels.

It is difficult to know where necessity begins and freedom ends.[29] Engels points to several sources of marital un-freedom that are obstacles to the achievement of families based on genuine feelings. First, children must obtain their parents' consent for the match in many countries. This is problematic in itself (for it means that one's own consent does not rule) and in that parents consider extraneous criteria (such as property, reputation, or career ambitions) when granting permission. Second, within marriage women are placed in a degrading and subordinate position backed by law and custom. Women manage the household for free, while men enrich themselves in the world of creative labor. This "gives him a position of supremacy without any need for special legal titles and privileges." Some special titles and privileges augment his position, so that women are denied voting rights, the right to inherit or own property, sexual freedom, and other privileges men have. "Within the family he is the bourgeois, and the wife represents the proletariat."[30] Women are indoctrinated to see the beauty in sacrificing themselves and to see dedication to the family as their first duty; they come to respect men as the "natural" leaders of the home and to see their place as in the home. The merely "natural" sexual division of labor persists into the modern world, but with the difference that man's conquest of nature has undercut the environment in which people submit to nature. This "false consciousness" leads to the perpetuation of gender stereotypes and to degrading self-images among women.

The most prominent and troubling aspect of woman's condition is, for Engels, the sexual double standard, as it is complicated by class conflict and the subordination of woman. Chastity is a duty for women because it ensures the smooth passing of heritable wealth to a man's offspring. While female chastity is necessary for this, male chastity is not; men take advantage of their privileged position to exercise their "right of conjugal infidelity," sleeping around as much as men and women both had before the pairing marriage.[31] This double standard is an emblem for the subordination of women under capitalism. Women cannot do anything about this degrading double standard because mores and material conditions prevent them from exercising independence from the family in productive work; a woman cannot complain because she has nowhere to go if her complaints are ignored. This double standard puts a lie to talk about "domestic bliss" or ethical love as the basis of the family. Engels' point is that these aspects of bourgeois ideology must be lies because the family is a reaction to the needs of the capitalist order. Engels' method seems to be: figure out what the capitalist order demands of the family (certain paternity for heritable wealth) and we can figure out what the family is *really* about. Marriage will be "founded on the open or concealed domestic slavery of the wife" as long as the conditions of consent are not secured, as long as the domestic supremacy of the man within monogamous marriage persists, and, finally, as long as the capitalist order persists.[32]

How much necessity must be purged to make marital consent genuine, and what would genuine consent look like? The marital ideal Engels puts forward is based on "individual sex love" (*die individuelle Geschlechtsliebe*), the "greatest moral advance" in world history. Individual sex love melds medieval chivalry and modern capitalism. Chivalry as practiced by Germanic tribes allowed women independence from family duties and placed them on a pedestal. Modern capitalism is based on the appearance of contract. Add these poses together, in the proper way, and individual sex love emerges. Sex love contains a belief in "personal beauty," an aspiration toward "close intimacy," a "similarity of tastes and . . . the desire for sexual intercourse" so that men and women are not "totally indifferent" about whom they sleep with. These ideas, as old only as the Middle Ages, are not sufficient for this ideal. Sex love is based on "subjective inclination," not "objective duty"; it comes from inside those experiencing it, not from the outside influence of parents, children, money, property, religion, or artificial social roles. Such love is genuinely consensual, so it presupposes that women and men are "on an equal footing." It is risky and intense, so lovers "feel that non-possession and separation are a great, if not the greatest calamity." Sex love accompanies a new standard of judgment for marital relationships: "We do not only ask, was it within or outside marriage, but also, did it spring from . . . reciprocated love or not?" To put this another way, "every marriage is immoral which does not rest on mutual sexual love and *really* free agreement of husband and wife."[33]

Individual sex love does not necessarily go together with monogamous marriage. From stories of chivalrous love in the Middle Ages to French novels that glorify adultery and show "wedded life" to be "leaden boredom," modern peoples acknowledge that conditions for genuine love are often outside marriage.[34] Monogamous married couples mouth praise for individual sex love, but marriage's origin in the regime of private property means that monogamy is, in reality, conceived in external things and in calculations of value.[35] Boring institutions, children, long-term obligations, property calculations, worries about employment, and other small stuff have tainted love under capitalism. At the deepest level, this is why Engels likens monogamous marriage to prostitution: a monogamous marriage is a "marriage of convenience" or a fleeting alignment of interests. While the ideal of individual sex love was mouthed previously, it is possible as a social ideal only when the monogamous family is abolished as an economic unit. The purity of love—the purging of every consideration from love aside from whether one has passion and affection for one's partner at this time—requires that economic and social considerations be pushed aside. Engels sees a glimpse of this pure love in the proletariat of his day, a group, he claims, that is without private property. Without that prop for male supremacy, women in the proletariat family can separate if they prefer.[36] Engels wants to universalize the experience of the proletariat in this respect. Such is the final emancipation of the individual from all forms of necessity, and, for the first time, the "free development of each" emerges.[37] The process begun (for our purposes) with Locke—the attempt to emancipate human beings from the givens of nature—seems to culminate with the genuinely free sharing of individual sex love.

Individual sex love is consensual, and consent is, much as in Rousseau—who is at least a moderate advocate of romantic love—the proof and guarantor of love. Engels is no Rousseau, however. He strips Rousseau's romantic love of the austerity of consent, the need to subordinate subsequent passion to the passion that exists when one first consents. Marriage based on sex love, for Engels, must neither respect the initial choice nor reflect an unshakeable will. In this, Engels parallels Mill, whose defense of choice within marriage allowed spouses to act on the reevaluation of previous choices. For Engels, individual sex love need not be "materialistic" in the sense of involving only the physical acts of love, yet it seems to depend on actual sex to a far greater degree than Mill's more austere account. Engels follows the logic of sex love. Since only marriages based on love are moral, only marriages "in which love continues" are moral. Divorce, separation, serial monogamy, cohabitating outside of marriage, or "hooking up" are options for free people. Engels offers two visions of what will happen to relationships after the ethic of individual sex love is the accepted norm. Perhaps genuinely consensual marriages will arise and we will truly eliminate the sexual double standard, since women now will be in material position to demand that their husbands be faithful. Perhaps the realization of individual sex love will consist of a string of short-term trysts as women are freed from constraints placed on them by the sexual double standard. Engels refuses to guess whether men will come to act more like women or women like men.[38] It will be up to the next generation—one influenced only by the idea that real individual sex love grounds genuinely equal marriage and, presumably, one shorn of ideas bred by the regime of private property and male dominance—to decide what the new face of marriage or relations will be.[39] What seems certain is that individuals will be free to follow their passionate interests and will always be able to remove consent once it is given.

> The intense emotion of individual sex love varies very much in duration from one individual to another, especially among men, and if affection definitely comes to an end or is supplanted by a new passionate love, separation is a benefit for both partners as well as for society.[40]

For Engels, marriage neither creates its own obligations (as in Rousseau) nor does it cause other obligations, such as those to children, to arise (as in Locke) and it certainly is not concerned with extraneous matters such as property and children (as in Hegel and Locke). Individual goods of affection and intense emotions become the grounds for and the ends of marriage.

If individual sex love is the proof of consent and consent is the proof of love, then Engels has not really solved the problem of identifying when the conditions of genuine consent exist. This is where Mill seems to have left it. Mill favors disbanding the legal superstructure for male dominance and forming a public opinion open to "experiments in living" so that individuals can choose their family form. As we have seen, he seems open to the possibility that men and women would choose to perpetuate the sexual division of labor. For Engels, genuinely consensual marriages must eliminate the sexual division of labor, which necessarily fosters dependence and inequality and undermines conditions for genuine consent. Women may think they choose their domestic vocations, but they are *really* enslaved to them and their choice has been surreptitiously coerced by patriarchal public opinion. If women perform the housework while men earn a living, men enrich themselves and their wives are vulnerable and must put up with male infidelity, oppression, orders, and rule. Women must, under such circumstances, conform to ideas that men have for them—they must be agreeable and deferential, and, being this, they are slaves. Consent is impossible in such a context: the woman lacks the material prerequisites to leave the marriage and thus cannot genuinely consent to stay. Following from this problem of consent is what Engels sees as the dilemma of the modern woman. Modern women are divided or conflicted: "If she carries out her duties in . . . her family, she remains excluded from public production and unable to earn; and if she wants to take part in public production and earn independently, she cannot carry out family duties."[41]

One can find this dilemma in Mill's thinking as well. No earning power, no dignity and independence for women; no dignity and independence for women, no genuine consent in marriage.[42] The more radical reading of Mill is that he favors abolishing the sexual division of labor by encouraging women, as much as men, toward separate lives of productive labor in the marketplace. This solution still does not go far enough for Engels, in part, I assume, because Mill does not explain who will do the housework while both spouses are working. Engels cuts the Gordian knot by suggesting that household work, child-rearing, and all occupations must be made public activities and that the monogamous family, at least as an economic unit, be abolished altogether.[43] Somehow members of what used to be the family must still be provided for after wives and mothers enter employment in public industries: their food, drink, and shelter provided, the housekeeping done, and the children cared for. Since there will be no private family to meet such needs, meeting the needs must become a social or public activity. "With the transfer of the means of production into common ownership, the single family ceases to be the economic unit of society. Private housekeeping is transformed into a social industry. The care and education of the children become a public affair; society looks after all children alike, whether they are legitimate or not."[44]

While the household is transformed into a "social industry," women enter the world of industrial society or public production. In this sense, the economic system that gives rise to the monogamous family has been preparing gravediggers for the monogamous family as well as for itself.

> The emancipation of woman will only be possible when woman can take part in production on a large, social scale, and domestic work no longer claims anything but an insignificant amount of her time. And only now has that become possible through modern large-scale industry, which does not merely permit the employment of female labor over a wide range, but positively demands it, while it also tends towards ending private domestic labor by changing it more and more into a public industry.[45]

Three factors lead industrial capitalism to kill its creature, the monogamous family. First, the introduction of tools leaves out the need for brute, natural strength where men seem to have a clear advantage over women.[46] Second, modern industry demands that women participate in the production of social goods. This may mean that modern capitalists seek to expand the labor pool so that they can drive wages down and profits up. If this is so, modern liberal feminism is the perfect ideology, in the Marxist sense, for industrial capitalism, for it dilutes wages by increasing the available labor pool. Third, "private domestic labor" is changed "more and more into a public industry." What Engels means by this is unclear. It may mean that the family continues to lose functions to other public institutions, so that family life is concerned with less and less and can wither for lack of something to do. It may mean that domestic employment of women is easier due to the advances in tools, so that women are freed from the onerous demands of housekeeping. (The electric oven and refrigerator, for example, erase the need for much housekeeping.)

The abolition of private property puts an end to the calculations, insecurities, and uncertainties that pervade the private sphere. Communism "removes all the anxiety about the 'consequences' [of sex], which today is the most essential social—moral as well as economic—factor that prevents a girl from giving herself completely to the man she loves." Engels hopes that this will suffice "to bring about the gradual growth of unconstrained sexual intercourse and with it a more tolerant public opinion in regard to a maiden's honor and a woman's shame."[47] An early draft of the *Communist Manifesto* contains Engels' thoughts on the relationship between communism and the independence that sustains true individual sex love. Communist society, Engels writes,

> will transform the relations between the sexes into a purely private matter which concerns only the persons involved and into which society has no occasion to intervene. It can do this since it does away with private property and educates children on a communal basis, and in this way removes the two bases of traditional marriage, the dependence rooted in private property, of the woman on the man and of the children on the parents.[48]

Extraneous institutions, Engels suggests, get in the way of love's flourishing. Engels never explains in much detail what transforming private housekeeping into a public industry means. It is necessary to ask, again, what will happen with the children.

There are major and profound unanswered questions in Engels' theory at this juncture. Who will these public caretakers be? What will the goals of their caretaking be? Who will oversee the caretakers to ensure that they achieve their goals? Families have been the ultimate overseers of their children's education because families have an intimate interest in the education of their young. The interest families show in their children may be a source of injustice *outside* the family, as parents love their own children more than they love the best children and the inequalities among families redound to the benefit or detriment of their children. These sources of injustice serve the important public purposes of educating youth to character, knowledge, and self-control. Engels would rid society of the injustice *outside* and *inside* the family by abolishing the family. Engels promises equal treatment for children once the family is abolished ("The care and education of the children becomes a public affair; society looks after all children alike"). In this context, I must raise the issue Aristotle raised about Plato's communism in the *Republic*. "What belongs in common to the most people," Aristotle writes, "is accorded the least care."[49] Richard Krouse puts a finer point on the educational problems derived from Engels' "abstract collectivism." "In order to emancipate women from the ghetto of the home," Krouse writes, "Engels would relegate children to the ghettos of the state (or its postrevolutionary equivalent)." It is not clear that the "values of individual autonomy and self-consciousness prized in the more reflective versions of the Marxian ideal would flourish in this context."[50]

Aristotle and Krouse think the common care of children will be done poorly, and it is difficult to imagine that so obvious an objection had not occurred to Engels or Marx. What explains their confidence that common education will not be a ghetto experience for children? Provision for children would be met in the same way as the provision of production under postrevolutionary communism. The governing principle of Marxist communism is "from each according to his ability; to each according to his needs." The motive for production after the elimination of private property is not to earn profit and glory or to obtain subsistence, but because producing things is a release of the essential human penchant for productive labor. Each becomes what is unique in the human species in this laboring; all people realize the universal trait of the human species in themselves. Much the same must happen with the children. The first stage involves transferring power from the monogamous family to public institutions. With this in mind, Marx and Engels suggest, as a half measure tending toward the abolition of the family, one of their ten planks for promoting communism: "Free education for all children in public schools."[51] Public schools represent the transferring of educational responsibility from the prejudiced, oppressive private bourgeois family to communal institutions, and this shift can contribute to wearing away class distinctions (especially if private education and homeschooling are forbidden). Public education, as it is practiced in America and throughout the Western world, does not, for communists, go far enough in eliminating the division of labor or in abolishing its connection to the wage economy: motives for providing education remain tainted by self-interest and professional interest. Eventually, humanity must provide for the needs of children—humanity understood as loyal, competent, benevolent people spontaneously arising to meet each other's needs.

Individuality and the Marxist Perspective

Marx and Engels believe that the state will eventually wither away and that all will come together to meet human needs, including the needs children have for care and education. The state and the family continue to exist because the persistence of class conflict makes a coercive authority necessary to protect the few from the many. Ultimately, the problem is that capitalism alienates our labor from our life: people under capitalism think of life beginning where laboring ends because their labor is not their own. Engels and Marx insist that the abolition of capitalism and the establishment of communism go with the abolition of the family and the establishment of conditions for individual sex love. "The supersession of individual economy is inseparable from the supersession of the family." Only by wiping away private property and the class conflicts that it engenders can we expect "alteration of men on a mass scale" and the "revolutionising of the existing world." The transformation of human affairs brings about the "liberation of each single individual."[52] This is the Marxist notion of freedom without alienation, or individual freedom enjoyed with perfect socialization. Man is self-determining, self-conscious, and productive; one meets one's own needs (for food, water, shelter, procreation) out of a genuine desire to labor, not as it was under previous modes, when one was compelled to work so that one's needs could be met. Man also meets the needs of others as the "brotherhood of man" becomes a reality and as all people experience the same needs.[53] Human beings will enjoy full emancipation when they gain control of nature, including their own nature. History, it seems, has set for human beings the "task of replacing the domination of circumstances and of chance over individuals by the domination of individuals over chance and circumstances."[54] Thus, for the first time, after this transformation, we have the flourishing of human individuality exercised in tandem with man's extraordinary power over nature.

No longer will human beings be caught between freedom and duty, conscience and needs, passion and reason, work and free time, or family and work. Marxist theory presupposes that human affairs will be radically, fundamentally, and irrevocably (if not abruptly) transformed so that human needs will be met spontaneously by the freely provided labor of others. Consider Marx's most famous portrait of a life of the free individual.

> In communist society, where nobody has one exclusive sphere of activity but each can become accomplished in any branch he wishes, society regulates the general production and thus makes it possible for me to do one thing today and another tomorrow, to hunt in the morning, fish in the afternoon, rear cattle in the evening, criticize after dinner, just as I have a mind, without ever becoming hunter, fisherman, shepherd, or critic.[55]

Such a vision might be consistent with the care and education of children if children grew up spontaneously and the demands children made on adults were negligible. Marx and Engels seem to think otherwise, suggesting that the needs of children are genuine and require the attention of adults, if not family members. How will the needs of children be met in an environment where individuals can choose to parent some of the time without ever becoming a parent or give care some of the time without ever becoming a caregiver? The needs of children, such as they are, will apparently be met the same way that the needs of all human beings will be met: through the spontaneous, temporary, freely chosen labor of those interested in providing it. It will not be love, pride, duty, or obligation that moves people to provide for children, for all of these concepts presuppose conflicts within individuals or society. Society under Marxist communism resembles a more robust Big Brothers Big Sisters association, in which those that care for children at a particular time spontaneously provide the needs of those children. This may sound ridiculous, but Marxist theory depends on the permanent transformation of human beings.

What convinced Marx of the possibility of a permanent transformation of human nature was his quasi-Hegelian belief that History can resolve the contradictions that have defined human life. "Communism," he writes in 1844,

> equals humanism, and as fully developed humanism equals naturalism; it is the genuine resolution of the conflict between man and nature and between man and man—the true resolution of the strife between existence and essence, between objectification and self-confirmation, between freedom and necessity, between the individual and the species.[56]

The elimination of alienation and contradiction marks the absorption of man into himself and the species. Free human beings are completely socialized to a liberated human community—there is no longer a conflict between the public and the private.[57] Only when all tensions, all sources of alienation, and all boundaries have withered is the future of freedom realized. Much has been written on the difficulties involved in Marx's understanding of human liberation as the elimination of strife.[58] I want to emphasize that love does not survive the elimination of human alienation, neediness, and tension. As Hegel teaches, love begins with a feeling of incompleteness or deficiency in one's own person that leads one to seek another. This expression of neediness culminates in the mysterious ethical love found in family life. Love is not self-contained and self-sufficient; its nature, however, arises from the neediness and insufficiency of individuals as such. Marx and Engels put forward the idea that such a condition is overcome after the revolution. Love is not possible or necessary if the entire species is contained already within oneself, after all. The resolution of contradictions, the removal of alienation, the movement toward a time free of contradictions, the hope that the abolition of private property will inaugurate an epoch of abundance, the belief in the natural provision of all necessary human goods—all of this, I submit, is inconsistent with the idea that we are incomplete and needy. This forces Marxist theory to reduce love to a physical act. Erasing the contradictions that define human history heretofore, Marx and Engels also erase the possibility of love. This makes Marx's theory, in this respect as in many others, more a wish than a science.

But what a wish! The Marxist vision of human liberation and individual sex love is enchanting to modern peoples, and the pervasive acceptance of this vision would have, and arguably *has* had, profound implications for family life. The Marxist vision points to the eclipse of family life and duties by personal relationships. It promises the emancipation of individuals from the force of necessity, broadly understood to include the forces of nature, economic calculation, social pressure, and the consequences of previous choices or the tyranny of (one's own) past. It contains a promise of freedom, rooted in modern political thought from its inception, yet often tempered by other considerations. This is just the point. The intrusion of "other considerations," such as children and the formation of one's own character, in other modern thinkers shows that freedom understood as the conquest of nature (broadly construed) is not the only human good. Human goods conflict with one another—and this makes family life much more enduring, important, and indispensable than Marx and

Engels had thought. Human beings are irreducibly complex, which confounds the Marxist contention that human life will, at some point in the future, be freed from conflict and alienation. It takes terrible insight to wish the problems of human nature away. No matter how many times we resolve contradictions or remove tensions, others arise or the same ones come back.

Chapter 8

Freud, Russell, and the Liberated Family

One of the questions left in the wake of Durkheim's argument for marriage concerns the need for the social control of male sexual passions. Especially Protestant traditions long held that human beings are prone to lust that can be remedied in marriage. Durkheim's defense of marriage institutions fits with that tradition. Marriage can be a proper remedy to naturally errant sexual passions only if marriage is strong enough to control those passions. For Durkheim, a marital bond, weakened by the institution of divorce by mutual consent, would not be able to tame the male's "desire for the infinite." The subsequent anomie would contribute to social deviance, crime, and suicide. Durkheim's approach begs several questions. Has he understood the depths of human desire and depravity? Is marriage the proper remedy for desire and depravity? Is control necessary to human happiness?

Mere utterance of the name Sigmund Freud suggests that Durkheim did not have the final word on these questions. Freud deals institutions of social control quite a blow by his suggestion that they cause more harm than good. This contention rests on a more radical understanding of the place and power of sexuality in human experience than the one offered by the seemingly asexual Mill and by the scientific Durkheim. Intellectual trends and philosophic discourse following from Freud's principles see the conjugal family as a source of distortions and repression inimical to human thriving, freedom, and equality. Entailed in this critique is a new understanding of human nature stripped of its rationality and self-control, of the desirability of social control, and even of its apparent freedom.

Sigmund Freud (1856–1939) was the oldest of seven children. He married Martha Bernays upon completion of his studies in 1886, and they promptly had six children in nine years. They were married for over fifty years, until Sigmund's death. If Freud's marriage itself was, in these respects, not unconventional, his thinking was. His hostility toward religion, as seen in his *Future of an Illusion* (1927), combined with his theories of human sexuality and his understanding of what civilization is, made him perhaps one of the great, and certainly one of the most influential, intellectuals of the twentieth century. The family lies at the center of human life for Freud, and his reinterpretation of what it means to be human gave expression to Bertrand Russell's critique of the family. I trace Freud's thought around the structure of his *Civilization and Its Discontents* (1930), the *locus classicus* for his critique of family and his account of human development. I refer to his other works as needed to flesh out his thinking.

Native Instincts and the Mediation of the Family

Freud begins *Civilization and Its Discontents* by responding to a friend's critique. While the friend is sympathetic to Freud's conclusion about the illusory character of religion, he worries that Freud ignores the "true source of religious sentiment," which lies, according to this friend, in a sensation of, or a desire for, the eternal or a feeling that there is something "limitless, unbounded" or even "oceanic" for which human beings long.[1] This desire accounts for the energy people invest in efforts of faith; once the wellspring of faith dries up, one might suspect that people will undertake millennial efforts to bring heaven to earth. Like Durkheim, Freud thinks religious sentiments are remediable elements of human life. Freud takes a reductive, arguably more scientific tack in answering his friend's question. He returns to first principles to show that the longing for the infinite is an effect of an even earlier cause. Babies see things in terms of their own pleasure. They gradually distinguish pleasures in their bodies (e.g., releasing excrement) from pleasures outside their bodies (e.g., their mother's breast). The introduction of this "reality principle"—the importance of outside limits on human egoism—forces babies to separate their egos from the external world, and this separation shrinks and tames the ego. In those manifesting a "desire for the infinite," the tamed, more mature ego-feeling coexists with the infinite ego-feeling that seeks a limitless expansion of the ego.[2] The carcass of the infinite ego-feeling is not scented in every psyche, so that rare and weak oceanic feeling cannot be the source for energetic religious practices. "After all," Freud writes, "a feeling can only be a source of energy if it is itself the expression of a strong need."

The strong need that gives rise to religion comes in response to the "infant's helplessness and the longing for the father."[3] This understanding of where religion comes from is prototypical for Freud. "High" achievements such as religious longing are grounded in "low," often sexual, impulses or longings. Nowhere is this reduction of the high to the low more evident than in Freud's crypto-teleological account of human happiness. Human beings desire happiness above all, and happiness is modeled on the pleasures that accompany sexual climax.[4] For Freud, smiles are foretastes of, or analogues to, orgasms. "What we call happiness," Freud writes, "in the strictest sense comes from the (preferably sudden) satisfaction of needs which have been dammed up to a high degree."[5] Sexual love furnishes the most "intense experience of an overwhelming sensation of pleasure" and "a pattern for our search for happiness."[6]

Families, the first movement to civilization, form in the name of this quasi-orgasmic understanding of happiness. "The founding of families was connected with the fact that a moment came when the need for genital satisfaction no longer made its appearance like a guest who drops in suddenly, and, after his departure, is heard from no more for a long time, but instead took up its quarters as a permanent lodger." Due to this inexplicable, mysterious, evolutionary increase in sexual appetite (Freud cites Darwin here), men and women strike a marriage bargain, in which men get to use women as sex objects while women entice men to help raise children.[7] Love, understood as a man's desire for sexual satisfaction and a woman's love for a child that has separated from her, and necessity, understood as the compulsion to work, are parents of civilization. One might expect an ever more effective satisfaction of genital needs after the marriage bargain is struck, and therefore that civilization would serve the needs of love, and that love would blossom in civilization.

Yet love does not thrive in civilization in an uncomplicated way. The family is a move to civilization. Social organization, moral restrictions, and religion, other moves toward civilization, arise only after sons revolt from their father's unlimited rule in the precivilized family. Freud's account of this seminal event is found is his *Totem and Taboo* (1913), on which he relies in *Civilization and Its Discontents*.[8] A taboo, for Freud, is a cultural prohibition on actions that human beings are inclined to indulge. The most important such taboo is the prohibition on incest, the "most drastic mutilation which man's erotic life has in all time experienced."[9] The incest taboo is coeval with the establishment of totems, or primitive clans, whose central act is animal sacrifice. In the beginning, there were no limits on sexual freedom. Sons engaged in an unstated rivalry with their fathers over sexual access to their mothers, even as the sons admired their fathers for providing life's needs.[10] The sons' resentment is understandable because the precivilized "violent and jealous father" hoarded "all of the females" and drove away his sons as they matured in order to keep control of his harem. The father's jealous and greedy control over his women created an excess of males without sexual outlets. One day, Freud continues, the exiled brothers banded "together, killed and devoured their father and so made an end of the patriarchal horde." These precivilized "cannibal savages" ate their fathers hoping to ingest his virtue and strength, and this meal was made the centerpiece of primitive totem societies.[11] Their ambivalent attitudes toward their father—the respect and affection they felt for him even as they resented him and ate him for dinner—led them to feel guilty about their actions. To appease this guilt, they forbade the killing of the totem animal and renounced the fruits of their revolt by forgoing their father's women. The sons realized that giving rein to sexual desire would lead them to a "struggle of all against all." They "had no alternative" but to prohibit incest if they were to live together in peace.

> Totemic religion arose from the filial sense of guilt, in an attempt to allay that feeling and to appease the father by deferred obedience to him. All later religions are seen to be attempts at solving the same problem . . . and are reactions to the same great event with which civilization began.[12]

Religions based on animal images are replaced by monotheistic religions where the father is worshipped as sovereign. Monotheism, guilt, civilization, and the incest taboo arise together. "The most extreme denial of the great crime" becomes "the beginning of society and of the sense of guilt."[13]

Human beings establish families by differentiating one group from another and by initiating marriages across totems. This sounds innocuous, but it is a wrenching, guilt-ridden, and unnatural happening that violates human instincts in two ways. First, it demands the suppression of the unlimited sexual instincts that existed before the onset of the incest taboo. As religion spreads, more restrictions follow and distortions of the human sex drive lead to a civilization-wide mental health crisis. Second, the sons feel guilty about their innate drive to aggression and violence, and their efforts to repress it contribute to civilization's discontents. "If civilization imposes such great sacrifices not only on man's sexuality but on his aggressivity, we can understand better why it is hard for him to be happy in that civilization."[14]

Freud's discussion of the incest taboo illustrates a poetic truth. The incest taboo and civilization itself originate when human beings master their imperious *aggressive* instincts and promiscuous *sexual* instincts.[15] An instinct is "*an urge inherent in organic life to restore an earlier state of things* which the living entity has been obliged to abandon under the pressure of external disturbing forces"; it expresses "the inertia inherent in organic life" and shows the "*conservative* nature of living substance." Instincts point people back to an original state and reflect a desire to return to the satisfactions of the origin. Freud again seems to embrace an ancient understanding of ends when he claims that an accurate investigation of instincts make "it possible to specify this final goal of all organic striving."[16] Historical research, complemented by psychoanalysis, reveals the goal. Unlike Hegel's projecting vision, and in the manner of state of nature theorists, Freud means historical research in the old-fashioned sense: an investigation into the "*old* state of things."[17] Freud's project of reconciliation sees happy individuals merge with the most primitive aspects of their nature. That instincts move to first things means that they move to a fixed target. Aggression and sexual passions are intractable facts of human life; the discontents related to them are intractable features of civilization.

Consider aggression, "an original, self-subsisting instinctual disposition in man."[18] When aggression points to the external world, it seeks to destroy, dominate, and kill. Destructiveness points inward too. Internal destructiveness is part of the death instinct or wish. The claim that human beings have an instinct for death, Freud recognizes, may seem odd, since human beings love life. The desire for self-preservation is, on Freud's reading, a desire to avoid death *on another's terms*. The death instinct, which gives rise to recklessness and aggression, comes from the human desire to return to their original inanimate state. In the beginning, there was inanimate matter and some mysteriously unknowable force brought that matter to life. Tension arose as "what had hitherto been an inanimate substance endeavoured to cancel itself out," and this tension still threatens to rip civilization apart.[19]

The sexual instinct poses more serious difficulties for Freud. It initially appears that sex instincts are connected to a desire to lengthen and continue life, or a "life instinct." Freud introduces a clever distinction between the kinds of matter that exist among the first things so that he can maintain that human beings have life and death wishes. Some matter (he calls it the soma) is brought to life and is subject to natural death; another part of matter (the germ-cells) is "potentially immortal," in that it can reproduce and surround itself with new soma. Sex instincts aim at "the coalescence of two germ-cells which are differentiated in a particular way." An aspiration for immortality, linked to the existence of primitive germ-cells, lurks in the sexual instinct.[20] Freud again has recourse to first things to explain that form of sexual desire because the distinction between the sexes does not exist in these initial germ-cells. Freud seems to have in mind Aristophanes' speech in Plato's *Symposium* stating the view that sexuality involves a desire to restore an earlier state of things. In this earlier state, most human beings were bisexual (and they still are to an extent), and they were split up; now they search the earth for their other half.[21]

Body and soul, human beings desire life and death and fighting and loving. This "pre-eminently dualistic view of instinctual life" does not lead to a synthesis between the two antagonistic features, nor do they cancel each other out. Aggression and sexuality unsettle civilization as people vainly seek a return to their initial state. These features mingle and neither develops in a straight line, and the sound sense, or at least the anti-utopianism, in Freud is that these tensions and desires are sown in human nature. Freud recommends his audience familiarize themselves "with the idea that there are difficulties attaching to the nature of civilization which will not yield to any attempt at reform."[22]

Freud insists on his account of origins though it sounds "fantastic" and has a "monstrous air."[23] Given its strange beginning and our intractably uncivilized instincts, it is no surprise that tragedy lurks in civilization. "Love comes into opposition to the interests of civilization . . . [and] civilization threatens love with substantial restrictions." The first problem is that the family will not give its children up—this happens both because the family is tightly knit together to serve the needs of children and because mothers see their children as parts of themselves. Families are extreme partisans on their children's behalf and against the interests and needs of the community's justice. These problems, as old as the political community itself, are not the half of it. The family is sexually charged, with sons having their first sexual experiences at their mothers' breasts and daughters fixated on their fathers. Sons are taken with the "Oedipus complex" after they are weaned from the teat; they want to know their mother and they resent their father. Daughters have a different complex, in which they imagine they will become pregnant from their father after they are weaned; the weaning estranges the girl from her mother, and she fears her mother has stolen her penis. Eventually, for both the boys and the girls, their fear of losing the parent that they are led to resent leads them to internalize their resentment.[24] Sexual charges operate in the other direction as well. Mothers may be horrified to know it, but their caresses, their midnight feedings, and their attentions show that their baby is "a substitute for a complete sexual object." Children understand this loving and their earliest anxieties involve losing the person who has loved them—they fear the dark, for instance, because they cannot see this person.[25]

The second problem is that civilization displaces or mutilates human erotic life.[26] The incest prohibition points family members beyond the walls of their own family and toward the broader civilization for sexual gratification. Freud agrees with Marx that advances in civilization bring restrictions on sexual freedom, but not for the reasons Marx thought. Men expend sexual energy to build civilization, though building civilization may not gratify their libidos. Greater restrictions on sexual freedom accompany advances in civilization until, as in modern Western Europe, civilization turns against sexual instinct itself. Society can and should proscribe sexual practices in childhood, but it is a "source of serious injustice" to accept sex only in the context of a "solitary, indissoluble bond between one man and one woman" who engage only in approved sexual practices and who see sex as a duty to the species.[27] When people violate these principles, they are apt to have pangs of conscience. To use Freud's terms, the socially conditioned superego turns against the ego.

Sexual instincts do not disappear and they are not renounced; they are *sublimated*—they are pushed below the surface and are expressed in nonsexual ways.[28] People seek "substitutive satisfaction" in commercial enterprises, politics, union organizing, church, and other places where their restless, anxious desire to be busy finds an outlet. Political life takes on greater urgency and modern society's "unbridled pursuit of money and possessions, and its immense advances in the field of technology" take the place of sex. The sublimation of sexual desire does not derive from the private property regime. Social conventions sublimate sexual instincts, but natural instincts toward aggression are sublimated too. Any theory, such as Marx's, based on the belief that aggression is removable from the human condition is built on "an untenable illusion." If private property were abolished, if "complete freedom of sexual life" were established and sexual rivalry eliminated, aggressiveness would remain.[29] On the basis of sublimated aggression, human beings seek to overcome the power of nature and the feebleness of our own bodies. Human beings become members of "a human community, and, with the help of a technique guided by science, [go] . . . over to the attack against nature and subject her to the human will."[30] Science is sublimated aggression. To put a fine point on Freud's point, Marx's utopianism is cured by reading a little Nietzsche, who saw how human beings turn the will to power on themselves in creating a conscience and on nature through scientific conquests. Attempts to transform society and the family must account for intractable instincts; radical attempts that wish aggression away are bound to fail.

Civilization tames sexual and aggressive instincts, but how much should it do so? To what extent can society control them without making people miserable? This question goes to the heart of family life because the attitude toward sexual instinct indicates a proper relationship between the individual, the family, and the civilization in which the family is embedded. Because the unlimited paternal family did not embed the family in civilization, for instance, it allowed free rein to incestuous sexual instincts. So amorphous is the sexual instinct that we must realize that sex *can be* kept inside the family; civilization dislodges it. This dislodging limits sexual freedom, takes the sexual charge from the family, and empowers the community. Does civilization demand the substitution of sexual instincts so that human energy is displaced to meet the requirements of justice and "progress"? Does civilization annihilate individual passions and reconstruct the family only to suit its needs? Is civilization worth it?[31]

Neuroses, Repression, and the Goodness of Civilization

Civilization channels sexual instincts through the family by providing outlets for sexual energies. Rules accompany civilization, first from external authority provided by the sons that revolted against their greedy fathers and then from internalizing that rule. This process of "setting up an agency" in people to watch over them "like a garrison in a conquered city" moves people away from instinct and toward the rule of the superego, or conscience. As the superego expands, civilized people suspect themselves and their sexual instincts. "Every renunciation of instinct becomes a dynamic source of conscience and every fresh renunciation increases the latter's severity and intolerance." The superego threatens, dominates, and represses sexual instinct; its internalized rules make people ashamed, disgusted, and guilt-ridden about their instincts.[32] As conscience demands more, morality becomes stricter; as morality becomes stricter, individuals suppress sexual passions and aggression more; the more individuals suppress, the more they become violent and unhappy and civilization becomes neurotic. The "sense of guilt" is "the most important problem in the development of civilization"; "the price we pay for our advance in civilization is a loss of happiness through the heightening of the sense of guilt."[33]

The "harmful suppression of the sexual life of civilized peoples" causes serious nervous illnesses.[34] Neuroses especially abound in societies, such as Freud's Europe, that link sex, reproduction, and marriage. Within five years, Freud thinks, "marriage becomes a failure in so far as it has promised the satisfaction of sexual needs." The task "of mastering such a powerful impulse as that of the sexual instinct by any other means than satisfying it is one which can call for the whole of a man's forces," but the best way of "mastering" the sexual instinct is to indulge it. This is true especially for men, who benefit from the double standard in sexual morality and can sublimate sexual energy into productive labor. Women fear the consequences of sex, internalize cultural prohibitions against extramarital relations, and enter marriage with an unhealthy ignorance of sex, so it is little wonder that they become disillusioned. Disillusionment leads women "to fall ill of severe neuroses which permanently darken their lives." Women face a Hobson's choice. Either they face the ire of their superego by seeking a "cure for nervous illness" through "marital unfaithfulness," or they swim against the tide of female nature and try to "dam-up" their libidos and seek substitutive satisfactions without becoming neurotic.[35]

Under normal conditions in civilization, man's initiative is diverted from sex and women become cold and asexual.

> To the uninitiated it is hardly credible how seldom normal potency is to be found in a husband and how often a wife is frigid among married couples who live under the dominance of our civilized sexual morality, what a degree of renunciation . . . is entailed by marriage, and to what narrow limits married life—the happiness that is so ardently desired—is narrowed down.[36]

"American Gothic" marriages bequeath joyless neuroses to their offspring. Unsatisfied wives become overtender and overanxious toward their children; distant fathers watch their cold wives chill as they spend their energies on newborns instead of with their husbands. Oversolicitous mothers awaken sexual precocity too early among their children, and they make strict demands on seemingly abnormal children. The cycle of neuroses rolls on to the next generation with no end in sight.

Freud, for whom marital unhappiness is a great concern, does not provide an extended or thematic discussion of divorce, nor does his concern about the relationship between the generations lead him to discuss inheritance. Freud ignores these problems because he thinks he sees through Durkheim's superficial account of sexual passions. Durkheim held out hope that people could enjoy liberty in the service of self-improvement, and for this it was necessary that people pull themselves out of the stream of natural instincts. The "conservative" part of Freud—his view that human instincts move backwards and that there is little we can do to remedy the fundamental problems of civilization—is of a piece with his denial of human freedom. Instincts drive people in a direction and civilization diverts those drives or represses them in the name of the superego. The rebellious sons who founded civilization were forced to do so by feelings of sexual desire, aggression, and guilt. Even the works created by an artist or the findings discovered by the scientist are results of displaced libido and sublimated instinct brought about from an institution human beings were forced to create. Freedom, for Freud, is one's urge to follow one's instincts that are inhibited by civilization.[37] The most crucial aspect of Freud's denial of human freedom is his equation of love with sexual gratification. This understanding of freedom means that people appear to themselves to be trapped in their own instincts, unable to attain the distance from self necessary to share deeper unity or an ethical love with another. Attempts to move love beyond sex rest on an affirmation of human freedom that goes beyond the urge to follow an instinct.

Given his denial of freedom, it is fair to ask what can be done or why we should even ask what can be done. Freud *seems* noncommittal. He does not ask if we are "justified in reaching the diagnosis that, under the influence of cultural urges, some civilizations, or some epochs of civilization . . . have become 'neurotic,'" but his view on this matter is clear: Western civilization makes people sick. Freud disclaims any intention "to express an opinion upon the value of human civilization,"[38] yet the advances of civilization are detrimental to most individuals and to civilization as such (because a civilization cannot be healthy if its citizens are neurotic). He "certainly" does not believe that it is a "physician's business to come forward with proposals for reform,"[39] but his protests are not credible. If neuroses are akin to tuberculosis, as Freud claims, there must be a psychoanalytic equivalent to antibiotics.[40]

There is no radical prospect for improving our situation, nor are radical solutions such as Marxist communism able to bring man happiness. The latent causes of discontent are sown in man's instincts and in his relation to the world around him. For Freud, there are three sources of human suffering: our weakness in comparison with nature, the feebleness of our bodies, and the "inadequacy of the regulations which adjust the mutual relationships of human beings in the family, the state and society."[41] Much had been done to alleviate the first and second sources of human misery by Freud's time and much more has been done since (though neither source of suffering has been completely erased). Advances in science have lengthened our lives and brought more of nature under our control. Still, human beings cannot understand the problem of social institutions, much less find a solution to it. Freud concentrates on that problem. The greatest, most reliable source of and model for human happiness is sexual gratification. Civilization demands that people sublimate or repress sexual instincts; all civilization is repression. Freud's claim is that Western society represses more than it needs to for the purposes of civilization—we have, in Herbert Marcuse's delicious phrase, "surplus-repression."[42] Man's search for happiness in civilization centers on finding outlets for individual desire while accommodating the group's cultural claims. Limits placed on sexual desire in the Western world are too radical and profound (e.g., prohibitions on homosexuality, incest, premarital sex, non-procreative sex, contraception, and polygamy). The exaltation of a solitary, indissoluble bond between a man and a woman in which the sexual instinct is connected to its "natural" purpose of procreation seriously undermines our ability to achieve happiness. Civilization's idea of family forces individuals to sacrifice happiness and is the "source of serious injustice." Modern civilization pursues a Christian ideal of loving one's neighbor and one's enemies, the accomplishment of which is so impossible that members feel guilt-ridden and depressed. People have traded direct instinctual gratification for security and longevity in civilization, with discontent, malaise, and unhappiness thrown in for good measure.[43]

Freud develops a typology of regimes as they relate to the sexual instinct. In the first and loosest, any expression of the sexual instinct is legitimate. In the second, only sex related to reproduction is legitimate. In the third and strictest, legitimate sex aims at "*legitimate* reproduction."[44] If "civilized" countries exist on the third level and society is the cause of misery and serious injustice, reform involves moving toward the second regime and perhaps the first. Members of Western society need more purely sexual outlets for their sexual passions. Freud never connects these dots. He maintains the stance of a mere analyst and a somewhat conservative scientist who recognizes his limits. Everything—his nonjudgmental attitude toward what he calls perverse expressions of sexual desire, his detachment of sexual instinct from procreation, his equation of love with sexual love, his view on the centrality of sex to human happiness, his critique of excessive family unity, his worries about female frigidity and male repressions, his view that some societies might suffer from collective neuroses—everything, I say, in his thought points to a society existing at the first level.

We find confirmation of this in his treatment of contraception. He generally opposed the contraception methods of his day.[45] He feared they caused psychological problems because they interfered with sexual gratification. Yet he held out hope.

> We possess at present no method of preventing conception which fulfils every legitimate requirement—that is, which is certain and convenient, which does not diminish the sensation of pleasure during coitus and which does not wound the woman's sensibilities. This sets physicians a practical task to the solution of which they could bend their energies with rewarding results. Whoever fills this lacuna in our medical technique will have preserved the enjoyment of life and maintained the health of numberless people; though, it is true, he will also have paved the way for a drastic change in our social conditions.[46]

If such a thing could be found (and it *was*, on Freud's own terms, in the birth control pill), contraception would have the effect of accomplishing what sexual instincts demand: separating sexual satisfaction from procreation and other social purposes, thus justifying the deregulation of the sexual instincts. Freud favors contraception for the reason Durkheim opposed it. Freud hopes to achieve the maximum amount of sexual gratification on the level of civilization. To realize this goal it is necessary to allow sexual indulgence while divorcing such indulgence from its natural and social consequences. What this means for marriage and child-rearing Freud does not venture a guess. On what that "drastic change in our social conditions" might have been, I believe that Bertrand Russell's thought is a good place to start.

Marriage and Morals in Russell's Social Thought

Bertrand Russell (1872–1970), famous British logician and polemicist, was the son of a prominent, radical British family. His father, Viscount Amberley, was, along with Mill, an early advocate for contraception, and his marital practice was broad-minded, for the viscount consented to his wife's affair with Bertrand's tutor. Russell himself was first married in 1894, but that marriage fell apart after seven years; after years of separation, during which time he carried on a series of overlapping trysts, Russell divorced in 1921. He married his pregnant girlfriend six days after his first divorce was official. This second marriage bore Russell two children, but after eleven years that marriage too fell apart. It may have fallen apart because Russell was following a family tradition of having an affair with the children's governess, whom he married in 1936 and then divorced in 1952, after siring another child. Russell refused to let the dream die; he quickly married a fourth time, and the fourth marriage proved a charm, lasting until his death in 1970.

His most important book on the family is *Marriage and Morals* (1929), an extended argument for a new morality based on Freud's critique of bourgeois marriage. Its position is pro-love, anti-divorce (in some circumstances), anti-fatherhood, and pro–open marriage. With this last position especially we break some new ground, and we must understand what it is and how it fits in with all of the other purposes and institutions of marriage. For Russell, open marriage takes two forms. First, open marriage is a conjugal relationship that does not "exclude other sex relations." It is a mellow, nonexclusive marriage, untainted by primitive jealousy by which one seeks to control one's spouse. Jealousy is a vice, after all. Marriage stripped of jealousy would be free of this destructive and controlling vice, and it would exist on a more rational plane. Marital happiness requires "complete equality," "the most complete physical and mental intimacy," "a certain similarity in regard to the standards of values," and "no interference in mutual freedom."[47] Second, borrowing from Ben Lindsey's *Companionate Marriage* (1927), Russell would allow men and women to enter and exit marriage, without penalty and by consent, until they had children. Lindsey advocated creating a marriage-lite in which couples without children could live together, have access to birth control, and be able to part without alimony. Russell would make the marriage even liter, in that he would forbid any state acknowledgment of private relations until children arrived.[48] These two understandings of open marriage are not necessarily in conflict. Man and woman can be free to enter a loose relationship before the arrival of children, and then, once children arrive, they can live together and raise children without making unreasonable demands about sexual exclusivity. Russell separates marriage from the need to be sexually exclusive.

Sexual fidelity is, for many thinkers and even for many human beings, important, if not a *sine qua non*, to married life. Stability in marriage, Russell holds, is best accomplished "by distinguishing between marriage and merely sexual relations." Marriage and exclusive sexual relations were joined by Christian theology. According to the Christian tradition, as Russell reads it, sex is dirty and ugly, and is to be avoided except where it is the intention of the parties to procreate. This position leads Christianity to condemn sex education, nudity, contraception, and other liberating institutions. There is in the modern world, Russell contends, "a certain antagonism between religion and love" due to the fact that "the Christian religion, unlike some others, is rooted in asceticism."[49] It is here that Russell builds on Freud's thought, though in a way that suggests that there is more to love than sexual gratification. World-denying, sex-condemning, guilt-ridden Christianity, with its more secular expression in the Protestant work ethic, represses sexual desires on which a genuine connection between two people is built. Those who do not experience these joys displace their sexual longings and their genuine desires for intimacy into an "envy, oppression, and cruelty" that leads to patriotic wars, cutthroat industrial competition, censorious public opinion, and puritanical legislation. Allowing more expression of sexual desire enriches the profound experience of love, in which there is "an instinctive and not merely conscious extension of egoistic feeling so as to embrace the other person." He even worries about a habit among "modern emancipated people" of "dissociating sex from serious emotion and from feelings of affection," for this would mean that love was incapable of bringing profound satisfactions and fulfillment.[50] Russell opposes "rigid barriers" that would prohibit men and women from wandering, yet he somehow does not want to devalue sex in the fashion that a culture of "hooking up" does. Sexual intercourse is to be "regarded primarily as experimentation with a view to love."[51]

This encomium about the connection between sex and love would seem to lead Russell to the traditional position in defense of marital fidelity. Russell's departure from this position is occasioned by his understanding of what the conditions for genuine love are. Here he melds Mill and Freud. Love is "free and spontaneous" and it dies when it is seen as a duty. Uninhibited sexual passions are sown in human nature, and love is "an anarchic force which, if it is left free, will not remain within any bounds set by law or custom."[52] Attempts to tame this anarchic force lead us to view marriage as a cold duty, foster unhappiness in marriage, and eventually result in diverting the sex drive in destructive ways. Sexual passion is too strong to be safely directed, and love too based on free spontaneity to be burdened with commitment. Every time a partner wanders, it is a sign that he is shopping for a better mate; comparison shopping need not be a problem. If partners would rid themselves of the expectation that love is lasting, they could be free and easy in their relationships and disburden themselves of the sadness, jealousy, and resentment that can accompany a breakup. In fact, Russell seems to suggest that love is concerned with the happiness and good of the other person, while jealousy is merely demanding one's own good. A true lover would embrace a partner's search for happiness and the good wherever it leads, not stifle it by selfishly demanding sexual exclusivity. By expecting each partner to find erotic outlets outside of marriage, marriage can be less disrupted by unreasonable passions.

It is remarkable, given the unreliable nature of human sexual desire, that Russell maintains the institution of marriage at all. On this point he plays a Lockean tune. Russell regards "marriage not primarily as a sexual partnership, but above all as an undertaking to cooperate in the procreation and rearing of children."[53] Any lingering traditionalism in Russell is connected to this point, yet he almost immediately abandons it, arguing that there are ways to separate child-rearing from marriage. The movement to separate education from parenthood is underway, in fact. Throughout modernity, family functions with respect to children have gradually devolved on the state. In modern times, the functions normally associated with the father have slowly been taken over by the state, and "to this process of substituting the State for the father no clear limit can be set." The abolition of child labor, the rise of compulsory education and health legislation, the coming state provision of economic support (and perhaps child care), and the inevitable move toward economic independence for women through their working outside the home—all these factors interact so that fatherhood "loses its *raison d'etre.*" Russell likens the movements afoot in modernity to the abolition of the family seen in Plato's "city in speech" from *The Republic.*[54]

There are several reasons Russell believes "the substitution of the State for the father . . . is in the main a great advance." Fathers unreasonably tend to insist on knowing that the children they are raising are indeed their own. A decline in wifely fidelity means that it will be difficult to establish paternity, so it would be foolish to rely on fathers to provide for their "children." A larger problem involves the tight emotional intimacy of the family. "The modern small family, unadulterated, is too stuffy and confined for healthy development during the early years."[55] The syndrome of sexual repression in which children have been typically raised adds to the family's repressive stuffiness. Mothers, dissatisfied with their husbands, redirect sexual longings toward their young children. Frustrated fathers oppress and repress their children.

Russell slices off Freud's "conservative" theory of enduring instincts, which had in fact been destabilized by Freud's belief that civilization sublimates sexual drives toward the conquest of nature.

Freud's Effect on the Family and the Search for Meaning

Let us put Freud's thought in context, for, in some respects, it marks a turn in how modern thinkers view the family. Insisting on the intractability of instinct, Freudian analysis shows that human personality exists independent from culture; Freud opposes the optimism about the triumph of an enlightened culture over dark instinct (seen in both Mill and Marx) and Durkheim's positivism, which reduces human beings to products of cultural forces.[56] Freud accepts Durkheim's view of how culture works: human beings internalize cultural norms and these have a profound effect on human passions.[57] The intractability of instinct in culture means that mental conflict, neuroses, and sublimation are endemic to the human condition; this accounts for Freud's anti-utopianism.

Freud's account of *why* instincts are intractable and the mind is restless and anxious is self-contradictory and implausible. Freud's theory of instincts rests on his contention that human beings long to return to their native nothingness and to the immortality connected to soma, and few thinkers today take these theories seriously or see them as improvements on what Freud himself considers superstitious explanations. This seems to be what Freud's critics see as his foundational "biological determinism." What is more, sexual practice is very mutable on Freud's account, and, in principle, his analysis can lead to the conclusion that instincts themselves are the product of history. It took so many mental gymnastics for Freud to maintain his theory of instincts that, eventually, it failed the laugh test. Beauvoir, one of Freud's insightful critics, sees that Freud's doctrine "demands the indefinite and arbitrary multiplication of secondary explanations" and that "when observation brings to light as many exceptions as instances conformable to the rule, it is better to give up the old rigid framework." This rigid framework is precisely Freud's theory of instincts, the ballast of his thought, the maintenance of which led Freud to adopt "strange fictions," such as the story of revolt from *Totem and Taboo*.[58] The effectual truth of Freud's thought is Russell's embrace of liberation.

Freud inverts previous ideas about the educative effects of modern marriage. Locke focused on the progress of self-control as essential to rational liberty; Durkheim, on how social control tames modern man's tendency to anomie. Freud's thought provides a scientific basis for criticisms of institutions, virtues, mores, habits, and social practices limiting the human expression of instinct. Chief among these is the unified family, even in its attenuated bourgeois form. Habits of self-control become, under Freud, debilitating repressions and deflected distortions. Monogamous marriage creates frigid, unhappy wives and disappointed husbands. Child-raising appears to be a perverse way to register sexual passion, and a sick mother that spends too much time with her children is hardly preparing them for a life of rational liberty. Freud and Mill land a one-two punch against the tightly knit family. Mill shows that such a family could only be built on revocable choice, while Freud shows that the marital and familial unity is hardly as moral as it appears. When combined with Mill's critique of male tyrannical violence and dehumanizing female submission, Freud's theory about repression and diverted sexual passions put the bourgeois family on the defense, and it has not recovered. Despite his conservative-seeming anti-utopianism and endorsement of sex differences, Freud's critique of the family was essential to getting women to see the problem in the unified marriage: marriage could not be reformed to promote human happiness, and marriage and sex were excessively centered on children. However much feminist thinkers see Freud as part of the patriarchal tradition, his critique of family life paves the way for the feminist critique of patriarchy; much of his thought survives their criticisms. Liberation is good for human beings because it is consistent with intractable human instincts for sexual gratification and aggression. Feminist thinkers borrow Freud's critique of motherhood while rejecting his "biological determinism" so that something could be done about the condition of motherhood. His theory could be adopted by utopians because Freud's science was so questionable.

This points to Freud's vision of what a human being is—the deepest level at which Freud's theory is controversial. If human beings are governed by instinct, then they can hardly be blamed for their actions. Instincts can be *diverted*, or *repressed*, or expressed, or indulged, but they cannot be avoided, and there would be little possibility for genuine self-government if Freud's vision were to be correct. The most interesting revolts against Freud, we shall see, come in the name of self-government and human freedom.

Chapter 9

Feminism and the Family

Feminist thinking flows from the belief that maleness and femaleness, and gender roles as such, are products of society.[1] Modern feminists complete Mill's more tentative effort to show that society gives individuals their particular shape. "One is not born, but rather becomes, a woman," as Simone de Beauvoir writes;[2] "anatomy is not destiny" could well be the motto. Neither is history destiny, at least insofar as history reveals that sex differences are seen in almost all times and places and appear natural. If there are human universals such as natural sex differences, if those universals are rooted in human biology, and if human biology is stable, then attempts to improve the condition of women, as feminists understand it, are doomed.

If sex differences *have* been universal, feminists respond, they need not continue to be so. In rising to the challenge of history and anatomy, feminists explain why sex differences have been universal in order to make it plausible that the sexes could be otherwise. While conceding that our biology may be stable, they must show that the *conclusions* we draw from biology need not be the same yesterday, today, and forever. While conceding that history and sociology mostly repeat the same story of sex differences, feminists must show that a new era is dawning that will overturn history's inexorable conclusions. Feminists seek to show that culture and ethics have changed, and with them the meaning of masculinity and femininity and the place of family among human goods.

The crux of feminist concerns centers around the sexual division of labor as it has been historically understood. It enslaves women, it keeps women from becoming full-fledged citizens, and it assigns women tasks below their pay grades. The sexual division of labor, seemingly so central to family unity, is artificial, debilitating, infantilizing, patriarchal, tyrannical, and worse. What follows from this criticism of the sexual division of labor is a proposal to reform how the family divides labor that also changes the meaning of family life for men and women. Some feminists aspire to make a gender-neutral society along the lines described by Susan Muller Okin.

> A just future would be one without gender. In social structures and practices, one's sex would have no more relevance than one's eye color or the length of one's toes. No assumptions would be made about "male" or "female" roles; childbearing would be so conceptually separated from child rearing and other family responsibilities that it would be a cause for surprise, and no little concern, if men and women were not equally responsible for domestic life or if children were to spend much more time with one parent than the other. It would be a future in which men and women participated in more or less equal numbers in every sphere of life, from infant care to different kinds of paid work to high-level politics.[3]

The aspiration to create a gender-neutral society carries with it assumptions about nature, anatomy, psychology, and history. In order to lay bare these assumptions, we must turn to the work of Beauvoir, whose *Second Sex* is, by widespread consent, the founding book of mainstream modern feminism.[4]

Identifying and Deconstructing Patriarchy

Beauvoir provides the deepest and most systematic critique of how deeply patriarchy has shaped the ways of traditional women and perpetuated their status as "the second sex." What is remarkable in Beauvoir is how self-creating human beings are. "Man is defined as a being who is not fixed, who makes himself what he is. . . . Man is not a natural species: he is a historical idea." She echoes the same ideas about the relation between nature and history near the end of her tome: "Humanity is something more than a mere species: it is a historical development; it is to be defined by the manner in which it deals with its natural, fixed characteristics."[5] Anatomy, psychology, economic conditions, custom, technology, culture, and other limits of our situation seem important, but "in themselves" they "have no significance" because human beings have great power to put a new interpretation on their situation and to rearrange things to achieve freedom. If human beings are undefined by nature, then either their situation defines them or they can define themselves. Until yesterday women were passive and defined by their situation; now it is time for women to define themselves.

Beauvoir's unique contribution to developing the modern idea of freedom as exerting power over nature is her distinction between transcendence and immanence. Transcendence, for Beauvoir, is the freedom to "engage in freely chosen projects."[6] Transcendent freedom expresses itself in different ways. Transcendence involves laboring, creating, and remodeling the face of the earth. Not satisfied with the givens of nature or culture, transcendent beings aspire to be sovereign over life instead of stupidly repeating ancestral ways. This aspiration is responsible for technologies that transform the human situation. The "reality of man is in the houses he builds, the forests he clears, the maladies he cures."[7] Transcendence also involves creativity in the sphere of values, the special province of independent artists and philosophers. Artists create principles to define their interests and their situation; they have powers of reinterpretation that free them from cultural chains. More artist than artisan, Beauvoir's own transcendence is expressed in the sphere of values. She chooses her word carefully—human beings are *transcendent*, or are akin to gods, in asserting this latent creative capacity.[8]

Immanence, in contrast, involves submission to the species, biological necessities, and customs that seem to grow from biology. Immanent action expresses itself in different ways too. Those subject to immanence treat biological processes as givens, thereby enslaving themselves to the perpetuation of life and values. Women, for instance, are immanent when they see themselves as essential to the reproduction of the species. Men and women are immanent when they submit to rules of religious orthodoxy or follow "natural" desires or adhere to "natural law." In short, immanent action, shorn of ideas or principles or choices or spirit, resembles a passive acceptance of mere life or tradition.

The border between transcendence and immanence is unstable. Yesterday's immanence is overcome or reinterpreted tomorrow, and it is difficult to know where the limits of human power lie because we have only begun to tap our power to remake the world. Beauvoir finds it difficult to identify genuine human choice in action as well. Women, for instance, can choose to become pregnant, bear children, and rear children. Women can choose to spend precious time dolling themselves up, or they can exert themselves by playing the helpless coquette in order to win a man.[9] The power to choose in these cases implies the power to choose among alternatives. Women can be mothers, nuns, or laborers, and the fact that they can choose among different life scripts is the source of their claim to freedom. Yet, for all their choices, motherhood, for Beauvoir, (probably) represents a form of "voluntary acquiescence" and not a free, transcendent action because mothers (often) do not invent or implicate a truly chosen or principled end in becoming mothers. To anticipate the language in our next chapter, mothers are "choosing" among cultural scripts written by others instead of writing their own. Their actions are not truly free unless *their* project is *truly* chosen: Beauvoir seems to equate truly choosing with artistic invention.

Women have in the past been immanent.

> What peculiarly signalizes the situation of woman is that she—a free and autonomous being like all human creatures—nevertheless finds herself living in a world where men compel her to assume the status of the Other. They propose to stabilize her as object and to doom her to immanence since her transcendence is to be overshadowed and forever transcended by another ego which is essential and sovereign.[10]

Beauvoir uncovers male sovereignty in nearly every aspect of life. Consider Beauvoir's treatment of male and female sex organs. People "treat the infantile penis with remarkable complacency," while "mothers and nurses feel no reverence or tenderness toward [a girl's] genitals." Boys are told to urinate while standing up, encouraging them to see that "the penis can be manipulated" and "it gives opportunity for action." Girls must uncover themselves but hide their organ while urinating, "a shameful and inconvenient procedure."[11] The male erection is seen as an "affirmation of his subjectivity, his transcendence" and he takes pride in his size and stamina, while girls hide their sex organ, shrouded in passivity, shame, and mystery.[12] The penis and other male toys are symbols "of autonomy, of transcendence, of power," while the girl is stuck playing with dolls.[13] Boys experience nocturnal emissions, which are interpreted as signs of future potency and action, while girls begin to menstruate, which makes them feel envious, embarrassed, and defective.[14] Even and especially the physical act of love equates the male with the active and strong and the female with the passive and weak. A male comes to possess a woman—to "have her," in the common expression—by penetrating her, and this penetration is "an essential element" in patriarchy's "general frame." "Like the female of most species, she is *under* the male during copulation. . . . The woman lies in the posture of defeat. . . . She always feels passive: she is caressed, penetrated; she undergoes coition, whereas the man exerts himself actively."[15]

Penises and vaginas, and the action that takes place with them, are interpreted thus because men have written the cultural script. These ideas are "imposed upon [a girl] by her teachers and by society."

> Everything helps to confirm this hierarchy in the eyes of the little girl. The historical and literary culture to which she belongs, the songs and legends with which she is lulled to sleep, are one long exaltation of man. . . . Children's books, mythology, stories, tales, all reflect the myths born of the pride and the desires of men; thus it is that through the eyes of men the little girl discovers the world and reads therein her destiny.[16]

Freud is one of Beauvoir's main theoretical opponents because he perpetuates the cultural idea that the male is normal and strong, while the female is weak and envious of his position. Beauvoir offers a more humanist ethics than Freud because of her refusal to give into scientific or historical determinism and her emphasis on the "idea of *choice*."[17] In her emphasis on freedom (or transcendence), Beauvoir seems to eschew the idea of a determinative positive science from Durkheim's sociology; Beauvoir displays the tension between freedom and science, two of the modern world's deepest commitments.

The arc of Beauvoir's treatment of the patriarchal tradition suggests that what has been written by men can be rewritten. Values cannot be based on physiology; "rather the facts of biology take on the values that the existent bestows upon them. We must view the facts of biology in the light of an ontological, economic, social, and psychological context."[18] Women can reinterpret patriarchal interpretations bestowed on biological "facts." The cramping pains of menstruation, Beauvoir writes, may be "due to psychic causes" arising from a "moral tension" between the female's hope for transcendence and her reality of immanence.[19] Perhaps today's independent women can stand up and pee like the Egyptian women of Herodotean fame,[20] or at least the act of sitting down to urinate could be ennobled by a new cultural script. As to the ideas surrounding sex, women should avoid the posture of defeat by hopping on top,[21] by refiguring what sexual relations between men and women mean, or by avoiding sex with men altogether.

Much the same is true of sex differences in athletics. Men appear to be faster, stronger, more competitive, and more aggressive by nature than women, but Beauvoir insists society causes these differences. A girl is not "given the encouragement accorded to her brothers," and custom renders independence and aggressiveness "difficult for them." Passivity, timidity, femininity, maternity—these mark the woman; true women never sweat. A new destiny awaits, if women would invent a new cultural script.

> Let her swim, climb mountain peaks, go out for adventure, and she will not feel before the world that timidity which I have referred to. It is in a

> total situation which leaves her few outlets that her peculiarities take on their importance—not directly, but by confirming the inferiority complex set up in childhood.[22]

Traditional ideas of a more voluptuous feminine beauty give way to a more athletic vision. Women transform from the immanent, passive other to an active, transcendent, powerful absolute.

Beauvoir sees these changes in sexual behavior and physical fitness as indispensable parts of a broader political and economic reform. Women are not supposed to leave their new aggressive selves in the bedroom or the gymnasium: aggression, competition, potency, and transcendence should redefine their lives. Let us follow the same technique, showing how Beauvoir's vision of transcendent marriage and motherhood follows from her critique of immanent marriage and motherhood. Much has changed since primitive times, but two things remain true of marriage. A woman marries because "she must provide society with children" and because she must "satisfy a male's sexual needs and . . . take care of his household."[23] Because women take care of the household, men are free to leave the home and to find transcendent action in the workplace. The effects of this sexual division are moral and economic. Man, Beauvoir writes, is

> the productive worker, he is the one who goes beyond family interest to that of society, opening up a future for himself through co-operation in the building of the collective future; he incarnates transcendence. Woman is doomed to the continuation of the species and the care of the home—that is to say, to immanence.[24]

Her days are filled with necessitous activities or housework, about which Beauvoir writes a scathing and memorable critique. There are always dishes to wash and put away, meals to cook, clothes to wash, fold, and put away, messes to clean up or prevent, and goods to buy. "Few tasks are more like the torture of Sisyphus than housework."[25] Household tasks are "meticulous and limitless" and "tiresome, empty, monotonous"; they do "not even tend toward the creation of anything durable"; and they "[produce] nothing," and are "boring." After all, as Beauvoir writes, "the battle against dust and dirt is never won." So devoid of meaning are household tasks that immanent housewives pitifully invest them with supernatural meaning: "In her war against dust, stains, mud, and dirt she is fighting sin, wrestling with Satan."[26]

> It has been said that marriage diminishes man, which is often true; but almost always it annihilates woman. . . . Her true sentiments become clear; she sees that her husband could get along very well without her, that

> her children are bound to get away from her and to be always more or less ungrateful. The home no longer saves her from empty liberty; she finds herself alone, forlorn, a subject; and she finds nothing to do with herself.

Again, "The tragedy of marriage is not that it fails to assure woman the promised happiness . . . but [that] it mutilates her; it dooms her to repetition and routine . . . her life is virtually finished forever."[27]

It is difficult to capture the depths of despair that accompany the boredom, pitiableness, annihilation, mutilation, and meaninglessness of the housewife's life when lived according to the traditional sexual division of labor. Not that there is anything wrong with being a housewife! She longs to be transcendent, but is stuck with the dishes. She yearns for a project, but folds piles of laundry. Thirsting for freedom, she tastes only a repetitive life of necessity. The meaning associated with these grim tasks was connected to the beautiful home and to the family life to which they contributed. It was once thought that the sexual division of labor was an important, if not an indispensable, element of a loving marriage, a shared life committed to common projects. Housework itself is a repetitive, Sisyphean task, and no one ever thought matching socks was a transcendent activity. It was part of a total situation in which a man and a woman united in love and each made unique contributions to raising a family and building a common life. Beauvoir unmasks these old visions as claptrap disguising male dominance. The reality of marriage has changed. She even questions whether family life can still constitute a common project. The best contemporary marriages subsist because the "man and wife reach a compromise. They live side by side without too much mutual torment, too much lying to each other. But there is one curse they very rarely escape: it is boredom." Marriage is like housework, and women and men suffer the "slow assassination of a dull marriage."[28]

Motherhood is every bit as Sisyphean as housework and as deadening as marriage with the added problem that it constitutes dangers for society at large. Beauvoir seems to think of motherhood as the essence of immanence: the cycle of reproduction limits the freedom of women and seems to put them in the service of the species. Why is it that women are stuck bearing the children? And even if they have to, why must women *rear* them? The real problem is that the cultural script of motherhood is so readily available and that often the woman's "choice" to be a mother really reflects acquiescence to a cultural script. By acquiescing in motherhood connected to marriage, women take "an easy road"[29] and rob themselves of the arduous task of constructing their own futures, of designing their own projects, and, finally, of being completely human.

We see an ambiguity creep into Beauvoir's thinking with her most pro-motherhood statement in *The Second Sex*. "The child is an enterprise to which one can validly devote oneself; but it represents a ready-made justification no more than any other enterprise does; and it must be desired for its own sake, not for hypothetical benefits."[30] A *valid* selection of motherhood would not implicate biological determinism or social pressure. It would not involve trapping a man to supply one's economic security by securing him a child. Crude contractual thinking, so prominent in the marriage bargain, denigrates the capacities of women and seals their subordination to men.[31] Too often, the way things are presently organized, women are motivated by such immanent concerns. The result is to put children at risk, as Beauvoir, armed with Freudian insights, argues.

> The great danger which threatens the infant in our culture lies in the fact that the mother to whom it is confided in all its helplessness is almost always a discontented woman: sexually she is frigid or unsatisfied; socially she feels herself inferior to man; she has no independent grasp on the world or on the future. She will seek to compensate for all these frustrations through her child.

This makes mothers domineering, "sadistic," and "capricious."[32] Sexually dissatisfied themselves, mothers divert their sexual energies to their children. They lash out at a world that does not provide them space, or they displace their desire for power on their children, the only beings that women can, for a time, dominate. They often produce coddled and spoiled children who are unable to aspire for transcendence and are willing to submit to the vilest tyranny in politics. They are the reason our civilization has lost its dynamism. Thus the structure of the family is a matter of urgent public concern.

The Independent (and Transcendent) Woman and Her Family

The result of Beauvoir's distinction between transcendence and immanence is an almost Manichean dualism, finally promising, it seems, liberation from the dictates of nature. Human beings long to be free or transcendent, but they are stuck with bodies, necessity, and immanence. The reality of immanence seems inescapable in family life. Marriage seems to be based on a mutual dependence connecting one's identity to another's, so freedom and independence are compromised. Living in a common abode seems to require that the abode be an object of common care; this necessitates some division of labor in the family, and this labor is often divided along sexual lines. Having children means conforming, to a degree, to the reproductive cycle, which limits human freedom and (perhaps) equality. Beauvoir recognizes these problems in their depth and complexity; she offers a vision of family life that nevertheless promises independence and equality for men and women. She draws admiringly on Mill.[33] As her diagnosis of the problems associated with the subjection of women goes deeper than Mill's, however, her account of how women rise from their status as the second sex goes beyond what Mill, on one level, thought necessary.[34] Beauvoir worries that Mill's abstract principles secure women only a negative liberty. Genuine reform must assist women in freeing themselves from immanence associated with biology and social conventions.[35] This distinguishes the first wave of feminist thinkers such as Mill from the next wave, represented by Beauvoir.

The Hollow Liberal Victories

Beauvoir believes that marriage is in a "period of transition."[36] Mill's legal revolution has been implemented, and men and women are now practically equals with regard to the "abstract, theoretical rights they enjoy."[37] Women have secured the vote. Gainful employment and productive labor are open to women. Marriage unions originate in consent, and, in most places, either party can sue for divorce on the same grounds. Contraception is more or less available to women. Women have the legal authority to own and bestow property.[38] For all these advances, however, women still do not get paid as much as men, they work in drudgery, they are subservient to their husbands, they perform most household tasks, they do not practice sexual freedom as much as men do, and they do not use contraception. Mill built a legal regime to undermine unified marriages, but women did not immediately dismantle that vision of marriage. We are back to the distinction between the freedom to choose and content of the choice. Women have secured only a negative or formal freedom, and this alone does not secure substantive equality with men: "She remains bound in her condition of vassalage,"[39] even if she formally chooses to embrace that condition.

Liberalism fails to grasp the deep sources of oppression. Marxist historicism, with its emphasis on the influence of changes in the mode of production, provides an essential part of Beauvoir's analytical framework for understanding the oppression of women. Changes in law have not freed women. Woman's condition has improved due to two factors: she now shares in productive labor, and she has been "freed from slavery to reproduction."[40] The aim of these changes is to "free [women] from domestic bonds." Despite these gains, women are still "only halfway there."

Beauvoir approves of the Comintern's 1924 statement: "The Revolution is impotent as long as the notion of family and of family relations continues to exist."[41] As long as women live privately in families, they construct no class consciousness or sense of sisterhood; fragmented and dispersed, they seem unaware of their collective oppression.[42] Woman's "liberation must be collective," for without it a few women struggle somewhat pitifully against their immanent sisters, but they get nowhere.[43] "What is extremely demoralizing for the woman who aims at self-sufficiency is the existence of other women of like social status, having at the start the same situation and the same opportunities, who live as parasites."[44] The critique of the housewife is intrinsic to Beauvoir's efforts to construct the collective sense of sisterhood necessary to achieve woman's liberation. Housewives are standing obstacles to the cultivation of a collective feminine consciousness.

The New Working Mother

The importance of women establishing themselves in the workplace cannot be overstated. Despite Mill's aspirations for great results from a legal revolution expanding opportunities for women, the removal of obstacles did not achieve what Mill had hoped or as much as Beauvoir would have liked. Mill thought the "*power* of earning is essential to the *dignity* of a woman";[45] women must be free to earn a living if they are to be considered equal to men. Mill, as we have seen, does not discuss what will be done with the children if women work or if men are not around, and he does not insist that women *actually exercise* that power of earning. For Mill, women must have options, one of which is to seek gainful employment, but they would still be free even if they let their husbands provide. Beauvoir goes further than Mill in a parallel statement: "Only independent work of her own can assure woman's genuine independence."[46] In her insistence that women work for a living, Beauvoir sees the need to eradicate the sexual division of labor because, shorn of a meaningful horizon of marital unity, it is mired in immanence.

It is not a cheap shot to repeat that Beauvoir's ideal for how the relations between men and women should be structured is found in the *promise* of the Soviet Revolution. Her statement is worth relating at length:

> A world where men and women would be equal is easy to visualize, for that precisely is what the Soviet Revolution *promised*: women raised and trained exactly like men were to work under the same conditions for the same wages. Erotic liberty was to be recognized by custom, but the sexual act was not to be considered a "service" to be paid for; woman was to be

> *obliged* to provide herself with other ways of earning a living; marriage was to be based on a free agreement that the spouses could break at will; maternity was to be voluntary, which meant that contraception and abortion were to be authorized and that, on the other hand, all mothers and their children were to have exactly the same rights, in or out of marriage; pregnancy leaves were to be paid for by the State, which would assume charge of the children, signifying not that they would be *taken away* from their parents, but that they would not be *abandoned* to them.[47]

Maternity, for Beauvoir, must be a voluntary action, or "a rationally integral part of [a woman's] life."[48] Abortion and contraception ensure the separation of sex from reproduction that is so important to a woman's freedom and equality; few press the freedom to terminate pregnancy as far as Beauvoir does. The end of the stigma against non-marital births promotes sexual and reproductive freedom as well. The woman would still seem to need a man to become pregnant, and this tends to make her dependent on him; however, the availability of artificial insemination may portend independence from any man.[49] This is one of the final frontiers in the effort to divorce sex and reproduction. Such a separation is part of Beauvoir's effort to make maternity as voluntary as possible. Women should be able to avoid pregnancy when they have sex (for this, contraception and abortion), and they should be able to become pregnant without being dependent on a man (for this, artificial insemination and, perhaps, genetic engineering).

Economic considerations must also not impinge on a woman's decision to have a baby. This can be accomplished by state policies. First, mandatory paid pregnancy leave from their jobs ensures that women remain independent, well supported, productive, and free throughout their maternity.[50] Paid leave fosters the integration of maternity into a chosen life plan while making sure that women do not lose out at work as a result of making that choice. Second, the state obliges women to work for their own freedom and independence. Third, the state would assume the charge of the child after the mother returns to work.[51] This is a win-win solution for the mother and the child. Mothers win because they are freed up to pursue their own projects and to struggle and cultivate "the richest individual life" possible. Children win because an independent and self-sufficient woman "will have the most to give her children and will demand the least from them. She who acquires in effort and struggle a sense of true human values will be best to bring them up properly."[52] Beauvoir has little to say about how to reconcile the fact that children are charges of the state with the fact that mothers are still bringing children up, and she has little to say about what would go on in the state-run day cares. Perhaps women contribute most to their children's upbringing by leaving them to state experts, thereby freeing children from their motherly oversight. An independent woman is needed to raise an independent child, but the independent woman will not be around overmuch. Independent career women are not as frustrated by the conflict between transcendence and immanence that defines their traditional sisters. No longer frustrated by consignment to the home, they will not take their frustrations out on their kids.[53] This benefits children by making them stronger and more independent and more able to follow their own projects.[54] The new mother spends much less time and energy on her children, for the sake of the children.[55]

Beauvoir makes a remarkable concession in this context. "There is one feminine function that it is actually almost impossible to perform in complete liberty. It is maternity." Despite the availability of contraception and the advances in family leave and day care, "having a child is enough to paralyze a woman's activity entirely," and it forces her to take on "burdens hardly compatible with a career."[56] Beauvoir's reference to pregnancy and motherhood suggests an ambiguous understanding of nature. At the outset the book, she answers the question "what is a woman?" with "woman is a womb." It is difficult to blame patriarchy for this fact, and the fact that men do not have wombs suggests that this is a natural source of sexual difference that may be masked or mitigated by technology, but that cannot be erased.[57] Is there room for this understanding of nature in Beauvoir's analysis? Elsewhere she adopts an attitude suggesting that "nature" is a ruse invented by men to idealize and perpetuate their rule. This reading of nature suggests that patriarchy or sexual difference is remediable, if we would stop thinking of woman as the other. Is there an eternal feminine attachment to a child that will always make choosing one's own projects difficult and burdensome? Can Beauvoir account for traces of immanence in the mother-child relationship? Are there limits to the human power of redefinition? Beauvoir does not pursue these thoughts, but, as we shall see, this intractable element of immanence points to some hard truths about the human condition.

The Demands and Limits of Socialism

Beauvoir follows Marx and Engels in many of her recommendations and in her mode of analysis. She sees the family as part of a syndrome of oppression for women, though she does not think that Engels' analogy between the proletariat class and women holds. She favors abolishing norms that favor sexual exclusivity and hopes that widespread availability of contraception and abortion can assist in promoting freer sex love. Promiscuous women can avoid dependence on any particular man. She wants to introduce women to the world of work and choice and to abolish the sexual division of labor. She would relieve women of the burdens of child-rearing and, if possible, child-bearing, and, in principle at least, turn children into charges of the state.[58] She also suggests that fundamental changes in how the economy is organized are necessary to free women even when they are laborers. "Only in a socialist world would woman" attain liberty by working.[59] By "a socialist world," Beauvoir means the end of exploitation of workers connected with private ownership of the means of production and the abolition of classes and class conflict. Truly free or socialist work is separate from motives that "forced" people to work under the capitalist system (the desire for profit or glory or the need to earn money for food and shelter). Free labor is chosen because one has a desire and an ability to labor in a particular way. Engels was also concerned to turn private domestic industry or housework "more and more into a public industry," though it is not clear that Beauvoir sees this in Engels. Beauvoir does not see the effort to abolish housekeeping as part of the normal socialist agenda, and she sees this as a failure in the Marxist mode of analysis.

For Beauvoir, the question is not whether socialism is desirable or whether it is a live human possibility—it is both. She asks whether establishing socialism *does enough* to foster women's liberation. Marxist analysis is correct in identifying the ultimate historical character of human being, but it does not properly identify history's moving forces. Marx and Engels thought changes in the mode of production moved history. Beauvoir holds that the abolition of classes is a necessary, but *insufficient*, condition for the emancipation of women.[60] Marx and Engels, it seems, ignored challenges posed by the differences between women and the proletariat in assuming that the abolition of private property would suffice to bring about the abolition of the private family. The private family has an economic expression but is based on deeper values and meanings.

> A truly socialist ethics, concerned to uphold justice without suppressing liberty and to impose duties upon individuals without abolishing individuality, will find most embarrassing the problems posed by the condition of woman. . . . For a democratic socialism in which classes are abolished but not individuals, the question of individual destiny would keep all its importance—and hence sexual differentiation would keep all its importance. The sexual relation that joins woman to man is not the same as that which he bears to her; and the bond that unites her to the child is *sui generis*, unique. She was not created by the bronze tool alone; and the machine alone will not abolish her. To claim for her every right, every

> chance to be an all-around human being does not mean that we should be blind to her peculiar situation. And in order to comprehend that situation we must look beyond the historical materialism that perceives in man and woman no more than economic units.

Beauvoir demands the establishment of socialism while recognizing that socialism is not radical enough; her Marxist stew needs a pinch of existentialist choice. Why is socialism too timid? We are left with the same puzzle we saw in the previous subsection on working motherhood. Perhaps the tools of socialism are simply not suitable for eradicating the cultural problems posed by women's situation under patriarchy and other tools are needed to emancipate women.[61] Abolishing private property or promoting life-enhancing technologies alone will not cure the maladies caused by woman's biology, but a revolution in values might do the trick. In this case, technology and economic changes must be "integrated into the totality of human experience" through a revolution in how we value those changes.[62] A sisterly vanguard might create a new horizon to liberate women—one that interprets their biology in such a way as to lead to their emancipation.

A second possibility lingers. Perhaps the way women have a unique bond with their children or the differences between men and women are immutable features of the human situation.[63] This suggests that the immanent reality of our bodies remains even after a revolution in values and that Beauvoir would not be denying the importance of sex differences in the psychological makeup of men and women; perhaps something (nature?) puts fuzzy limits on our "indefinitely open future." Beauvoir encourages readers to think that men and women may overcome the deficiencies of socialism in the field of values so that all are encouraged to eradicate conventional sex differences. The transcendent field of values, however, may not be as flexible or "indefinitely open" as she hopes, and we may once again reach the mortifying limits to transcendence.

The New "Marriage"

Beauvoir's ambiguity on the relationship between transcendence and immanence pervades her treatment of love and marriage. Like Mill, Beauvoir thinks men and women need complete freedom to enter and exit marriage, yet she goes further than Mill in criticizing the institution of marriage. Women must learn what men have, apparently, long known: those who seek meaning in marriage and family life are destined to dull, frustrated lives. As a consequence, marriage is truly chosen by neither men nor women. Traditional marriages are "not generally founded upon love" and do "not assure [the individual's] personal happiness," but rather aim "to make the economic and sexual union of man and woman serve the interests of society." Marriage enslaves men and women to the demands of society. Marriages founded on convenience are unlikely to produce genuine love. Mundane concerns lead to mundane relationships that never reach the lofty heights of transcendence. It is equally absurd to expect that two people could satisfy each other sexually throughout their lives, especially those who share so many mundane interests.[64] Nor can marriages based on the idea of providing a legal framework for reproduction provide happiness, for they imagine women as breeders of children and men as hucksters pursuing a business transaction. Marriage as a legal and moral arrangement is overrated. Dating an artist sounds more intriguing than being married to a woman who folds the laundry or a man who mows the lawn. Relationships should be more fluid; individuals in relationships should be more autonomous and less needy and dependent.

Female equality and freedom mean that women should not look to men for financial support or help in raising the kids or to provide patterns for their development. What else are men good for? Let us work backwards from Beauvoir's picture of the ideal relationship to see what, if anything, will continue to unite men and women.

> The ideal . . . would be for entirely self-sufficient human beings to form unions one with another only in accordance with the untrammeled dictates of their mutual love. . . . This balanced couple is not a utopian fancy: such couples do exist, sometimes even within the frame of marriage, most often outside it. Some mates are united by a strong sexual love that leaves them free in their friendships and in their work; others are held together by a friendship that does not preclude sexual liberty; more rare are those who are at once lovers and friends but do not seek in each other their sole reasons for living.[65]

First notice that "unions" are made up of two "entirely self-sufficient human beings." Self-sufficient people form fundamental projects without relying on another person; they find life's meaning outside their relationship with another person. What holds these couples together if not the most important thing? Some are in it for the sex, and they find their friendships and meaningful work outside the sexual relationship. Others are held together by a friendship, perhaps one developed around a shared project, but they do not insist that the friendship develop into a sexually exclusive relationship. The highest, or at least most rare, relation hits the daily double, including both an exclusive sexual relationship and friendship, but this highest relation is not all-encompassing. Friendship between mates grows around a shared ideal or project; in the project, mates find meaning. A man and a woman, for example, work together in a resistance movement to expel a foreign occupier and have a sexual affair while they engage in that project. Their life would be defined by this project; sex is almost beside the point for such comrades. Erotic attachments tend to die "in an atmosphere of esteem and friendship, for two human beings associated in their transcendence, out into the world and through their common projects, no longer need carnal union; and because the union has lost its meaning they even find it repugnant."[66]

Beauvoir recognizes that sex involves "hav[ing] to put up with" the limit to human power that is "one's body."[67] Men recognize that they do not have rational control over their genitals, nor do women. Sexual relations seem to signify our incompleteness, our neediness, and the limits of our power; it is difficult to imagine transcendent or truly free sexual relations. "The fact is that physical love can be treated neither as an end in itself nor as a mere means to an end; it cannot serve as a justification of existence; but neither can it be justified extraneously. That is, it should play in any human life an episodic and independent role. Which is to say that above all it must be free."[68] Few people see sex as an "end in itself," let alone as a "justification of existence." More prominent is the view that sex is a means to reproduction, to getting a man to stick around, to satisfying animal pleasures, or to building and signifying a loving relation. Beauvoir rejects these views: sex plays an "independent role" when it is separated from other goods. Perhaps this is why free sex occurs episodically. It is unconnected to other endeavors, following only the human will when and where it leads. The challenges posed by sex are even deeper when we recall the image of the passive woman and a woman's horror at being impaled. Sex has long been a weapon used to keep women in the posture of defeat, a symbol of male dominance and immanence.

The problem of male dominance is more easily solved than the challenge of sexual immanence. Sex can be made more consistent with woman's equality once women overcome their passivity and establish reciprocity with their partners. For this to occur, men and women must first establish conditions of equality in "concrete matters."[69] The demands of reciprocity are more difficult to satisfy. Men have sought dominion in sex; complicit in their subordination, women have sought to establish a bond of togetherness through sex instead of establishing a reciprocal relationship.[70] Can sex ever be reciprocal on Beauvoir's principles? Few insist that sex leads to the objectification of women as "the other" more stridently than does Beauvoir.

Sexual desire makes one vulnerable to conquest by another, to dependence on another, to being overtaken by erotic passions, and to one's partner not respecting one's freedom and dignity.

An older solution to this theoretical problem was to see *eros* as a movement toward another person indicating one's need for another's love. *Eros* seems to be an immature expression of this deeper spiritual bond, and it is *one way* people come to feel a need for that deeper love. This deeper love is the joining of two people into a common mission, of which family life often is a central preoccupation. Beauvoir caricatures and ridicules the idea of marital unity. She sees the couple not aspiring for unity or a deeper spiritual love, but rather as becoming "for one another the *Same*" and hence not needing to exchange a gift of love to one another. She sees sex not as an impossible-to-satisfy longing for love between two subjects, but as a shameful act of "joint masturbation."[71] The tenor of Beauvoir's argument or redefinition is that the old idea of two becoming one makes the idea of love as a gift-love impossible: we do not give gifts to ourselves, after all.

Beauvoir thinks her principles yield better results, which demand that she explain love while maintaining throughout the reality of otherness. The estrangement of one human being from another cannot be overcome, but that does not mean that relations between two human beings must be hostile. "The relation of the *other* still exists; but the fact is that the alterity has no longer a hostile implication, and indeed this sense of the union of really separate bodies is what gives its emotional character to the sexual act." Lovers enjoy pleasure in common, which means that each feels pleasure in his or her own body while realizing that another aids in giving the pleasure. Each feels a boundary of separateness and seeks unsuccessfully to overcome that boundary. Ultimately, for Beauvoir, erotic charm is built on "a mutual generosity of body and soul."[72] Its generosity seems to lie in the fact that each receives an unexpected pleasure bestowed by another. A partner comes to realize that a lover views the flesh as given by the other. In giving myself as a gift to another, I can know myself as a free subject able to give myself to another. My ability to give such a gift to another means that I have constructed a project for myself and found a way to integrate sex into it. One certainly need not construct a project in this way; nothing in nature suggests that it is integral to a good life.

"In the midst of the carnal fever," Beauvoir writes, lovers "live out in their several fashions the strange ambiguity of existence made body." Each sex participates in "the same drama of flesh and the spirit, of finitude and transcendence."[73] Each being is carnal and passive, but longs for freedom from carnality and transcendent action; each is an object of desire, and longs for subjectivity and sovereignty; and each longs for satisfaction, but soon becomes sated. "In a genuinely moral erotic relation there is . . . a moving struggle to regain liberty in the midst of sexuality but this is possible only when the other is recognized as an individual, in love or in desire,"[74] and recognition is ambiguous and dramatic even then. Truly free sex appears as a mystery revealing the *true* human mystery of a desired but unfulfilled love.

Sex and love pose problems on a number of levels. As we have seen, patriarchy distorts sexual relations by promoting male dominance and female passivity. Women are humiliated by penetration and they become frigid and impervious to sexual pleasure as they assume the posture of defeat; men seek a dominance that always eludes them and this leaves them unsatisfied.[75] Beauvoir argues for economic and cultural reform so that the problem of patriarchy, when it comes to sex and love, can be resolved (or at least mitigated).[76] Promoting equality in other spheres of life and divorcing sex from human concerns such as marriage, reproduction, and economic well-being encourages women to see sex as empowering. This problem of patriarchy masks the more intractable ambiguity regarding transcendence and immanence, freedom and sexuality, body and soul, and otherness and unity (of some sort). "Every human existence involves transcendence and immanence at the same time,"[77] and nowhere is this dualistic contradiction more evident than in sexual relations. Love is a free outward movement toward the other, but our un-free, passive bodies ensnarl love's overtures. Transcendent human beings seek to lose themselves in their projects; immanent human beings are stuck with their unchosen bodies. Despite Beauvoir's anti-immanence, this problem seems to be an inescapable, permanent, and revealing feature of human life.

Beauvoir claims that human existence involves transcendence and immanence, yet she is embarrassed by the persistence of the immanent. "Every time transcendence falls back into immanence, stagnation, there is a degradation of existence into the '*en soi*'—the brutish life of subjection to given conditions—and of liberty into constraint and contingence." Immanence as such seems to be an "absolute evil." Human beings "wish that . . . transcendence may prevail over immanence." The "true problem for women is to reject . . . flights from reality and seek self-fulfillment in transcendence."[78] Beauvoir may want us to redefine what is regarded as immanent and this would imply that she does not necessarily have contempt for the body.[79] The immanent is part of human life, human life is linked to the body, and there are limits to how much human beings can reinterpret their immanence. Beauvoir rejects the idea of human essence, but seems to show that there is a human essence or a fundamental human situation. Beauvoir aspires to complete self-sufficiency, but shows that it is impossible. Her critique of motherhood, marriage, and love is based on the principled difference between transcendence and immanence, but she shows that human life mixes these two elements. Whither, then, her critique of motherhood, marriage, and love?

This leads to Beauvoir's most controversial claim on the meaning of love and sex. Beauvoir solves the problem of patriarchy by promoting the idea that it is necessary for human beings to be "entirely self-sufficient" if they are to enjoy pure love. Complete self-sufficiency, earnestly pursued, obscures us from our ambiguous situation, in which we can never achieve self-sufficiency despite our aspirations and in which our dependence on our unchosen bodies and on our partner's are inescapable facts. The problem of patriarchy is solved by making sure women do not see themselves as "the other." The contradiction of love shows that we are always, in a sense, "the other" to others, and the effort to solve the problem of patriarchy obscures this fact. These observations lead to the fundamental question: does feminism erase love?

Love and the Limits of Feminism

This issue concerns many feminist thinkers, and it is necessary to survey some prominent feminist thinkers in trying to figure out what implications feminism has for love and marriage. Love is a mystery, and it is a trap. Do we rid ourselves of the mystery when we try to spring from the trap? Beauvoir oversells the capacity to transcend immanence in her effort to rid women of patriarchy, and in so doing she provides a framework that distorts our view of ourselves. Her efforts complicate the quest for self-knowledge by breeding contempt for our inevitable human immanence. Anatomy may not be destiny, but it is something. Efforts to define existence cannot so easily leave essence behind, even at the definitional stage.

Beauvoir's effort to cultivate self-sufficiency calls into question our need for love. Independence cannot be reconciled with love, which implies dependence on another and a lack in oneself. Beauvoir is committed to human independence, which suggests that a human being has no need for another. The part of Beauvoir aimed at dismantling patriarchy repels her commitment to transcendence. Transcendence in general implies that one is *dis*satisfied with oneself and that one wants something more. Insofar as feminism advocates for independence, it is hostile to the claims of motherhood, fatherhood, and marriage, since all of these imply the presence of love and dependence. Insofar as feminists advocate transcendence, they run up against the limits of nature and demonstrate our incompleteness or lack of self-sufficiency as individuals. Beauvoir's attempt to solve the problem of patriarchy and the problem of sex as such by the same means reveals a tension fundamental to the human situation. The presence of the desire for transcendence shows our longing for completion and perfection and our inability to achieve either; it shows both our greatness and our humiliation as creatures.

The arc of this problem is also seen in Okin's *Justice, Gender and the Family*, a more liberal iteration of Beauvoir's existentialist vision. Okin puts forward a vision of a future in which gender would be as important a fact to human beings as eye color or toe length. The crucial move in Okin's argument is that women are vulnerable on three different levels, and their vulnerabilities reinforce the social construction of traditional sex differences. First, women are vulnerable by anticipation, which means that they choose roles and life plans for which society deems them suitable. Evidence for this is that women choose nurturing professions and have lower educational expectations and career aspirations than men.[80] Second, women are vulnerable within marriage because men have the economic earning power to dictate what happens in the family. Social pressure reinforces this vicious cycle. Men earn more than women because of sexism, so it pays to have men work; since men earn more, families make a prudent economic decision to keep the wife in the home doing "boring and unpleasant" household chores.[81] Third, women are made vulnerable by separation because they are deprived of earning power, and they do not cultivate their job skills as they are minding the house. This makes them hesitate to leave an unpleasant, abusive, or neglectful husband for fear of the economic consequences.[82]

To relieve these cascading vulnerabilities, Okin recommends policies that encourage the creation of a gender-neutral family and woman's independence from family roles. These policies include the end of employment discrimination on the basis of sex; paid parental leave for mothers and fathers; reduced working hours for parents until their children are in school; requiring large employers to provide quality, on-site day care; government day care for everyone through subsidies; the *practice* of employment discrimination or affirmative action in employment areas that are thoroughly gendered today (quotas for women as school superintendents and for men as kindergarten teachers); educational policies that break down sexual stereotypes; and the provision of quality after-school programs for children so parents can work longer hours.[83] She advocates these programs because they tend to make members of the family more independent of one another by keeping men and women in paid work despite the traditional definition of family obligations.

The promotion of independence fosters justice, in Okin's view. Justice demands true choice, not false socialization or coercion based on vulnerability, to govern the arrangements in the family. True choice cannot be realized unless there is already an equal distribution of paid and unpaid work, leisure, physical security, and economic resources between men and women.[84] With the economic conditions for independence, justice, and true choice come the psychological conditions for independence. Until women *see themselves* as independent they will not be so. Until women see that housework can be evenly divided and that they are not uniquely suited to be mothers, they will not be independent. Until women find their identities outside the family and see themselves as "discrete persons with their own particular aims and hopes" instead of as "members of families" who "care about one another and share common ends," they will not be independent. Until women see that the practice of "self-sacrifice and altruism" in a unified marriage is "better labeled a lack of foresight than nobility," they will not be independent.[85] This emphasis on independence and this critique of "self-sacrifice and altruism" encourage women (and men) to hold something back from marriage and family life in the name of justice and self-protection; the ethic of care—and a life dedicated to motherhood—is dangerous to women. Okin seems to believe "the *highest* of virtues" in marriage and family life are built on justice, their "most *essential*" element.[86]

Much like Mill's idea of marriage, Okin's idea holds that any dependence in the family is built on a foundation of prior, always retrievable independence. This view commits her to ignore the status of children or to assume that the interests of independent mothers and the interests of children coincide.[87] Her "love" risks no dependency. This raises the fundamental issue. Love and marriage are about depending on another for support; Okin and Beauvoir insist that women stop depending on men and rely on themselves (and the state). Why would people participate in a just family life or, to say the same thing, a family life without love? The feminist vision points to the family's end.

Much the same conflict is seen in Betty Friedan's influential *Feminine Mystique*. Drinking at the well of post–World War II psychology, Friedan envisions women leaving the empty nothingness of housewifery behind and developing "a sense of identity, the firm core of self or 'I' without which a human being, man or woman, is not truly alive."[88] Self-actualization makes love possible. Love had been defined, according to the dictates of marital unity, "as a complete merging of egos and a loss of separateness—'togetherness,' a giving up of individuality rather than a strengthening of it." Friedan spends much of her book showing how this idea led women to physical and psychological distress and a fruitless search for meaning through housework or sex or femininity. A woman can break up this feminine mystique by seeking "something more," which is "creative work of her own." Women are not opposed to "lifelong commitments," but those commitments are to their professions.[89] The new and improved love between self-actualized people will not be "motivated by the need to make up for a deficiency in the self; it [is] more purely 'gift' love, a kind of 'spontaneous admiration.'"[90] Self-actualized people are not deficient, yet their cup may run over in providing gift-love for others.

There are reasons to be dubious of an independent love or a love that is consistent with self-sufficiency. Let us look at this thought from the angle of Beauvoir's artistic understanding of transcendence. The old love of feminine immanence and otherness is based on the idea that human beings need each other—especially the idea that women need men and children need parents, but also the idea that men need women; the old love involves dependence. Love arises because a self-sufficient life is not fully satisfying and we hope to find happiness in and with another. Love stays because two people living a common life manage to put the elements of love—sex, their need for one another, their mutual growth, their individual growth—in proper order. Such a love may never be fully satisfying, but its deficiencies point to a more complete and satisfying object of love—to a love that is more genuinely transcendent, perhaps, in some sense. Beauvoir redefines love to make it consistent with independence. Would a rose by another name smell as sweet?

The Philosophical Dilemmas of Beauvoir's Feminism

Beauvoir's framework of immanence and transcendence implies that there are no limits to the feminist project and that the creation of the gender-neutral society is possible; transcendence is possible if we leave the body behind. By pursuing the problems with her framework, we reach the limits of transcendence and therefore the limits of her thinking and perhaps the limits of modern political thought. Many other thinkers, including some of the deepest feminist thinkers, have noticed this problem in Beauvoir, but they have not recognized its ramifications for the feminist account of the family. Many continue to endorse Beauvoir's aspirations while showing the limits of her principles. They continue to believe gender is socially constructed. They continue to view marriage and motherhood and sexual relations with men as traps or sources of oppression and to confine motherhood to the narrower bounds. They insist that housework exists within a horizon of oppression. They are critics of sentimental love. So they drink from the same well, but they do not go as deep. Can Beauvoir's policies and principles be divorced?

I have been pointing to hard truths, strange ambiguities, or fundamental tensions in Beauvoir's thought throughout my discussion with the aim of exposing the limits of her thought. Beauvoir's thought points to these dilemmas, but it cannot on its own terms overcome or resolve them. Any satisfying account of the family in modern political thought must come to grips with these antinomies—I consider it a tribute to Beauvoir's depth of purpose that she brings these aspects to the fore.

Anatomy or Immanence and Destiny or Transcendence

Feminists correct extreme formulations of sex difference put forward by Hegel, Comte, Freud, and, to a lesser extent, Durkheim by pointing out that anatomy is not destiny. Destiny, for Beauvoir, stands in for transcendence, the project or principle we freely choose; anatomy stands in for immanence, the limits to our freely chosen projects. As Beauvoir's analysis shows, human life mixes transcendence and immanence. This has two underappreciated implications for attempts to understand the family. First, anatomy does shape human destiny to an extent, and this means that the differences—anatomical, chemical, psychological—between men and women must have weight in any account of the family. Whether anatomy affects human life so much that it calls into question the prospect of a gender-neutral society is an open question. Second, Beauvoir's own contemptuous evaluation of immanence must be reevaluated in light of how inevitable human immanence is, unless we are willing to contend that feminism is misanthropic. Immanence cannot be a "degradation of existence" or an "absolute evil" if we are to appreciate its role in human life.

Transcendence and Independence

Human independence is not the same as human transcendence. Independence suggests self-sufficiency, while the aspiration for transcendence suggests consciousness of insufficiency. This problem affects our understanding of love. Love and independence are mutually repellent, while love and the aspiration for transcendence can be complementary. Love implies a need for transcendence and, perhaps, our dependence on that for which we aspire. Insofar as feminism emphasizes independence, it undermines love. Insofar as feminism emphasizes transcendence, it is consistent with the idea that love is crucial to human life so long as we appreciate the ways in which our immanent selves contribute to that love.

The Goodness of Independence

Are self-sufficiency or independence, as Beauvoir understands them, good for human beings? Modern thinkers such as Locke, Rousseau, Hegel, and Mill emphasize independence or individuality as central to the experience of human happiness; independence appears, in some sense, as a condition for achieving human happiness. Beauvoir goes further than previous thinkers in equating independence with human fulfillment. More poignantly than any of the modern thinkers covered in this study, Beauvoir forces us to confront the question of what independence is good for. She spills little ink on this question, other than to contend that independence is used for projects of one's own making. She puts forward a belief in human transcendence that it is void of a concern about what is transcendent. So her thinking cries out for a concern about the nature of transcendence and the place of human independence.

The Conquest of Nature

Feminism is a manifestation of the modern attempt to conquer nature. Feminists demand the conquest of sex differences even if those sex differences are natural. As Okin writes when arguing for erasing sex differences, "Our laws do not allow kleptomaniacs to shoplift, or those with a predilection for rape to rape."[91] Nature inclines us in directions that our laws do not allow us to go, and human law and custom must go against the grain of pernicious expressions of nature. Okin's thought ends in this moral position about the conquest of nature, and it is our object in the subsequent chapters to understand this morality with all its complications and limits. Feminists smuggle, perhaps, a teaching about what is of transcendent importance and that is the liberation from natural restraints and the capacity to build a gender-neutral future.

Responses to Beauvoir's feminism come from those emphasizing the importance of anatomy and those emphasizing the importance of destiny. It is to these sociologists and philosophical-Catholic thinkers, respectively, that I turn in the next chapters.

Part IV

The Old Family and a New Nature

Chapter 10

Positivism Supplemented
Anatomy, Evolution, and the Family

Naturam expellas furca, tamen usque recurret.
—Horace

What an opportunity family decline has been for sociologists! Few social trends are as well documented as those surrounding the decline of the modern family. Compared with a century ago, non-marital births are up, divorce rates are up, fertility rates are down, cohabitation has risen as marriage rates have declined, adults marry later in life and have children later, abortion rates are up, families are smaller and more fluid, people spend less of their lives in a stable family, the number of single-parent families is up, the percentage of children who have their family life disrupted by divorce or desertion is up, and polls across the industrialized world suggest that people find less personal satisfaction from family life than they once did and that people are less defined by their places within the family than they were earlier in modernity.

These findings concern social scientists because of the negative social effects that accompany family decline. David Popenoe, one of today's eminent family sociologists, sees this pattern. The first chapter of his *Life without Father* (1996) catalogues the "remarkable decline of fatherhood and marriage" and the second describes the "human carnage of fatherlessness."

Popenoe and other marriage movement scholars show that children are more likely to have emotional and behavioral problems,[1] to need professional help from psychologists, to have health problems, to have poor academic performance, to drop out of school, to divorce when they marry, to have less satisfying interpersonal relationships, to commit crimes, to spend time in jail, to be abused, and to live in poverty when they are not raised by two married, biological parents. Many are upset about the connections established between family decline and "human carnage." The great accomplishment of the marriage movement social science is to establish such connections beyond reasonable doubt.[2]

Why have marriage and the family declined so? Social scientists answer with sociological theory derived from Durkheim's assumptions. Family form is the product of culture. Culture changes, so the institutions that defined culture yesterday (hereditary monarchy, strong centralized church, and a guild-based economy, for instance) are not today's cultural institutions. Today's culture is more taken with ideas of individual freedom and female equality than yesterday's. The subtitle of James Q. Wilson's *The Marriage Problem: How Our Culture Has Weakened Families* tells the story of family decline. From the perspective of positivist social science, human nature provides little direction in how culture shapes family life; nature poses problems for the family and provides the almost useless materials through which culture shapes the purposes of marriage. The fact of cultural diversity suggests that there is nearly infinite variety of family forms, and there is little in human nature to limit the power of culture to shape these institutions. Cultures give us scripts, and we are versatile actors playing our parts on the stage. If there is something wrong with family life, there is something wrong with the script from which today's individuals read; any restoration of family life requires a rewrite of that script.[3]

Taking a long view and with the aid of anthropological research, the general findings of social science positivism are as follows. (1) Marriage is a social institution whose primary purpose is the procreation and education of children. (2) Marriage is the most successful institution in which to raise children. (3) Marriage has mostly divided the labor up between men, who are inclined to be public faces and providers for the family, and women, who are more inclined to be homemakers and caregivers.

Must marriage always be these things, however? Might not another institution—the state, for instance, in some form—take care of children? Are two parents *really* essential to the education of children?[4] Why is there a relationship between natural fathering and the actual job of educating and supporting children? Is the sexual division of labor necessary to procreate and to educate and care for children? Might a more informal cohabitation arrangement suffice to raise children? Might stepfamilies or adopted families be as successful, in the aggregate, as a family with two biological parents? Must sexual exclusivity be a part of married life and family life? There may be *no necessity* behind the two biological parent institution and other institutions may arise to achieve the old goals. If culture changes, the family changes too, if the assumptions of social science positivism are correct. Perhaps family decline, as marriage movement social scientists define it, presages a better future for children. Perhaps, as Mill suggests, social disorder caused by the revolution in family life will be a temporary blip. If social roles are scripts, new scriptwriters may arise to make today's assumptions consistent with social order, women's equality, and human happiness. Perhaps, as Beauvoir suggests, an artistic redefinition of human happiness as transcendence will convince people to lower the family and rise up some new, feminist ideal that can remake the moral world.

These objections to social science positivism *as a means of guiding our thinking about the family* are grounded in assumptions about expanding the vistas of human control. Many of the modern thinkers hold that nature *can* be conquered, and their view culminates in the triumph of culture as that which gives meaning to life. Culture or, to say the same thing, History bends human beings to the demands of their time. The principles of modern social science do not permit social scientists to say anything against the deep and hostile questions from the previous paragraph, but Popenoe, among others, articulates a philosophic objection to his own social science in order to show that the family has an irreducible core of meaning. Seeking a way to defend the family against cultural trends hostile to it, Popenoe and others seek to show that the family is natural. Against their feminist critics, they hope to show that the obligations of family life go with the grain of human nature so that people can once again respect and appreciate the family in modern times.

From Durkheim to Darwin: The Place of Nature in Family Sociology

Popenoe understands the challenges to positive social science as it tries to guide social action. He begins his deepest account of the place of family in the modern order by raising a series of questions similar to those raised above.

> Could it be that the era of fatherhood is at an end, that the fatherhood problem can be resolved by simply getting rid of fathers and perhaps

> substituting someone or something else in their stead? . . . Have we become so free and individualized and prosperous that the traditional social structures surrounding family life no longer have the importance that they have had in all of human history to date?[5]

Popenoe admits that fatherhood is not as necessary as it once was, given provisions of the welfare state, various technological changes, and the entry of women into the job market. He also writes, with the next stroke of his pen, that such argument against the traditional family is "fundamentally wrong."[6] How can he be so sure that changes that have rocked the family since the onset of modernity will not and *should not* proceed apace?

Popenoe's account of family decline begins with a normal sociological trajectory. He identifies a variable that signifies family decline: fatherlessness (children growing up apart from their biological fathers). Nearly 40 percent of American children do not live with their biological fathers, and that number has been climbing.[7] Two "proximate reasons" for the surge in fatherlessness are divorce and out-of-wedlock births, and a "single phenomenon underlies them both: a decline in the institution of marriage."[8] As marriage trends down, alternatives to marriage trend up; fewer children are born, and more children live without fathers. Marriage has declined for economic reasons (the ability of women to earn their own money and the declining significance of a husband's salary), technological reasons (advances easing the burden of housekeeping and better health provision for women and children), and for reasons of government policy (such as the rise in welfare provisions), but "the main underlying cause of the decline of marriage and fatherhood" is "the cultural shift toward self-fulfillment."[9] Economic and policy changes derive from this cultural shift, the *true* and *efficient* cause of family decline.

The problem is culture. Culture is "the values and beliefs that give coherence and meaning to life—our shared ideas about what is good and bad, right and wrong, desirable and undesirable, and the basic assumptions about reality we take for granted." American culture, and Western culture generally, used to value sacrificial love, duty, commitment to others, communal goals, and the needs of vulnerable children. Abetted by today's affluence, there is an increasingly prominent strain in American culture that embraces (in Popenoe's words) a "radical, expressive, or unencumbered individualism" bent on "self-aggrandizement at the expense of the group" and on achieving "personal goals, self-expression, sexual freedom, and even impulsiveness."[10] Feminism as Beauvoir articulates it is an expression of this cultural shift. One could peel the onion of efficient causality one more layer. Popenoe's chapters sometimes conclude with elliptical codas about the decline of a religious belief that used to support a culture of sacrificial love and restrained the culture of individual spontaneity.[11] Decline in religion leads to decline in a loving, sacrificial culture that religion sustained; this contributes to a decline in committed marriages.[12] There is a tragic twist in Popenoe's account in which a religious culture of love and self-sacrifice has given way to an apparently beneficial, somewhat deleterious secular spirit of individualism. Popenoe seems to embrace religious decline but worries about its effects. What emerges from the process is the new cultural script of expressive individualism, written by no one and everyone.

Much like Hegel, who worried about the imperialism of subjective liberty, Popenoe and marriage movement scholars think that this new, more radical spirit of individualism causes the decline of family life. They also think that marriage and family life are worth preserving as *indispensable* means to securing socially important goals. Popenoe is caught between two competing claims. On the one hand, he endorses the central tenets of sociology (and of Beauvoir's feminism), namely the malleability of human nature and the immense power of culture to define human institutions. Family form is shaped by the strength of religious belief, government policies, and economic forces, which themselves are determined by cultural attitudes of individualism. Nothing is permanent in the world of culture; alternative institutions displace outmoded ones, and the family appears to be one such outmoded institution. On the other hand, Popenoe thinks there are limits to the shaping power of culture. The limits are these: children are better off living with and being raised by their biological parents, and marriage is a nearly universal cultural institution designed to sanction sexual congress between men and women and to attach men and women together and to their common offspring.[13] Marriage's importance derives from the fact that it is linked to the well-being of children, whose long period of maturation means that they cannot be treated as adults. Culture cannot define away or creatively reinterpret these facts.

Other marriage movement sociologists rest content promoting traditional family scripts against modern and postmodern alternatives.[14] Popenoe *resolves* this tension between the power of culture and its limits in accord with the dictates of modern natural science, but outside traditional sociology.

> Even though family life today is heavily shaped by a massive layer of culture, the predispositions of our biological makeup are ever present. It is almost certainly the case that families are more than just arbitrary social constructs that can be redesigned at will; they are partly rooted in biology,

> especially because they intimately concern what is most basic to life—the reproduction of the species.[15]

In an important sense, Popenoe departs from feminist, Millian, Hegelian, and sociological tenets in turning to man's biological makeup and especially to the importance of natural sex differences. Mill seemed to think, and modern feminists (as I define them) think, that sex differences are products of cultural forces that can be changed by transforming the modern regime. Sociology as practiced by Durkheim emphasizes the decisive role played by culture, though he defends social goods served by a "traditional" culture more than Mill or feminists. Even Hegel embraces the idea that most human attributes are acquired historically, though like the early sociologists he (somewhat inconsistently, perhaps) tempers emphasis on History with a dose of nature. All of these principles suggest that family life can be organized however a culture decides it should be organized.

Against the overwhelming direction of such intellectual opinion and almost against his professional training, Popenoe asserts the persistence of nature.[16] He returns to the idea that human nature has roots in human biology, an idea widely accepted before the twentieth century.[17] Popenoe arrives at the nature of nature through studies showing the historically constant attributes of family life, traits of men and women, and needs of maturing children. Nature does not have a particular destiny or direction; it does not point to a *telos* or invite us to wonder about the *meaning* of the historically constant. On a deeper level, Popenoe unites with his sociological colleagues, seeing human beings as fundamentally caused and viewing the family as an instrument for social purposes. Popenoe's revised model includes a relatively stable human nature in addition to culture as a force determining human life.

Nature's Character and Its Implications for Marriage

Nature provides marriage and family life with a core; culture determines what surrounds that core and how strong the core is. The core of nature poses challenges for the family; it also limits how cultural institutions take the family into account. We have returned to the complex idea, found in Locke, of nature's givens. Nature presents the following conundrums. For women, childbirth is arduous and somewhat debilitating, and mothers seem to be suited to care for young children much more than men. Children are unable to take care of themselves for many years (and the greater the demands of society, the more time they need to prepare themselves for independence). Men, who are less attached to the family by nature, value sex more than women do; men are stronger and less interested in caring for children than women are; and men want to be certain that they are fathers of their own children.[18] Following the pioneering work of Edward Westermarck, marriage movement sociologists show how Marxist and feminist scholars have exaggerated the supposed diversity of social institutions to deal with these conundrums for the ideological purpose of weakening the natural family.[19] These natural facts *constrain* cultures to follow rules and patterns in the organization of family and marriage. Universal patterns exist around what is prohibited or discouraged (e.g., incest, adultery) and what exists (e.g., marriage in some form, acknowledgment of paternity, the sexual division of labor).

Let us take one of nature's givens and see how it affects marriage and family life in practice. "Our underlying biological nature dictates that every society faces the problem of how to keep men in the reproductive pair-bond."[20] The male resistance to settling down in marriage and family life is rooted in male biology. Like Rousseau, Popenoe contends that men and women have different sexual strategies because they have, at bottom, different genitals.[21] All people strive to perpetuate their genes through reproduction and to boost their numbers of surviving offspring, but men have countless sperm and women have a finite number of eggs and fewer child-bearing years. Men can spread their genes more widely by siring children with many women; women will spread their genes just as effectively by sleeping with one man or by sleeping around like men. Because their pregnancies are debilitating and they must spend effort and time nurturing their children, women try to capture help from men for the task of childrearing or to transform men from "cads" to "dads."[22] For this transformation, society or culture is needed. Motherhood almost flows from the hand of nature, while fatherhood is, more or less, a product of culture. Women can capture male energy and protection for their children by establishing a permanent sexual relationship with the man (marriage) by appealing to man's strong sexual desire. Men invest themselves because they gain sexual access to their wives and because they are confident in the paternity of their children.[23] Biology may point men away from family life more than it points them toward it, but men still have "a biological predisposition to assist with child-rearing" and "to a certain extent" to live in monogamous relationships, and this predisposition must be fostered by culture.[24]

Men and women contribute differently to child-rearing, and these differences relate to their unique psychological and emotional constitutions. Cross-cultural studies find that men are more aggressive than women, more abstract in their thinking, and less empathetic in personal relationships.

Supporting Hegel's view about sex differences and child-rearing, studies show that the actions of men emphasize competition, risk-taking, independence, discipline, challenges, and the development of self-control, and it is more difficult to interest men in providing the warm, sympathetic caretaking necessary for infants and very young children.[25] Women are better suited to these tasks. Children need both of these parts, and Popenoe argues that people should not expect a gender-neutral society to arise because nature gets in the way. Ultimately society should expect children to need their mothers at an early age and to need their fathers as well as their mothers after the age of three. Almost every society on record, from today's most "advanced" to the most primitive, follows this pattern of dividing the labor along sexual lines.[26]

A detailed cataloguing of Popenoe's evidence for these propositions need not detain us. Popenoe relates this evidence to advance what he takes to be a healthy mixture of culture and nature in our thinking about family life. He wants both men and women to experience the benefits of modern culture (e.g., career opportunities for women, more egalitarian and companionate marriages) and the fulfillment that comes from labor in an atmosphere of equality without creating an environment harmful to children and to families with children. The desires to labor and to reason are natural human traits, though they conflict with other natural traits. Modern marriage seems based, as Mill, in part, promised, on companionship, romantic love, and sexual attraction. Companionship emphasizes the similarity and compatibility between husband and wife. Romantic love seems to emphasize that men and women are different and complementary. Marriage is not based on a consistent application of social androgyny or gender neutrality. Neither companionship nor romance necessarily prompts us to think about the kids. To those taken with modern marriage, Popenoe, in effect, pleads: if men and women must be complementary to experience romantic love, perhaps they can also be complementary in the rearing of children and in the social ecology of child-rearing. He hopes to resurrect a "modified traditional family," in which people may marry later, have fewer children, and perhaps even live together before marriage, and in which women will pursue careers before and after they nurture their children, but which would still be "child-centered." This family requires couples to share household labors more, but wives would probably have child care responsibilities for the first years of each child's life. Popenoe is a moderate feminist, in that he believes women should have more opportunities for careers than they were afforded by the traditional man-as-breadwinner/woman-as-homemaker model. Changes in culture have made housekeeping a less onerous task.

It is still important and valuable, especially as it relates to childrearing. A mother is indispensable for early childhood development, and wives and husbands may have to split the chores differently than they did in the past to accommodate each other.

This arrangement may prove too "traditional" for today's feminists, if not most modern people. Popenoe insists, however, that data teach us to recognize the intractability of nature: "Rather than strive for androgyny and become continuously frustrated and unsettled by our lack of achievement of it, we would do much better to more readily acknowledge, accommodate, and appreciate the very different needs, sexual interests, values, and goals of each sex."[27] Note, again, that nature is not beautiful or purposive or connected to higher human ends or a cause for wonder or normative in an ultimate sense: it *is*. The cross-cultural data reveal that nature and cultures that ignore nature will have an unfulfilled and unhappy populace.

This argument is incomplete, for it assumes the intractability of natural sex differences and hence of nature as such. Why are natural givens considered given? Above all, as they appeal to universal patterns, Popenoe and his allies have not yet shown that the marriage bargain encapsulated by the traditional family must long endure. He depends on an argument about the endurance of the natural givens he identifies; since his sociological principles make such an argument difficult to sustain, he turns elsewhere.

Nature's Evolutionary Basis

Popenoe and others turn to biology to find the solid findings on which a dependable version of nature can be built. In this, they repeat the pattern seen in Comte. Against modern feminism, Popenoe embraces a variation on the theme that anatomy *is* destiny, up to a point (or perhaps that anatomy is not insignificant); he turns to beginnings to find what is intractable in the human condition, basing his treatment on Darwinian evolution. Popenoe approves the dictum: "Nothing in biology makes sense except in light of evolution."[28] Evolutionary processes point to the elements of our nature that cannot be changed without overhauling our hard wiring or through a dramatic reignition of the evolutionary process.

Human beings and their environment form a system that determines the concept of human nature, but both human beings and the environment are moving targets; they evolve as they interact with one another. The study of how biological and environmental conditions interact forms the heart of the nature that sociobiologists study. Human nature is an equilibrium between our organically unstable, genetic development and the changing conditions of our social, moral, and physical environment.

Chance variation (accomplished through mutation) changes the organism, while natural selection is the principle from the environment that changes an organism. Chance variation reveals the reproductive process, perhaps the most stable mechanism in nature and one of the strongest evidences of natural species or essence, as *the* instrument whereby a species changes. Natural selection, the testing mechanism that ensures that the strongest survive, "decides" which adaptations survive and which die. This world of flux would not seem a promising place to find stability to ground morality, but the interaction of these mechanisms produces a relatively stable picture of human nature.[29]

One such adaptive mechanism is the natural desire to have and raise children. This engrained desire serves our natural biological interests. "If we accept Darwin's theory of evolution by natural selection, which favors those functional adaptations that promoted survival and reproduction in evolutionary history," Larry Arnhart writes, "it would seem likely . . . that the desire to care for children is a natural adaptation for human beings."[30] No one consciously has children to pass on genes or for the sake of the species' survival: parents have a natural desire "rooted in hormonal and neural systems" to do so. So strong is this natural desire that suppressing it may create "an emotional cost that will be unendurable for most people."[31] The natural desire to give parental care manifests itself differently in males and females, just as the biological interest in reproducing differs. These natural differences ground the sexual double standard, the different reproductive strategies adopted by men and women, and the sexual division of labor—all objects of bitter complaint from feminist critics of the modern nuclear family. Let us explore these concepts to grasp the underlying commitments in this move to biology.

Males and females adopt different reproductive strategies and have different natural desires because they have different interests in reproductive fitness. To repeat, human beings, like all creatures, seek to perpetuate their genes, and females invest more in each child than males do. Men need only sire children, while women carry and nurse them. To father a child is easier and less time-consuming than to mother a child. Men can also sire many more children than women can have, which gives men a reproductive interest and inclination to sexual promiscuity. Women can parent fewer offspring than men, and the high investment cost of each child means that women must be devoted to each child.[32] If a child is a shared interest bringing men and women together, they are committed to the child, and to each other, for different reasons and in different ways.[33] In fact, the marriage bargain struck by men and women involves not a little chicanery:

> Males and females are constantly playing games with each other, males seeking to maximize the number of their sexual partners and females seeking the fittest male who can provide for them and their offspring. The male has strong incentives to pretend that he will provide resources and loyalty when he has no intention of doing so, while the female has a strong incentive to detect this deception. The female . . . has a strong incentive to make sure her children are fathered by a male with the best possible genes, regardless of whether he is the one actually providing for her economically, while the male has a strong incentive to avoid being cuckolded and wasting his resources raising someone else's offspring.[34]

We have moved from complementary sexes to the battle of the sexes. Natural desires point men toward promiscuity and women toward secure, status-seeking men. Men want young and attractive maidens with child-bearing hips and promising nursing abilities; women want strong, successful, perhaps older men. These different natural desires and needs have led to the almost universally acknowledged sexual double standard. Women put up with some male infidelity in exchange for support and security, but men will not raise the children of other men: men need guarantees. Natural desires do not point to a stable family form and fidelity.[35] Nature presents *problems* more than it provides a basis for solving them.

Marriage appears to be more a temporary alliance or a convergence of interests between a man and a woman than a permanent union dedicated to a genuine common good. To put this another way, the natural desires of men lead to a weak commitment to marriage and the family, while women think of men as security blankets for themselves and for their children. Men use women for sex; women use men for security. This mutual use is what evolutionary theorists might call "love." Darwinian theorists perceive this problem, and they think the problem of weak male commitment and divergent interests is solved by culture or education. Consider the following. Francis Fukuyama sees the male role in the family as "fragile and subject to disruption"; the "extent to which males will stay in monogamous pair-bonds and play an active role in the nurturance of children will depend less on instinct than on the kinds of social norms, sanctions, and pressures that are brought to bear on them by the larger community."[36] James Q. Wilson thinks "nature has played a cruel trick on humankind" by making "males essential for reproduction but next to useless for nurturance" and by making such nurturance essential for children to "grow up in an orderly and safe environment."[37] Even Arnhart, who tries to show the sufficiency of nature more than other Darwinian theorists, realizes that marriage is a "social" bond in addition to being a natural one because nature itself does not limit male promiscuity.[38] Darwinian scientists suggest that men can be brought to limit their sexual passions out of a heightened sense of their own desires and happiness. There is no call to a higher duty or to a human good. The problems of nature are solved by appeals to individual self-interest rightly understood, insofar as cultural institutions support that appeal.

Sexual difference is another persisting element of differential reproduction. Men and women have different physical endowments, including, but not limited to, their different roles in reproduction. There are also well-established differences in their neural and endocrine systems.[39] By looking at today's men and women in light of our closest relatives in the animal kingdom, we can make inferences about how evolutionary processes "selected" the sexes we see today. Let us take two important groups of adaptation. At some point in the human past, women differentiated themselves from apes in the manner of their ovulation, and both men and women became different in how they had sex. In the beginning, human women could reproduce and attract males only seasonally, when they were in heat. This meant that males would have less of a reason to stick around to help with their offspring because they could not constantly have sex. With the disappearance of estrus and the evolutionary adaptation of menstruation, men and women could have sex anytime, and men were inclined to hang around to see if they might get lucky. In the beginning, vaginal canals tilted backwards and human beings copulated in the manner of dogs. Such copulation does not prove as preoccupying, personal, or intimate as face-to-face sex. Apes also have much smaller penises than men. Evolution favored forward-tilting vaginal canals so that human beings could have face-to-face and hence more personal and intimate sexual experiences. It also favored larger male penises (at least when compared to the apes), which adds to sexual intensity, pleasure, and coupling. These evolutionary adaptations contributed to making men more interested in loving a woman and hence in raising a child with her,[40] and helped meld individual interests to the long-term interests of the species.

Women have different chemical constitutions than men, and their differences relate to childrearing. Women have increased levels of oxytocin and prolactin during pregnancy and while breastfeeding. These hormones act as natural opiates, helping women get more in touch with and attached to their children; children receive these hormones through breastmilk and become in turn more attached to their mothers. Men, on the other hand, have androgens that block the effects of hormones associated with nurturing; men have high levels of testosterone and reduced serotonin activity in the frontal cortex of the brain, leading them to be more aggressive and risk-taking than women. These chemical expressions of sexual difference derive from the environment of evolutionary adaption when human beings were distinguished from the beasts. Infants would not have survived without constant attention from their mothers, so mothers with high levels of oxytocin and prolactin had children that survived; women were attracted to the men best able to protect and provide for them in an era of scarcity and danger, so abler and tougher men reproduced.[41] Evolutionary biology shows that physical and chemical expressions constitute nature's givens and that these expressions render nature's givens, for practical purposes, inescapable.

These givens supplement positivism by pointing to natural desires and attributes that shape and underlie cultural traditions and institutions. Traditions that do violence to these natural desires and attributes contravene human nature; traditions that deal well with them are consistent with human nature. Good family life takes account of the different ways the sexes provide care for children, the different approaches men and women take to sexual experiences, and the long-term needs of children. To put this differently, human beings are endowed with a powerful natural desire to parent, and this desire to parent "is a fundamental norm of Darwinian natural right,"[42] though this desire is not as active in men as it is in women. Similarly, sexual coupling and the sexual division of labor represent deep-seated, long-engrained natural desires that satisfy our biological interest in reproduction and constitute a norm in a common human pattern.

Efforts to change these elements of family life radically are bound to fail. Those interested in supplementing the findings of social science positivism with a dose of sociobiology often cite the experience of the failed Israeli kibbutz movement, a modern effort to conquer the natural desires around which the family arises.[43] The kibbutz movement sought to break down traditional gender roles and familial forms through a form of communism. Founders of the kibbutz insisted that children be placed in houses apart from their parents (especially their mothers) and raised by experts who were not blood relations. Kitchens, laundries, and other household tasks were held in common; members provided according to their abilities what each needed. Men and women were supposed to share the work evenly, and children were to be raised in a gender-neutral way. Today, kibbutz institutions involving the family are moving in the way that sociobiologists would expect. "Granddaughters of women who 75 years ago insisted on being released from domestic chores are now the leading force within the kibbutz for more parental involvement in the upbringing of young children and for allocating women more time at home with their families."[44] Why this change? Women insisted on it, and children were suffering without it, and the change was passed over the mild objections of the kibbutz's men. Since the change, the women spend more of their time in spontaneous interaction with their children than their husbands do. Popenoe may see the Swedish family as facing a similar crisis arising from its willingness to have children brought up by government-sponsored day care and its commitment to imposing a strict gender equality. Perhaps, as David Blankenhorn seems to argue, the movement to accept same-sex marriage as equivalent to heterosexual, monogamous marriage puts modern countries in a similar crisis, for such a movement decouples family life from marriage.

The failure of such radical attempts to change the structure of family life reveals the power of nature. Communities dedicated to doing away with supposedly constructed differences between males and females see those differences emerge nonetheless. Parents still want to care for *their* children, and children want special attention from *their* parents. The human carnage of fatherlessness itself suggests that there are natural needs that modern society has tried to suppress or distort, to the detriment of children. This suggests that these aspects of family life are not merely constructed. The same questions arise. How do we differentiate the constraints *really* in nature from those that merely appear to be there? Most decisively, presuming our ability to identify nature, what should our underlying attitude toward nature be? Should we respect or conquer it?

The Traditional Family and Spontaneous Order

Thinkers who emphasize the formative power of culture still want to show that some elements of family life are unchangeable. The *natural* element of the family is the unchangeable element; natural constraints limit the cultural institution. For both Hegel and Comte, the natural constraints are, in part, the sex differences between men and women. As we saw in chapter 5, Comte's evidence for the persistence of sex differences came from the science of phrenology. Sociobiology occupies the same place among some of today's marriage movement advocates that phrenology did in Comte's social philosophy. This is not meant as a cheap shot. Today's science appears to have more sophisticated modes of identifying chemical, neurological, anatomical, and psychological differences between the sexes than did yesterday's crude measurement of cranium sizes. Today's sociobiology cannot be waved off like phrenology. It provides an account of nature that limits the power of social institutions and allows for an evaluation of those social institutions. These advances in the study of nature explain why marriage movement advocates turn to Charles Darwin.[45]

The emphasis on biological evolution does not suffice to explain how human nature has arrived at its current destination. Cultures evolve too, and cultural evolution reverberates on biological evolution; the street goes both ways. Our biology poses permanent problems to which cultures adapt. When disruptions in culture are great, human beings write different cultural scripts to deal with natural problems and givens, but they need not do so in ways that follow yesterday's patterns. What is crucial, according to this way of thinking, is that the patterns arise *spontaneously*. The neoliberal family is attached to a belief in spontaneous order.

Spontaneous Order

Sociobiology's connection to evolutionary theory raises the philosophic issue about nature's status as a *permanent* limit on the power of culture. Recall Durkheim's dynamic phrenology. In the beginning, according to Durkheim, men and women had similarly sized craniums; as culture demanded more from men, their craniums grew, while women's craniums did not. The disproportionate growth in men's brains proves the formative power of culture and circumstance, though bigger brains also limit what can be expected in a culture at a particular time. Brains do not grow bigger or shrink overnight; however, what has changed could change again. Culture shapes "nature" just as "nature" forces the hand of culture. The stale debate between nature and nurture or (what is the same thing) culture is ill-conceived. The relation between them is dynamic, with nature limiting culture and culture affecting nature.

As long as the order arises from the mutual adjustment of individuals, nature, and culture, the social order that arises is consistent with human freedom. Antithetical to this system is a system of centralized command or constructive rationalism, whereby a vision of nature or culture is imposed on individuals.

Consider how the theory of spontaneous order addresses the question of how long marriage should last. Marriage is a universal pattern for raising children, but different times call for different marriage customs. The most common reasons to end a marriage involve infidelity and infertility, both of which strike at what evolutionary theorists see as the heart of marriage: the procreation and education of children. Other factors shape marriage mores as well. In agrarian societies, wives and husbands are economically codependent, so divorce is rare. In industrialized and urban societies, men and women are or can be more independent of one another, and divorce becomes more common and accepted. Add a generous welfare state to industrialized, urban conditions and divorce will be even more accepted, for economic independence is even more within the reach of women and children. Societies went from condemning divorce to tolerating it to, perhaps, celebrating how it promotes personal growth. Marriage mores adjust to conditions.

Consider also changes in motherhood. Not only the birth control pill, but also great advances in antibiotics, prenatal and obstetric care, and our ability to produce mass amounts of baby formula have reshaped the human habitat so women can more easily leave the home. Indoor plumbing and electronic inventions such as refrigeration have freed women from the need to milk cows, grow food, visit the well, and wash clothes down by the river. Women are now free to pursue some of their own creative projects without necessarily sacrificing the attention due to their families, or they can reorder their lives so that family life is no longer as high a priority as it once was.

The natural human desire for sexual mating and parental care limits the changes: we do not expect a thoroughly random, promiscuous future in which children are raised by the state or in extra-familial settings. We expect those who cheat on a spouse to be more roundly condemned than those who divorce for lesser reasons, because fidelity is closer to the heart of family life. There may continue to be extra excitement around a couple getting married or having a child, even if we no longer condemn someone for "shacking up" with a lover or having a "bastard child." Monogamous relationships will represent a norm because of the power of nature, no matter how weak the cultural support for monogamous marriages may be.

The most famous proponent of spontaneous order theory is Friedrich Hayek. The theory is based on the insight that order emerges from the interaction of individuals pursuing their own designs within the framework of relatively simple rules of action. Order does not emerge from someone who imagines a wonderful or equitable world and then implements this abstract plan in the real world. Nor does order arise from the slow unfolding of a predetermined, providential plan. Order arises from the spontaneous adjustment of people living and acting with one another. The most famous and visible application of spontaneous order theory appears in the free market's pricing system. Briefly, the prices of goods float; supply, demand, cost, and the desire for profit constitute the price, and these factors fluctuate, so prices fluctuate. Prices arise spontaneously, that is, as a bargain between a buyer and a seller and without the intrusion of an outside planner.[46]

For Hayek, what is true of prices is also true of morality and mores. Morality and mores arise spontaneously and signal the needs of dispersed people in their attempt to live their daily lives. Hayek does not go into detail on these matters, but we can work out his reasoning. The feminism of Beauvoir and Okin bespeaks an unnatural and unspontaneous manner. Beauvoir and Okin posit a vision for a gender-neutral future and then use the coercive arm of the state to get human beings to live that vision. Okin's vision that all of society's jobs will be divided between the sexes is an abstract goal, precluding the mutual adjustment of culture and nature in a free-floating relationship. Adherents to the theory of spontaneous order make a formal critique of feminism's goals. Feminists are liberals in a hurry, violating the norms of liberty. Adherents to the theory of evolution and spontaneous order are dedicated to liberty and are willing to wait a while for whatever changes arise spontaneously. They prefer the change of mores brought on by the refrigerator or the antibiotic to the change wrought by the Civil Rights Act or Title IX.

Spontaneous Disorder

Whether spontaneous order can serve as a basis for defending the family is open to serious question, especially in light of events. Spontaneous order is connected to the idea of creative destruction. Spontaneous advances destroy parts of the old order (such as old companies or indissoluble marriage or the discouragement of premarital sex), yet tomorrow *will have some* institutions and morality tending to promote order. According to Hayek, modern civilization arose with the support of a belief in property and the practice of monogamous marriage and bourgeois family life. For a variety of reasons, "traditions" of respect for property and dedication to family have made the dynamic, innovative Great Society of the modern world possible. Rational justifications for property rights are too difficult for people to understand, and even if they could understand, many would be tempted to violate property rights when they can get away with it. The same is true of monogamous marriage. People sense the immediate benefits of giving into sexual temptation if it will not immediately hurt them. Religion supports a respect for property and marriage where the long-term reasons for such respect are beyond the grasp of most. This leads to Hayek's controversial claim that civilized free societies must be "tradition-bound" societies.[47]

> We owe it partly to mystical and religious beliefs, and, I believe, particularly to the main monotheistic ones, that beneficial traditions have been

> preserved and transmitted at least long enough to enable those groups following them to grow, and to have the opportunity to spread by natural and cultural selection. This means that, like it or not, we owe the persistence of certain practices, and the civilisation that resulted from them, in part to support from beliefs which are not true—or verifiable or testable—in the same sense as are scientific statements and which are certainly not the result of rational argumentation. . . . *The only religions that have survived are those which support property and the family.*

Hayek admits that there is a "*historical* connection between religion and the values that have shaped and furthered our civilisation," but he hesitates to suggest that "there is any *intrinsic* connection between religion and such and such values."[48] We may be able to dispense with the religious support for these moral rules.

This distinction between historical and intrinsic causes can be expanded. Perhaps there is no "*intrinsic* connection" between the rise or maintenance of civilization and family values. Perhaps, that is, civilization can survive and adapt to times when respect for family, marriage, and even property might wither. Hayek is open to this possibility. He writes, "I ought however at least to mention that I believe that new factual knowledge has in some measure deprived traditional rules of sexual morality of some of their foundation, and that it seems likely that in this area substantial changes are bound to occur."[49] It is difficult to know what this "new factual knowledge" is. It may relate to the ability of society to adjust to technologies such as the birth control pill or legal changes such as easier access to divorce. Whatever it is, Hayek indicates that free societies may not need to remain bound by the traditions of monogamy or nuclear families. Ideological policies inimical to nuclear family life have arisen in the past decades and may contribute to the "human carnage of fatherlessness." Hayek's "go-slow," spontaneous approach to new mores could lead to the same destination without the carnage. If new mores arose spontaneously, Hayek, in my view, could not object to those new mores or the new moralities that arose.

In any event, the sexual revolution shows that traditional morality as understood by Hayek need not last. Here our guide is Fukuyama, whose *Great Disruption* (1999) applies the theory of spontaneous order to the period following the sexual revolution. Fukuyama takes seriously the biological findings of Darwinian conservatism, and he takes cultural evolution as seriously as he takes biological evolution. Yet marriage movement sociologists have little to cheer in Fukuyama's book. Fukuyama begins by noticing that families are reconstituting because members of society realize once again how important a stable family life is for children: divorce rates, birth rates, and illegitimacy rates, for instance, have leveled off, and there are cultural indicators suggesting that family life is, if not on the rebound, not declining as fast at it did in the time between the 1950s and 1990s. The reconstituted family is no "return to Victorian values"; religious norms regarding sex, reproductive freedom, marriage, and the importance of family life are no longer the key. "No one is about to propose making birth control illegal or reversing the movement of women into the workplace." In the beginning, women were less promiscuous for fear that they would be saddled with an unwanted pregnancy. "Unregulated sex" need no longer lead to pregnancy. Women can now exchange their acquired domesticity and sexual modesty for a freedom once safe for men only. The movement of women into the workplace is part of a more general trend away from the importance of paternity. In the beginning, if a woman had a child out of wedlock, she and her child would both suffer "destitution, if not early death" for lack of a provider and protector. Today, the dangers of life without father are mitigated through a combination of "female incomes and welfare subsidies." Men are almost superfluous now, and they have reacted to this by going less frequently where they are not needed. These two developments suggest that "the importance of kinship as a source of social connectedness will probably continue to decline, and the stability of nuclear families is likely never to recover fully."[50]

Sociobiologists such as Arnhart and others teach that the relationship between mother and child is natural, while fathers are attached to the family weakly, mostly through culture. To secure their children, mothers have been willing to trade sexual access for security, and men, concerned about perpetuating their genes and names, have been thus led to the family. Modern society renders this old marriage bargain obsolete: women do not need men around and men prefer not to be there anyway. Fukuyama ridicules the fashionable nostrum that children thrive in all kinds of families, but there seems to be little gluing the nuclear family together. Consider his most optimistic gloss on the modern nuclear family.

> Norms governing the behavior of men and women with respect to families changed dramatically after the 1960s in ways that ended up hurting the interests of children: men abandoned families, women conceived children out of wedlock, and couples divorced for what were often superficial and self-indulgent reasons. The interests of parents and the interests of their children frequently conflict: time spent taking a son or daughter to sports or school is time spent away from a job, a girlfriend, or leisure activity; living with a less-than-perfect spouse for the sake of the children gets in the way of new opportunities for companionship and sex. But parents will

> also have a strong natural interest in the well-being of their children. If it can be demonstrated to them that their behavior is seriously injuring the life chances of their offspring, they are likely to behave rationally and to want to alter that behavior in ways that help their children.[51]

It is not clear what this means. First, Popenoe and others have shown that parents who prefer their own good to their children's good seriously injure their children. Other social institutions could arise to replace the family in this respect; the times and their generally flexible understanding of evolution lead to the conclusion that other institutions could arise or are already arising. Second, what Fukuyama means by behaving rationally is unclear, since the interests of adults and children frequently conflict. Men used to have a reason to "behave rationally" and rear their children: they wanted sex. Now they can have sex without behaving rationally in that sense. Women used to "behave rationally" and modestly to keep their men around. Now rational behavior leads women to forge an independent life.[52] In any event, Fukuyama's understanding of "nature" is rather a restatement of the fundamental problem. One understanding of nature (the parents' natural interest in their child) seems to point beyond the individual, while the second, more modern understanding points to an independent life.

This is not quite how Fukuyama and the sociobiologists see it. These are not two different understandings of nature, but two ways of registering the same understanding of nature. Men and women are not united in marriage by a common good, manifested in a union and a child, to which each contributes in a unique way. Marriage emerges as a pact for mutual interest whereby men and women use each other to serve their own interests. Human beings are not social animals so much as individuals that are dependent on others to achieve their interests. Men and women are concerned with their own survival and with the survival of the species, though the primary concern of each is for individual survival and happiness. As modern life makes it easier to shunt children aside and pursue one's own interests, it seems implausible that we will be able to "demonstrate" to a parent shirking his duties that his behavior is injuring his children. It seems equally implausible that he will be "likely" to behave differently in the face of global evidence about how such behavior harms children. The ways of registering natural desires are not equal.

The Reemergence of the Dialogue between Union and Contract

Social science positivism needs the supplement provided by evolutionary theory to explain stability. Cultural institutions respond to biological needs, and those needs are relatively unchanging, given human genetics. As Fukuyama shows, the biological data need not point to family life in a traditional or meaningful sense. Human carnage associated with fatherlessness can be a temporary blip on culture's moral progress resulting from a temporary victory of constructive rationalism or ideology. In the dialectic between culture and biology, culture is more powerful and instructive than biology, especially in an age dedicated to the conquest of nature and especially because the data of biology are, in the end, fundamentally ambiguous.

Nature in the modern sense does not allow us to transcend the challenge posed by the cultural commitment to individualism. Why should a man prefer his children to leisure time or his wife to a series of girlfriends? Why should a woman forgo career possibilities and invest time in her children? Why should children express gratitude to their parents? Our genes and our natures point toward independence and dependence, and modern conditions make going in each direction equally possible (if not equally attractive). Social science data show that "married people are happier, healthier, and better off financially,"[53] but appeals to self-interest rightly understood are open to the liberal objection that each individual understands his or her interest best. "Divorce may be harmful in some cases, but not in mine," or so say many who divorce. "Having children out of wedlock is often a problem, but not for my kid," says the mother of a child conceived outside the confines of marriage. The data of social science positivism show the personal and social benefits of strong family life to all, but this self-interest rightly understood moves few to change their behavior in this realm of life.

Sociobiology does not limit the modern understanding of nature. Sociobiology is interesting because it attempts to temper modern individualism by showing that a social nature is hardwired into mankind. Our "social nature" and our morality are discovered by figuring out what a good long-term survival strategy would be and how the good of the individual comports with the good of the species. There is a line from our natural passions to our interests to morality, and the narrow pursuit of our self-interest conflicts with our long-term interests. These are the facts that purport to make us "social" animals, but they really show that we are strategizing and aggressive individualists with subrational motives grounding our rational choices. We need society for the better realization of our individual needs. Sociobiology is more in line with the social contract tradition than with the Aristotelian tradition of man being a political animal.

Let us return to first things. The evolutionary mode, in both its biological and its cultural varieties, shares enemies with Beauvoir's feminist existentialism—both deny the existence of human essence and both think the human condition is a state of flux, though in different ways. Beauvoir's feminism is based on the idea that there is no such thing as natural sex roles or natural purposes in human life; men with social power have constructed gender roles and women have become "the second sex." Beauvoir believes human beings have reached a point where they can take control of their own immanence, their own nature, their own biology; the past's unplanned, oppressive evolution can be brought under the control of transcendent individuals. Evolutionists taken with the idea of spontaneous order emphasize the limits of our ability to design our nature and point out the need to go slow by allowing change to arise naturally. They show that human beings are much more "hardwired" by nature (e.g., toward living in families or as men and women) than feminists thought. This is interesting and important in itself. Evolutionists sometimes go further in adopting a policy of self-denial in light of these hardwired limits. Rapid changes brought about by revolutionary technologies may rock "natural" institutions such as the family, but retrenchment follows. The *status quo ante* is not restored, but a new morality will replace the old and rise to the challenge caused by the intersection of our evolving nature and culture. To use Fukuyama's example, the family is reconstituted after the "great disruption" as a thinner, more unstable, less demanding, more individualistic community than the old family, but it too will represent certain norms and attitudes serving the species' long-term interests (until the next reconstitution).

Sociobiology's counsel of restraint and self-denial is prudent; will people heed it? If E. O. Wilson, the founder of sociobiology, is correct, spontaneous development will be abandoned and progress will be led by a vanguard of change once human beings come to seize their own destiny. Wilson writes near the end of his classic *On Human Nature*:

> The human species can change its own nature. What will it choose? Will it remain the same, teetering on the jerry built foundation of partly obsolete Ice-Age adaptations? Or will it press toward still higher intelligence and creativity, accompanied by a greater—or lesser—capacity or emotional response?

Wilson's answer comes from the very framing of the question. The evolution of the human species is now (or may soon be) a conscious "exercise of will," in which we either deny or assert ourselves.[54] Self-knowledge helps us "distinguish safe from dangerous future courses of action with greater precision" so that we can decide "which of the elements of human nature to cultivate and which to subvert." Once "our descendents . . . learn to change the genes themselves," the hardwired "biological substructure" itself can change.[55] After seeking to conquer nature and showing that nature does not provide aspirations for human life, it is late in the game to welcome nature home and ask modern people to respect her limits or to deny themselves the power to remake her. Absent an account of why nature's limits are good in themselves or meaningful or revealing, it does little good to tell modern people to respect nature's limits. Wilson, the biologist, seems to understand the political implications of sociobiology better than the adherents of sociobiology in the field of political science.

There are deeper problems endemic in the sociobiological perspective. Social science and sociobiology tell an important, integral part of the story of why the effort to construct a gender-neutral society has led to family decline. Family decline marks the revenge of the body against feminist attempts to show that anatomy is not destiny. Sociobiology follows the scientific method and tends to see human behavior and norms as adaptations or as fundamentally *caused* things rather than as *chosen* things. The problem is not so much with social science's reductive method; it is rather with its expunging of explanation and freedom from the human experience. Against this scientific perspective, the feminists' emphasis on transcendence seems to do greater justice to human nature than the sociobiologists' emphasis on biology, even if feminism itself goes too far from the body. Beauvoir's injunction in *The Second Sex* after she has presented the "data of biology" reflects more than a little truth: "It is not upon physiology that values can be based."[56] Sociobiology shows biology's intractability, while Beauvoir insists that we cannot escape the question of what our attitude to biology and nature should be. We need an "ontology of biology," or an account of what our attitude toward biology should be, that sociobiology does not, in itself, provide.

If the sociobiological perspective provides its own ontology, it is one tending to destabilize or deinstitutionalize the family. Sociobiology and feminism provide a one-two punch in knocking out the idea that we can find meaning behind the biology of human beings. Beauvoir's feminism adheres to the idea we can interpret human biology in any different number of ways. Sociobiologists point to the instability that exists in nature and to the possibility that we may be able to construct a new biology after the truth of sociobiology is revealed. Neither culture nor nature is stable, which leads to the conclusion that all is flux in human life and that there are not natural givens. The end of modern political thought reveals the end of the family. How can we find meaning amidst this flux, or can we perceive the meaning of the flux itself?

Human beings nevertheless resist the conclusions of sociobiology because they sense that to belong to a family cannot be reduced to the biological fact of procreation. Biology alone doesn't make the family. Sociobiology shies away from seeing family life in light of ultimate values because it reduces the goods associated with family life to the status of a means to achieve complex and important biological ends. Human beings marry, have children, form communities, divorce, and so on to secure the manifest goods of human action. These human goods are not reducible to drives or instincts or genetic tendencies. These goods have status independent of the biological goods they secure; they are phenomena, not epiphenomena. Feminism presumes people are too free; a limiting sociobiology presumes people are too biologically determined or too free (depending on which strain of it is emphasized). Each opposes a disposition toward nature that seeks meaning from the limits endemic to the human condition because each opposes the idea of permanent limits.

Philosophy articulates the common goods associated with family life and how these goods relate to the limits seen in human biology. We see a role for philosophy in sociobiology's understanding of marriage and family life. Marriage arises, according to sociobiology, from the different sexes pursuing the reproductive strategies derived from their different natures. The good that men and women share is, from the standpoint of the species, reproductive fitness. This good does not require a permanent union or even marital fidelity. In fact, as the trends that I mentioned at the beginning of this chapter suggest, the common good of reproductive fitness hardly requires much of a mutual commitment between a man and a woman. Sociobiology conceives of marriage as a temporary meeting of the minds instead of as a durable union. We must ask the following questions. Are the goods of marriage reducible to biological goods? Are there, as Hegel and others held, *independent* moral goods connected with seeing the family as the home of ethical love? Does sociobiology provide a genuine account of morality in its model of self-interest rightly understood?

In an important sense, Darwinian sociobiology occupies the same theoretical place that religion used to occupy. Darwinian sociobiology attempts to regulate and evaluate family life from outside cultural practice, and it reflects the hope that what is outside of practice is stable enough to provide a perch from which to evaluate practice. The natural, "unchangeable" limits of cultural evolution, while not as constant as Almighty God, seem durable and constant enough to allow for judgments about the family today. Darwinists and adherents to the theory of spontaneous order often have seen religious belief as reinforcing sensible moral codes and teaching believers to act in a way that benefits the group.[57] This is not, of course, to say that religion is the same kind of a limit as sociobiology. Jesus Christ is the same yesterday, today, and forever, but our evolved nature is not the same today as it was yesterday, and we do not know what it will be tomorrow; we cannot talk about forever when discussing our nature, as sociobiology understands it.

Sociobiology seems a fitting place to seek stability in our skeptical age. Modern thinking seems destined to ride this seesaw of culture and nature, of human power and its limits. This is its destiny, in part, because both positions are reasonable and are furnished by evidence. Nature poses limits, and those limits are often transgressed; we cannot say for sure where those limits lie, though we are pretty sure that they lie somewhere. The modern way of viewing marriage and the family is problematic as well because modern people often implicitly adopt a technological way of looking at the family, seeing it as a tool to achieve other goods. Few seem willing to see it as reflecting independent, moral goods. Most modern thinkers (with the partial exception of Hegel) think love greases the wheels of reproduction. Most modern thinkers seem to think that there would be little need to regulate the family (in law or opinion) were children not involved; the state is concerned about love and marital unity only insofar as it is concerned about children. This is why sociobiology and the theory of spontaneous order seem to foster liberty: the place and depth of familial commitment can float with the needs of the times.

The findings of sociobiology and social science positivism provide ample ground for wonder. Human beings live on many different levels, and we are mixtures of many different and contradictory elements: our genetic codes are similar to the animals, but we are unique creatures; we stand over and control the natural world, but we are part of the natural world as well; we are a mixture of dependence and independence; and we have a rich inner life and a complex outer life. Efforts to come to grips with our proper attitude toward our biology must assimilate these findings. Figuring out our special place in the cosmos depends on our ability to reconcile or at least explain these antinomies.

The modern thinkers that attenuate the unity of the family denigrate love because love is dangerous and because it is difficult to grasp what love is. Love is, or can be, the common good of marriage and family life. Love is, or can be, an end of marriage and family life. If love is an end of human endeavor, it is a mysterious one. Seeing love as a means to reproduction clarifies things; seeing reproduction as a means to love is difficult to follow. Modern thinkers are, almost without exception, united in seeing marriage and family life as means to socially useful ends. If they are means, it is difficult to demonstrate that they are, in certain forms, *indispensable* means for the ends they serve; the idea of family is the history of shedding the connections between the family and the goods to which it seemed connected. Modern defenders of the family (e.g., Locke, Durkheim, Popenoe) offer ever-thinner versions of the family because the family appears to be indispensable for fewer and fewer goods.

The claims of love and Christianity seem to stand or fall together. Marriage's move from sacrament to contract is a move from love to reproduction and from mysterious unity to individualism. So deep has modern thinking penetrated our minds that we cannot quite explain what love is. It is time for a new look at these old questions: what is love, and what does it have to do with marriage?

Chapter 11

A Second Sailing?

Recovering Marital Unity and the Purposes of the Family

Beauvoir's feminism poses the most serious challenge to the existence of family life. It is no coincidence that the concerns about family decline articulated by social scientists are increasing in post-Beauvoir, later modernity. Yet the social science positivists whose hearts are with the family do not aspire to defend the family as such and do not paint a different picture of nature or immanence than Beauvoir. Popenoe and the sociobiologists try to show that nature's givens are inescapable and that we must build social institutions after recognizing this fact. They think feminism puts ideology before sound science. They do not argue that nature is good or connected to the human good; nature *is*, and it demands that we realistically adapt to it.

Feminists hold a trump card against this argument when they, in effect, ask, "Who is being realistic here?" The argument melding social science positivism and evolutionary biology is vulnerable to the claim that we cannot really distinguish the natural from the artificial. Since our understanding of nature is dynamic, the institutions we forge to deal with nature are dynamic. Conceptions of nature have changed in large part because human beings have taken upon themselves the task of conquering nature or transforming the meaning of nature's givens. Seeking permanence in nature's givens leaves us with insoluble controversies. We see flux in nature and history, both of which appear to be canvasses for human power to forge meaning amidst flux. We keep repeating the critique that Rousseau made of Locke's understanding of natural givens. That move—that historical developments erase a static understanding of nature—is repeated throughout modern political thought on the family. Mill tried to show that what Hegel and Comte thought were natural sex differences were, in part at least, due to social circumstances and hence subject to change. Beauvoir tried to show that the natural meaning Rousseau and Freud imputed to the sex organs was, in fact, a story that could be revised by a different scriptwriter. Beauvoir and Engels thought Mill's culture of choice did not suffice to erase immanence or natural sex differences. Modern political thought has been a battle over the character and the meaning of nature, and it culminates with feminism's characterization of nature as immanence. This attitude toward nature is not *necessarily* present at the creation of modern political thought, but the criticisms of early modern thinkers by later modern thinkers seem to lead to this conclusion. The embrace of human power, seen in the earlier thinkers, seems to lead inexorably to these conclusions as well.

Defenders of the family have data but insufficient philosophical depth to defend their ideas of permanence in human affairs; opponents of the family have philosophical depth but are plagued with philosophical problems, not the least of which is that their teaching leads to the family's end and sees human life as devoid of any intrinsic meaning. The crisis in family life is connected to the crisis in modern political thought.

Is there a way out? A "way out" must be consistent with modern principles and the human situation, insofar as these are consistent with one another. Few understand the connection between modern principles and the human situation more deeply than Karol Wojtyla, later Pope John Paul II (henceforth John Paul), whose understanding of the crisis in modern political thought is central to his articulation of Catholic faith in modernity. John Paul articulates the principles of marriage and family life in an effort to instruct people of the dangers to marriage and family life afoot in the modern world. Practical errors affecting the family are related to deep philosophic errors about the meaning of being human. Modern people do not understand what a human being is because they have forgotten how to find meaning. John Paul responds to this crisis by showing people how to think about what human being means and then by showing what this means for love, sex, family, and marriage.

I approach his teaching on the modern crisis of love and the family mostly through his *Love and Responsibility* (1960). Perhaps we would not read this book of pastoral advice if Wojtyla had not been made pope in 1978. There is another possibility: perhaps Wojtyla would not have become pope if he had not written this book. This thought was put forward by John Paul himself when the book was reissued in 1980. Upon his ascension, he delivered a series of weekly meditations on love and marriage, released under the title *Man and Woman He Created Them: A Theology of the Body* (1979–1984), and he also released the apostolic exhortation *Familiaris Consortio* (1981), a *Letter to Families* (1994), and other works. I reference these works when it is necessary.

John Paul's thinking on these matters is part of his effort to explicate the church's teaching in Vatican II and to meld the traditional positions of the Church with an emphasis on what is called personalism. I aim to present his understanding of the modern crisis, to show how that crisis affects family life, and to show how he draws on our experience of the human situation, among other things, to remedy this crisis. John Paul was trained as a philosopher, and his treatment of these issues arises from his understanding of how Christian faith provides a response to the crisis in modern thinking. It may be helpful for some to think of this chapter as an explication of a Christian script on the family or as a portrait of what a universe of meaning that *could* inform our observations of the world looks like. John Paul's understanding of love, marriage, and the family does not seem to come from revealed truth alone. In any event, it is not helpful to think of reason and revelation in an either/or manner. His position on the deep and interesting question of how reason and revelation relate to one another emerges through this discussion.

Love, Sex, and the Human Person

The crisis in modern thinking spawns confusion, anxiety, and trouble for family life.[1] Like marriage movement scholars, John Paul peppers his writings with indications that we have reached a crisis.

> In the conditions of modern life we find that the family in its traditional form—the large family relying on the father as the breadwinner, and sustained internally by the mother, the heart of the family—has reached a state of crisis. The fact that married women must or at any rate are able to take up regular employment seems to be the main symptom of the crisis, but it is . . . not an isolated symptom.[2]

If married women must seek work, it is a sign that the modern economy no longer makes room for family life (by paying a "family wage") as it did in the past. If women choose to seek work, it may be a sign that men and women no longer value family life as they once did. Either way, it seems that the family, the particular, intense order of love in most lives, is losing its privileged spot in the human heart. His later diagnoses contain much familiar to those worried about family decline combined with several unique aspects of the Catholic tradition. Signs of family degradation include the growing number of divorces, the acceptance of free love and non-marital cohabitation as equivalents to marriage, a decline in respect for motherhood, the erosion of parental authority, recourse to sterilization, widespread popular acceptance of contraception, portrayals of women in the mass media as sex objects, and a widespread acceptance of abortion.[3]

Causing these ills, John Paul sees a civilization of technology embodying individualist and utilitarian attitudes toward nature obscuring a civilization of love. Modern thinkers put forward a dualistic understanding of man, in which man is a body separated from a soul, leading to a focus on each apart from the other. This problem is nearly as old as the faith itself.

> The human family is facing the challenge of a new Manichaeism, in which body and spirit are put in radical opposition; the body does not receive life from the spirit, and the spirit does not give life to the body. Man thus ceases to be a person and a subject. Regardless of all intentions, and declarations to the contrary, he becomes merely an object. This neo-Manichaean culture has led . . . to human sexuality being regarded as an area for manipulation and exploitation rather than as the basis of . . . primordial wonder.[4]

John Paul's critique elicits agreement from non-Catholic thinkers such as Hans Jonas, Leon Kass, and Martin Heidegger.[5] Nature and natural facts can be overcome by exertions of human will. Direction for our use of objects comes from outside of nature, from the consciousness of freedom or transcendence that allows us to put objects in the service of our chosen projects. Other animals may run like machines, but human beings possess this special something that allows them to carve their own path. Conceiving of nature as object or "standing reserve" (to use Heidegger's phrase) is connected to a mind-body dualism; consciousness is the ghost in the machine that makes the machine what it wills. Human beings sense their power, consciousness, and essential humanity by laboring in a hostile world. The conception of nature as object or standing reserve, the modern scientific method, and the promotion of technology stand together.

> The development of contemporary civilization is linked to a scientific and technological progress which is often achieved in a one-sided way, and thus appears purely positivistic. Positivism . . . results in agnosticism

> [about deeper meaning] in theory and utilitarianism in practice and in ethics. In our own day . . . *utilitarianism* is a civilization of production and of use, a civilization of "things" not of "persons," a civilization in which persons are used in the same way as things are used.[6]

By positivism, John Paul means the promotion of technology without reflection on how it affects human life and the attempt to divorce action from moral context. Positivism, or social science shorn of its historical foundation, appears to be the culmination of modern science in that it imputes to nature only the meaning created by human beings. As a result, human beings are ever more powerful to make nature bring forth and are also more alienated from a world in which they cannot find themselves.

Emblematic of this problem is the concept of "biological order." From the view of the biological order, the sexual urge (about which more below) is a "sum of functions" directed toward reproduction.

> If man is the master of nature, should he not mould those functions—if necessary artificially, with the help of appropriate techniques—in whatever way he considers expedient and agreeable? The "biological order," as a product of human intellect which abstracts its elements from a larger reality, has man for its immediate author. The claim to autonomy in one's ethical views is a short jump from this.[7]

Most, if not all, of the thinkers we have canvassed up until this point prioritize the spirit over the body in a "conscious utilitarianism" that John Paul diagnoses as modern dualism.[8] This is manifest in modern defenses of the birth control pill. No longer fearing pregnancy, the natural consequence of sex, people fit pregnancies (or the lack thereof) into their plans and can be responsible for their reproductive behavior. Birth control puts the choices of human beings in control by ensuring that each child is consciously willed or chosen by its mother (and, perhaps, father). We have reproductive systems like the animals, but, unlike the animals, we can control those systems; therefore, the elements of humanity that confer moral standing and set human beings apart from the animal world seem to be reason, will, and the consciousness of freedom. The body is immanent, or the dimension that functions on behalf of the conscious self, or left over stuff of nature that we are stuck with. Integrating our bodies into our chosen life plans, we bring our body alive and make it human.

This is modernity's incomplete conception of human being. John Paul's treatment of human being appears at the onset of *Love and Responsibility* (1960) and in his *The Acting Person* (1969), a philosophical account of the person.[9] His starting point is the person because we must know what loves and what has sex if we are to build a nonutilitarian approach to sex and love.

From the Individual to the Person

Modernity suffers a "crisis of truth," which is also a "crisis of concepts." Words such as love, freedom, gift, and person have ceased to convey their essential meanings, and these are central concepts for understanding marriage and family life. "Only if the truth about freedom and the communion of persons in marriage and in the family can regain its splendour, will the building of the civilization of love truly begin."[10]

John Paul begins his articulation of the civilization of love by establishing foundations for the human person. All human beings, all of nature, all that exists in bodily form are objects. A gulf exists between the "world of persons" and the "world of things" or objects. Persons possess the "ability to reason," a potentially rich "inner life" or spiritual life, and a special kind of striving.[11] The dynamic composite of object and person or subject arises from reflection on human experience. Sometimes we appear to ourselves as immanent, or mere objects—we are acted upon by others or by nature, and we have bodies. Other times we sense our ability to make decisions, to act on them, and to affect the world by our plans. John Paul's sense of human personality and subjectivity pits him against social science positivism, Marxist materialism, and Freudian analysis, all of which see human beings primarily as objects acted upon by forces beyond their own making. Appealing to experience in opposing these inhuman doctrines, he forms an alliance with modern existentialism in defending human freedom (or subjectivity).

That alliance with existentialism is only temporary for two reasons. First, our aspiration to be free is more than, or not even, a desire for autonomy and self-sufficiency. Human beings choose to act, and they realize genuine freedom when they choose the good and true. Human beings desire transcendence; transcendent knowledge and goodness are objects of our freedom. More specifically, our inner life exists on vectors of reason and desire: our reason demands that we seek the cause of all that exists, while our aspiring character leads us to ask what it means to possess goodness. Man's inner life is, in a sense, a continuation of his outer, animal life. The fact that we desire food and drink for our bodies is connected to the fact that we desire knowledge or goodness or love. We desire and aspire. The fact that we calculate how to achieve the objects of our desire enables us to raise questions about whether those objects really satisfy us. John Paul's treatment of love traces human beings from the earliest awakening of animal-like desires to their more profound inner expressions. The high does not stand without the low, to borrow from C. S. Lewis.

Human beings relate to one another as objects and subjects, or as self-determining beings capable of choosing ends. When we relate to one another merely as bodies, we treat each other as objects. When we relate to one another on an intellectual or spiritual plane through speech or by sharing a common good, we treat each other as subjects. The fact that human beings are objects and subjects poses a difficulty for our ability to understand human sex. Sex involves the body intensely, so we are tempted to understand sex as part of the world of objects and to view human sex as akin to animal sex: a woman is the object of man's sexual passions and a man the object of a woman's, and the purpose of sex is the propagation of the species. Beauvoir, as we have seen, thought human beings remained objects for one another and this made sex an intrinsically immanent, alienating activity, to her mind.

Beauvoir's emphasis on subjectivity or transcendence betrays the opposite problem in its obscuring of human immanence. It forgets the body, or it fails to see how the body is integral to the human person. This is the second problem John Paul identifies with existentialism, the effectual truth of man's alienation from nature. It may seem strange that John Paul, whose concern is with the souls of his flock, is the one pointing out the importance of the body. Bodily life is not made for the person, and it is not the home of the person's real identity. *But* it is essential to our identity. Human beings are man and woman, for instance—sexuality is not a trap; it is part of who we are. On this insight that a person is body and soul hinges John Paul's attempt to meld important insights of modern and late modern philosophy (an emphasis on the person and human freedom) with morality and love, the great Christian virtue, and thus to solve the riddles I posed at the completion of the chapter on Beauvoir. His goal is to articulate a sexual and marital ethic consistent with viewing human beings as objects and subjects, as bodies and free beings. Playing a Kantian tune, John Paul's bedrock principle is that subjects should not be exploited as objects, or that "a person must not be *merely* the means to an end for another person."[12] In fact, "anyone who treats a person as the means to an end does violence to the very essence of the other, to what constitutes its natural right."[13] To avoid the temptation to exploit another, the potentially "using relation" must become a loving relation in which the lovers share a common good. A common good "unites the persons involved internally, and so constitutes the essential core around which any love must grow." Loving relationships are built on a "footing of equality," since love grows as a couple commits to the good around which they build unity.[14]

The sexual relationship illustrates this idea.[15] It is tempting to see sex as a relation in which partners use each other to experience pleasure. Sex contains the possibility, as Kant also recognized, that human beings will make themselves into things. This mutual use of genitals for the purpose of pleasure is not suitable for sex between subjects or persons. Kant's solution to the problem is a vision of marriage as two people owning each other without subordination "*in a manner equal to a thing*"; it is an "*equality* of possession."[16] This does not really unite the couple, and it does not stop them from using one another: it makes their using legal and equal and, presumably, non-exploitive. Kant cannot ascend from the world of things because he radically juxtaposes the realms of nature and freedom; sex, existing in the world of things and nature, is divorced from love and freedom. Nature appears as standing reserve or meaningless mechanism, while freedom exists in the absence of nature (in the noumenal world). John Paul, in contrast, takes this physical act of sex as an indicator of what sex really means. Nature points to human longings for the presence of genuine love and common good. Sex is consistent with freedom when each lover serves the lovers' common good. Sex and love, like motherhood and fatherhood, are "rooted in biology, yet at the same time transcend it."[17] In the case of sex, the common goods are procreation, "the ripening of the relationship between two people," and the "legitimate orientation of desire."[18] What distinguishes sex from the realm of objects is the desire for the good and its orientation toward love, two distinctively human traits.

Individualist and dualist thinkers—that is, *modern* thinkers—fail to grasp the logic of personhood, which demands, in Hegel's formulation, that marriage supersede the standpoint of contract by embracing a common good. Modern thinkers see human beings as trapped in their own selves, defining the goods outside of themselves with reference to their own pleasures or interests or society's interests. "The great danger" lies in the fact that starting from modern principles "it is not clear how the cohabitation or association of people of different sexes can be put on a plane of real love, and so freed from the dangers of 'using' a person." The best human relations can aspire to, under modern individualism, is a "harmonization of egoisms," in which partners live in harmony so long as they remain "mutually advantageous" to one another.[19] Thinkers, such as Locke, most concerned to secure this harmonization emphasize a conjugal life serving the ends of procreation and the education of children. Others, like Durkheim and Comte, emphasize how marriage can harmonize egos by taming male sexual passion and by exposing males to feminine virtues. Mill and Beauvoir, more radical than others, question the need to harmonize egos because such a harmonization risks subordinating women or enslaving them to immanence. Even Hegel, whose vision of ethical love mirrors John Paul's, seems to think that ethical love is a somewhat immature moment, overcome in achieving a fully rational, human life.

Previous thinkers saw love as dangerous, unduly partisan, a somewhat immature human passion, conducive to dependence, or inimical to the exercise of rational liberty, and they reject John Paul's priority of love over ego or liberty. John Paul's argument about the priority of unity and love over harmonization and ego depends on his defense of love. Why should human beings treat one another as persons? What is so great about love?

Love and Sex

Modern thinkers have failed to grasp the depth and complexity of what it means to be human. Getting half the person right, they cut it off from its full meaning. Perhaps they have built their idea of what it means to be human from their critique of love and Christianity, the religion of love, for the effect of their critique has been two opposite errors—the equation of love with sex and the romantic equation of love with spiritual companionship. John Paul insists that we understand the meaning and possibilities of personal relationships, which involves connecting sex and spiritual companionship in the person. Envisioning a unified institution, John Paul approaches the phenomenological method I discussed earlier in chapter 4 on Hegel. Phenomenology reflects an attitude of receptive charity toward the institutions of the world, and phenomenologists aspire to grasp what is genuinely true and meaningful about those institutions. Since human beings are part of nature, our minds must possess qualities that allow us to apprehend the world even as the world discloses or reveals itself to us. The phenomenological method "impresses the stamp of experience on works of ethics and nourishes them with the life-knowledge of concrete man by allowing an investigation of moral life from the side of its appearance." *Love and Responsibility* is, in part, a phenomenology of human sexuality. Yet John Paul is a Christian thinker, and, he writes, "the Christian thinker . . . cannot be a Phenomenologist."[20] The loving, receptive, contemplative investigation of the world cannot proceed accurately without objectivity provided by "different epistemological premises, namely, meta-phenomenological and even meta-physical premises."[21] Phenomenology illuminates within a consistent teleology, a developed system of natural law, or a context in which we know the truth about man's condition; it brings truth home. On one level, John Paul follows Hegel: he grounds his account of things in a system that brings meaning to it. On another level, there is a gaping gulf between Hegel's History and John Paul's system of teleology and revealed theology.

The metaphysical context in which John Paul interprets human sexual experience is personalism, a doctrine affirming the dignity of persons made in the image of God. In *Love and Responsibility*, he begins by asking whether the desire for sex is an instinct or an urge. At stake in this question is whether human beings can be responsible in their sex lives and whether they can build a common good of love from sex. As Freud understood, instincts are reflexive, beyond the control of conscious thought. An urge is an orientation given to man's desire that reason *can* control; human beings are responsible for what they do with urges. Consistent with the idea that human beings have an inner life, John Paul sees sexual passion as an urge, "a vector of aspiration, along which [human] existence develops and perfects itself from within."[22] Man and woman seek one another to fulfill this need and have the "physiological structure" to satisfy one another. In contrast to animals, human beings do not find sexual relations at this level satisfying; the physical union points to a deeper reality of two sharing common goods of body and spirit. The complementary sexual structure of man and woman and the sexual urge provide the material out of which deeper human aspirations spring. Here John Paul agrees, in part, with evolutionary biologists in seeing the "proper end of the sexual urge" as "the existence of the species *Homo,* its continuation, and love between persons, between man and woman . . . channeled by that purpose."[23] The sexual urge is neither evil in itself (as in the Manichean-puritanical interpretation of Christianity), for it is the material from which love grows, nor is it only for pleasure (as per Freud). The sexual urge is the first rung in a ladder leading to love, which we can climb so long as we do not stop at the first rung by interpreting sexual urges as uncontrollable instincts and as long as we do not view our actions through an individualist lens.

John Paul's metaphysical, psychological, and ethical analyses of love describe this ladder of love.[24] He identifies the elements of love while pointing to the limits of each element so that a complete picture emerges. Attraction, for example, involves thinking an object of desire is good and committing oneself to that object enough to act on its behalf. But attraction remains in the realm of the subjective, in that it does not ask whether the object of a lover's love is *actually* good and does not necessarily direct a lover to what is worthy in a beloved. With these limits in mind, John Paul concludes that attraction is "*of the essence of love and in some sense is indeed love, although love is not merely attraction.*"[25] The same pattern holds in his analysis of the other elements. Goodwill involves desiring the good of another, but goodwill does not necessarily manifest in action on behalf of that person and does not raise the question of the good. Sympathy is an emotion wherein we feel with another closely and intimately, but sympathy exists on the level of emotions and seems to be something that happens to us instead of being something we do. The creative power of the will plays a role in forming friendships and in uniting two around a common good, but friendship does not unite two in a common good.

We can see what is crucial here by comparing John Paul's likening of marriage and friendship with Mill's attempt to equate the two. For Mill, marital friendship does not supersede the standpoint of contract, for the partners must be apart from the union and free to exit the marriage if it no longer suits their needs as they understand them. This relation is unstable (given the mutability of passions) and subjective. John Paul sees marital friendship as a couple forging a greater integration of two into one served by the mutual surrendering of one free person to another and by their service to a common good. He calls marital friendship betrothed love, the essence of which is "self-giving, the surrender of one's 'I,'"[26] characteristics which Mill, it appears, associated with spousal abuse. Betrothed love, John Paul writes,

> is something different from and more than attraction, desire, or even goodwill. These are all ways by which one person goes out towards another, but none of them can take him as far in his quest for the good of the other as does betrothed love. "To give oneself to another" is something more than merely "desiring what is good" for another—even if as a result of this another "I" becomes as it were my own, as it does in friendship. Betrothed love is something different from and more than all the forms of love so far analysed, both as it affects the individual subject, the person who loves, and as regards the interpersonal union which it creates. When betrothed love enters into this interpersonal relationship something more than friendship results: two people give themselves each to the other.

Approximations of genuine dedication to another's good are seen in devoted teachers, or doctors, or mothers, who give of themselves for the good of others. Betrothed love involves giving oneself to another and experiencing the peace, joy, and trust that follow from a reciprocal gift.[27]

Betrothed love has a bodily expression. To be precise, giving oneself to another includes giving one's body as part of giving one's love. The human body has the facility to express love, and sex is love's natural language. "In the order of love a man can remain true to the person only insofar as he is true to nature. If he does violence to 'nature' he also 'violates' the person by making it an object of enjoyment rather than of love."[28] Children are signs of conjugal unity and betrothed love. These natural aspects of human life do not make human beings less free or transcendent. Freedom is a quality of persons, and persons are body, but not only body. Personhood is natural, which means that not all of nature is without meaning or dignity of its own, or not all is "standing reserve." With this acceptance of nature, and in the rejection of dualism especially, John Paul breaks with modern political thinking while preserving its dedication to freedom.

Marital Unity, Betrothed Love, and Indissoluble Marriage

An indissoluble marriage is home of betrothed love. John Paul is not the first modern thinker to see indissoluble marriage as essential to marital unity (Comte took marital unity beyond the grave). It is revealing to explore modern thinkers who limit access to divorce because they swim somewhat against the tide of individual autonomy, emphasizing responsibility in their defense of freedom. These modern thinkers see divorce as a problem either for society or for the individuals in the marriage, but they think about divorce apart from the idea of marital unity. Locke sought to limit divorce so that marriage could serve its chief ends of procreation and the education of children; once children were gone, there was no need for the marriage to continue. Divorce in Locke's case is limited by a need to adapt to the fact that children have a long period of nonage when they need parental support and guidance. Durkheim allows divorce and demands that a third party testify to a marriage's true estrangement before a divorce is granted. He limits access to divorce because otherwise the marital institution would no longer regulate male sexual passion, and men, especially, would be subject to a debilitating anomie. Divorce, though an individual desires it, is unhealthy for society and contradicts self-interest rightly understood.[29]

John Paul sees indissoluble marriage as "one of the cornerstones of all society" because it is essential for the personalistic norm and betrothed love.[30] His treatment of indissoluble marriage tracks Hegel's thought and then goes beyond it to better fulfill Hegel's aim of protecting ethical love from the dangers of caprice.[31] Marriages supersede the standpoint of contract and the perspective of mutual use by basing the union on "ethical love" (Hegel) and on an integrated, reciprocal love (John Paul). Love begins on a "subjective or psychological" level and aspires to be a "love in its full objective sense." Like Hegel, John Paul worries that moderns are tempted to understand marriage in the first subjective sense, so he aims to defend love in a second, ethical sense.[32] There is a difference between Hegel and John Paul on divorce, however. Hegel thinks marriage commitment is connected to unstable human passions that cannot be absolutely extinguished. As a result, for Hegel, though it is "indissoluble *in itself*," marriage contains "within it the possibility of dissolution." To uphold "the right of ethics against caprice," Hegel insists that an ethical authority testify to the total estrangement of the parties. Hegel relies on the words in Christ's discussion of divorce with the Pharisees to show that Mosaic Law allowed divorce "because of the hardness of their hearts."[33]

Like Hegel, John Paul thinks "marriage 'is' indissoluble."[34] The logic of the position is that marriage is a unity whereby two are joined into one, or become "one flesh," and unity implies indissolubility, for if the union were breakable, lovers would hold something back from the union. Children testify to and embody this unity, though it is implicit in the idea that two become one. Hegel and John Paul put indissolubility at the heart of marriage in part because marriage creates a unity defined by an ethical, mature, and stabilizing giving of oneself to another. For John Paul, Hegel's more permissive standard is an inessential concession to the enduring power of "use-thinking" and subjectivity in marriage. Consider a woman married to a serial adulterer to illustrate this divergence. Hegel discusses this case and holds that this woman can divorce him since they are estranged, if an ethical authority testifies to the estrangement.[35] John Paul also discusses this scenario,[36] and in such a situation "there is only one possibility—separation, but without the dissolution of the marriage itself," and without either remarrying. If divorce and remarriage were allowed in this case, one party, usually the woman, would be in danger of being "put in the position of an object for use."[37]

The personalistic norm *alone* cannot bear this argument. Marriage is based on objective or ethical love, but ethical love can break down, and that is why an ethical authority testifies to the estrangement. A separated couple is not practicing the integration of love, for the union of sympathy and friendship no longer unites a separated husband and wife; separation, it seems to me, is *objectively* the breakdown of integrated, betrothed love—there is no giving of oneself to another in that case. John Paul may be able to respond based on a slippery slope argument. Allowing divorces in some cases would open the door to allowing divorces many cases. If the ethical authority is able to grant divorces to couples separated due to adulterous actions, then couples merely unhappy in marriages will take advantage of this loophole and either have affairs or claim that they have had affairs so that they can divorce. This makes all marriages vulnerable to becoming based on the principle of mutual consent or perhaps even no-fault divorce (and such a shift would be abetted by an ethical authority that does not dig deeply into situations). Easily accessible divorce makes each member vulnerable to becoming an object for use. Most countries that have slowly liberalized their divorce laws—that is, that have moved from indissoluble marriage to fault divorce on limited grounds to no-fault divorce—have experienced such a slippery slope in the middle stages of the transition, and this has played a role in the move toward more liberal divorce laws.[38]

Careful attention to the context of John Paul's argument shows that something more is at work in his defense of indissolubility. This adultery scenario calls into question the application of the good of indissolubility to a time when a husband and wife live separate lives. He concedes that the personalistic norm *alone* does not lead him to conclude that separated couples should remain married.

> The commandment to love, as it occurs in the Gospels, is more than the "personalistic norm," it also embodies the basic law of the whole supernatural order, of the supernatural relationship between God and man. Nevertheless, the personalistic norm is most certainly inherent in it—it is the "natural" content of the commandment to love, that part of it which we can equally well understand without faith and by reason alone.[39]

The commandment to love takes one beyond reason as it takes one beyond personalism. The particular understanding of marital indissolubility is connected with the great mystery of love and unity in which marriage mirrors Christ's enduring relationship to the church.[40]

Questions remain. Is mutual surrendering of persons possible? Is it desirable for human beings to go this far in doing justice to their inner lives and personalities? When considered from the perspective of "the natural order," it "makes no sense to speak of a person giving himself or herself to another," especially in a physical sense. No matter how much one wants to surrender to another physically, one remains separate and distinct from that other; this body-to-body gap cannot be breached. The human person is inalienable—one cannot surrender oneself or be the property of another. "But what is impossible and illegitimate in the natural order . . . can come about in the order of love and in a moral sense." What Christ voices in the first gospel—that "he who would lose his soul for my sake shall find it again" (Matt 10:39)—is a view supported by reason. Human beings are enlarged and enriched "in a super-physical, a moral sense" by the giving of self to another. Gift-love elevates the inner self over the physical self and the order of persons over the order of nature.

John Paul and the Dignity of Love

No other modern thinker mirrors John Paul's concept of love more than Hegel. Each sees love relating to the spirit's deepest needs. For Hegel, love contains two moments (a moment of deficiency followed by a moment when we discover ourselves in another person) and an "immense contradiction" (a contradiction centering on the fact that we lose and find ourselves in love).[41] John Paul agrees. On the moment of deficiency, John Paul thinks that "desire presupposes awareness of some lack . . . it is simply the crystallization of the objective need of one being directed toward another being which is for it a good and an object of longing." On the moment of losing and finding oneself, he writes,

> Love forcibly detaches the person . . . from his natural inviolability and inalienability. . . . The person no longer wishes to be its own exclusive property, but instead to become the property of that other. This means the renunciation of its autonomy and its inalienability. Love proceeds by way of this renunciation, guided by the profound conviction that it does not diminish and impoverish, but quite the contrary, enlarges and enriches the existence of the person.

Whereas Hegel calls this an "immense contradiction," John Paul sees love as a "profound paradox" concerning the "'mystery' of reciprocity," or a "magnificent paradox."[42] The mystery exists on a number of levels. Betrothed love fulfills human freedom while involving a sacrifice or giving of self. It joins two separate, inalienable persons into one flesh. It contains a bodily expression in sex and procreation, because the body is part of the person, while still aspiring to a transcendent and spiritual good. Most of all, it is a profound human need. "Man cannot live without love. He remains a being incomprehensible to himself, his life is senseless, if love is not revealed to him, if he does not encounter love, if he does not experience it and make it his own, if he does not participate intimately in it."[43] Our desires point, beyond biology, beyond sexual urges, beyond daily needs, beyond social needs, beyond politics, to the need for love. They point to our need for communion with another person, and ultimately, it seems, to our need for God.

John Paul and Hegel part ways over the dignity or rank of love as a human concern. For Hegel, the family responds to the need for love, but an individual's participation in the rational state surpasses family life in dignity because only the state recognizes human beings as free, equal beings. Crucial for our purposes is the fact that Hegel's family is part of a rational constitution that represents the consummation of the will's movement in history. The triumph of the spirit, or freedom, elevates universal citizenship in the rational state. Hegel's family seems to represent a more primitive form of ethical life manifesting less mature psychological needs and aspirations. It may be a remnant of ancient communal life that serves the needs of universal citizenship and the state by creating a desire for belonging that is satisfied in the state. The state, the preeminent Hegelian institution, reconciles contradictions between the particular and the general, between immanence and self-reflection, and even between motion and rest.[44] Each will acts to create rational institutions in the world, whether consciously or not, and those institutions acknowledge and reflect the rationality of each will in the world. The rational state is the result of the rational will willing itself. Once rational institutions, including the ethical family, exist in the world, human beings are satisfied.[45]

John Paul subverts Hegel's order, contending that "freedom exists for the sake of love" because it is "by way of love that human beings share most fully in the good" and because "man longs for love more than for freedom."[46] We have reached a point of ultimate value, and we have been heading for this juncture since the outset of the book. John Paul works with some of Hegel's categories, yet, as we have seen, he melds freedom and nature in his conception of the person. Freedom is a characteristic of human will, yet the aspiring character of the human person obliges the will to seek goodness, including the greatest goodness, love. Modernity has been right to value freedom because it is a precondition for the genuine aspiration to goodness, but freedom is no guarantor of goodness. Like Aristotle, John Paul puts the question of the good life front and center in moral philosophy, and he concludes that human beings aspire to happiness properly understood.

Hegel sees the problems associated with an arbitrary, individualistic, and abstract understanding of freedom. Freedom without limits finds itself in free creativity, self-assertion, and the transgression of boundaries, but this is in reality pure arbitrariness and irrationality. Freedom presupposes limits to which free actions conform. Historicism allowed Hegel to escape the trap of arbitrary willfulness by purporting that human beings understand their actions in a larger historical context that gave meaning to their actions. Above all, he sought to reconcile discontented human beings by showing them that human desires were satisfied in the modern constitution. Hegel's reconciliation spins apart because man, as he sometimes recognizes, is fundamentally desiring and restless: we are restless, in Augustine's celebrated words, "until [our heart] rests in You [God]."[47] This restlessness is a reflection of man's loves, his aspiration for moral goodness, and the imperfect condition in which human beings dwell. Love underlies our desire for recognition as free and equal citizens as it shoots through our relations in the world. Hegel makes freedom, equality, and the glories of mutual recognition more satisfying than they are and human beings more satisfiable than they are. The ladder of love reaches higher than the state, and the institutions, such as the family, that respond best to that deep human need are higher in the human heart. The elevation of something as an object of human aspiration places John Paul outside the modern tradition as I have presented it, despite his embrace of freedom.

Sex Differences and the Meaning of Children

For Hegel, customs, laws, and state institutions must regard the family as a unity to secure ethical love, and this in effect means that the state recognizes husbands as heads of the family. State recognition of individuals in marriage introduces a corrosive individualism inimical to two becoming one. It is just for the state to follow the traditional formula of public man, private woman because sex differences suit men and women to do different things in the family. Hegel embraces the logic of marital unity: the more one conceives of the family as a unity, the more necessary it is to acknowledge sex differences and to have women especially find their vocation in the family.

Few thinkers take the idea of family unity as seriously as John Paul.[48] Does he accept the logic of sex difference and sex subordination as he advocates unity? John Paul rejects Hegel's idea that the state's recognition of unity requires a complex of family rights whereby the father represents the family in public forums. "There is no doubt," John Paul writes, "that the equal dignity and responsibility of men and women fully justifies women's access to public functions."[49] This is in keeping with John Paul's implicit criticism that Hegel overly politicizes human life. Because politics is not as important as Hegel thought, the way in which the state recognizes the family is not as important. Not the state's recognition but its provision of rights and opportunities matters. Among these are the rights to educate children in one's own traditions, to support one's children, to housing suitable to family life, and to wholesome recreation fostering family values.[50] Generally, John Paul suggests that "society must be structured in such a way that wives and mothers are *not in practice compelled* to work outside the home, and that their families can live and prosper in a dignified way even when they themselves devote their full time to their family."[51] Some of his most faithful adherents see in his thought a certain flexibility in how families divide the labor,[52] but they are uncompromising on the question of unity.

It is a question of prudence how and how far a political community can, should, and must go to recognize marital and family unity.

John Paul sees marriage as a "mutual surrender of both persons, of their belonging equally to each other."[53] Mutual surrender is possible as each serves the common goods of marriage—accepting and educating children, building a unifying love, and orienting desire legitimately. Men and women seem to provide different things as they surrender to each other in serving these common goods. On a psychological level, men are generally more sensual than women and women more sentimental and intimate than men. For John Paul, this shows that the sensualist, the sentimentalist, and the craver of intimacy are unprepared to build a betrothed love. There is no automatic correction of one sex by the other—sentimentality does not balance out sensuality, nor does sensuality elevate intimacy. These features must be self-consciously integrated, and men and women are co-creators of such "objective love."[54] Not everything hangs on whether John Paul gets male and female psychology correct. His purpose in this context is to describe the incompleteness of each loving expression and the need for man and woman to participate fully in the creation of their own love. Men and women may also experience parenthood differently, and this difference requires that they transcend themselves in unique ways. Parents are co-creators of their children. By this John Paul means that parents take initiative with one another and with God the creator in bringing a child into existence. Parenthood is "an internal attitude" of betrothed love crystallized in a new being. Nor should parenthood occupy a different space in the life of the husband or the wife. Women are by nature more physically and psychologically connected to the child, for they sense their own role as a creator of the child more intensely since they give birth.

> Woman's constitution differs from that of man; in fact, we know today that it is different even in the deepest bio-physiological determinants. The difference is shown only in a limited measure on the outside, in the build and form of her body. . . . The whole exterior constitution of woman's body, its particular look . . . are in strict union with motherhood.[55]

Men's bodies, on the other hand, do not scream "fatherhood." This makes it is necessary for "paternal feelings" to be "specially cultivated and trained, so that they may become as important in the inner life of the man as is maternity in that of a woman."[56] (That fatherhood is more culturally variable than motherhood is a central finding of social science positivism and evolutionary sociobiology.) Again, everything does not hang on whether this analysis is absolutely correct: if men need more training to become engaged in the inner lives of their children, cultures should provide such training. If John Paul is incorrect about how men and women experience parenthood, perhaps all he has said is that men and women must be equally engaged in their children's inner lives.

But this would understate the ways in which sex differences relate to the idea of marital unity. To understand the connection, we must return to the idea that human beings are persons, unities of body and soul. Because body is essential to personhood, human sexuality is a dimension of (not merely incidental to) the human person. Human sexuality is not a product of human will—men and women do not decide to become "man" or "woman." Nor is human sexuality simply the product of a cultural environment; cultures suggest different clothing styles and different behaviors for men and women, but these are manifestations of the basic reality of sex differences. It is a modern delusion to think that sex differences are products of human acts or cages of natural determinism. This delusion derives from the idea that real human activity exists on a plane of freedom or spirit against the dead hand of nature, or, more modestly, from the dualism between body and soul characteristic of modern thinking, which leads to a denigration of sexual identity because that identity is not the product of choice. Here John Paul's position aligns with the conclusions of modern evolutionary biologists. Not only are there differences between the sexual organs, there are differences in the structure of the tissues and in the chemicals that are found in men and women. Remember the title of John Paul's series of talks on the family: *Man and Woman He Created Them*. The sexes are physically complementary in the sexual act and for procreation. Such physical expressions do not exhaust the meaning of complementariness for men and women, though they point to its character. It is not good for either to be alone, and each inclines toward the other as a means of achieving unity and serving the other in love. There are psychological tendencies in men and women that make interpersonal union possible. Respect for the idea that men and women are complementary nourishes respect for the idea that men and women form a deeper marital union.

Opening up oneself to another means opening up to everything that one's spouse is and has; such openness requires openness to receiving life. Giving oneself to another means giving one's all, including one's fertility. John Paul offers extensive advice on sexuality while also showing how sex integrates the "order of nature" with the "personal order." He instructs husbands to be tender and patient and wives to be warm and engaged.[57] This involves ensuring that the couple has a proper disposition toward sex, namely a spirit to serve one another and a willingness to bear children, the natural fruits of sex.

John Paul's teaching on contraception and continence arises from the collision of these attitudes. Recall the position of Sigmund Freud, another modern thinker opposed to contraception, in a manner. Freud worried that contraception inhibited sexual satisfaction, yet he hoped that a mode of contraception would arise that would enable human beings to experience sexual satisfaction and avoid unwanted pregnancies. We may have reached that day. Unlike marriage movement positivists, who worry about the demise of the family but see no problem with the use of contraception, John Paul sees connections among the acceptance of artificial birth control, a civilization of use, and family decline. When a couple wants to express its love through sex but does not want children, John Paul recommends periodic continence. If sex is disconnected from its natural purpose, the relationship risks sliding toward a sexual union for mutual use instead of being a union of persons for the experience of love. If partners are unwilling to become parents,

> sexual intercourse between them will have no full objective justification. . . . If the possibility of parenthood is deliberately excluded from marital relations, the character of the relationship between partners automatically changes. The change is away from unification in love and in the direction of mutual, or rather, bilateral, "enjoyment." . . . When a man and a woman rule out even the possibility of parenthood their relationship is transformed to the point at which it becomes incompatible with the personalistic norm.[58]

There *seems* to be hedging in John Paul's formulation. Using artificial contraception takes away the "full justification" for the sex act, but may leave a partial one; it moves sex "in the direction" of bilateral enjoyment, but perhaps not all the way. It *may seem* that John Paul is open to contraception being acceptable as long as the couple has the proper attitude toward one another during sex; contraception may make that attitude more difficult to achieve, but it may not rule it out.

This is not John Paul's meaning.[59] "The moral aspect of any procedure," writes John Paul in *Familiaris Consortio*, "does not depend solely on the sincere intentions or on an evaluation of motives. It must be determined by objective standards," which in this case concerns the presence of artificial birth control techniques. Use of birth control reflects a denial of sex's procreative purpose. Even the rhythm method *could* be condemned based on a totality of the circumstances and an evaluation of the motives of the parties. Separating the procreative meaning from the unifying meaning of sex is the problem.

> When couples, by means of recourse to contraception, separate these two meanings that God the Creator has inscribed in the being of man and

> woman and in the dynamism of their sexual communion, they act as "arbiters" of the divine plan and they "manipulate" and degrade human sexuality—and with it themselves and their married partner—by altering the value of "total" self-giving.[60]

John Paul's vision contravenes the aspirations of modern thought on the family in at least two ways. First, unlike most modern thinkers, John Paul is concerned to defend marriage as a unity by defending the indissolubility of marriage and by seeing children as concrete manifestations of marital unity and as gifts instead of as burdens. Experiences of marriage and family life are seen against this unity, lending meaning and dignity to activities that may otherwise seem mundane. Marriage precedes parenthood because marriage's self-giving is a model for the self-giving of parenthood; absence of the one puts the other at risk; the presence of marriage readies one to be a parent.

Second and more radical yet, John Paul argues that respect for marital unity goes together with respect for nature's purposes in sex. The ideas that nature has a purpose and that we should respect nature cleave together. We have seen, beginning with Locke's stance toward Eve's curse, that modern thinking takes an adversarial relation to nature's givens. Nature is not for John Paul a series of obstacles. He does not seek to make man master; he redefines a respectful mastery as fitting for man. "Mastery over nature," he writes, "can only result from a thorough knowledge of the purposes and regularities that govern it." Artificial contraception achieves mastery by subverting a woman's biological system and disrespecting the natural (created) order. Mastering the sexual urge really means that we accept its purpose in marriage and its procreative potential while conforming our actions to its patterns. One way to look at his position here is this. Nature is two-sided. Human beings have "natural" sexual instincts or urges and they have reproductive systems. By controlling the system, people can give vent to natural instincts or urges. Have people thereby conquered nature or been conquered by natural, untutored desire? An ethic of continence subordinated to the personal order conforms to nature while demonstrating that it is human nature to be more than mere nature. John Paul insists that this position is available to reason, though "it is much easier to understand the power of the natural order . . . if we see behind it the personal authority of the Creator."[61]

It is not that reproduction is the only purpose of marriage, nor must marriage culminate in reproduction, nor is marriage accidental to reproduction; rather, betrothed love is connected to procreative sex within the bond of marriage.[62] Marriage, in its essence, buckles sex reproduction and betrothed love together. In defending this unity against the modern tendency to separate, John Paul reveals himself at his most radical. Why the institution? People *can* physically reproduce without love and without marriage, and people purport to love one another without marriage. These deinstitutionalizing actions, detrimental to sound family order, do violence to the personal order and to the revealed order. As I mentioned at the outset, John Paul's worries about the family combine most of the worries of social science positivists with much that is distinctive in the Catholic tradition. That the rise of contraception and the decline of the family occur at the same time is suggestive evidence that these aspects together constitute an institution or a complex of attitudes and actions. This is what *has happened*; it is also what was *bound to happen* given the relationship among these goods. Along with the availability and accepted use of contraception comes a mentality allowing promiscuous sex, abortion, divorce, infidelity, crime, child abandonment, and family dissolution. Contraception makes the relations between the sexes less centered on children and more centered on mutuality and sexual pleasure, and pleasure relations between the sexes are less likely to be marital or unifying than child-centered relations. The availability of contraception affects the expectations of men and women. Traditional, sexually modest women are put at a competitive disadvantage, and promiscuous women no longer can depend on a shotgun marriage to attach men to their children. The result is that more or less traditional women have children without the benefit of marriage, while less traditional women have abortions. The availability of contraception hence fosters more illegitimacy and abortion because it promotes more non-unitive sexual relations. It lowers the physical cost of infidelity within marriage, making it more common. Not tethered to women through marriage, young men commit more crimes, do more drugs, and, in general, act less responsibly, and this behavior redounds to the next generation.[63]

Contraception and the rationale justifying its use disrupt connections among marriage, sex, and procreation—contraception tries to separate goods that are connected. This is a problem if connections among these goods are salutary for individuals and society alike. Contraception allows hedonistic impulses to triumph in human relations: women become objects for men's use and men become objects for women's use. Less concerned about a woman's physical or psychological well-being and about the children, men are more likely to be in a relationship for the sex. It is conceivable, as "conservative" contraception advocates hold, that contraceptive sex promotes marital bonding.[64] In principle, however, contraception violates the personal norm; as a societal norm, contraception brings with it a complex of attitudes and behaviors that disrupt family life and marital unity. Sex and procreation remain connected insofar as they involve the deeper commitments of betrothed love and common goods—the weakening of these commitments serves to prove that sex and procreation are connected.

This idea has implications for same-sex marriage. Same-sex marriages could link betrothed love to sex without the sex differences that culminate in procreation. A same-sex couple needs no artificial contraception to prevent pregnancy, of course, as homosexual sex is closed to the possibility of procreation. This issue of same-sex marriage raises a fundamental question: why is sex open to procreation an essential part of betrothed love in marriage? The answer to this question requires us to delve into the nature of love and sex. Sex naturally admits in procreation, though it has other subordinate purposes. Mastering sexual passions means subordinating sex to this natural end—it is an exercise of human responsibility. Marriage leads to the subordination of sexual urges to this natural end, so it consists with personalism and divine right. Sex outside of marriage and non-procreative sex combine the same dangers about our inability to master sexual passion and the same errors about how institutions cling together.

The Persistence of Marital Unity

John Paul's central insight concerns the threat posed to the personal norm by the utilitarian, object-for-use attitude afoot in our age. Sexual relations are vulnerable to the object-for-use attitude,[65] so it is first of all necessary to show how the personal norm interprets our experiences of sex and love better than other modes of thought and then to show how it goes with certain attitudes, behaviors, and institutions. John Paul reaches these conclusions through the use of a phenomenology informed by personalism and the revealed fact that human beings are free creatures living in a created order.

John Paul defends the personal order to rejuvenate a culture of love. When viewed from Hegel's perspective, this ambition involves a deprecation of politics, as we have seen in John Paul's treatment of sex differences. Unlike Hegel, John Paul does not question the suitability of women to free and equal citizenship, and he tries to show how the order of love can thrive without the institutions of male headship to which Hegel attached ethical love. Hegel's ethical love becomes problematic because Hegel puts it in a system that elevates the realm of politics above family life; his family precludes state recognition of female independence and personhood, but it makes state recognition the pinnacle of human existence. This does an injustice to the capacities of women. In contrast, John Paul sees the order of love as more important than the state and accommodates family life to a variety of political orders. Public recognition of familial unity is still vitally important for John Paul, but recognition of independence and equality by the state pales in comparison to the order of love, so that any solvent from state institutions does not necessarily wear away the order of love.

John Paul's skepticism about the morality of progress and liberation reflects a view that the human world is supported by standards from the outside. This makes his theory less liable to "development" than Hegel's. Hegel's theory, we have seen, is subject to the objection that History has left the institution of family and ethical love behind. John Paul sees society as subject to natural laws of operation and the family as an institution that is the cornerstone of society. In conceiving of marriage as an institution, he sees it as a series of connections, or buckles. It buckles betrothed love to marriage, marriage to parenthood, and sex to procreation. Modern political thought, with partial exceptions, initiated a revolution in marriage at the level of betrothed love. Modern thinkers questioned whether such a total self-giving was healthy, possible, or consistent with individual liberty and equality. Once that understanding of love is no longer the basis of marriage, a host of subsequent developments follow. Once marriage no longer involves a total giving of the self, the preparation ground for the self-giving that is parenthood erodes. Once marriage is not a total self-giving, divorce seems more tenable. Once parenthood becomes less important or less central to a marriage's mission, couples elevate other goods as the purpose of marriage; this elevates sex divorced from procreation as a good of marriage. Once procreation ceases to be the purpose of sex, marriage itself loses a major justification; fewer marriages form, more marriages end in divorce, and fewer children are born. Break the first link and the rest of the chain breaks as well. This is why John Paul emphasizes the civilization of love in his writings on the family. Other thinkers concentrate on the implications of family's decline or wish to have strong marriage but do not criticize the use of contraception (for instance); John Paul gets underneath both phenomena, concentrating on what causes the decline of marriage and the acceptance of contraception. It is at least suggestive evidence in favor of John Paul's views that his predictions of what would happen if we abandoned the civilization of love and personalism have indeed come to pass.

John Paul shows the logic of love: accept the initial premise about the nature and goodness of total self-giving and the rest of his argument about the nature of the institution follows. Love continues to draw people in our age of freedom. There is always reason for hope because human beings need each other, no matter how much we try to talk ourselves out of that fact. We still love, but most today have lost the language to understand what we are doing. We give ourselves, but we do not know what it means to love. There will be reason for hope as long as we do not lose the material for hope—the actual experience of marital unity and betrothed love. As this is the most attractive aspect of the family's end, advocates of marriage may do well to articulate the goods of marriage in this vein and to worry about drawing out all of the implications of this view later.

Could, would, and should we want to bring about a new kind of family or the family's end? In line with evolutionary biologists, John Paul implies that biological sex differences limit the amount of change we can expect from the attempt to bring about the family's end. The most dramatic obstacle to the reconstitution of family life involves the human need for love. Human beings would not want to be alone because they long for the satisfying love consistent with the personal order. Aware of their lack, they sense the need to fill. Others have tried to account for this lacking in ways that point to the triumph of politics or personal projects. John Paul's radical position is that this lack is what it seems to be—a thirst for love. Bringing about the family's end is likely to disrupt the most sensible, reachable, and desirable institution that constitutes a rung on the ladder of love. Family and marriage are social institutions that are part of the created order; they conform to the created order for the benefit of human beings and society. Human beings will recognize this and they should. That is John Paul's untimely meditation about covenantal marriage.

Chapter 12

What Is to Be Thought?
Tensions and Lessons

Thinking on the family turns on the question of whether society is a collection of individuals or a collection of families. This vision of what society is often depends on an evaluation of mutual dependence in family life. The view that mutual dependence is connected to the human good lends itself to seeing the family as the basic unit of society. The view that dependence is inimical to a good life is connected to the view that society is a collection of individuals. All hands agree that marriages must originate in consent and that marriage's mutual dependence must be voluntary; today's debate on the family concerns whether couples supersede the point of view of contract *in* marriage.

Among other things, this study has presented an unfolding of the modern concept of liberty and how it affects the family. The conception of liberty decomposes old institutions and reconstitutes new ones. The theoretical frame of reference associated with modern liberty revolutionizes our moral universe; it does not easily comprehend goods associated with nature, immanence, mutual dependence, and love, and thus the goods accompanying modern liberty seem incommensurate with the goods of family and marital unity. The transcendent independence embraced by Beauvoir, to use the most extreme example, invites a critique of motherhood, sexual or marital fidelity, mutual dependence, pregnancy, and love. This incommensurability of goods need not be cause for alarm: many, if not most, human goods are irreconcilable to others. The imperialism of modern liberty—its crowding out of human goods inconceivable on the basis of modern liberty—is the cause for concern as we contemplate the family's end.

My judgment that this is a deep problem has its basis in the belief that the modern democratic regime dedicated to limited government and individual liberty must be balanced if it is to be sustainable. Consider how the modern democratic world is experiencing a steady decline in the number of live births. Decreases in birth rates generally arise with, and may be traceable to, the ethic of modern liberty (emphasizing the goods of spontaneous individuality, personal independence, and the conquest of nature).[1] Availability of modern contraception techniques accelerate population decline, yet the decline antedates modern contraception, which appears to be as much an effect of the cultural factors causing population decline as its cause. Modern contraception expands the empire of choice by allowing couples (or, perhaps, women) to choose the number of children they want and to avoid having children during seasons of their choice. Individuals have become masters of the reproductive process, and, all over the Western world, people are, in the main, having fewer children than their ancestors. Such population decline, on such a wide scale and in the absence of pestilence and warfare, is unprecedented. While we grasp public policy, social, and economic problems associated with population decline, we are not sure how to counteract it or whether to counteract it. We assert power over the reproductive process in the name of greater individual and sexual liberty (in a manner), yet our mastery may come to inhibit the pursuit of prosperous, productive lives.

Examples multiply. Stronger families keep government limited by providing services, in the raising of children and in how a husband and a wife share a life, that government otherwise might have to provide. It produces citizens more likely to be moral, relatively self-sustaining, and law-abiding. It answers a deep human need for belonging, unconditional acceptance, love, and mutual recognition that might otherwise find unhealthy outlets.[2] Marriage and family life are ballasts that serve individual happiness and contentment and lend meaning to our freedom and equality. Many theories (such as Beauvoir's) tending toward the family's end also point to the end of limited government. On the level of ideas and in practice, the future of the family is connected with the future of limited government, in part because they share theoretical opponents and in part because they serve and reinforce one another.

Our coming demographic challenge and these other potential ills arise because of the separation of marriage from procreation, of sex from love, and of sex from procreation. The persistence of their connection is also evident, for often with less of one (marriage and lifelong love), we get less of others (sex and children). For Locke, "Procreation and the bringing up of Children" are the chief ends of conjugal society.[3] Today's most authoritative, or most modern, public statements about marriage see procreation and the education of children as outside marriage's ends.[4] Marriage today appears as a sign of commitment and affection, as a "close relationship" defined by the persons involved.[5] I have tried to explain the philosophical underpinnings of this transformation from Locke to contemporary opinion. Let me begin this discussion of what we should think about the family by tracing the career of modern liberty. Generally, modern liberty leads to the separation of values and goods that were connected. Unified marriage and family life fasten marriage to parenthood, parenthood to education, love to sex, sex to procreation, and marriage to mutual economic dependence. Unified marriages are sums greater than these connections, for they imply monogamy, sexual exclusivity, and a large measure of permanence as measures that secure these connections. Modern thinkers pressure marriage and family life by making each connection and trait testify at the bar of reason and pass the tests of individual freedom and sexual equality. The modern notion of liberty is the impetus to see our condition as progressively independent of traditions, nature, and other human beings, and to assert human control over the merely natural. It tends to find human freedom in our capacity to *separate* what once was joined or to disentangle inessential traits from essential traits.

The Career of Modern Liberty

What began in Locke as an antipatriarchal effort to separate civil government from the family and civil society results in the separation of freedom from nature, or perhaps the separation of freedom from nature is implicit in Locke's separation of family from civil government. Locke separates civil government from civil society, whose chief institution is the family, in order to correct the mis-education and partisanship born of unifying the family, politics, and property. Marriage and family life, for Locke, no longer constitute a permanent, dependent relation between husband and wife and between parent (or father) and child. He distances marriage and family life from their origins in religious orthodoxy and articulates grounds for separating the nuclear family from a larger extended family. Acknowledging sexual equality by basing marriage on mutual consent, Locke's nuclear family centers around the natural needs of procreation and education. His nuclear family can dispense with marital permanence because marriage can end after its chief end, the procreation and education of children, is accomplished.

Rousseau, Hegel, Comte, and Durkheim questioned Locke's initial effort to found marriage on a contract open to divorce, though each accepted Locke's view that parental authority is temporary. These divergent defenses of marital unity, offered with an eye to the limits of modern liberty, defend unity on controversial, and ultimately unstable, grounds. Rousseau, after calling attention to the social construction in Locke's understanding of nature, grounds marital unity on the imagination informed by the natural complementariness of the sexes. Hegel, thinking that imagination alone could not justify marital unity, shows that unified marriage and family life answer human needs and are represented in historical institutions; our understanding of needs and the institutions that represent them changes precisely because they are not, as Hegel himself had thought, grounded solely in nature, or because nature does not prove as strong as History as a force in human life. Durkheim, recognizing the continuing destructive and reconstructive power of History to transform the merely natural, tries to defend an attenuated marital unity with positive social science by showing that some marital institution is necessary for social health and individual self-control; Durkheim is open to the possibility that other institutions will arise or are arising to tame man's desire for the infinite, if that desire genuinely persists. Each thinker recognizes the human power to make History; each unsettles the understanding of nature on which he relies and makes it more difficult to identify stable principles from which to understand family life.[6]

Subsequent theorists of the family targeted the social vision of marital unity as inimical to individual liberty, sexual equality, and individual flourishing. Mill and Durkheim are essential in furthering modern separations with respect to the family. Mill pays comparatively little attention to the needs and status of children as he envisions a family built for adult sexual equality and independence, while Durkheim extends Locke's critique of patriarchal partisanship by separating parenthood from education and justifies marriage for what it does to and for men. Mill and Durkheim see marriage centered on adults: Mill emphasizes loosening marriage to secure greater equality and independence for women, while Durkheim emphasizes maintaining marriage as an institution necessary (for now) to cultivate self-control in men (Freud calls into question the goodness of that self-control or "repression"). Mill separates sex from reproduction in his defense of contraception; his defense of divorce calls into question the need for marital permanence; his willingness to allow spouses to define the terms of marriage makes a defense of fidelity more difficult; and his understanding of the economic basis of individuality leads him to separate marriage from mutual economic dependence. Connections stand in the way of human choice; essential marital traits stand in the way of spontaneous individuality.

From the perspective of Beauvoir and Marx, Mill fails to tame the twin powers of ideology and nature. Mill separates in law and opinion, but more radical measures are necessary for separations in fact. Modern backers of contraception, from Mill to Freud, Russell, and Beauvoir, separate procreation from sex and perhaps also sex from love. Separating procreation from sex serves personal independence by empowering women to control their reproductive cycles and by allowing women to pursue creative work of their own without the burdens of bearing children. Part of this effort to secure woman's independence is to separate birthing children from household work and child-rearing. Freed from such drudgery, women can achieve equality and transcendence. They can also be creative workers while children learn, from their absence, valuable lessons on how to be independent. Motherhood is a replaceable institution, as the state can provide. Beauvoir, Russell, and, implicitly, Freud separate sex from dampening, depressing, dependence-creating monogamous love. Beauvoir recommends what used to be called adultery as a way of preventing dependence on any one man; Freud seeks sexual outlets for Western civilization's "surplus repression." The principles behind Beauvoir's more radical separation of things are present in nascent form, as we have seen, even in modern defenders of marital and familial unity. Like her modern predecessors, Beauvoir separates transcendent or free activity from immanent, or natural, unfree action, and she locates family life in the realm of nature and unfree action.

Modern thinkers defend marriage as an institution with reference to the naturally different needs and abilities of the sexes, though they undermine our ability to see these natural differences as permanent or essential by embracing the inexorable power of History to redefine the moral environment of humanity. Is there a necessary connection between marital unity and the sexual division of labor? Is there a way to defend marital unity without recourse to these unstable grounds?

A "New Deal" for Marital Unity?

Recall the logic of marital unity. When marriage and family life concern serious, time- and resource-intensive common goods, it is necessary for a couple to divide up their collective labor to accomplish the ends of the family. The more the family practices the division of labor in accomplishing its ends, the more it likely practices the sexual division of labor, because men and women seem suited to play different roles in the family. The sexual division of labor and marital unity seem so closely connected that the sexual division of labor *defines* "traditional" family life in much academic and social scientific writing, even writings sympathetic to relatively traditional forms.[7] Such writings mistake a relatively ugly (by contemporary lights) means (the sexual division of labor) for an arguably more desirable and defensible or indispensable end (unified marriage and family life). The unified family has been left behind by today's family debates that concentrate on removing the sexual division of labor. We can grasp why this is. Rousseau, Hegel, and Comte found it necessary for political communities to recognize men as the public faces of the family so that the corrosive influences of individualism and calculating reason would not detract from marital and familial unity and the communal nature of the family would be respected. The sexual division of labor is subordinate in importance, for these thinkers, to the formation of unified marriage and family life, and the natural differences between the sexes serve to show that the unified family did not unjustly lock women out of politics, as it reflected the sexual division of labor. The response to such defenses of unity (especially in Mill, Marx, and Beauvoir) is to accept the modern *logic* of marital unity, but to question whether the family needs to be concerned about serious time- and resource-intensive *common* goods. Less intense family life requires less division of labor, and less intense families are less likely to practice or need the *sexual* division of labor. Women, like men, can be free, independent, and equal if marriage and family life demand less commitment, time, and energy. Contemporary moves to deinstitutionalize marriage and to define marriage apart from children are the latest, and greatest, movements in this direction.

Modern critics of the sexual division of labor had another path available to them. They could have accepted the "serious family" and its division of labor, but have criticized the need to divide labor along *sexual* lines.[8] Building and maintaining a marriage, like building and caring for a home and household, takes investment of time, consumes mental and physical energy, presupposes and builds love and sharing of goods, requires resources from outside of the family, and demands countless other products of human creativity and character. Couples can, in principle, divide time- and resource-intensive labor how they see fit. This open-ended adjustment would allow women to pursue economic opportunities outside the home, and men to attend to the home and household, according to the specific desires of the couple. It is also based on the recognition that tending the household may not be as time- and resource-intensive as it once was due to advances in technology (such as the refrigerator) and the rise of mandatory, highly subsidized public schooling. The workplace in advanced modern economies often provides more flexibility to men and women so that they can, by structuring hours creatively, meet demands of career, marriage, and family. This "new deal" would have maintained unified marriage and family life while being more flexible in how unity is achieved. It would have allowed men and women to "have it all," or at least to have more venues for different fundamental human capacities, including those associated with unified marriage and family life.

Modern critics did not pursue this "new deal," in part, because of problems and paradoxes associated with the idea of consent. Consent signifies choice, and consent to marriage makes the marriage consistent with individual liberty. A "yes" given under duress, however, is not a "yes." What is duress? A gun pointed to a woman's head makes void her "I do." Are there moral equivalents to having a gun put to a woman's head? If women have a Hobson's choice between marrying under conditions of legal inequality and starving, the choice to marry is not really a choice. Mill's prescription—changing laws to allow women to own property, to vote, and to divorce—promises to provide a legal structure for genuine consent. Mill also had to explain why women endured their subordination so long. He held that women were educated into apolitical submissiveness and that their education was designed by males to benefit males; their choices, made pursuant to social conditioning, were not free. Critics of Mill's "formal freedom" think his critique of the social construction of gender is inconsistent with his legal or political prescription or his endorsement of a mere formal liberty. Mill's legal revolution failed because too many women and men continued to "choose" traditional roles. If society "forces" them to "choose" traditional roles, genuine choice can be achieved by limiting society's power or by marshaling the power of the modern state to propound a new social vision. As Beauvoir and some other feminists argue, residual "chosen" sex differences prove that a reconstruction of gender requires more radical measures, including, but not limited to, state action to relieve women of the burdens of raising children. Genuine consent may necessitate the suspension of "formal liberty" so that we can secure substantive equality because these thinkers *know* or *think* residual inequalities are evidence for the persistence of social conditioning. Securing *substantive* equality between men and women would produce conditions for genuine consent and would provide evidence that genuine consent is possible.

Yet achieving *substantive* equality, between men and women and among human beings generally, has proven to be more than a little difficult. How can we know when the conditions for genuine consent exist if society keeps presenting inequalities or differences between the sexes? If persisting inequalities or differences are evidence of a skewed environment, only equality of result proves the existence of equality of opportunity. Since equality of result is elusive, the effort to achieve the conditions for genuine equality of opportunity can never cease. Thus the idea of consent fosters the continual decomposition and recomposition of the modern family. If we do not presume that a substantive equality is the only just outcome, how can we know when the inequalities or differences that exist are products of genuine choice? How much inequality or difference results from individual choice, individuals following their nature, or individuals doing what they do best? There is an insurmountable theoretical problem in identifying the conditions for genuine consent: as we define consent up, it is elusive and increasingly illiberal in its bent to social engineering; as we define it down, it may countenance systematic prejudice.

The idea of consent contains another paradox. How does consent extend in time? An individual consents to the obligations entailed in marrying. Is that consent sufficient for a lifetime? Must vows be renewed? If so, how often? We should view the projection of consent into the future along a continuum. On one side is continuous consent favoring an idea of liberty as spontaneity. This idea allows people to ask whether old institutions and commitments still serve their needs; when institutions or commitments are inconsistent with one's personal development as one comes to understand it, nothing in the idea of continuous consent deters an individual from leaving them behind. Continuous consent liberates from the dead hand of the past, especially one's own. Commitments are contingent upon their ability to serve one's present ends, and there is no guarantee that one will want to keep today's promises tomorrow. People change, and it takes courage to shed accustomed habits and pursue one's transcendent self. On the other side of the continuum is a view emphasizing that society and individuals cannot secure and (hence) should not want to secure continuous consent. Consent is meaningless without duration—handshakes, vows, and promises are absurd if the consenting parties could instantly pull out. Durable consent assures our reciprocal ability to depend on one another and to secure the goods (such as love) associated with mutual dependence. It is clear that we cannot foresee all that a marriage will entail, so it is difficult to put a time limit or conditions on one's consent as per a contract. The presence of children, along with our inability to predict when they will come along, makes circumstances of marriage and family life subject to chance. The idea of liberty as spontaneity embedded in continuous consent also seems inconsistent with any durable concept of self-government. It fosters arbitrariness, irrationality, immaturity, and irresponsibility, while durable consent opens one to the rule of reason, to the government of one's passions, and to development and self-improvement.[9]

Late modern critics see an association of socially constructed gender, "formal liberty," and durable consent with marital unity. Unified marriage and family life are consistent with neither continuous consent nor a radical understanding of conditions for genuine consent. Emphasis on the two radically loosening conceptions of consent leaves only the standpoint of contract (or less), where marriage and family life are less able to transform or stabilize individuals. Continuous consent is inconsistent with the promise or vow creating marriage (for vows and promises presume that consent extends over time), and it promotes a way of thinking in which individuals do not give themselves to another. Viewing parenthood from the perspective of continuous consent makes it difficult to sustain interest in, and responsibility for, children.

Defending marriage and family life demands that we expose the intellectual extremism in these partial conceptions of consent. This does not send me careening to the opposite side, in which I allow a mere Hobson's choice for women or in which I demand that marriages be indissoluble in practice. If we see dangers on only one side of consent, we risk sliding into the vices contained on the other. All these conceptions, at their most extreme, are unsound as principles of action and ideas of the family. Unified marriage and family life require an account of why we should accept some substantive inequalities or differences in family life along with a defense of the goods associated with durable consent and responsibility.

The best evidence marshaled by evolutionary biologists suggests that modern feminists misjudge the conditions for genuine consent in seeking equal outcomes between men and women. Men and women *tend to* choose *somewhat* differently. The fact that a fifty-fifty split does not exist among kindergarten teachers or in child care arrangements for young children is *not* dispositive evidence that an environment of free choice does not exist. Nearly all plumbers, truck drivers, auto mechanics, and carpenters are men, and few complain about sexual discrimination in these professions. Attempts to approximate a fifty-fifty split between men and women in some kinds of housework and employment are unrealistic. Science and philosophy and individuals generally distinguish accidental or contingent, socially conditioned inequalities between the sexes from durable ones. Few today doubt that legal obstacles to woman's advancement must be removed and that equal opportunity in education and employment should be secured. I am open, in principle, to the possibility that some of today's inequalities are remnants of a social construction of gender. Inequalities that linger are not, however, *ipso facto* evidence of persisting patriarchy; they may reflect decisions based on honest self-evaluation, inescapable biological realities, or differences in native ability. As a theoretical matter, the effort to secure a gender-neutral practice can be an exercise in social construction that the advocates for a gender-neutral society (rightly, in part) condemn. Studies show that spouses divide household tasks more equally than they did in previous generations (suggesting that there is variability in how tasks are divided), yet studies also show that some traditional sexual division of labor persists despite efforts to eliminate it and despite the strains this puts on mothers of the young.[10] Some sexual division of labor will, probably, persist in a society that adopts a public stance of gender neutrality and that strictly divides public from private.

The theoretical problems implicated in partial ideas of consent open the door to a "new deal" for marital unity. The alternative to the family's end is not necessarily the restoration of family life defined by the "traditional" sexual division of labor. We will probably have families that (to an extent at least) practice the sexual division of labor less rigidly than their predecessors, and this result does greater justice to the capacities of women and vindicates human spontaneity more than previous forms of the family. The sexual prejudices of Hegel and Comte are refuted by experience: modern states are no more in danger with modern women in charge than they are with modern men in charge. Wives and mothers will work outside the home more, and husbands and fathers will share more household tasks and/or spend more quality time with children than they once did (even if what is done with their quality time is different from what is done with a mother's). Differences related to the bodies of the sexes will not disappear—and women, and especially young mothers, will have different needs based on pregnancy, birth, and their ability to care for small children. Something suits the sexes to do different things and be different, even if they can legally do most anything.

The families practicing a less rigid sexual division of labor are not necessarily new families. The future of the family depends on whether modern families can work out a "new deal" for marital unity and cut off its logic earlier than its modern defenders had. Serious family life involves commitment, mutual service, teamwork, interdependence, and the division of labor in the family in the service of serious ends, but its division of labor need not be a traditional *sexual* division of labor. Couples can divide most family labor, and they can share responsibility of earning family resources, in a variety of ways; they can adjust how they divide tasks over time in their life courses. Such flexibility can accommodate the desires of each sex to exercise rational faculties inside and outside the family. Central to marital unity is the relative permanence, trust, and fidelity of spouses living a common life: this involves the creation of an enduring union. The flexibility concerns the means used to fulfill the family's serious ends. Family members can see their outside activities serving their family's ends, and they all, in different ways, provide the attention, time, reflection, and love necessary for these "new families" to achieve the family's ends.[11] These activities can be baptized by seeing marriage and family life within a universe of meaning wherein unity and its mutual dependence is embraced and valued. The crucial question revolves around how we interpret these experiences.

There is a Hegelian riposte to this more or less gender-neutral *modus vivendi*. State recognition of individual liberty outside of marriage tends to introduce a corrosive individualism into the family, and unified marriage is more difficult to maintain once individualism has been invited indoors. Communal attitudes require public support, and supporting communal attitudes within the family was a primary justification for coverture laws, prohibitions on easy or no-fault divorce, and male headship for voting purposes, among other things. The "new deal" for unity assumes that Hegel overstates how much unified marriage and family life are connected to a public recognition of the sexual division of labor. Hegel's argument erodes the distinction between private and public by showing how *public* recognition shapes *private* ideas. The "new deal" for marital unity depends on resurrecting this distinction between private and public as a necessary means to protect marital unity. It is based on the assumption that people are social in that they need social bonds with others, but not political in the sense that their ideas of justice and human good flow directly from their political community.

The Goods and Bads of Dependence

Why should we seek a "new deal" for unified marriage and family life? Modern thinkers have subjected such ideas of unity to persistent withering criticisms. As successful as these criticisms have been, they must reflect a genuine human desire for something more or other than unified family life. As Locke worried, excessively unified families pose problems for politics by instilling a debilitating partisanship and by inculcating habits of mind subversive of self-government. Excessive family unity can also subvert individuality by preventing the rise of one's own identity. The attempt to put marriage and family life on a contractual basis is based on a criticism of unity based on self-sacrifice. An ethic of self-sacrifice or self-denial runs too counter to human nature by demanding that we take the being of others more seriously than we take our own. Family life based on sacrificial love stands on an unsteady, undependable foundation—the virtues of family life unendowed. Unified marriages, insofar as they rest on sacrificial love, disrupt family life as much as or more than individualism because, in the main, the commitment of self-sacrifice can be as fleeting as a spontaneously chosen dependence. Marital unity, insofar as it relies on divine law, goes against the grain of modern life. Contractual marriage has the benefit of providing an organizing principle for marriage and family life consistent with the individualism of modern life.

The view of marriage as a contract represents a natural perspective, one in which human beings are the creators, definers, and preservers of the marital bond. There is much in the idea of marriage that lends support to this view. The marriage contract is flexible and the interested parties negotiate the terms of the relationship. Marriage begins as a bilateral voluntary agreement, just like a contract. Even the greatest modern critic of the contractual view of marriage, Hegel, agrees that marriage "begin[s] from the point of view of contract," in which the persons uniting appear to themselves as self-sufficient or independent. The consensual beginning of marriage also bespeaks the equality of the partners: each creature enjoys the rationality to enter into the agreement (thus modern societies set an age of consent for marriage and for engaging in consensual sex). Divorce by mutual consent also reflects the contractual character of marriage. Contractual marriage is designed to ensure that marriage serves the individuals in the marriage by securing independence for each. It limits parental authority to determine marriage partners and even parental veto over marriage partners. Individuals are the best judges of what is in their interest, so they should determine whether a particular marriage proposal is in their interest. The betrothed may still ask for parental consent or advice, but even parents with strong reservations yield to the wishes of their children. Asking others to validate our sentiment of love would be like asking someone to feel our pain or to live our life. Consent buckles love to marriage and is evidence of that love.

Yet the idea that consent secures individual independence carries potentially corrosive implications if that independence is never surrendered upon entering marriage. Beauvoir takes independence furthest. Independence entails legal equality, economic sustenance outside of marriage, freedom from children, sexual freedom through contraception, and the elimination of the sexual double standard. An independent person does not need any other particular person and has no need for the institution of marriage. Beauvoir severs things that were connected by tradition and nature and argues for designing one's life for oneself. There is something intensely spiritual about this emphasis on independence in consent. Marital relations arise from our ideas and visions, not from our bodies or from bonds suggested by the body. Sex has the meaning we decide to give it, so even the most intensely physical act receives its meaning from the spirit.[12] This autonomy grounds many of the separations in modern thinking on the family, for it involves the separation of soul from body. The desire for independence contains a radical philosophical position, articulated by Beauvoir, emphasizing the independent human creation of meaning as, in a sense, the essence of humanity. This means human beings can invent and reinvent the institutions of human life free from internal or external control. This independence as autonomy leads to the view that human beings make their own laws and institutions to suit their visions of self. Independence applied to the family means that a husband or wife puts self above spouse and children.

Only after understanding this desire for independence in all its depth and complexity can we begin to see its limits and ambiguities. Is autonomy so understood humanly possible? How much autonomy is good for human beings? No one, not even the sociobiological defenders of the family, articulates the goodness of the alternative pole implicating the goodness of dependence (though they do argue for the necessity of sex). When today's arguments obscure a genuine human good, it is necessary to defend the place of that good in the hope of arresting the trend and to show the limits of the alternative principle.

Consider first a philosophic problem in emphasizing the pole of independence as autonomy. For advocates of autonomy, the human future is undefined and undefinable. Autonomous creatures favor the open-ended pursuit of ends; the institutions made for such creatures cannot limit open-endedness; and institutions are deinstitutionalized *in principle.* Embracing autonomy leads to declines in the value of goods in permanence, stability, and dependability. People cannot be certain what to expect from their most intimate associates. Eschewing institutions imposed by the tradition of family unity, modern thinkers are susceptible to an unmoored politics of imagination that privileges arbitrary humors asserted by the will over rational self-government.[13] Freedom as autonomy leads to arbitrariness or subjectivity unless it is dependent on reason to an extent. To say the same thing, autonomy without direction or opposition from the outside fosters human creativity divorced from reason. This internal critique of autonomy implies that a form of human *dependence* on unmade things is part of human life and that we cannot recognize human freedom apart from the existence of these unmade things.

Most modern thinkers, quietly acknowledging this problem, embrace the seed of autonomy while seeking to limit its growth with a conception of nature. Whether it is the natural givens in Locke, the natural differences between the sexes leading the imagination in Rousseau, or the natural psychological sex differences in Hegel, Comte, Durkheim, Freud, and sociobiology, these notions of nature form the basis for the continuation of the family as an institutional limit within which the free, creative power of human labor operates. These thinkers also conceive of nature as an unstable something that can be changed or overcome through science, subsequent acts of human labor, acts of the imagination, history, alternative institutions, or advances in technology. Nothing stable emerges from their sensible attempts to limit autonomy and lend stability to family life due to their unsettling conception of nature. Nature appears as a challenge or as an object of standing reserve subject to human manipulation, not as a permanent limit or reflection of a deeper moral reality. The crisis of family unity derives from this understanding of nature and the concept of autonomy to which it is tied.

A defense of human dependence requires that we leave the modern concept of nature. The most philosophically confident defenses of unified family life arise from organized religion, and the fruitful practice of marital and familial unity is associated, in the West, with natural law and religious belief generally and with Christianity in particular. Why this is so is connected to the understanding of the goodness of the created order or nature associated with, but analytically distinct from, religious belief. On a general level, dependence involves connecting the human desire for freedom or autonomy with the question of the good. Autonomy, in this regard, serves goods beyond itself, and exercises of autonomy are judged with reference to these goods. Human beings are free to strive for the good; that freedom is a means to the good marks the form of human dependence on the good. Let us consider these claims. From the modern view, the family and human institutions in general are human creations in flux. Under this conception, there are no safe, calm harbors for morals or human institutions amidst the flux of nature and human life. Yet human life, from another point of view, appears remarkably steady and constant, if we do not demand certainty. Human beings strive for justice, love, virtue, wisdom, pleasure, equanimity, victory, nobility, strength, beauty, and other goods. People are free to range among these goods, so these goods do not appear to be created arbitrarily or posited merely by the will. Ranging among them leaves plenty of room for argument (and even for difference) about which good is most essential or highest. At their noblest, free human beings strive to investigate these peaks of existence. Striving requires that we recognize the range of goods on which human beings are dependent and for which they aspire. Striving is common to diverse human beings, and deliberation consists in considering the world in relation to these goods.

People are drawn to lives dedicated to pleasure, lives dedicated to honor, lives dedicated to practical arts, lives of moral excellence, political life, family life, lives of religious devotion, and philosophic life. These ways of life are not necessarily inconsistent with one another, nor are they necessarily opposed to one another. Either out of frustration at our inability to discover for certain which of these goods is the highest, truest, or best, or from a desire to expunge the goods associated with Christianity, modern thinkers embark on a project emphasizing independence and human creativity. Seeing man increasingly as a historical being, modern thinkers see human striving as a desire for sovereignty or autonomy. This aspiration is self-defeating, however. It is best to realize that our freedom is not so constrained, yet also constrained, by our concern for goodness or happiness. This view brings with it more quiescence about revolutionary change, because we desire to preserve the freedom of others to range among these goods to find their own.

Marriage and family life are competitors among these human goods because they implicate one of the great, if also one of the greatly disputed, human goods: love. Lovers are dependent on a beloved, and unified family life necessarily entails a range of dependencies. Instead of denying that marriage and family life involve dependencies, I would acknowledge and embrace that reality. Family life entails the dependencies of love. More than a few feminist critics of marriage and family life put love in the dock as a "pivot of women's oppression."[14] This is true in a sense and false in another. Love is "oppressive" (if that is the right word) or dependency making; it makes claims on our being; it involves changing our identity; it points to our lack of self-sufficiency. It is false, however, in that love's chains are neither arbitrary social constructions, nor unchosen, nor unworthy of choosing. Love resembles a universal language; its experience knows no boundaries, nor is it consigned to a particular era.

Marriage is founded in consent; it forms a loving, mutually dependent relation that *supersedes* the point of view of contract. Consent leads to a transformation, for true marriage supersedes the more contractual, individualist rendering of reciprocity—"I will do something for you if you do something for me." Recall how the idea of contract is limited as a conceptual tool for thinking about and experiencing marriage and family life. Whereas contracts spell out terms, marriages concern unforeseeable uncertainties that force the adaptation of plans for the relationship. Health changes, people get different jobs or lose jobs, and our individual identities change as we adapt to living with another. Few are so blessed with foresight to predict all that a marriage will involve ten months hence, much less ten years. The arrival of children changes priorities and, once again, leads couples to supersede the point of view of contract. The supposed need for spouses (especially wives) to achieve economic independence from the other illustrates the limits of the contractual view. To an extent, couples and families practice a community of property. Money goes into a common pool from which communal property is purchased; houses, furniture, books, appliances, and all other household items are acquired with a family's resources, and all members of the family have access to these items. There is not much of a "tragedy of the commons" problem in this situation, however, since members care about the upkeep of commonly owned items. They care about the property because they are members of the family and the family owns the property. Even if men and women seek financial independence from their spouses as a matter of protection, they generally do not think twice about placing their earnings in a common pool for the purposes of eating, lodging, driving, and taxation. Divorce, a testament to the contractual view, is complicated because it is difficult to divide the things created by the marriage. The family is, for theoretical and practical reasons, a communal institution; its members are unable to figure out where "mine ends" and "yours begins." Many women seek a more enriching range of experiences rather than independence, and their seeking may reflect a laudable effort to "have it all" that need not be inconsistent with unified family life. The ideology of contract obscures these realities.

This mutual dependence within a community of sharing goes much deeper, for it leaves out the application it has to children and the physical act of love. Children are "wholes" created from the "parts" provided by parents, and there is no way to divide children if the parents want out of the relationship. While spouses may agree to have a child, children are not and cannot be parties to this contract, and spouses rarely agree to have a particular child. Sex is another mutual dependence difficult to capture with the ideology of contract. Men and women need each other for sex. Sex is often mutual use for the purpose of individual pleasure; sex is consensual. The ideology of contract captures such manifestations of sex. Yet it explains neither *all* sex nor sex connected to its biological result. Sex can join two people into one, either literally through the creation of children or figuratively in the sharing of a life.

The role sex plays in mutual dependence leads us to consider how human beings are dependent in another profound, specifically natural way. Human beings are bodies as well as creative spirits or souls. The family, love, and sex make sense only if we integrate and appreciate this reality at the foundation of our thinking. Again, our tendency is to *separate* procreation from sex and from marriage; what we mean by the separation in each of these cases illustrates the basic premises of the ideology of contract. When modern peoples separate procreation from sex, it is an effort to define the meaning of sex for ourselves instead of mutely following nature's orders. Those engaging in sex determine its meaning or even whether it will have meaning; sex creates bonds that lovers invent and to which they consent. Sex is spiritualized or less bodily as it is divorced from procreation. Likewise with the separation of procreation and marriage. Not the body, but the spirit, imagination, and mind define and create marital bonds. Contemporary conceptions of marriage result not only from the separation of marriage from procreation, but also from privileging the spiritual creative aspect over the procreative. With greater "realism" ascertaining the essence of marriage, contemporary thinkers leave dependence on the body behind.

While we may be able to conceive of financial independence within marriage (though it is difficult to achieve it), the idea of sexual independence is an oxymoron. Low bodily needs and passions—the need to eat and drink, sexual desire, for instance—lead human beings outside of themselves while testifying to our dependent and social nature. Infant children manifest this dependence most obviously, for these children must first be (re)produced by the body and then sustained by others. No human being escapes these realities, and the household arises to meet them. Individuals also depend on one another in sex, and they depend on their bodies to perform it. Sex is intensely physical, though not only that. Sex indicates that we want or love another particular person, that we may depend on another for satisfaction, fulfillment, and enrichment. Higher aspirations grow from these lower needs and passions, and they can only arise after some of these lower needs are satisfied. Marriage and family life need not be a realm of necessity or un-freedom. Instead, in and through them, we see our anxious, dependent, social nature. The "necessities" of marriage and family life are necessary if we fail to learn how to love another freely. Assertions of human independence, such as those of Beauvoir, depend on suppression of these facts and a failure to connect them to what is highest.

This sharing of goods, procreation, parenthood, mutual adaptability, and mutual dependence speak to how the marital union transforms individuals. Part of this transformation involves deepening mutual dependence in marriage. This deepening is what love is; the goodness of dependence is tied to the idea that love itself is a great human good. Perhaps genuine liberal freedom, recognizing the incommensurability of human goods, sees the family as a venue wherein the goods come into conflict and seeks to reconcile them, knowing full well that upsetting the balance risks undermining genuine goods.

The Family's End(s)

It is necessary to think through the goals of marriage and family life in order to give an adequate account of their proper form. Marriage and family life appear as stark illustrations of *modernization*. As the family loses functions and authority, people seem less committed to it and invest less in it. As they invest less in it, people see themselves more as individuals apart from the family and come together only for an increasingly narrow range of tasks revolving around companionship, affection, and offering psychological support.[15] *Companionate marriages* are built around these ends.[16] Spouses sharing experiences in the workplace and in the family, on this view, are more likely to regard one another with empathy and to understand one another; relationships will be less hierarchical, leading to greater interpersonal intimacy and sympathy; and sex, aided by modern contraception, need not lead to unwanted pregnancies so that gender roles can be more open-ended. This vision of marriage lends itself to the *contractual* reading of marriage. Wives and husbands see themselves as agents with independent interests bargaining over their roles in the "household." Persons with independent interests in the relationship (we leave the exclusive language of legal marriage at this point) may renegotiate the terms of marriage to suit changes in interest, ambition, and ability, and leaving the relationship is always an option when it no longer secures the mutual support, companionship, and affection that first brought the couple together.[17] This process almost seems as if it is beyond human control. As society grows more institutions (especially including the state), the family loses its functions, and as it loses its communal functions, it loses it communal *raison d'etre*. As marriage loses its functions, it loses its communal form, and this fosters the deinstitutionalization of marriage. The legal development of seeing living together as equivalent to marriage follows from this moral revolution about the family's end.

Social science shows that cohabitation accomplishes the thin emotional goals it sets for itself less well than marriage.[18] Studies show that neotraditional, communal marriage (practicing a division of labor centered around more intensive family ends and rooted in communities centered around religious faith) is at least as satisfying as, and probably more satisfying than, companionate marriage.[19] These findings scream out for theoretical elaboration, for they defend more communal institutions in the name of the thin ends set for the family in late modernity. The real question, I submit, concerns whether we should understand the ends of marriage and family life in the thin terms of late modernity and how we can recover a language that does justice to the continuing experience of marital and familial unity.

The thin, mostly psychological and individualistic ends set for married life in contemporary thinking eschew the underlying community of married life because they seek to maintain individual independence within an inescapably dependent relationship. They reflect a desire to consent to a marriage, but to consent as little as possible and to be able to rescind one's consent. They reflect a paramount concern to maintain equality within the family. Husbands and wives contract for "mutual support, and Assistance" and "Care, and Affection" (Locke), "sympathy in equality" (Mill), cultivating self-control (Durkheim), or "facilitating each member . . . in the process of discovering, and becoming, himself" (Carl Rogers).[20] The parties to the marriage understand themselves as contracting for mutual use, ensuring that the relationship remains in the realm of subjectivity.

While these psychological conditions are part of love, neither alone nor added up do they capture the experience of marriage and family life. Love makes the family, and love has a particular character. In the nature of love, and how it relates to marriage and family life, we come upon the manner of limiting modern and contemporary efforts to deconstruct and reconstruct these institutions.[21] Hegel is an appropriate guide for thinking about the nature of marital love. Love begins with a longing, reflecting a sense of human deficiency. The reaction to this longing at first appears to be a self-forgetting, self-effacing, self-denying joining with another filled by the unconditional gift of oneself to another person. This is not quite what goes on. There are genuinely sacrificial moments in this joining with another, yet the uniting is not sacrificial but rather a life-enhancing, life-enriching experience. It adds another to one's being without demanding that one lose one's own.

The concepts of affection, care, sympathy, self-fulfillment, and self-control do not do justice to what love, in its totality, is and creates because none of them demand that we leave the standpoint of contract. Love presents genuine reciprocity, trust, peace, and joy to the couple experiencing it. I aim not to pile up adjectives but to illustrate that the thin ends of late modernity are parts of a larger whole. Conceiving of marriage in terms of affection and sympathy is not wrong, so long as we do not leave it at that. Affection (an emotional warmth for and desire to be near another) and sympathy (a passive emotional fellow feeling) are the ingredients out of which love is built. Standing alone they are insufficient and unstable, because they do not call forth common goods outside the individual around which to create a durable relation. Affection and sympathy are the inclinations out of which friendship grows. Attempting to build marriage only out of affection and sympathy, or mistaking these parts of love for the whole of love, leads people to fall out of "love" before they have a chance to build it. Friendship involves desiring another's good and acting to achieve it, and Mill's equation of friendship and marital love is not wrong. Love is, in a sense, friendship with benefits. The benefits are not sexual access, or not just sexual access. Sensual experiences are tip-offs to what the benefits that accompany friendship are. Lovers transcend merely subjective emotions or passions in desiring the good of a beloved above their own. Children also show how subjective passions point beyond themselves to the creation of a self-transcending reality. Man and wife take action to ensure that their love lasts and that their children thrive, and this taking action demonstrates that love and parenthood do not remain on the passive, subjective level characteristic of late modernity's public understanding of marriage.

Contemporary human beings exercise a tremendous power over nature and over their life courses, and this destabilizes the boundaries of nature and the human institutions designed for our happiness. In the face of this uncertainty, spouses take responsibility for building their love and projecting it into the future. Children, again, are emblematic of this responsibility. Parents bring children into the world, parents sustain and educate them, and parents maintain an intense concern for their well-being into the future. Our human future is in doubt if we lack human beings willing and able to act on their concern about the continuation of the human future. We cannot understand a parent's responsibility for a child or a spouse's dependence on a beloved apart from the love and self-giving that are involved in marriage and family life. Responsibility is the virtue of owning an uncertain future, and anyone who risks love must be responsible in this way. Love is an enriching, self-transcending virtue whereby we gift ourselves to others as we build a common life. Love is the reason we seek responsibility for the future. Responsibility and love—these are the virtues, I say, that define marriage and family life. They are high exercises of human freedom, and without them as the family's ends we may reach the family's end.

Notes

Chapter 1

1 Consider, e.g., E. J. Graff, *What Is Marriage For?* (Boston: Beacon, 1999); Judith Stacey, *In the Name of the Family: Rethinking the Family in a Postmodern Age* (Boston: Beacon, 1997); Linda McClain, *The Place of Families* (Cambridge, Mass.: Harvard University Press, 2006); Martha Fineman, *The Autonomy Myth* (London: New Press, 2005); and Stephanie Coontz, *Marriage, a History: From Obedience to Intimacy, or How Love Conquered Marriage* (New York: Viking, 2005).

2 Consider, e.g., Linda J. Waite and Maggie Gallagher, *The Case for Marriage: Why Married People Are Happier, Healthier, and Better Off Financially* (New York: Broadway, 2000); David Blankenhorn, *Fatherless America* (New York: HarperCollins, 1996); David Popenoe, *Life without Father: Compelling New Evidence That Fatherhood and Marriage Are Indispensable for the Good of Children and Society* (New York: Free Press, 1996); and Kay S. Hymowitz, *Marriage and Caste in America* (Chicago: Ivan R. Dee, 2006).

3 Compare David Blankenhorn, *The Future of Marriage* (New York: Encounter, 2007), with Jessie Bernard, *The Future of Marriage* (New York: Bantam, 1973).

4 Alan Wolfe, *One Nation, After All* (New York: Penguin, 1999), 9–10, defines the freedom coming with modernity as "the freedom to construct one's own life as one best sees fit. Concretely, that means not accepting God's commands regarding right and wrong, but developing one's own personal ethical standards. It means thinking of marriage as a union of consenting equals to be dissolved when it oppresses one or both of the parties involved." See also Michael Sandel, *Democracy's Discontent* (Cambridge, Mass.: Harvard University Press, 1996).

5 For the first part of this shift, see Emile Durkheim, "The Conjugal Family," in *Durkheim on Institutional Analysis*, ed. and trans. Mark

Traugott (Chicago: University of Chicago Press, 1985), 229–39; and for the second part, see Law Commission of Canada, "Beyond Conjugality" (2001), http://www.samesexmarriage.ca/docs/beyond_conjugality.pdf; James Smith, *Beyond Monogamy* (Baltimore: Johns Hopkins University Press, 1974); Mary Ann Glendon, *The Transformation of Family Law* (Chicago: University of Chicago Press, 1989), chap. 2; and Fineman, *Autonomy Myth*, 99, 106–8, 134–36.

6 James Q. Wilson, *The Marriage Problem* (New York: HarperCollins, 2002), 83–105; Law Commission of Canada, "Beyond Conjugality," xxiii; and Robin Fretwell Wilson, ed., *Reconceiving the Family* (Cambridge: Cambridge University Press, 2006), chaps. 14–17.

7 Glendon, *Transformation of Family Law*, chap. 4; and American Law Institute, *Principles of the Law of Family Dissolution: Analysis and Recommendations* (Philadelphia: American Law Institute, 2002), chap. 6.

8 Michael Walzer, *Spheres of Justice* (New York: Basic Books, 1983), 218–19.

9 David Popenoe, *Disturbing the Nest* (New Brunswick, N.J.: Transaction, 1988), chap. 7; and Glendon, *Transformation of Family Law*, 291–98.

10 American Law Institute's *Principles of the Law of Family Dissolution* is an American version and follows the policy of "Beyond Conjugality," though without its lengthy justification for the policies.

11 Law Commission of Canada, "Beyond Conjugality," 7. Also Graff, *What Is Marriage*, 36–48, 113–17.

12 Law Commission of Canada, "Beyond Conjugality," 12–17.

13 Law Commission of Canada, "Beyond Conjugality," 113. See also McClain, *Place of Families*, 191–215.

14 Blankenhorn, *Future of Marriage*, 12–21, surveys journalistic and legal opinion on the matter of what marriage is and concludes that most think that "marriage is exclusively a private relationship, created by and for the couple, essentially unconnected to larger social needs and public meanings." See also McClain, *Place of Families*, 151–54; Pepper Schwartz, *Love Between Equals* (New York: Free Press, 1995), 10–11, 181–85; Graff, *What Is Marriage*, 70–71, 113–17; Robert P. George, "What's Sex Got to Do with It?" in *The Meaning of Marriage*, ed. Robert George and Jean Bethke Elshtain (Dallas, Tex.: Spence, 2006), 145; Glendon, *Transformation of Family Law*, 2, 144–45, 297.

15 John Witte, *From Sacrament to Contract* (Louisville, Ky.: Westminster

John Knox, 1997), cf. 3–4 with 10–11 and chap. 1 with chap. 5 to see the outer limits of this transformation. See also Wilson, *Marriage Problem*, 88 ("The Enlightenment laid the groundwork for replacing a sacrament with a contract and then a contract with an arrangement"); and Glendon, *Transformation of Family Law*, 26–34.

16 Cf. John Locke, *Second Treatise of Government* (henceforth *2T*), in Locke, *Two Treatises of Government*, ed. Peter Laslett (Cambridge: Cambridge University Press, 1960), ¶78, with Nena O'Neil and George O'Neil, *Open Marriage* (New York: M. Evans, 1972), 43.

17 We will consider the arguments of Rousseau, Hegel, Comte, Durkheim, and John Paul II below, all of whom are critics, in one way or another, of overemphasizing personal independence in marriage and family life. Those who see contemporary advocates of retrenchment as alarmist sometimes point to the *Boston Quarterly Review* (1859): "The Family, in its old sense, is disappearing from our land, and not only our free institutions are threatened but the very existence of our society is endangered." See Graff, *What Is Marriage*, 88; and Phillip Longman, *The Empty Cradle* (New York: Basic Books, 2004), 151.

18 Popenoe, *Life without Father*, 52–78; Blankenhorn, *Fatherless America*, 25–48; Patricia Morgan, *The War between the State and the Family* (New Brunswick, N.J.: Transaction, 2008), 22–48; Paul Amato and Alan Booth, *A Generation at Risk: Growing Up in a Time of Family Upheaval* (Cambridge, Mass.: Harvard University Press, 1997), 20, 216–21; Waite and Gallagher, *Case for Marriage*, 124–40; Judith Wallerstein, Julia Lewis, and Sandra Blakeslee, *Unexpected Legacy of Divorce, A Landmark 25 Year Study* (New York: Hyperion, 2000), xxiii–xxv, 294–316; Elizabeth Marquardt, *Between Two Worlds* (New York: Three Rivers, 2006); Barbara Defoe Whitehead, *The Divorce Culture* (New York: Vintage, 1998); Mary Eberstadt, *Home-Alone America* (New York: Penguin, 2004); W. Bradford Wilcox, *Why Marriage Matters*, 2nd ed. (New York: Institute for American Values, 2005), 10–33; and Marsha Garrison, "Marriage Matters," in Wilson, *Reconceiving the Family*, 322–27.

19 Blankenhorn, *Future of Marriage*, 17 ("Without children, marriage as an institution makes little sense"), 99–105; Alan Carlson, *Conjugal America* (New Brunswick, N.J.: Transaction Publishers, 2007), 5–22; Wilson, *Marriage Problem*, 25–44, 218–22; James Q. Wilson, "Marriage, Evolution, and the Enlightenment" (lecture, American Enterprise Institute, May 3, 1999), ¶2 ("If the human infant were born able to move about and feed itself, as is true of sharks," Wilson notes,

"marriage would not exist"); Brigitte Berger, *The Family in the Modern Age: More Than a Lifestyle Choice* (New Brunswick, N.J.: Transaction, 2002), 139–73; Jennifer Roback Morse, *Love and Economics* (Dallas, Tex.: Spence, 2001), 83–158; Garrison, "Marriage Matters," 319–20.

20 For discussions of this modified nuclear family, consider David Popenoe, *The War over the Family* (New Brunswick, N.J.: Transaction, 2008), 182–85; Blankenhorn, *Future of Marriage*, chap. 8.

21 Popenoe, *War over the Family*; and Brigitte Berger and Peter Berger, *The War over the Family: Capturing the Middle Ground* (New York: Doubleday, 1983).

22 See Coontz, *Marriage, A History*, 113–18, 145–49; Graff, *What Is Marriage*, 2, 11–16, 92–99; Wilson, *Marriage Problem*, 41; Berger, *Family in the Modern Age*, 74–80; Waite and Gallagher, *Case for Marriage*, 44–46, 117.

23 Cf. the U.S. Supreme Court in *Eisenstadt v. Baird*: "The marital couple is not an independent entity with a mind and heart of its own, but an association of two individuals each with a separate intellectual and emotional makeup."

24 Mark 10:8; see also Genesis 2:24, Matthew 19:5, and Ephesians 5:31.

25 Pedro-Juan Viladrich, *The Agony of Legal Marriage* (Pamplona: Servicio de Pulicaciones de la Universidad de Navarra, 1990), 182.

26 George, "What's Sex," 146–53; and Viladrich, *Agony of Legal Marriage*, 200–202.

27 Survey the prefaces and acknowledgments to nearly every academic book and find repeated testimony to marital love and mutual dependence involved in marriage, even among those professing no particular attachment to these goods.

28 David Hume, "Of Polygamy and Divorce," in *Essays Moral, Political and Literary*, ed. Eugene Miller (Indianapolis, Ind.: Liberty Fund, 1987), 189. Consider also Blackstone, *Commentaries on the Laws of England* (Chicago: University of Chicago Press, 1979), 1:430: "By marriage, the husband and wife are one person in law: that is, the very being or legal existence of the woman is suspended during marriage, or at least is incorporated and consolidated into that of the husband: under whose wing, protection, and *cover*, she performs every thing."

29 Glendon, *Transformation of Family Law*, 103–10.

30 Glendon, *Transformation of Family Law*, 125, 116–35; and Garrison, "Marriage Matters," 307–15, esp. notes 22 and 24.

31 Hegel, *Philosophy of Right*, 1633R. All italicized words within quotations are in the original unless otherwise noted.

32 Evidence for the idea that marriage is transformative is summarized by the comparison between marriage and cohabitation in Waite and Gallagher, *Case for Marriage*, 17, 22–35, 54, 67–68, 73–77, 83–88, 94–96, 99ff.; and Garrison, "Marriage Matters," 307–15.

33 Consider especially Sandel, *Democracy's Discontent*, 108–15; Garrison, "Marriage Matters," 327–29; and Glendon, *Transformation of Family Law*, 144–47.

34 See Alexis de Tocqueville, *Democracy in America*, trans. Harvey C. Mansfield Jr. and Delba Winthrop (Chicago: University of Chicago Press, 2000), 483 (2.2.2); and Pierre Manent, *A World beyond Politics?* trans. Marc LePain (Princeton, N.J.: Princeton University Press, 2006), 111–16.

35 Morse, *Love and Economics*, 53–61.

36 Consider, for instance, Waite and Gallagher, *Case for Marriage*, in light of Tocqueville, *Democracy in America*, 501–3 (2.2.8).

37 Elizabeth Fox-Genovese, *Marriage: The Dream That Refuses to Die* (Wilmington, Del.: ISI Books, 2008); also Glendon, *Transformation of Family Law*, 297 ("The legal imagery of separateness and independence contrasts everywhere with the way most functioning families operate and with the circumstances of mothers and young children in both intact and broken homes").

38 Berger likewise thinks "every theory of the family implicitly contains a set of assumptions about human nature." *Family in the Modern Age*, 72.

39 Tocqueville, *Democracy in America*, 518 (2.2.15).

40 Stacey, *Name of the Family*, 122–27 (Consider especially 127: "If we begin to value the meaning and quality of intimate bonds over their customary forms, there are few limits to the kinds of marriage and kinship patterns people might wish to devise. . . . Two friends might decide to marry without basing their bond on erotic or romantic attachment. . . . Or, more radical still, perhaps some might dare to question the dyadic limitations of Western marriage and seek some of the benefits of extended family life through small-group marriages arranged to share resources, nurturance, and labor"); Fineman,

Autonomy Myth, 134–36; David A. J. Richards, *The Case for Gay Rights* (Lawrence: University Press of Kansas, 2005), 131–38; and McClain, *Place of Families*, 162–70, 181–82.

41 Consider, especially, Jonathan Rauch, *Gay Marriage: Why It Is Good for Gays, Good for Straights, and Good for America* (New York: Henry Holt and Company, 2004), 89–93, 24; and Andrew Sullivan, *Virtually Normal: An Argument about Homosexuality* (New York: Vintage, 1996), 179.

42 See Blankenhorn, *Future of Marriage*.

43 George, "What's Sex," 149–57.

44 Tocqueville is the last thinker to fall on the cutting room floor, and I could write a book on why that is. Most everything that is important and excellent in Tocqueville's treatment of the family appears in Hegel's account (though Tocqueville's treatment may rest on different foundations), and the dissolution of Tocqueville's family happens for the same reasons that Hegel's family dissolves. What Hegel accomplishes more excellently than Tocqueville, in my judgment, is explicitly to articulate the psychology that leads to the satisfactions of marital and familial unity and the legal regime on which it rests.

45 Some writers, such as Comte, Mill, and Marx, write at approximately the same time, so it is difficult to determine the proper chronological order.

Chapter 2

1 Consider Witte, *From Sacrament to Contract*, 192–93; and Allan Bloom, *The Closing of the American Mind* (New York: Simon & Schuster, 1987), 110ff.: "The nation as a community of families was a formula that until recently worked very well in the United States. However, it is very questionable whether this solution is viable over the very long run" (112). Thomas L. Pangle, *The Spirit of Modern Republicanism* (Chicago: University of Chicago Press, 1990), puts forward a variation on this theme: "Locke is not of course the sole source of the powerful forces which have since his time steadily eroded the patriarchal family. . . . But he abetted and vastly strengthened those forces by giving them their most powerful theoretical justification and most sober rhetorical dress" (242). See also Wilson, *Marriage Problem*, 83, 88; Peter Augustine Lawler, *Homeless and At Home in America* (South Bend, Ind.: St. Augustine's, 2007), 95–100; and Peter

Augustine Lawler, *Stuck with Virtue* (Wilmington, Del.: ISI Books, 2005), 217–34.

2 See Peter Laslett, *Family-Life and Illicit Love in Earlier Generations* (Cambridge: Cambridge University Press, 1977), 102–59; Gordon Schochet, *The Authoritarian Family and Political Attitudes in 17th Century England* (New Brunswick, N.J.: Transaction, 1987), 54–84; Gordon Schochet, *Patriarchalism in Political Thought* (New York: Basic Books, 1975); and Lawrence Stone, *The Family, Sex and Marriage in England, 1500–1800* (New York: Harper & Row, 1977), 628–36, 645–48.

3 Tocqueville, *Democracy in America*, 228 (1.2.6).

4 Consider Blankenhorn, *Future of Marriage*, 26–27.

5 Locke, *2T* ¶8. I will refer to Locke's works by the following abbreviations: *1T* = *First Treatise of Government*, in *Two Treatises of Government*, ed. Peter Laslett (Cambridge: Cambridge University Press, 1960) (followed by paragraph); *2T* = *Second Treatise of Government*, in Laslett, *Two Treatises* (followed by paragraph); *ECHU* = *Essay Concerning Human Understanding* (New York: Dover, 1959) (followed by book, chapter, and paragraph); and *STCE* = *Some Thoughts Concerning Education*, ed. Ruth Grant (Indianapolis, Ind.: Hackett, 1996) (followed by paragraph).

6 Locke, *2T* ¶105–7.

7 Locke, *2T* ¶79.

8 Locke, *2T* ¶80; also Locke, *1T* ¶90.

9 Locke, *1T* ¶54.

10 Peter C. Myers, *Only Star and Compass* (Lanham, Md.: Rowman & Littlefield, 1999), 199.

11 Locke, *2T* ¶65, 80.

12 Blankenhorn, *Fatherless America*; and Popenoe, *Life without Father*. This "male problematic" is a hallmark of the contemporary literature on sociobiology. See especially David Buss, *The Evolution of Desire* (New York: Basic Books, 1975), and chapter 10 below.

13 Locke, *ECHU* 1.3.9; also Locke, *1T* ¶54–56.

14 Locke, *1T* ¶56; and David Foster, "Taming the Father: John Locke's Critique of Patriarchal Fatherhood," *Review of Politics* 56 (Fall 1994): 659.

15 Locke, *2T* ¶110. See Melissa Butler, "Early Liberal Roots of Feminism: John Locke's Attack on Patriarchy," in *Feminist Interpretations of John*

Locke, ed. Nancy J. Hirschman and Kristie M. McClure (University Park: Penn State University Press, 2007), 112; and Lee Ward, "The Natural Rights Family," in *Nature, Woman, and the Art of Politics*, ed. Eduardo Velasquez (Lanham, Md.: Rowman & Littlefield, 2000), 156–61.

16 Locke, *1T* ¶47–49; Locke, *2T* ¶74, 105, 106, 112.

17 What follows in this paragraph borrows from Foster, "Taming the Father," 664–67. As representatives of the tradition, consider John Calvin, *Institutes of the Christian Religion*, trans. Henry Beveridge (Grand Rapids: Eerdmans, 1957), 2.8.35–38; Robert Filmer, *Patriarcha and Other Writings*, ed. Johann Sommerville (Cambridge: Cambridge University Press, 1991), 12; Samuel Pufendorf, *On the Duty of Man and Citizen According to Natural Law*, ed. James Tully, trans. Michael Silverthorne (Cambridge: Cambridge University Press, 1991), 126–27; Aristotle, *Nicomachean Ethics*, trans. Martin Ostwald (New York: Macmillan, 1962), 1163b15–29; and Cicero, *De Officiis*, trans. Walter Miller (Cambridge, Mass.: Harvard University Press, 1913), 1.17.

18 Exodus 20:12 (KJV). Butler, "Early Liberal Roots," 106–7; Schochet, *Authoritarian Family*, 6–7, 72ff.; and Foster, "Taming the Father," 665. Foster points out that both Luther and Calvin present their teachings on obedience to government within the context of their discussions of this commandment. See Luther, "Explanation of the Fourth Commandment" in *Small Catechism* (St. Louis: Concordia Publishing House, 1943), 6; and Calvin, *Institutes*, 2.7.35.

19 Locke, *ECHU* 2.28.11, 1.3.26, and 4.20.17.

20 Locke, *1T* ¶88.

21 Locke, *2T* ¶4.

22 Locke, *2T* ¶78.

23 Consider Robert Paul Wolff, "There's Nobody Here But Us Persons," in *Women and Philosophy*, ed. Carol C. Gould and Marx W. Wartofsky (New York: Penguin, 1976): "Despite all the treatises on education in the liberal tradition, there is little recognition that childhood is an essential stage in the life of each person, and not merely an irritating infirmity, symmetrical with the infirmities of old age, save that childhood, unlike old age, is to be got over as quickly as possible" (132).

24 Myers sees the ends of marriage in procreation and the education of children, both of which lend stability to the household and point "toward the moderation inherent in Locke's understanding of marriage as a voluntary, contractual relationship." *Only Star and Compass*, 205.

25 Locke, *2T* ¶75.

26 Ward, "Natural Rights Family," 157; Pangle, *Spirit of Modern Republicanism*, 172–74.

27 Locke, *1T* ¶47.

28 Locke, *2T* ¶106.

29 Locke, *2T* ¶94.

30 Cf. Foster, "Taming the Father," 660, with Jean Bethke Elshtain, *Public Man, Private Woman* (Princeton, N.J.: Princeton University Press, 1981), 125.

31 Locke, *2T* ¶82.

32 Cf. Schochet, *Authoritarian Family*, 275.

33 In this, Locke aligns with many contemporary marriage advocates by seeing the procreation and education of children as the "chief" reasons for marriage, as against those who see marriage as a relationship of affirmed love and commitment between adults. See Blankenhorn, *Future of Marriage*, 26–27; Wilson, *Marriage Problem*, 83; and Witte, *From Sacrament to Contract*, 186–93.

34 See Mary Lyndon Shanley, "Marriage Contract and Social Contract in Seventeenth Century Political Thought," in Hirschman and McClure, *Feminist Interpretations*, 31–34; Carole Pateman, *The Sexual Contract* (Stanford: Stanford University Press, 1988), chap. 4; and Butler, "Early Liberal Roots," 105.

35 Locke, *2T* ¶83; also Locke, *1T* ¶47.

36 Cf. Locke, *1T* ¶64; also *1T* ¶65, 66, with Locke, *2T* ¶83.

37 Consider especially Locke's comments on the education of girls: "I will take the Liberty to say, that . . . the nearer they come to the Hardships of their Brothers in their Education, the greater Advantage will they receive from it all the remaining Part of their Lives" (*STCE* ¶9). That Locke is no simple patriarch or that his teaching in this regard is open to feminist development or even that Locke is not fully candid about the full and liberating implications of conceiving of marriage as a contract between equals is the emphasis of a whole strand of arguments, including Ward, "Natural Rights Family," 164–75; Myers, *Only Star and Compass*, 202; and Butler, "Early Liberal Roots," 115–18.

38 Jacqueline L. Pfeffer, "The Family in John Locke's Political Thought," *Polity* 33 (2001): 607–8, 610ff.

39 So, for instance, Graff, *What Is Marriage*, 123ff., argues that the idea

that children need fathers really boils down to the idea that they need two people (or one?) with enough resources.

40 Locke, *STCE* ¶96.

41 Locke, *2T* ¶173, 139.

42 Locke, *2T* ¶56, 173. See Foster, "Taming the Father," 646n13. Locke treats education as the duty of parents (see *1T* ¶90, 93; *2T* ¶169), while he does not consider law or government to effect the purpose of education (*1T* ¶93; *2T* ¶87–89, 123, 173).

43 Locke, *2T* ¶83, 78.

44 Locke, *2T* ¶123.

45 Locke, *2T* ¶61.

46 Locke, *2T* ¶63.

47 Pfeffer, "Family," 598–600.

48 Locke, *STCE* ¶130.

49 Locke, *STCE* ¶106.

50 Locke, *ECHU* 2.21.48; also 2.21.51, 2.21.54.

51 Locke, *STCE* ¶56, 61, 31–39. See Nathan Tarcov, *Locke's Education for Liberty* (Chicago: University of Chicago Press, 1989), 86–93, 132–36.

52 Locke, *2T* ¶65.

53 Locke, *2T* ¶83.

54 Locke, *2T* ¶65.

55 Locke, *1T* ¶97. Also Locke, *2T* ¶67; and Locke, *STCE* ¶4, 5, 34, 107.

56 See Leonard Sax, *Why Gender Matters* (New York: Doubleday, 2005); and Steven E. Rhoads, *Taking Sex Differences Seriously* (New York: Encounter, 2004), chaps. 4, 8.

57 Pangle, *Spirit of Modern Republicanism*, 236; Foster, "Taming the Father," 667; and Bloom, *Closing of the American Mind*, 114–15. For a similar view, consider Karl Marx and Friedrich Engels, *The Communist Manifesto*, ed. Samuel H. Beer (Wheeling, Ill.: Harlan Davidson, 1955), 12–13, 27–28.

58 Locke, *2T* ¶67–68.

59 Locke, *2T* ¶72–73.

60 Locke, *2T* ¶72–73.

61 Locke, *2T* ¶73, 120. According to Forrest McDonald, *Novus Ordo Seclorum* (Lawrence: University Press of Kansas, 1986), 11n5, debates surrounding a 1776 act abolishing entail on estates had to respond to

the charge that the abolition "does injury to the morals of youth, by rendering them independent of and disobedient to parents" as well as discouraging parents from cultivating and improving the land itself.

62 Locke, *1T* ¶91–92, 111–18.

63 Locke, *STCE* ¶40. Cf. Pangle, *Spirit of Modern Republicanism*, 238: "Inheritance . . . proves to be *the* tie that binds maturing young people to society, both familial and civil" (emphasis added); and Ward, "Natural Rights Family," 170.

64 Locke, *STCE* ¶40; also ¶41, 42, 96; ¶96–99 generally.

65 Locke, *STCE* ¶96.

66 Locke, *STCE* ¶97.

67 Locke, *STCE* ¶96.

68 Locke, *STCE* ¶97.

69 Locke, *2T* ¶73.

70 Locke, *STCE* ¶99.

71 Niccolo Machiavelli, *The Prince*, trans. Harvey C. Mansfield Jr. (Chicago: University of Chicago Press, 1985), 66. Cf. Ward, "Natural Rights Family," 164–75, who does not emphasize the limits of Locke's reliance on inheritance.

72 Locke, *2T* ¶83; also *2T* ¶81.

73 Ward, "Natural Rights Family," 166ff.

74 Locke, *2T* ¶78.

75 Locke, *2T* ¶81.

76 Locke, *2T* ¶82.

77 Locke, *2T* ¶78, 83, 65.

78 Myers, *Only Star and Compass*, 205–6.

79 Locke, *2T* ¶223, 226.

80 Pangle, *Spirit of Modern Republicanism*, 241–42.

81 Theresa Brennan and Carole Pateman, "Mere Auxiliaries to the Commonwealth," in Hirschman and McClure, *Feminist Interpretations*, 62ff.; Diana H. Coole, *Women in Political Theory*, 2nd ed. (Boulder, Colo.: Lynne Rienner, 1993), 73.

82 See Ward, "Natural Rights Family," 167–71.

83 Locke, *2T* ¶83, 78.

84 Locke, "Virtus," in *Political Writings*, ed. David Wootton (Indianapolis, Ind.: Hackett, 2003), 241–42.

85 See Pfeffer, "Family," 608–10.

Chapter 3

1 Jean-Jacques Rousseau, *Second Discourse*, in *The First and Second Discourses*, trans. Roger Masters and Judith Masters (New York: St. Martin's, 1969), 102.

2 Rousseau, *Second Discourse*, 120–21.

3 The deepest account of how fluid the concept of childhood is can be found in Philippe Aries, *Centuries of Childhood* (London: Jonathan Cape, 1962), esp. chaps. 1–2 and the conclusion of pt. 1 in chap. 5.

4 Rousseau, *Second Discourse*, 116. To highlight the ambiguous place occupied by the good of a female for the savage, consider that, in his *Essay on the Origin of Languages*, Rousseau contends that natural man lives "only to sleep, to vegetate, [and] to rest." *Essay on the Origin of Languages*, trans. John H. Moran (Chicago: University of Chicago Press, 1986), 38n4.

5 Joel Schwartz, *The Sexual Politics of Jean-Jacques Rousseau* (Chicago: University of Chicago Press, 1985), 13.

6 In *Emile*, Rousseau denies that men are, or at least children are, by nature sexual beings:

> The senses are awakened by the imagination alone. Their need is not properly a physical need. It is not true that it is a true need. If no lewd object had ever struck our eyes, if no indecent idea had ever entered our minds, perhaps this alleged need would never have made itself felt in us, and we would have remained chaste without temptation, without effort, and without merit. . . . I am persuaded that a solitary man raised in a desert, without books, without instruction, and without women, would die there a virgin at whatever age he reached. (*Emile*, trans. Allan Bloom [New York: Basic Books, 1979], 333)

7 Rousseau, *Second Discourse*, 135.

8 "For a man who had no idea of merit or beauty, every woman would be equally good, and the first comer would always be the most lovable." Rousseau, *Emile*, 214.

9 Rousseau, *Second Discourse*, 134, 135.

10 Cf. Nicole Fermon, *Domesticating Passions* (Middletown, Conn.: Wesleyan University Press, 1997), 89, who uses romantic and conjugal love interchangeably.

11 Rousseau, *Second Discourse*, 141. See Eileen Hunt Botting, *Family Feuds* (New York: SUNY Press, 2006), 34.

12 Rousseau, *Second Discourse*, 146–47.

13 Rousseau, *Second Discourse*, 150–51. In the *Essay on the Origin of Languages*, Rousseau calls this time "a golden age" (33).

14 See the discussion of natural in the savage state and natural in civil society, Rousseau, *Emile*, 406. Susan Moller Okin, *Women in Western Political Theory* (Princeton, N.J.: Princeton University Press, 1979), 106–39, proceeds as if there is no ambiguity or tension in what Rousseau means by nature, and this problem leads her to accuse Rousseau of misogynistic inconsistencies. Going in the opposite direction, Penny Weiss and Anne Harper, "Rousseau's Political Defense of the Sex-Roled Family," *Hypatia* 5 (1990): 92–93, 105, contend that Rousseau's wildly different conceptions of nature hide the fact that he is a moral utilitarian.

15 Botting, *Family Feuds*, 35; and Deborah Winkle, "Convention and Constraint in the Education of Rousseau's Natural Woman," in Velasquez, *Nature, Woman*, 184–85.

16 See Rousseau's letter to Mme de Berthier (Jan. 17, 1770): "In vain I seek where one can find true happiness; if, indeed, it is at all on earth, my reason shows me it can only be [in the family]; . . . if the life of a bourgeois household is distasteful to you, and if common notions have you under their thumb, then rid yourself of the thirst for happiness that is tormenting you, for you will never appease it." In *Citizen of Geneva: Selections from the Letters of Jean-Jacques Rousseau* (Oxford: Oxford University Press, 1937), 374–75.

17 Rousseau, *Origin of Languages*, 33, 45.

18 It is also clear that Rousseau is talking about the same families in both places, for the inbreeding family of the *Essay on the Origin of Languages*, like the family of the *Second Discourse*, is a place where "instinct held the place of passion; habit held the place of preference." *Origin of Languages*, 45.

19 Rousseau, *Emile*, 221.

20 Rousseau, *Emile*, 391.

21 Rousseau, *Origin of Languages*, 44–45. See Schwartz, *Sexual Politics*, 27ff., for an excellent discussion of these matters.

22 Rousseau, *Second Discourse*, 148. Cf. Rousseau, *Origin of Languages*, 45, with Rousseau, *Second Discourse*, 149.

23 Rousseau, *Emile*, 430.

24 It is his defense of natural sex differences that leads so many scholars to see Rousseau as a defender of the patriarchal tradition. See especially Okin, *Women*, 106–39; Zillah Eisenstein, *The Radical Future of Liberal*

Feminism (New York: Longmans, 1981), 55; Joan B. Landes, *Women and the Public Sphere in the Age of the French Revolution* (Ithaca, N.Y.: Cornell University Press, 1988), 67–69, 85–89; and Pateman, *Sexual Contract*, 53–54, 96–102.

25 Rousseau, *Emile*, 264. Also: "With so great an inequality in what each risks in the union, how can one fail to see that if reserve did not impose on one sex the moderation which nature imposes on the other, the result would soon be the ruin of both, and mankind would perish by the means established for preserving it?" Rousseau, *Emile*, 358–59.

26 Rousseau, *Emile*, 360.

27 Rousseau, *Emile*, 358.

28 Rousseau, *Emile*, 361. Rousseau asks, rhetorically, "if all the austere duties of the woman were not derived from the single fact that a child ought to have a father." *Politics and the Arts: Letter to d'Alembert on the Theater*, trans. Allan Bloom (Ithaca, N.Y.: Cornell University Press, 1968), 85.

29 Rousseau, *Emile*, 357 (emphasis added). In the *Letter to d'Alembert*, Rousseau imagines a scenario in which the order of sexual attack and defense were reversed and concludes that mankind would die out (84).

30 Rousseau, *Emile*, 358.

31 Rousseau, *Emile*, 360, 358.

32 See Rousseau, *Emile*, 377: "In the harmony which reigns between them, everything tends to the common end; they do not know who contributes more. Each follows the promptings of the other; each obeys, and both are masters."

33 Rousseau, *Letter to d'Alembert*, 47, 84.

34 Rousseau, *Emile*, 361. For Rousseau's discussion of how women are enslaved to public opinion for the purposes of securing feminine modesty, consider, e.g., *Emile*, 369 ("All their lives [women] will be enslaved to the most continual and most severe of constraints—that of proprieties") and 377.

35 Rousseau, *Emile*, 408. See also *Emile*, 371, 393. The stronger may appear to be the master but "actually depends on the weaker" due to "an invariable law of nature which gives woman more facility to excite the desires than men to satisfy them. This causes the latter, whether he likes it or not, to depend on the former's wish and constrains him to seek to please her in turn. . . . Women possess *their empire* not because

men wanted it that way, but because nature wants it that way" (*Emile*, 360, emphasis added).

36 See Okin, *Women*, 101, where the characterization of Rousseau's woman as "both a virgin and a prostitute," while typically splenetic, is not entirely beside the point.

37 Rousseau, *Emile*, 407.

38 Jean-Jacques Rousseau, *Discourse on Political Economy*, trans. Judith R. Masters (New York: St. Martin's, 1978), 219 . Elshtain, *Public Man, Private Woman*, 158, calls this a "surprisingly tedious conclusion."

39 Rousseau, *Emile*, 363.

40 "The whole education of women ought to relate to men. To please men, to be useful to them, to make herself loved and honored by them, to raise them when young, to care for them when grown, to counsel them, to console them, to make their lives agreeable and sweet—these are the duties of women at all times and they ought to be taught from childhood" (Rousseau, *Emile*, 365).

41 Rousseau, *Emile*, 371, 383.

42 Rousseau, *Emile*, 377. See also 386–87.

43 Seeing Geneva as a model of vice may seem incorrect, as his *Letter to d'Alembert* appears to defend Geneva's rustic simplicity and its separation of the sexes from Paris' corrupting combinations. While Rousseau thinks that the theatre would corrupt Geneva, he suggests in section 11 of the letter that Geneva institute grand balls, dancing festivals, and beauty and singing contests in order to introduce what he elsewhere condemns as a spirit of gallantry into the cold and phlegmatic city. Geneva looks good next to Paris, but all is not well in Geneva. People are fleeing (*Letter to d'Alembert*, 132). Cf. Botting, *Family Feuds*, 37–38, who sees Rousseau's account as much more one-sidedly anti-Paris.

44 Rousseau, *Letter to d'Alembert*, 99.

45 Rousseau, *Emile*, 374. Pamela Jensen, "Dangerous Liaisons," in *Love and Friendship*, ed. Eduardo Velasquez (Lanham, Md.: Lexington, 2003), observes that the men and women of Geneva "don't seem to like each other very much, and their single sex entertainments reflect this mutual wariness" (203). Cf. Okin, *Women*, 101.

46 Consider, in this context, John Paul II [Karol Wojtyla], *Love and Responsibility* (San Francisco: Ignatius, 1981), 57–61, in which he shows that rigoristic interpretations of the sex drive are quite foreign to Christianity's emphasis on love.

47 See Rousseau, *First and Second Discourses*, 229–30, notes 1 and 3; and Fermon, *Domesticating Passions*, 67–76, who, in my view, represents the typical reading of Rousseau as endorsing Genevan institutions.

48 Rousseau, *Emile*, 406.

49 Rousseau, *Emile*, 406.

50 Rousseau, *Letter to d'Alembert*, 128.

51 Rousseau, *Letter to d'Alembert*, 131.

52 Rousseau, *Emile*, 400.

53 See especially Jensen, "Dangerous Liaisons," 211–22.

54 See, e.g., Rousseau, *Letter to d'Alembert*, 83, 85; Rousseau, *Emile*, 386, 389, 391.

55 Rousseau, *Letter to d'Alembert*, 81.

56 Rousseau, *Letter to d'Alembert*, 71–72. "Men will always be what is pleasing to women; therefore, if you want them to become great and virtuous, teach women what greatness of soul and virtue are." Rousseau, *First Discourse*, in *The First and Second Discourses*, trans. Roger Masters and Judith Masters (New York: St. Martin's, 1969), 52.

57 Rousseau, *Letter to d'Alembert*, 88, 101–4. Tocqueville, *Democracy in America*, 574 (2.3.12).

58 Rousseau, *Letter to d'Alembert*, 85.

59 Rousseau, *Letter to d'Alembert*, 87–88.

60 Ultimately, Okin's feminist criticisms of Rousseau depend on her privileging of the world of politics and her dismissal of Rousseau's vision of a closely knit family life.

61 This is the implication of the discussion in Rousseau, *Emile*, 45–49; and in Weiss and Harper, "Sex-Roled Family," 98–100.

62 See especially Rousseau's discussion of mercenary tutors, *Emile*, 48–49.

63 Rousseau, *Emile*, 388. Allan Bloom, *Love & Friendship* (New York: Simon & Schuster, 1993), emphasizes romantic love at the expense of the motherhood part of Rousseau's teaching, thus understating the difficulties in Rousseau's portrait.

64 Rousseau, *Letter to d'Alembert*, 83, 82.

65 Rousseau, *Emile*, 46.

66 Rousseau, *Letter to d'Alembert*, 83.

67 "The most ancient of all societies, and the only natural one, is that of the family." Rousseau, *On the Social Contract*, trans. Judith R. Masters (New York: St. Martin's, 1978), 47.

68 Rousseau, *Emile*, 363.

69 Rousseau, *Letter to d'Alembert*, 101. I join Schwartz, *Sexual Politics*, 99ff.; Elizabeth Rose Wingrove, *Rousseau's Republican Romance* (Princeton, N.J.: Princeton University Press, 2000), 3–23; Mira Morgenstern, *Rousseau and the Politics of Ambiguity* (University Park: Penn State University Press, 1996), 181–234; and Botting, *Family Feuds*, 46–59, who, in different ways, connect Rousseau's teaching on the family to his republicanism.

70 "Ancient politicians incessantly talked about morals and virtue, those of our time talk only of business and money" (Rousseau, *First Discourse*, 51). This critique must apply equally, if not more so, to Britain than to France and Geneva.

71 Rousseau, *Emile*, 447.

72 Rousseau, *Emile*, 391.

73 As George Bernard-Shaw famously said, "Love consists in overestimating the differences between one woman and another."

74 Rousseau, *Emile*, 447–48.

75 Rousseau, *Emile*, 479.

76 Locke, *2T* ¶78.

77 The husband is "a master for the whole of life" (Rousseau, *Emile*, 404). I draw this argument partly from Bloom, *Love & Friendship*, 117–18.

78 See esp. Carol Blum, *Rousseau and the Republic of Virtue* (Ithaca, N.Y.: Cornell University Press, 1989), 204–15. Cf. Elshtain, *Public Man, Private Woman*, 162 (also 165–66), who argues that this vision "never existed nor could it be brought into existence if for no other reason . . . than the fact that women, placed as Rousseau places them, within an intolerable hothouse of propriety, piety, and chastity, will inevitably constitute an unhappy, repressed, and hence subversive population."

79 See Rousseau, *Emile*, 360.

80 Richard Velkley, "The Tension in the Beautiful: On Culture and Civilization in Rousseau and German Philosophy," in *The Legacy of Rousseau*, ed. Clifford Orwin and Nathan Tarcov (Chicago: University of Chicago Press, 1997), 72–76.

Chapter 4

1 Hegel, *PR* ¶258. Textual citations are abbreviated as follows: *PR* = *Elements of the Philosophy of Right*, trans. Allen Wood (Cambridge: Cambridge University Press, 1991) (followed by paragraph); and

PH = *Philosophy of History* (New York: Dover, 1956) (followed by page numbers). Twenty-three paragraphs in Hegel's most directly political work, *Philosophy of Right*, concern the family, while over one hundred concern the state. The state is the apex of human civilization and the key to reconciling the divisions that plague human existence. "It is only through being a member of the state that the individual himself has objectivity, truth, and ethical life," and it is only through participation in the state that individuals fulfill their "destiny" (i.e., *Bestimmung*) of leading a "universal life" (*PR* ¶258).

2 Since spirit in and for itself is *reason*, and since the being-for-itself of reason in spirit is knowledge, world history is the necessary development, from the *concept* of the freedom of spirit alone, of the *moments* of reason and hence of spirit's self-consciousness and freedom (Hegel, *PR* ¶342).

3 Hegel, *PR* ¶144. See Seyla Benhabib, "On Hegel, Women, and Irony," in *Feminist Interpretations of G. W. F. Hegel*, ed. Patricia Jagentowicz Mills (University Park: Penn State University Press, 1996), 28–29.

4 Hegel, *PR* ¶157; *PR* ¶158; Hegel, *PH* 42.

5 Hegel, *PH* 18. Hegel may be the founder of the "loss of function" or "law of contraction" school of family sociology made famous later by Durkheim, "Conjugal Family"; and Talcott Parsons, *Family Socialization and Interaction Process* (New York: Free Press, 1955), 16–17.

6 Hegel, *PR* ¶182R; *PR* ¶152.

7 Peter J. Steinberger, *Logic and Politics* (New Haven, Conn.: Yale University Press, 1988), 166.

8 Hegel, *PR* ¶142. "The *right of individuals* to their *subjective determination to freedom* is fulfilled in so far as they belong to an ethical actuality; for their *certainty* of their own freedom has its *truth* in such objectivity; and it is in the ethical realm that they *actually* possess *their* own essence and their *inner* universality" (*PR* ¶153).

9 Hegel, *PR* ¶153A.

10 Hegel, *PR* ¶161A.

11 Hegel, *PR* ¶163. "The ethical determination of marriage . . . consists in the fact that the consciousness emerges from its naturalness and subjectivity to concentrate on the thought of the substantial. Instead of further reserving to itself the contingency and arbitrariness of sensuous inclination, it removes the marriage bond from this arbitrariness. . . . It thereby reduces the sensuous moment to a merely conditional one—conditioned, that is, by the true and ethical charac-

ter of the relationship, and by the recognition of the marriage bond as an ethical one" (*PR* ¶164R).

12 Consider, also, John Paul II, *Love and Responsibility*, 80–82, 96–100, and 101–35 on the relationship between sensualism and objective love.

13 Hegel, *PR* ¶75R; *PR* ¶163; *PR* ¶162. "The *ethical* aspect of marriage consists in the consciousness of this union as a substantial end" (*PR* ¶163).

14 Hegel, *PR* ¶162; also *PR* ¶169.

15 Joan B. Landes, "Hegel's Conception of the Family," *Polity* 14 (1981): 17ff., never discusses how Hegel's understanding of love transcends feeling, and hence misapprehends the reasons behind, and the true significance of, Hegel's treatment of the differences between men and women.

16 Hegel, *PR* ¶162R.

17 Consider Denis de Rougemont, *Love in the Western World* (Princeton, N.J.: Princeton University Press, 1956), 306–11; and Morse, *Love and Economics*, 62–82.

18 Hegel, *PR* ¶163.

19 Hegel, *PR* ¶158A.

20 Michael O. Hardimon, *Hegel's Social Philosophy* (Cambridge: Cambridge University Press, 1994), 180. The other time Hardimon uses this formulation is when Hegel discusses sex differences, about which more will be said later. Cf. Landes, "Hegel's Conception," who underplays Hegel's endorsement of oneship and the communal marriage.

21 See Hardimon, *Hegel's Social Philosophy*, 180; and Betty Friedan, *The Feminine Mystique* (New York: Norton, 1997), chaps. 3, 12–13.

22 Hegel, "Fragment on Love," in *Early Theological Writings*, trans. T. M. Knox (Philadelphia: University of Pennsylvania Press, 1971), 305.

23 Schlomo Avineri, *Hegel's Theory of the Modern State* (Cambridge: Cambridge University Press, 1974), 140.

24 Hegel, *PR* ¶162.

25 Hegel, "Fragment on Love," 308.

26 Hegel, *PR* ¶158.

27 Hegel, *PR* ¶170, 171, 174.

28 Popenoe, *Disturbing the Nest*, 148.

29 Hegel, "Fragment on Love," 305, 307.

30 Hegel, *PR* ¶173, 173A.

31 Hegel, *PR* ¶174A, 175.

32 Hegel, *PR* ¶177, 175A.

33 Locke, *2T* ¶65, 78, 80, 83.

34 Hegel, *PR* ¶178.

35 Hume, "Of Polygamy and Divorce," 188–89.

36 Hegel, *PR* ¶164. Consider St. Augustine's playful suggestion that consummating a marriage is "right and honorable," but that it is still done in private and is the object of some public shame (*City of God*, 14.18, in *Political Writings*, trans. Michael W. Tkacz and Douglas Kries [Indianapolis: Hackett], 105–6). Hegel's account is consistent with the view that shame about human nakedness reflects an inner understanding that our sexual passions and acts are but incomplete expressions of deeper desires for recognition.

37 Hegel, *PR* ¶164A.

38 Hegel, *PR* ¶163, 163A; *PR* ¶176; *PR* ¶163A.

39 Hegel, *PR* ¶158A.

40 Landes, "Hegel's Conception," 14.

41 Hegel, *PR* ¶168R.

42 Hegel, *PR* ¶168, 168A.

43 Hegel, *PH* 42.

44 This is the deepest congruence between Tocqueville and Hegel. Like Hegel, Tocqueville sees the family as one of the most enduring and hence useful ways of curbing the typically democratic vice of excessive individualism (which Tocqueville defines as a drawing into oneself). Human attachments and mutual dependence in democratic times arise from needs, and more serious attachments and dependencies arise from enduring needs. On the tendency of democracy to independence and isolation, see Tocqueville, *Democracy in America*, 483–85 (2.2.2–3); and 643 (2.4.3). On the reduction of bonds to needs interpreted through the lens of self-interest rightly understood, see *Democracy in America*, 503, 506–9 (2.2.8–9).

45 Hegel calls marriage an "ethical duty" (*PR* ¶162R). See Steinberger, *Logic and Politics*, 187–88.

46 Hegel, *PR* ¶175, 175A. I take it that this is the significance of Hegel's likening men to animals and women to plants (*PR* ¶166A). See Popenoe, *Life without Father*, chaps. 5–6; Sax, *Why Gender Matters*; and Rhoads, *Taking Sex Differences Seriously*, chaps. 4 and 8, for reviews of the literature on the distinctive contributions to the rearing of children made by fathers and mothers.

47 Hegel, *PR* ¶165.

48 Hegel, *PR* ¶166.

49 Hegel, *PR* ¶166; *PR* ¶171. Here, again, Tocqueville's treatment mirrors Hegel's. Tocqueville seems to endorse the traditional sexual division of labor (he really only says that this is how Americans think that "nature had established such great variation between the physical and moral constitution of man and that of woman" [Tocqueville, *Democracy in America*, 574 (2.3.12)]) as an essential part of maintaining the family in the modern world. The modern democratic family is held together by needs and affection, which are apparent because men and women bring distinctive things to the union. Remove the need, and the affection withers. Remove the difference, and the need withers. This means, as Alice Behnegar writes, that "the family can endure only where sexual difference endures, institutionalized in—indeed, I might go so far as to say, exaggerated if not created by—the sexual division of labor" ("Women in Tocqueville's *Democracy in America*," in Velasquez, *Love and Friendship*, 346).

50 Steinberger, *Logic and Politics*, 188, reflects a broadly held view that Hegel's theory of gender can be excised from his conception of the family without doing substantial damage to his theory of marital unity. I believe that this discussion misses the underlying logic that marital unity and the communal family are, for Hegel, made possible by the persistence of natural sex differences. Hegel might be wrong about this, but the view is indeed Hegel's position.

51 Susan Moller Okin, *Justice, Gender and the Family* (New York: Basic Books, 1991), 32: "When we recognize, as we must, that however much the members of families care about one another and share common ends, they are still discrete persons with their own particular aims and hopes, which may sometimes conflict, we must see the family as an institution to which justice is a crucial virtue." The logic here is Hegel's. The more a woman thinks of herself apart from the family, the less she is concerned with love or common ends of family life. What thinking herself apart from the family means is dropping the traditional sexual division of labor. Others in this camp, I will argue, include Simone de Beauvoir and John Stuart Mill.

52 Consider Waite and Gallagher, *Case for Marriage*, 172–73.

53 Okin, *Justice, Gender*, 171.

54 McClain, *Place of Families*, 77. McClain is willing to tolerate a

diversity of divisions of labor in the family, it seems, *but* there are, as she puts it, "limits to toleration" (79).

55 Okin, *Justice, Gender*, 177; also Amy Gutman, *Democratic Education* (Princeton, N.J.: Princeton University Press, 1999), 112–15.

56 Supreme Court Justice Ruth Bader Ginsburg, for instance, contends that "motherly love ain't everything it has been cracked up to be. . . . To some extent it's a myth that men have created to make women think that they do this job to perfection." Quoted in Biskupic, "Ruth Bader Ginsburg: Feminist Justice," *Washington Post*, April 17, 1995.

57 The feminist critique of nature goes beyond the denial that nature exists. Even if masculinity were natural, feminist theorists deny that nature should be controlling or normative. Consider how Okin likens a masculine nature to antisocial predilections: "Our laws do not allow kleptomaniacs to shoplift, or those with a predilection for rape to rape. Why, then, should we allow fathers who refuse to share in the care of their children to abdicate their responsibilities?" (Okin, *Justice, Gender*, 39).

58 "The natural determinacy of the two sexes acquires an intellectual and ethical significance by virtue of its rationality" (Hegel, *PR* ¶165).

59 The parallel with Tocqueville is striking. Tocqueville emphasizes how individuals must realize their own interests in the family for it to be strong. See Behnegar, "Women in Tocqueville," 347, 356–58.

60 Hegel, *PR* ¶166.

61 Hegel, *PR* ¶170. Interestingly, Hegel's account of the family's communal property resembles a proposal made by that great anti-Hegelian Susan Moller Okin. Okin suggests that traditional couples (the man of the house is the breadwinner and the woman is the homemaker) should have their paychecks written out differently than nontraditional couples. Traditional couples could receive part of the check for the man and part for the woman. Hegel, I think, would rather suggest that paychecks could be written out to the family instead of to the individual worker (lest he be tempted to consider the money his). See Okin, *Justice, Gender*, 180–81.

62 Hegel, *PR* ¶170R.

63 Benjamin Barber, "Spirit's Phoenix and History's Owl," *Political Theory* 16 (1988): 19–22.

64 Hegel, *PR* ¶258.

Chapter 5

1 Auguste Comte, *The Positive Philosophy of Auguste Comte*, trans. Harriet Martineau (London: Calvin Blanchard, 1855), 25. Henceforth cited as *PP* followed by page number.

2 Comte, *PP* 2.

3 Comte, *PP* 28, 407.

4 Comte, *PP* 409, 414, 420, 415.

5 Comte, *PP* 36–37, 416–17, 431.

6 Consider the discussion of Comte in Leo Strauss, "What Is Political Philosophy?" in *What Is Political Philosophy?* (Chicago: University of Chicago Press, 1988), 18.

7 Comte, "Sentimental Characteristics of the Positive Method in the Study of Social Phenomena," in *The Essential Comte*, ed. Stanislav Andreski (London: Harper & Row, 1974), 137–98.

8 Comte, *PP* 26.

9 In *System of Positive Polity*, Comte calls it "the most serious of all anarchic symptoms of modern society" (Comte, *System of Positive Polity*, trans. John Henry Bridges [London: Longmans, Green, 1875–1877], 3:153). Henceforth cited as *SPP* followed by volume and page number.

10 Comte, *SPP* 3:153; also Comte, *PP* 502.

11 Comte, *PP* 503–4.

12 Comte, *PP* 498–515; and Comte, *SPP* 3:150–81.

13 In marriage, "the active and the affective sex, each without laying aside its proper qualities, must unite in a bond, at once exclusive and indissoluble, one surviving even death" (Comte, *SPP* 3:157–58). See also Comte, *PP* 502.

14 Comte, *SPP* 2:159.

15 Contrast Comte's language of "mutual service and perfection" with Locke's "mutual Support, and Assistance" (*2T* 78); Comte's "attachment, veneration, and love" (*SPP* 3:157) with Locke's "Care, and Affection" (*2T* 78); and Comte's "complete fusion of two natures in one" (*PP* 502) and "moral completeness" (*SPP* 1:188) with Locke's "Communion of Interest" (*2T* 78).

16 Again, contrast Comte's formulation with Locke's, in which the "chief,

if not the only reason" for the conjugal bond is the "Procreation and Education" of children (*2T* 80–81).

17 Comte, *SPP* 1:188–93.

18 Comte, *SPP* 1:189.

19 Comte, *SPP* 1:188–93; also *SPP* 1:169, 180 ("Women's minds no doubt are less capable than ours of generalizing very widely, or of carrying on the long processes of deduction. They are, that is, less capable than men of abstract intellectual exertion. On the other hand, they are generally more alive to that combination of reality with utility"); and Comte, *PP* 505.

20 Nicholas Capaldi, *John Stuart Mill: A Biography* (Cambridge: Cambridge University Press, 2004), 171.

21 Comte, *PP* 505.

22 Comte, *SPP* 2:155, 1:178–79, 1:188–89.

23 Comte, *SPP* 2:163.

24 Mill to Comte (June 15, 1843), in Comte and Mill, *The Correspondence of John Stuart Mill and Auguste Comte*, ed. and trans. Oscar Haac (New Brunswick, N.J.: Transaction, 1995), 165; and Comte to Mill (July 16, 1843), *Correspondence*, 179.

25 These quotations or insights are drawn from Comte to Mill (October 5, 1843, and November 14, 1843), in *Correspondence*, 188–92, 206–11.

26 Internal citations in this section to Durkheim's works are as follows: *ME* = *Moral Education* (New York: Free Press, 1973); *CF* = "The Conjugal Family"; *DMC* = "Divorce by Mutual Consent," in Traugott, *Durkheim on Institutional Analysis*; *DL* = *The Division of Labor in Society* (New York: Free Press, 1997).

27 Emile Durkheim, *Montesquieu and Rousseau: Forerunners of Sociology* (Ann Arbor: University of Michigan Press, 1960), 3–4.

28 Durkheim, *Montesquieu and Rousseau*, 3–4.

29 Durkheim, *Montesquieu and Rousseau*, 7ff. especially.

30 Durkheim, *Montesquieu and Rousseau*, 10, 7. See also Durkheim, *Montesquieu and Rousseau*, 43: "In consequence of the society's particular situation, communal life must necessarily assume a certain definite form. This form is expressed by the laws, which thus result with the same inevitability from the efficient causes. To deny this is to assume that most social phenomena, particularly the most important, have no cause whatsoever." Pierre Manent, *The City of Man*, trans. Marc A. LePain (Princeton, N.J.: Princeton University Press, 2000),

52–77, provides a penetrating analysis and elaboration of this "sociological viewpoint."

31 Durkheim, *Montesquieu and Rousseau*, 48–49. Durkheim calls this an effort to "describe and explain social types on a historical basis."

32 Emile Durkheim, *Suicide* (New York: Free Press, 1997), 361–70.

33 Durkheim, *Suicide*, 362.

34 See Durkheim, *DL* 226–38; and Durkheim, *Suicide*, 336ff., for accounts of how the gods and family tradition wore away in preparation for the coming of civilization. I elide two things that Durkheim separates in referring to this phenomenon as anomie. Egoistic suicide and anomic suicide are based on two different experiences. Egoistic suicide results from the disappearance of objects of devotion and intense concentration (e.g., larger families or political causes) beyond the self which throws the individual back only on himself, a situation many find intolerable (*Suicide*, 210ff.). Anomic suicide results from the psychological ascendancy of unrealizable goals or our inability to regulate desire (e.g., those born of divorce) (*Suicide*, 269ff.). Both "spring from society's insufficient presence in individuals" (*Suicide*, 258).

35 "Like everything else, man is a limited being: he is part of a whole. Physically, he is part of the universe imposed on every hand. Indeed, everything that is most basic in him partakes of this quality of partialness or particularity. To say that one is a person is to say that he is distinct from all others; this distinction implies limitation." Durkheim, *ME* 51.

36 Durkheim, *ME* 49–51; and Durkheim, *Suicide*, 270–71. See also *Suicide*, 247–51, 253.

37 Cf. Jennifer M. Lehmann, "Durkheim's Theories of Deviance and Suicide: A Feminist Reconsideration," *American Journal of Sociology* 100 (1995): 911–12.

38 Popenoe, *Disturbing the Nest*, 18–21; and Mary Ann Lamanna, *Emile Durkheim on the Family* (Thousand Oaks, Calif.: Sage, 2001), provide support for the view that Durkheim was concerned about the family throughout his career.

39 This quotation is drawn from a work of Durkheim's related by Lamanna, *Durkheim on the Family*, 95. Cf. Durkheim, "Introduction to the Sociology of the Family," in Traugott, *Durkheim on Institutional Analysis*, 219: "Today's family is neither more nor less perfect than that of yesterday."

40 Durkheim, *CF* 229.

41 See Durkheim, *Suicide*, 78–79. This "loss of functions" mode of analysis figures in Popenoe's *Disturbing the Nest*, chapter 4, "The Rise and Fall in the West of the Modern Nuclear Family."

42 Durkheim, *CF* 234. See also Durkheim, *Suicide*, 377: "Formerly domestic society was not just a number of individuals united by bonds of mutual affection; but the group itself, in its abstract and impersonal unity. It was the hereditary name, together with all the memories it recalled, the family house, the ancestral field, the traditional situation and reputation, etc. All this is tending to disappear."

43 Consider especially Tocqueville, *Democracy in America*, 1.1.3.

44 Durkheim, *CF* 234, 230.

45 See also Durkheim's similar but even more impassioned argument in "Professional Ethics and Civic Morals," in *Readings from Emile Durkheim*, ed. Kenneth Thompson (New York: Routledge, 1985), 156–58.

46 Durkheim, *CF* 236. It is not clear how far Durkheim would go in this direction, though the implications of this proposal, taken to their logical conclusion, would be quite immense.

47 Durkheim, *CF* 238. "Only this group [the professional group]," Durkheim suggests, "is able to perform the economic and moral functions which the family has become increasingly incapable of performing." "A Durkheim Fragment," *American Journal of Sociology* 70, no. 5 (1965): 535. This fragment is a translation of Durkheim's seventeenth and final lecture course, delivered in 1892.

48 See Durkheim, "Professional Ethics," 154 .

49 Durkheim, *ME* 146–47, 48–51.

50 Durkehim, *ME* 146–49.

51 Locke, *2T* ¶69, 81; Durkheim, *ME* 146.

52 Locke, *2T* ¶72, 67.

53 Durkheim, *CF* 239; Popenoe, *Disturbing the Nest*, 19.

54 Lamanna, *Durkheim on the Family*, 139.

55 Durkheim begins his "Divorce by Mutual Consent" (1906) by noting the rapidity with which the proposal to adopt a mutual consent, no fault regime was gripping France (*DMC* 240). Such a regime was adopted in France more than fifty years later.

56 Marriage's "principal reason for existing" is due to the fact that it exercises a "moderating and salutary effect" on the passions of those in

the marriage. Divorce by mutual consent, which purports to "lessen the moral miseries of the spouses, will have the result of demoralizing them and detaching them further from life" and many more will die by their own hands as a result (Durkheim, *DMC* 248). Also see Durkheim's review of a French book on divorce in *Emile Durkheim: Contributions to "L'Annee Sociologique,"* ed. Yash Nandan (New York: Free Press, 1994), 431: "The truth is that divorce cannot advance without threatening the institution of marriage; and it is the sufferings of the individual, caused by the sickness of the social and fundamental institution, that are coming to be translated in the yearly total of suicides."

57 Durkheim, *DMC* 247–48. Consider Waite and Gallagher, *Case for Marriage*, 47ff., who find that even today's thinner marriage leads to longer life expectancy and health for men and women.

58 "The institution of marriage has in itself a moral validity and has a social function, the implications of which go beyond concerns of the individual." From another review translated in Durkheim, *Contributions to L'Annee Sociologique*, 284.

59 Durkheim, *CF* 237; Durkheim, *DMC* 248.

60 Durkheim, *CF* 239.

61 Cf. Jennifer M. Lehmann, *Durkheim and Women* (Lincoln: University of Nebraska Press, 1994), 32, 33, 8, who sees Durkheim as largely silent on the question of women, yet she reconstructs Durkheim's portrait by reconstructing his "more latent than manifest, more immanent than articulate" antifeminist and patriarchal views.

62 Durkheim, *Suicide*, 215, 272, 385; see also Durkheim, *DL* 192 ("Woman is less concerned than man in the civilizing process; she participates less in it and draws less benefit from it. She more recalls certain characteristics to be found in primitive natures").

63 "The state of marriage affects the moral constitution of women only weakly. . . . She is a little outside the moral effects of marriage. As she does not profit much from it, she also does not suffer from it" (Durkheim, *DMC* 247). Also Durkheim, *Suicide*, 272, 275–76, 385–86. In *Suicide*, Durkheim found that married women took their own lives at a higher rate where divorce was not available than where it was available, though men committed suicide more where divorce was available. This condition led Durkheim to ask if "one of the sexes [must] necessarily be sacrificed, and [if] the solution [is] only to choose the lesser of the two evils?" (*Suicide*, 284). This sexual conflict of interest dissolves in

"Divorce by Mutual Consent," where Durkheim argues that divorce laws and marriage have no effect on women. His change on this important topic is occasioned by his revisiting of the statistical evidence on suicide, divorce, and marriage and his discovery that a third factor—living in Paris—that accounts for the apparently high suicide rate among married women (*DMC* 246). This growth in Durkheim's thought is traced in Lehmann, "Durkheim's Theories," 919–24.

64 This quotation is drawn from Durkheim's review of Marianne Weber (the sociologist wife of Max Weber), *Wife and Mother in Legal Development* (1907). Durkheim, "Review of Marianne Weber, *Ehefrau und Mutter in der Rechtsentwicklung*," in Traugott, *Durkheim on Institutional Analysis*, 141. Consider Durkheim's extended discussion of marriage in *Suicide*, 270:

> What is marriage? A regulation of sexual relations including not merely the physical instincts which this intercourse involves but the feelings of every sort gradually engrafted by civilization on the foundation of physical desire. For among us love is a far more mental than organic fact. A man looks to a woman, not merely to the satisfaction of the sexual impulse. Though this natural proclivity has been the germ of all sexual evolution, it has become increasingly complicated with aesthetic and moral feelings, numerous and varied, and today it is only the smallest element of the whole complex process to which it has given birth. . . . This is the function of marriage. It completely regulates the life of passion, and monogamic marriage more strictly than any other. For by forcing a man to attach himself forever to the same woman it assigns a strictly definite object to the need for love, and closes the horizon.

65 As Durkheim writes near the end of *Suicide*, 385, "in one sense [sex difference] was originally less marked than now, but from this we cannot conclude that it must develop indefinitely."

66 Durkheim, *DL* 18–21.

67 "If we reduce the division of labour between the sexes beyond a certain point marital life disappears, leaving only sexual relationships that are predominantly ephemeral. If indeed the sexes had not separated off from each other at all, a whole style of social living would not have arisen" (Durkheim, *DL* 21).

68 These quotations are drawn from those related by Lamanna, *Durkheim on the Family*, 175 (emphasis added).

69 These quotations are drawn from those related by Lamanna, *Durkheim on the Family*, 149.

70 David Hume, *The History of England* (Indianapolis, Ind.: Liberty Fund, 1983), 3:244.

71 Waite and Gallagher, *Case for Marriage*.

72 Consider also Eberstadt, *Home-Alone America*.

Chapter 6

1 John Stuart Mill, *OL* 18:257. Citations of Mill's works are to *The Collected Works of John Stuart Mill* (Toronto: University of Toronto Press, 1963–1991), followed by volume and page number. For clarity's sake, citations will be abbreviated as follows: *OL* = *Collected Works* to *On Liberty*; *S* = *The Subjection of Women*; and *OM* = "On Marriage." I drop the volume number after the first citation to each of these, but keep the abbreviation.

2 Mill, *S* 21:336. See Mill to Robert Barclay Fox (December 19, 1842): "It is becoming more & more clearly evident to me that the mental regeneration of Europe must precede its social regeneration & also that none of the ways in which that mental regeneration is sought, Bible Societies, Tract Societies, Puseyism, Socialism, Chartism, Benthamism &c will *do*" (*Collected Works*, 13:563); Mill to Parke Godwin (January 1, 1869): "The emancipation of women, and co-operative production, are . . . the two great changes that will regenerate society" (*Collected Works*, 17:1535); "Grote's History of Greece [review 5]": "The work which [Socrates] did requires to be done again, as the indispensable condition of that intellectual renovation, without which the grand moral and social improvements, to which mankind are now beginning to aspire, will be for ever unattainable" (*Collected Works*, 25:1164).

3 Capaldi, *John Stuart Mill*, 267. See also Bernard Semmel, *John Stuart Mill and the Practice of Virtue* (New Haven, Conn.: Yale University Press, 1984).

4 The feminist criticisms are found in Leslie Goldstein, "Mill, Marx, and Women's Liberation," *Journal of the History of Philosophy* 18, no. 3 (1980): 320, 328; Julia Annas, "Mill and the Subjection of Women," *Philosophy* 52 (1977): 190; Eisenstein, *Radical Future*, 115; Richard W. Krouse, "Patriarchal Liberalism and Beyond: From John Stuart Mill to Harriet Taylor," in *The Family in Political Thought*, ed. Jean Bethke Elshtain (Amherst: University of Massachusetts Press, 1982), 161–72; and Okin, *Women*, 226–27.

5 Mill, *OL* 261, 262, 264, 269. See also Mill, *OL* 220.

6 Mill, *OL*, chap. 4 (emphasis added).

7 Mill, *OL* 279. Joseph Hamburger, *John Stuart Mill on Liberty and Control* (Princeton, N.J.: Princeton University Press, 1999), 12–16, argues that Mill holds quite the opposite view. Moral offenders can, in Mill's words, be "justly punished by opinion" or "deservedly reprobated" or be "fit objects of moral reprobation" (*OL* 276, 281, 279). Hamburger (149–65, 171–80) explains this by referring to Mill's theory of historical progress: Mill's endorsement of liberation from public opinion suits his time, when Victorianism and Christian belief inhibit moral regeneration, but after his enlightened vanguard remakes public opinion, a virtuous, life-lending public opinion will justly constrain the choices of the less enlightened. For example, if we know that divorce was problematic, public opinion could justly stigmatize divorce. It seems to me that the evidence adduced by Hamburger points in the opposite direction. What should give way when expressing "our distaste" or standing "aloof from a person" makes that other's "life uncomfortable"? The principle behind our willingness to make others uncomfortable is societal confidence bred by moral consensus, and Mill's political teaching seeks to subvert this.

8 Mill, *S* 261. See also Mill, *S* 294–95, 340.

9 Mill, *S* 324.

10 Mill, *OL* 264–65.

11 Mill, *S* 331.

12 See Gertrude Himmelfarb, *On Liberty and Liberalism* (New York: Knopf, 1974), 176–83; and Alexander Bain, *John Stuart Mill, A Criticism* (London: Longmans, 1882), 108. Nadia Urbinati, "John Stuart Mill on Androgyny and Ideal Marriage," *Political Theory* 19, no. 4 (1991): 631–32, hints at this relationship. I develop the connection between *On Liberty* and *Subjection of Women* in what follows.

13 Mill, *OL* 261, 270; Mill, *S* 295. "The moral regeneration of mankind will only really commence, when the most fundamental of the social relations is placed under the rule of equal justice, and when human beings learn to cultivate their strongest sympathy with an equal in rights and in cultivation" (Mill, *S* 336).

14 Mill, *S* 264. "The present legal and moral subjection of women is the principal, and likely to be the latest remaining relic of the primitive condition of society, the tyranny of physical force" (Mill, *Collected Works*, 21:386) (written with Harriet Taylor, "Papers on Women's Rights").

15 Comte (1798–1857) and Mill exchanged letters concerning not only the foundations of science, but also the family and the importance and basis of sex differences. See *The Correspondence of John Stuart Mill and Auguste Comte*, especially letters 31–43. Mill also penned "Auguste Comte and Positivism" (1865), concerned with Comte's *System of Positive Polity*, as he was preparing *Subjection of Women*. Of Comte, Mill writes, "He admits that the marriage institution has been, in various respects, beneficially modified with the advance in society . . . but strenuously maintains that such changes cannot possibly affect what he regards the essential principles of the institution—the irrevocability of the engagement and the complete subordination of the wife to the husband . . . which are precisely the great vulnerable points of the existing constitution of society on this important subject" (*Collected Works*, 10:310–11).

16 Comte, *SPP* 1:188–93.

17 See also Hegel, *PR* ¶165–66, 170–72.

18 Comte, *SPP* 1:188, 182. See *SPP* 1:169, 180, quoted in chap. 5.

19 Mill praises the progressive California Constitution (brought on by the Compromise of 1850), that allows for women to own property within marriage and hopes that Britain will follow California's lead (*Collected Works*, 29:1149–50).

20 Mill, *S* 284. "By the common law of England, all that a wife has, belongs to the husband" (Mill, *Collected Works*, 28:160). English law, rendered by Blackstone, takes the legal point of view when thinking about the relationship between husbands and wives: "The very being or legal existence of the women is suspended during marriage, or at least is incorporated into that of the husband" (*Commentaries on the Laws of England* [Chicago: University of Chicago Press, 1979], 1:430). See also James Fitzjames Stephen, *Liberty, Equality, Fraternity*, ed. Stuart D. Warner (Indianapolis, Ind.: Liberty Fund, 1993), 136–39.

21 Mill, "Married Women's Property," in *Collected Works*, 28:283. Comte, as we have seen, is rightly counted among such people.

22 Men may tear all property "from her, squander every penny of it in debauchery, leave her to support by her labour herself and her children, and if by heroic exertion and self-sacrifice she is able to put by something for their future wants, unless she is judicially separated from him he can pounce down upon her savings, and leave her penniless. And such cases are of quite common occurrences" (Mill, *Collected Works*, 28:160).

23 Mill, *S* 284, 297.

24 Mill, *S* 297.

25 See Mill, "Woman's Suffrage," in *Collected Works*, 29:403; and Mill, *The Autobiography of John Stuart Mill*, in *Collected Works*, 1:207.

26 Consider Mill, *Collected Works*, 29:403; Mill, *S* 301, and *S* 294–95: "The family is a school of despotism, in which the virtues of despotism, but also its vices, are largely nourished."

27 Mill, *S* 301. See Elizabeth S. Smith, "John Stuart Mill's *The Subjection of Women*: A Reexamination," *Polity* 34, no. 2 (2001): 197–99.

28 Mill, *Collected Works*, 21:390.

29 Mill *S* 271, 285. See Mary Lyndon Shanley, "Marital Slavery and Friendship," *Political Theory* 9 (1981): 231–35.

30 Mill, *S* 284. Stephen, *Liberty, Equality, Fraternity*, 148–49. Stephen, Mill's astringent critic, observes that Mill does not account for the sources of true marital happiness and presupposes that his marriage will do it better than the unified marriage.

31 Mill, *S* 287, 289. Harriet Taylor, "Enfranchisement of Women" (1851), writes, "Such feelings often exist between a sultan and his favourites, between a master and his servants; they are merely examples of the pliability of human nature, which accommodates itself in some degree even to the worst circumstances, and the commonest natures always the most easily" (Mill, *Collected Works*, 21:411).

32 These words are Hume's. "Of Polygamy and Divorce," 189.

33 This discussion of "On Marriage" is necessary because it lays bare the historical foundation and culture-class analysis underlying Mill's subsequent work and also because it contains Mill's frankest and fullest discussion of human passions and divorce.

34 Mill, *OM* 21:38–41.

35 Mill, *OM* 21:38–41.

36 Mill, *OM* 39.

37 Mill, *OM* 40, 41.

38 Mill, *OM* 47–48.

39 Hamburger, *Liberty and Control*, 11–12; and Himmelfarb, *On Liberty and Liberalism*, 273–75, incorrectly, in my view, see Mill opposing single-party divorce in most circumstances.

40 Mill, *OM* 48.

41 Mill, *OM* 49. Mill writes (after November 9, 1855),

> My opinion on Divorce is that though any relaxation of the irrevocability would be an improvement, nothing ought to be ultimately rested in, short of entire freedom on both sides to dissolve this like any other partnership. The only thing requiring legal regulation would be the maintenance of the children when the parents could not arrange it amicably—and in that I do not see any considerable difficulty. (*Collected Works*, 14:500)

42 Mill, *OM* 38.

43 Nor is this the only instance in which Mill admits that the road to progressive ends is covered with heartache, conflict, intensified fanaticism, and, perhaps, even civil war. In *System of Logic*, Mill argues that the questioning of a society's fundamental opinions will cultivate "violent animosities" leading the state "virtually in a position of civil war," even though Mill defends such open questioning of society's pieties in *On Liberty*. One can only conclude that Mill believed that the price of such "violent animosities" and "civil war" that would follow from such questioning would be worth the progress it brings. See Hilail Gilden, "Mill's *On Liberty*," in *Ancients and Moderns*, ed. Joseph Cropsey (New York: Basic Books, 1964), 293–97, for this paradox. See Hymowitz, *Marriage and Caste*, chaps. 1, 2, 4, and 8 for how these two classes are affected by deinstitutionalizing marriage.

44 Mill writes,

> The arguments, therefore, in favour of the indissolubility of marriage, are as nothing in comparison with the far more potent arguments for leaving this like the other relations voluntarily contracted by human beings, to depend for its continuance upon the wishes of the contracting parties. The strongest of all these arguments is that by no other means can the condition and character of women become what it ought to be. (*OM* 49)

45 Mill, *OM* 42. Mill's silence on divorce in *Subjection of Women* follows, as he writes to John Nichol (August 1869), from "the obvious inexpediency of establishing a connexion in people's minds between the equality and any particular opinions on the divorce question" (*Collected Works*, 17:1634). Mill writes to William E. Hickson (March 19, 1850), "My opinions on the whole subject [of divorce] are so totally opposed to the reigning notions, that it would probably be inexpedient to express all of them and I must consider the portion of them which the state of existing opinion would make it advisable to express" (*Collected Works*, 14:48). That Mill was silent on the implications of his principles as he advocated for them is obvious in his

discussion with Comte. See Mill to Comte (December 18, 1841) in *Correspondence*, 42:

> You are doubtless aware that here an author who should openly admit to antireligious or even antichristian opinions, would compromise not only his social position . . . but also, and this would be more serious, his chance of being read. I am already assuming great risks when, from the start, I carefully put aside the religious perspective and abstained from rhetorical eulogies of the wisdom of Providence, customarily made even by unbelievers among the philosophers of my country. I rarely allude to such notions and, even as I try not to awaken any religious antipathy in the common reader, I believe I have written in such a way that no reader, be he Christian or unbeliever, can mistake the true nature of my opinions, though I admit I rather rely on that worldly prudence which, here in England, generally prevents religious writers from unnecessarily calling attention to the irreligion of any author of some scientific merit.

Also see Mill to Robert Barclay Fox (December 23, 1840), *Collected Works*, 13:454–55; Stephen, *Liberty, Equality, Fraternity*, 138–40; Smith, "Mill's *The Subjection*," 192–97; Urbinati, "Mill on Androgyny," 639–40; and Hamburger, *Liberty and Control*, chaps. 4 and 9, for accounts of Mill's almost esoteric presentation of issues in *Subjection of Women* and in his political career generally.

46 Mill's discussion of divorce in *On Liberty* appears in the context of discussing exceptions to the rule that consensual contracts must be kept. The two cases in which individuals cannot consent to a contract are when people sell themselves into slavery and enter into an indissoluble marriage. Further, Mill is correcting von Humboldt's "simplistic" views on the dissolubility of marriage by pointing out that marriage creates "expectations" and shapes "calculations" and that a new series of "moral obligations arise from the presence of children." Mill nevertheless does not believe that these complications make "*much* difference" from a legal point of view. It "necessarily make[s] a great difference" when viewed from a moral point of view, as people may be blamed for not giving "proper weight to those interests" (*OL* 300–301).

47 Mill, *S* 289, 295.

48 Thus my biggest disagreement with Urbinati, "Mill on Androgyny," who rightly, in my view, sees Mill endorsing an androgynous vision, but who, wrongly, in my view, compares Mill's ideal of marriage to the tightly knit classical *polis* (636) and sees it as rendering "the couple into a single being" (638). Against Urbinati, I argue that Mill's

egalitarian and androgynous visions intentionally undermine such a vision of marital and familial unity.

49 Mill, *S* 298.

50 Mill, *OM* 42. See, e.g., Friedan, *Feminine Mystique*, chaps. 12 and 13.

51 Mill, "Woman's Suffrage," 29:405.

52 Aristotle, *Nicomachean Ethics*, 1166b32, distinguishes a friend that is a second self and an equal with whom one has unabated contact from marital friendship, which is between unequals and in which each contributes something unique to the common store (1162a17–28). See Darrel Dobbs, "Family Matters: Aristotle's Appreciation of Women and the Plural Structure of Society," *American Political Science Review* 90, no. 1 (1996): 74–89. Urbinati, "Mill on Androgyny," 637–38, also makes this observation.

53 Cf. especially Montaigne, "Of Friendship," in *Complete Essays of Montaigne*, trans. Donald M. Frame (Stanford: Stanford University Press, 1957), 137–38, in which the Frenchman argues that the business aspects of marriage and the constraints that go with them are only two of the reasons that husbands and wives cannot be the best of friends. He continues,

> Besides, to tell the truth, the ordinary capacity of women is inadequate for that communion and fellowship which is the nurse of this sacred bond; nor does their soul seem firm enough to endure the strain of so tight and durable a knot. And indeed, but for that, if such a relationship, free and voluntary, could be built up, in which not only would the souls have this complete enjoyment, but the bodies would also share in the alliance, so that the entire man would be engaged, it is certain that the resulting friendship would be fuller and more compete. But this sex in no instance has yet succeeded in attaining it, and by the common agreement of the ancient schools is excluded from it.

54 Mill, *S* 336.

55 Michael St. John Packe, *The Life of John Stuart Mill* (New York: Capricorn, 1954), 317–20, lays out the position that "the sexual relation became for them revolting and unjust. It encouraged in the one sex pompous selfishness, and in the other, petulant servility: and it debased society to the level of a farmyard."

56 Shanley, "Marital Slavery and Friendship," 242.

57 William Edward Hartpole Lecky, *History of European Morals* (New York: Appleton, 1869), 2:300. Leo Tolstoy, in a letter to N. N. Strakhov, shares Lecky's view: "Should we permit promiscuous sexual intercourse, as many 'liberals' wish to do? Impossible! It would be

the ruin of family life. To meet the difficulty, the law of development has evolved a 'golden bridge' in the form of the prostitute. Just think of London without its 70,000 prostitutes! What would become of decency and morality, how would family life survive without them? How many women and girls would remain chaste? No, I believe the prostitute is necessary for the maintenance of the family" (quoted in Ernest J. Simmons, *Leo Tolstoy* [London: John Lehman, 1949], 328). Strakhov wrote a short rejoinder to Mill's *Subjection of Women.*

58 See the feminist criticisms cited in note 4 of this chapter.

59 Mill, *S* 297–98; and Mill, *OM* 43.

60 Shanley, "Marital Slavery and Friendship," 242.

61 Mill, *S* 336. See also *S* 276–77, 313. Disclaiming to know the natural differences between men and women could just as easily lead to a conservative stance toward traditional marriage: since Mill could not know that his day's conventions regarding the sexes were wrong, tradition could be seen as the safest ballast in our twilight of knowledge. I address this issue in the conclusion. If, as Urbinati, "Mill on Androgyny," 628ff., argues, Mill establishes the distinction between natural sex and socially constructed gender, he often denies that he knows where one begins and the other ends. This is a point Mill's "conservative" defenders stress and that Urbinati does not deal with.

62 Mill, *S* 277.

63 To be more precise, Mill believes that experience can show what women can do given the harsh conditions of patriarchy and that removing those conditions will open more untold vistas.

64 Mill, *S* 264–65.

65 Mill, *S* 338; see also Mill, *OM* 44–45.

66 Mill, *S* 318, 298, 326.

67 Mill, *OM* 43–44; Mill, *S* 326. Mill's feminist critics ignore that Mill envisions a "doubling of the mass of mental faculties for the higher services of humanity" from the emancipation of women (*S* 326; but see also 336), which indicates that women will work outside the household in numbers equal to men, at least in some jobs. As Smith, "Mill's *The Subjection*," 195, intimates, Mill's endorsement of the sexual division of labor is a means of "'softening the blow'" to the fence-sitting Victorians in favor of extending the franchise but worried about its effects on the family. See Urbinati, "Mill on Androgyny," 639–40.

68 Mill, *S*, chapter 3 and p. 313; see also *S* 304–5, 312, 280–81.

69 Mill, "Woman's Suffrage," 29:405.

70 Mill appeals to the interests of men and mankind as well in arguing for such an experiment. The contributions that women make to the project of progress might improve the attributes brought to the project by men. If women have nothing to add, there is no harm in having them try. If they add something, everyone gains. In either event, there is no harm in seeing what it is that women can do.

71 The only "natural differences" school that Mill addresses is the theory tracing natural differences to brain size, a crude and risible theory that Mill easily dissects (*S* 310–12).

72 Mill, *S* 305.

73 Mill, *S* 293.

74 Mill, *S* 298.

75 Mill, *OL* 224.

76 Mill, *S* 272.

77 Mill, *S* 269–70.

78 Mill, *S* 295.

Chapter 7

1 Karl Marx, *The Poverty of Philosophy*, in Karl Marx and Frederick Engels, *Collected Works* (New York: International Publishers, 1975–2005), 6:165: "The hand-mill gives you society with the feudal lord; the steam-mill, society with industrial capitalism." See also Marx, *The German Ideology* (Amherst, N.Y.: Prometheus, 1998), 42. Also Marx to P. V. Annenkov (December 28, 1846): "What is society, whatever its form may be? The product of men's reciprocal action. Are men free to choose this or that form of society for themselves? By no means. Assume a particular state of development in the productive forces of man and you will get a particular form of commerce and consumption and you will have a corresponding social structure, a corresponding organization of the family, of orders or of classes, in a word, a corresponding civil society. Presuppose a particular civil society and you will get particular political conditions which are only the official expression of civil society" (Marx and Engels, *Collected Works*, 38:95).

2 Marx and Engels, *Communist Manifesto*, 22 (end of pt. 1).

3 Marx, *German Ideology*, 81. Competition "destroyed as far as possible ideology, religion, morality, etc., and where it could not do this, made them into a palpable lie."

4 Marx, "On the Divorce Bill," in Marx and Engels, *Collected Works*, 1:307. Cf. Hegel, *PR* ¶163.

5 Marx and Engels, *Communist Manifesto*, 12: "The bourgeoisie has torn away from the family its sentimental veil, and has reduced the family relation to a mere money relation."

6 Marx and Engels, *Communist Manifesto*, 28.

7 Marx, *Capital*, ed. Frederick Engels (New York: Modern Library, 1906), 489.

8 See, for example, Marx, *German Ideology*, 38, 52.

9 Marx, *Capital*, 490 (emphasis added).

10 Frederick Engels, *The Origin of the Family, Private Property and the State*, ed. Eleanor Burke Leacock (New York: International Publishers, 1972), 71, from the first preface.

11 Cf. Engels, *Origin*, 87–88, 97. Of the savage state itself, Engels concedes that "we have no direct evidence to prove its existence, but once the evolution of man from the animal kingdom is admitted, such a transitional stage must necessarily be assumed," and of the era of unrestricted sexual freedom, Engels concedes that "we can hardly expect to prove its existence *directly* by discovering its social fossils among backward savages."

12 Engels, *Origin*, 103.

13 Engels, *Origin*, 111.

14 Engels, *Origin*, 159–60, also 215–16.

15 Engels, *Origin*, 113.

16 Marx, *German Ideology*, 38.

17 Engels, *Origin*, 160–61. "The division of labor is purely primitive, between the sexes only [in the gens]. The man fights in the wars, goes hunting and fishing, procures the raw materials of food and the tools necessary for doing so. The woman looks after the house and the preparation of food and clothing, cooks, weaves, sews. They each are the master in their own sphere; the man in the forest, the woman in the house. Each is the owner of the instruments which he or she makes and uses: the man of the weapons, the hunting and fishing implements; the woman of the household gear. The house-keeping is communal among several and often many families" (Engels, *Origin*, 218).

18 Schlomo Avineri, *The Social and Political Thought of Karl Marx* (Cambridge: Cambridge University Press, 1970), 103, paraphrasing Marx's *Grundrisse*.

19 Engels, *Origin*, 160. See also Marx, *German Ideology*, 38–39: "The slavery latent in the family only develops gradually with the increase of production, the growth of wants, and with the extension of external intercourse, both of war and of barter."

20 Engels, *Origin*, 117, 119–20. Also *Origin*, 220: "With the herds and the other new riches, a revolution came over the family."

21 Engels, *Origin*, 121.

22 Engels, *Origin*, 128.

23 Engels, *Origin*, 93, 125, 128.

24 Marx and Engels, *Communist Manifesto*, 14 (pt. 1).

25 Engels, *Origin*, 135–36.

26 Marx and Engels, *The Holy Family* (Honolulu, Hawaii: University Press of the Pacific, 2002), 231: "The labour contract is supposed to be voluntarily entered into by both parties. But it is taken to be voluntarily entered into as soon as the law has put both parties on an equal footing on paper. The power given to one party by its different class position, the pressure it exercises on the other—the real economic position of both—all this is no concern of the law. And both parties, again, are supposed to have equal rights for the duration of the labour contract, unless one or other of the parties expressly waives them. That the concrete economic situation compels the worker to forgo even the slightest semblance of equal rights—this is something the law cannot help." See also *Holy Family*, 47.

27 Kidnapping a wife or coercing marital vows under threats of death, for example, are not free.

28 Engels, *Origin*, 136: "The power conferred on the one party by the difference of class position, the pressure thereby brought to bear on the other party—the real economic position of both—that is not the law's business."

29 Consider also Graeme Duncan, *Marx and Mill* (Cambridge: Cambridge University Press, 1977), 151–52, and my discussion of this matter in the conclusion.

30 Engels, *Origin*, 137.

31 See Engels, *Origin*, 125 ("the right of conjugal infidelity"), 126 (monogamy is stamped "from the very beginning with its specific character of monogamy for the woman only, but not for the man. And that is the character it still has today"), 130, 131, 134, 138. In the *Communist Manifesto*, Marx and Engels assert, "Bourgeois

marriage is in reality a system of wives in common and thus, at the most, what the Communists might possibly be reproached with is that they desire to introduce, in substitution for a hypothetically concealed, an openly legalized community of women" (29).

32 Engels, *Origin*, 137.

33 Engels, *Origin*, 139–40,132, 143, 144 (emphasis added).

34 Engels, *Origin*, 134.

35 Engels, *Origin*, 144: "Full freedom of marriage can therefore only be generally established when the abolition of capitalist production and of the property relations created by it has removed all the accompanying economic considerations which still exert such a powerful influence on the choice of a marriage partner. For then there is no other motive left except mutual inclination."

36 Engels, *Origin*, 135.

37 The "free development of each is the condition for the free development of all" is the closing sentence of section 2 of Marx and Engels, *Communist Manifesto*. Consider Hal Draper, "Marx and Engels on Women's Liberation," *International Socialism* 40 (1970): 23–25.

38 Frances K. Goldscheider and Linda J. Waite, *New Families, No Families?* (Berkeley: University of California Press, 1993) suggest these two options for modern family arrangements.

39 Engels, *Origin*, 145.

40 Engels, *Origin*, 144–45. Cf. Mill, "On Marriage": "Marriage is but one continued act of self-sacrifice where strong affection is not; every tie therefore which restrains them from seeking out and uniting themselves with someone whom they perfectly love, is a yoke to which they cannot be subjected without oppression; and to such a person when found, they would naturally, superstition apart, scorn to be united by any other tie than free and voluntary consent" (*OM* 21:39).

41 Engels, *Origin*, 137.

42 Consider Mill, *S* 298: "The power of earning is essential to the *dignity* of a woman, if she has not independent property."

43 See also Engels, *Origin*, 221. Okin envisions just about the same kind of society in her feminist classic *Justice, Gender and the Family*, where she sees "a future in which men and women participated in more or less equal numbers in every sphere of life, from infant care to different kinds of paid work to high-level politics" (171). Okin does not go so far as Engels, however, in that she seems to retain the private money economy characteristic of modern capitalism.

44 Engels, *Origin*, 139.

45 Engels, *Origin*, 221.

46 See also Simone de Beauvoir, *The Second Sex*, trans. H. M. Parshley (New York: Vintage, 1989), 53–54.

47 Engels, *Origin*, 139.

48 Engels, "Principles of Communism," in *The Communist Manifesto*, trans. Paul Sweezy (New York: Modern Reader Paperbacks, 1968), 80.

49 Aristotle, *The Politics*, trans. Carnes Lord (Chicago: University of Chicago Press, 1984), 1261b32.

50 Krouse, "Patriarchal Liberalism and Beyond," 152.

51 Marx and Engels, *Communist Manifesto*, 32 (pt. 2).

52 Marx, *German Ideology*, 84, 60, 45, 49. Consider also Marx and Engels, *Communist Manifesto*, 28 (pt. 2): "The bourgeois family will vanish as a matter of course when its complement vanishes, and both will vanish with the vanishing of capital."

53 Marx, *Early Writings* (New York: Penguin, 1992), 176.

54 Marx, *German Ideology*, 482.

55 Marx, *German Ideology*, 53.

56 Marx, *Economic and Philosophic Manuscripts of 1844*, in Marx and Engels, *Collected Works*, 3:296.

57 Marx, "On the Jewish Question," in Marx and Engels, *Collected Works*, 3:168: "*All* emancipation is a *reduction* of the human world and relationships to *man himself*. . . . Only when the real, individual man re-absorbs in himself the abstract citizen, and as an individual human being has become a *species-being* in his everyday life, in his particular work, and in his particular situation, only when man has recognized and organized his 'own powers' as *social* powers, and, consequently, no longer separates social power from himself in the shape of *political* power, only then will human emancipation have been accomplished."

58 The most persistent criticism sees Marx's conception of freedom as presupposing the following fallacious syllogism: Socrates is a man. Man is a universal. Therefore, Socrates is a universal. The problem with this in logic and in application is that, for Marx, the attainment of freedom presumes the existence of "species-being," or universality, in each particular human being. As Elshtain writes in *Public Man, Private Woman*, "individual man and generic man must be identical if human emancipation is to be achieved" (192). See also Charles

Taylor, *Hegel* (Cambridge: Cambridge University Press, 2008), 557–58; and Duncan, *Marx and Mill*, 195–207.

Chapter 8

1 Sigmund Freud, *Civilization and Its Discontents* (New York: Norton, 2005), 36. Henceforth cited as *CD* followed by page number.

2 Freud, *CD* 40–41.

3 Freud, *CD* 46–47.

4 "Man's discovery that sexual (genital) love afforded him the strongest experiences of satisfaction and in fact provided him with the prototype of all happiness" (Freud, *CD* 89). See also Freud, *CD* 63.

5 Freud, *CD* 53. Freud also likened the beautiful to sexual stimulation. "There is to my mind no doubt that the concept of 'beautiful' has its roots in sexual excitation and that its original meaning was 'sexually stimulating.'" Freud, *Three Essays on the Theory of Sexuality*, trans. James Strachey (New York: Basic Books, 1962), 22n2.

6 Freud, *CD* 62–63. Consider the following example. "No one who has seen a baby sinking back satiated from the breast and falling asleep with flushed cheeks and a blissful smile can escape the reflection that this picture persists as a prototype of the expression of sexual satisfaction in later life." Freud, *Three Essays on the Theory of Sexuality* (New York: Basic Books, 2000), 48.

7 Freud, *CD* 86.

8 In *CD*, Freud relies on the account of the father story from *Totem and Taboo*, in Freud, *Complete Psychological Works*, 13:1–255 (see *CD* 133–35, 142).

9 Freud, *CD* 92–93.

10 See Freud, *Totem and Taboo*, 129–32, 143.

11 Freud, *Totem and Taboo*, 141–42.

12 Freud, *Totem and Taboo*, 145.

13 Freud, *Totem and Taboo*, 150.

14 Freud, *CD* 108–9.

15 Elshtain, *Public Man, Private Woman*, 262.

16 Freud, *Beyond the Pleasure Principle* (New York: Norton, 1990), 43, 45.

17 Freud, *Beyond*, 50, 45.

18 Freud, *CD* 118.

19 See Freud, *CD* 114–16; and Freud, *Beyond*, 46–47.

20 Freud, *Beyond*, 52, 54, 59.

21 Freud, *Beyond*, 49, 69ff.

22 Freud, *CD* 109–10.

23 Freud, *Totem and Taboo*, 141, 142n.

24 Freud, *CD* 19, 22.

25 Freud, *Three Essays*, 88–93.

26 "Society must defend itself against the danger that the interests which it needs for the establishment of higher social units may be swallowed up by the family; and for this reason, in the case of every individual, but in particular of adolescent boys, it seeks by all possible means to loosen their connection with the family—a connection which, in their childhood, is the only important one." Freud, *Three Essays*, 91.

27 Freud, *CD* 94–95.

28 Freud, *CD* 84. Freud describes the process of sublimation as enabling "excessively strong excitations arising from particular sources of sexuality to find an outlet and use in other fields, so that a not inconsiderable increase in psychical efficiency results from a disposition which in itself is perilous" (*Three Essays*, 104). "This capacity to exchange its originally sexual aim for another one, which is no longer sexual but which is psychically related to the first aim, is called the capacity for sublimation" (Freud, "'Civilized' Sexual Morality and Modern Nervous Illness," in Freud, *The Standard Edition of the Complete Psychological Works of Sigmund Freud*, ed. James Strachey (London: Hogarth, 1953–1974), 187.

29 Freud, *CD* 106–7, 118.

30 Freud, *CD* 55.

31 Freud, *CD* 81–82, 99.

32 Freud, *CD* 121, 128. See Freud, *Three Essays*, 36, 43, 57, 97.

33 Freud, *CD* 137–38.

34 Freud, "'Civilized' Sexual Morality," 183–86.

35 Freud, "'Civilized' Sexual Morality," 193–95.

36 Freud, "'Civilized' Sexual Morality," 201.

37 Freud, *CD* 57–58, 82.

38 Freud, *CD* 152, 153.

39 Freud, "'Civilized' Sexual Morality," 204.

40 See Freud, "Sexuality in the Aetiology of the Neuroses" (1898), in Freud, *Complete Psychological Works*, 3:263–65.

41 Freud, *CD* 67.

42 Herbert Marcuse, *Eros and Civilization* (Boston: Beacon, 1965), 46. Erich Fromm considers Freud's "criticism of middle-class mores, and the protest against them in the name of man and his development" to be "the most important—and radical element in Freud's system." Fromm, *The Crisis of Psychoanalysis* (Greenwich, Conn.: Fawcett Premier, 1971), 36.

43 Freud, *CD* 109.

44 Freud, "'Civilized' Sexual Morality," 189.

45 By contraception practices of his day, I mean coitus interruptus, the condom or sheath, the sponge or diaphragm, and abortion. See Angus McLaren, "Contraception and Its Discontents: Sigmund Freud and Birth Control," *Journal of Social History* 12 (Summer 1979): 514–16.

46 Freud, "Sexuality," 277.

47 Bertrand Russell, *Marriage and Morals* (London: Allen & Unwin, 1929), 142–43. Henceforth cited as *MM* followed by page number.

48 Russell, *MM* 157, 162–63, 165–66.

49 Russell, *MM* 239, 119–20.

50 Russell, *MM* 127. See Tom Wolfe, *Hooking Up* (New York: Farrar, Straus, & Giroux, 2000); and Bloom, *Closing of the American Mind.*

51 Russell, *MM* 128.

52 Russell, *MM* 140, 128.

53 Russell, *MM* 224; also *MM* 76, 129, 183, 235.

54 Russell, *MM* 204–9, 169. See also *MM* 9, 12, 89, 169, 178–79, 187, 218.

55 Russell, *MM* 216, 192.

56 Christopher Lasch, *Haven in a Heartless World* (New York: Norton, 1995), 76–77, 132.

57 Talcott Parsons, *The Structure of Social Action* (New York: Free Press, 1970), xi.

58 Beauvoir, *Second Sex*, 44–45.

Chapter 9

1 Few tasks are as fraught with peril as defining what feminism is. I boil it down to the beliefs that gender or sex differences are socially con-

structured, that the sexual division of labor must be remedied, and that modern peoples should aspire to create a gender-neutral society. This definition leaves out many groups, including "difference feminists" such as Carol Gilligan, whose *In a Different Voice* reflects the idea that women are naturally inclined to endorse an ethic of care instead of an ethic of justice. Consider the discussions of "humanist feminism" and "gynocentric feminism" in Browning et al., *From Culture Wars to Common Ground*, 2nd ed. (Louisville, Ky.: Westminster John Knox, 2000), 162–68.

2 Beauvoir, *Second Sex*, 267.

3 Okin, *Justice, Gender*, 171.

4 See Margaret Simons, "*The Second Sex*: From Marxism to Radical Feminism," in *Feminist Interpretations of Simone de Beauvoir*, ed. Margaret Simons (University Park: Penn State University Press, 1995), 243; Harvey C. Mansfield, *Manliness* (New Haven, Conn.: Yale University Press, 2006), 131; Sharon Krause, "Lady Liberty's Allure," *Philosophy and Social Criticism* 26, no. 1 (2000): 2, 16; Mark Kremer, "Simone de Beauvoir's *The Second Sex*," in Velasquez, *Love and Friendship*, 480; Browning et al., *Culture Wars*, 162. Shulamith Firestone even dedicated her most famous book, *The Dialectic of Sex*, to Beauvoir. Betty Friedan, who does not include Beauvoir in the index to her *Feminine Mystique*, still mentions Beauvoir's name secondhand once and refers to her concepts at crucial points in the argument (see *Feminine Mystique*, 19, 312, 314 [esp. n10], 322–25, 333–36, 375, 389). Later, Friedan admits to reading Beauvoir cover to cover near its release and to finding the book an epiphany of sorts. "I was," Friedan writes, "writing 'housewife' on the census blanks, still in the unanalyzed embrace of the feminine mystique. And the book's effect on me personally was so depressing that I felt like going back to bed—after I had made the children's breakfast in the suburban morning." See Friedan, "Sex, Society, and the Female Dilemma: A Dialogue between Simone de Beauvoir and Betty Friedan," *Saturday Review*, June 14, 1975, 16.

5 Beauvoir, *Second Sex*, 33–34, 716.

6 Beauvoir, *Second Sex*, xxxv. For a complete discussion of the distinction between transcendence and immanence, see Krause, "Lady Liberty's Allure," 3–7.

7 Beauvoir, *Second Sex*, 630.

8 Friedan, *Feminine Mystique*, 312–14, 344, discusses transcendence in

terms of personal growth within an existentialist framework akin to Maslow's hierarchy of needs. Frustrated, women still hope to "realize the full possibilities of their existence." The "unique human capacity to transcend the present, to live one's life by purposes stretching into the future . . . that is the distinction between animal and human behavior, or between the human being and the machine" (312). "This capacity to 'transcend the immediate boundaries of time,' to act and react and see one's experience in the dimensions of both past and future, is the unique characteristic of human existence" (313). "The only way for a woman, as for a man, to find herself, to know herself as a person, is by creative work of her own" (344).

9 Beauvoir, *Second Sex*, 259.

10 Beauvoir, *Second Sex*, xxxv.

11 Beauvoir, *Second Sex*, 271–73.

12 Beauvoir, *Second Sex*, 321.

13 Beauvoir, *Second Sex*, 278.

14 Beauvoir, *Second Sex*, 315–16.

15 Beauvoir, *Second Sex*, 321, 385, 386. See also Beauvoir, *Second Sex*, 373, 372, 377, 397. She summarizes these differences thusly: "Man dives upon his prey like the eagle and the hawk; woman lies in wait like the carnivorous plant, the bog, in which insects and children are swallowed up. She is absorption, suction, humus, pitch and glue, a passive influx, insinuating and viscous" (386). Consider also Barbara Ehrenreich, Elizabeth Hess, and Gloria Jacobs, *Remaking Love: The Feminization of Sex* (Garden City, N.Y.: Anchor, 1987), 202–3: "Heterosexual sex, and especially intercourse, is a condensed drama of male domination and female submission. The man 'mounts' and penetrates; the woman spreads her legs and 'submits'; and the postures seem to ratify, again and again, the ancient authority of men over women. . . . Sex, or women's role in it, is understood as a humiliation no man would want to endure."

16 Beauvoir, *Second Sex*, 280, 288. See also *Second Sex*, 597 ("We must only note that the varieties of behavior reports are not dictated to woman by her hormones nor predetermined in the structure of the female brain: they are shaped as in a mold by her situation."); 727 ("The peculiarities that identify her as specifically a woman get their importance from the significance placed upon them. They can be surmounted, in the future, when they are regarded in new perspectives."); and 329 ("The fact is that her resignation comes not from

any predetermined inferiority: on the contrary, it is that which gives rise to all her insufficiencies; that resignation has its source in the adolescent girl's past, in the society around her, and particularly in the future assigned her").

17 Beauvoir, *Second Sex*, 45, and 38–52 generally.

18 Beauvoir, *Second Sex*, 36.

19 Beauvoir, *Second Sex*, 697.

20 Herodotus, *The Histories*, trans. David Grene (Chicago: University of Chicago Press, 1987), 2.35. Egyptian society as Herodotus describes it is nevertheless thoroughly patriarchal by Beauvoir's standards.

21 Beauvoir, *Second Sex*, 401: "Full development requires that—in love, affection, sensuality—woman succeed in overcoming her passivity and in establishing a relation of reciprocity with her partner."

22 Beauvoir, *Second Sex*, 330–35.

23 Beauvoir, *Second Sex*, 427.

24 Beauvoir, *Second Sex*, 429–30.

25 Friedan's *Feminine Mystique*, chap. 10, contains one of the most memorable contentions that "housewifery expands to fill the time available" and the contention that "most housework" can be "capably handled by an eight-year-old child" (255–56).

26 Beauvoir, *Second Sex*, 451–59.

27 Beauvoir, *Second Sex*, 477, 478. See also Bernard, *Future of Marriage*, 38, 42–44, 48, and 51, who thinks that a housewife must be "slightly ill mentally" and "a nobody."

28 Beauvoir, *Second Sex*, 471, 476.

29 Beauvoir, *Second Sex*, xxvii. Friedan makes much the same argument in the language of Abraham Maslow's hierarchy of needs, though she does not hold women as responsible for their situation, as does Beauvoir. The feminine mystique, Friedan writes, has led women to motherhood's "stunting or evasion of growth" (*Feminine Mystique*, 77).

30 Beauvoir, *Second Sex*, 495.

31 See Beauvoir, *Second Sex*, 437.

32 Beauvoir, *Second Sex*, 512–14.

33 Beauvoir, *Second Sex*, xxix, 122, 133.

34 Against the tide of Beauvoir scholarship, Kremer, "Beauvoir's *The Second Sex*," 479–95, argues that Beauvoir never leaves Mill's bourgeois, liberal tradition for existentialism. I am open to the idea that Mill's

open-ended progressivism could not resist the radicalization of freedom found in Beauvoir.

35 Consider Beauvoir, *Second Sex*, 121, 133–36; and Simons, "*Second Sex*," 246–51.

36 Beauvoir, *Second Sex*, 426.

37 Beauvoir, *Second Sex*, 479.

38 Consider Beauvoir, *Second Sex*, 387, 425, 679, 680.

39 Beauvoir, *Second Sex*, 679.

40 Beauvoir, *Second Sex*, 121; see also 113 and 679 ("It is through gainful employment that woman has traversed most of the distance that separated her from the male; and nothing else can guarantee her liberty in practice. Once she ceases to be a parasite, the system based on her dependence crumbles").

41 Beauvoir, *Second Sex*, 127.

42 Beauvoir, *Second Sex*, 682. Consider Beauvoir, *Second Sex*, xxv: "The reason . . . that women lack concrete means for organizing themselves into a unit which can stand face to face . . . [is that] they have no past, no history, no religion of their own; and they have no such solidarity of work and interest as that of the proletariat. They are not even promiscuously herded together in the way that creates community feeling among the American Negroes, the ghetto Jews, the workers of Saint-Denis, or the factory hands of Renault. They live dispersed among the males, attached through residence, housework, economic conditions, and social standing to certain men—fathers or husbands—more firmly than they are to other women." See also especially Beauvoir, *Second Sex*, 58.

43 Beauvoir, *Second Sex*, 645–46. Also Jane Mansbridge, *Why We Lost the ERA* (Chicago: University of Chicago Press, 1986), 100: "Women can never hold half the economically and politically powerful positions in the country if a greater proportion of women than men withdraw from competition for those positions. More important, if even 10 percent of American women remain full-time homemakers, this will reinforce traditional views of what women ought to do and encourage other women to become full-time homemakers at least while their children are young. . . . If women disproportionately take time off from their careers to have children, or if they work less hard than men at their careers while their children are young, this will put them at a competitive disadvantage vis-à-vis men. . . . This means that no matter how any individual feminist might feel about child care and

housework, the movement as a whole had reasons to discourage full-time homemaking."

44 Beauvoir, *Second Sex*, 698–99.

45 John Stuart Mill, "The Subjection of Women" in *The Collected Works of John Stuart Mill*, 21:298.

46 Beauvoir, *Second Sex*, 475. Also 482: "It is for their common welfare that the situation must be altered by prohibiting marriage as a 'career' for woman." Beauvoir is even more direct in her interview with Betty Friedan later in life, where she says, "No woman should be authorized to stay at home to raise her children. . . . Women should not have that choice, precisely because if there is such a choice, too many will make that one. It is a way of forcing women in a certain direction." Friedan responds that she does not agree "politically, at the moment" (Friedan, "Sex, Society," 18).

47 Beauvoir, *Second Sex*, 724–25, also 126–28, 136. For Beauvoir, the problem with the Soviets was their backsliding when it came to rearranging the family.

48 Beauvoir, *Second Sex*, 121.

49 Beauvoir, *Second Sex*, 121.

50 See also Beauvoir, *Second Sex*, 425.

51 See also Beauvoir, *Second Sex*, 525: "In a properly organized society, where children would be largely taken in charge by the community and the mother cared for and helped, maternity would not be wholly incompatible with careers for women."

52 Beauvoir, *Second Sex*, 525.

53 Cf. Beauvoir, *Second Sex*, 513 with 525.

54 Women have, as Friedan sees it, caused a national crisis by leaving "a pattern of immature behavior on [their] children" by overprotecting them. There are, she writes, "frightening implications for the future of our nation in the parasitical softening that is being passed on to the new generation of children as a result of our stubborn embrace of the feminine mystique" (*Feminine Mystique*, 191, 197, 281). See also Friedan, *Feminine Mystique*, 186, 188, 298, 304–5.

55 This move is reminiscent of a discussion about the nature of balls in Jane Austen's *Pride and Prejudice*, chap. 11.

56 Beauvoir, *Second Sex*, 697.

57 Shulamith Firestone, *Dialectic of Sex* (New York: Bantam, 1970), 170ff.

58 Beauvoir, *Second Sex*, 58, objects to Engels' view that the family is abolished after the proletariat revolution, calling his view "an abstract solution" that slights the true problem. The experiences of Nazi Germany and Sparta also call into question the necessary connection between abolishing the family and emancipating women, though Beauvoir seems to hope that Soviet Russia might be able to do a better job.

59 Beauvoir, *Second Sex*, 680.

60 What this means Beauvoir relates in her dialogue with Friedan. Striking women at a LIP watch factory held out for higher wages and better hours, but they would still not carry on the night watch for the strike because their husbands wanted them home for the evening. This shows that revolutionary action in economics does not lead to desired and necessary changes in sex roles. See Friedan, "Sex, Society," 14–15.

61 See especially Beauvoir, *Second Sex*, xx–xxi. This possibility is indicative of those who see a Beauvoir who recommends that women abandon their old ways and adopt the transcendent ways of men and of those who see Beauvoir attacking the "ontological necessity" of the "binary gender system." For those in the first camp, see Elshtain, *Public Man, Private Woman*, 306–10. For those in the second camp, see Judith Butler, "Sex and Gender in Simone de Beauvoir's *Second Sex*," in "Simone de Beauvoir: Witness to a Century," ed. Helene Vivienne Wenzel, special issue, *Yale French Studies* 72 (1986): 45–47.

62 Beauvoir, *Second Sex*, 58–60.

63 See, for instance, Simons, "*Second Sex*," 251–59.

64 Beauvoir, *Second Sex*, 434, 435.

65 Beauvoir, *Second Sex*, 472, 479.

66 Beauvoir, *Second Sex*, 446.

67 Beauvoir, *Second Sex*, 472.

68 Beauvoir, *Second Sex*, 447; also 473.

69 Beauvoir, *Second Sex*, 401, 469.

70 Consider Beauvoir, *Second Sex*, xxiv–xxv, 64. See also Debra B. Bergoffen, "Out from Under: Beauvoir's Philosophy of the Erotic," in Simons, *Feminist Interpretations*, 189–91.

71 Beauvoir, *Second Sex*, 446.

72 Beauvoir, *Second Sex*, 401–2.

73 Beauvoir, *Second Sex*, 728.

74 Beauvoir, *Second Sex*, 440.

75 See Beauvoir, *Second Sex*, 389–99, 445–47, 465, 727–28.

76 Beauvoir, *Second Sex*, 402, 425

77 Beauvoir, *Second Sex*, 430.

78 Beauvoir, *Second Sex*, xxxv, 133, 51.

79 This is the thrust of Kristana Arp, "Beauvoir's Concept of Bodily Alienation," in Simons, *Feminist Interpretations*, 161–78.

80 Okin, *Justice, Gender*, 138–43.

81 Okin, *Justice, Gender*, 150; also 147–58 generally.

82 Okin, *Justice, Gender*, 170–71.

83 Okin, *Justice, Gender*, 176–77.

84 Okin, *Justice, Gender*, 31.

85 Okin, *Justice, Gender*, 32–33.

86 Okin, *Justice, Gender*, 28; also 29–30.

87 See also David Tubbs, *Freedom's Orphans* (Princeton, N.J.: Princeton University Press, 2007), 97–98; I suggest that Okin is much closer to Mill than Tubbs.

88 Friedan, *Feminine Mystique*, 305.

89 Friedan, *Feminine Mystique*, 344; also 348: "The only kind of work which permits an able woman to realize her abilities fully, to achieve identity in society in a life plan that can encompass marriage and motherhood, is the kind that was forbidden by the feminine mystique, the lifelong commitment to an art or science, to politics or profession. Such a commitment is not tied to a specific job or locality."

90 Friedan, *Feminine Mystique*, 323–24.

91 Okin, *Justice, Gender*, 39.

Chapter 10

1 The term "marriage movement" is their own moniker; see Institute for American Values, "The Marriage Movement: A Statement of Principles" (New York: Institute for American Values, 2000).

2 Many prominent feminists see David Popenoe, William Galston, and their marriage movement fellow travelers as the perhaps unwitting vanguard of a vast, right-wing conspiracy to reverse feminist achievements. Judith Stacey, *Name of the Family*, 52–62, for instance, initiated the argument that the family decline thesis has been propounded and aggressively publicized as part of the public policy discourse by

pro-family think tanks and their willing accomplices in the media. Stacey implies that the family scholars work from a thin data pool, and that through the machinations of a "feedback loop" wherein they cite one another's work, they create the impression that the pro-family position reflects a scientific consensus, even as they (allegedly) ignore important scientific counterevidence. Fineman, *Autonomy Myth*, 85; and McClain, *Place of Families*, 128–29, repeat Stacey's charge as conclusive or at least as weighty. While feminist thinkers have more than a few decisive points to make against social science positivism (as I think), their reaction in this respect is suggestive evidence that they put ideology in front of their scientific commitments. Would Stacey and the others offer such a critique of these scholars if their evidence had pointed in the other direction?

3 Consider the discussion of scripts in Blankenhorn, *Fatherless America*, 12–18, 65–69; Hymowitz, *Marriage and Caste*, 25ff., 72–88.

4 Consider Wilson, *Marriage Problem*, 41: "Marriage is a socially arranged solution for the problem of getting people to stay together and care for children that the mere desire for children, and the sex that makes children possible, does not solve. The problem of marriage today is that we imagine that its benefits have been offset by social arrangements, such as welfare payments, community tolerance, and professional help for children, that make marriage unnecessary."

5 Popenoe, *Life without Father*, 7–8. See also Wilson, *Marriage Problem*, 84: "The family was an odd institution. It arose out of our natural sexual appetite between men and women and was valuable in enabling children to be reared, but one could in principle devise alternatives to it. A child might be raised by an unwed parent, or a marriage designed to bring children into being might be terminated when they went off to become apprentices, or a man and a woman might live together without anything like a marriage agreement. Every human union that one can now see about us could be devised and assessed by reason alone."

6 Popenoe, *Life without Father*, 7–8.

7 Popenoe, *Life without Father*, 19. Also Blankenhorn, *Fatherless America*, 18–19.

8 Popenoe, *Life without Father*, 20, 23.

9 Popenoe, *Life without Father*, 43–44, 45. See also Popenoe, *War over the Family*, 12; Wilson, *Marriage Problem*, 102; Francis Fukuyama,

The Great Disruption (New York: Free Press, 1999), 5–6, 47–49, 72–76, 91.

10 Popenoe, *Life without Father*, 44. Popenoe gives an even deeper account of family decline along the same trajectory in *Disturbing the Nest*, 219–55. See also Fukuyama, *Great Disruption*, 77–91.

11 Consider Popenoe, *Life without Father*, 85, 116, 118–19, 227 ("Religion has long been a supporter of marriage and strong families"); and *War over the Family*, 110 ("If the accumulated sociological evidence is correct, religion has long played an important role in promoting marriage and family solidarity").

12 On this score, intervening variables such as feminism, therapeutic ideology, and secularism are part of the general category of individualism. See Popenoe, *Disturbing the Nest*, 22ff.

13 Against Marxists and other ideological opponents of marriage, Popenoe and other marriage movement social scientists argue that there is a universalism underlying human marital practice on precisely these points. See Popenoe, *Life without Father*, 37, 184–85 ("Marriage is one of the most important and certainly the most universal of social institutions"); Popenoe, *War over the Family*, 169 ("Marriage is one of the few universal social institutions, found in every known culture"); Wilson, *Marriage Problem*, 66 ("The family is not only a universal practice, it is the fundamental social unit of any society"); and Blankenhorn, *Future of Marriage*, 91, 104–5. Engels' conclusions about the existence of group marriages and matriarchal societies were challenged, successfully, by Edward Westermarck, whose magisterial *History of Human Marriage* (New York: Allerton, 1922), vol. 1, argues that almost all primitive societies were defined by monogamy, in one form or another; today's marriage movement scholars build on Westermarck's achievement in this respect and in others.

14 Popenoe, *Life without Father*, 10: "Being a father is much more than merely fulfilling a social role. Engaged biological fathers care profoundly and selflessly about their own children; such fatherly love is not something that can easily be transferred *or reduced to the learning of a script*" (emphasis added).

15 Popenoe, *War over the Family*, 95. Also Popenoe, *Life without Father*, 3: "More and more the question is being raised, are fathers really necessary? Many would answer no, or maybe not. And to the degree that fathers are still thought necessary, fatherhood is said by many to be merely a social role, as if men had no inherent biological disposition

whatsoever to acknowledge and to invest in their own offspring. If merely a social role, then perhaps anyone is capable of playing it. The implication is one of arbitrary substitutability." Popenoe seems to be arguing against his one-time colleague and marriage movement fellow traveler David Blankenhorn, whose *Fatherless America* (1995) is based on much the same data as Popenoe's *Life without Father* (1996) and with whom *it seems* that Popenoe was initially collaborating on a common book project. Blankenhorn does not delve into the biology or nature that might underlie scripts. His book argues against today's destructive "cultural scripts" (i.e., "The Unnecessary Father"; "The Old Father"; "The New Father"; "The Deadbeat Dad"; "The Visiting Father"; "The Sperm Father"; and "The Stepfather and the Nearby Guy") and in favor of a script for "The Good Family Man." Of "The Good Family Man," Blankenhorn, *Fatherless America*, 5, writes as follows: "I cannot imagine a good society without him, I offer him as the protagonist in the stronger script that I believe is both necessary and possible."

16 Popenoe, *War over the Family*, 177–78, writes, "Having been trained as a sociologist, I have long been partial to sociocultural explanations. But I must say, quite apart from the scientific evidence, that after a lifetime of experiences . . . I would be utterly amazed if someone were to prove that biology is unimportant to gender differences. . . . All human behavior represents a combination of biological and sociocultural forces." Also, Popenoe, *Life without Father*, 10.

17 Carl N. Degler, *In Search of Human Nature* (Oxford: Oxford University Press, 1993).

18 For an account of how nature poses these problems for cultural institutions, see Wilson, *Marriage Problem*, 29–32; E. O. Wilson, *On Human Nature* (Cambridge, Mass.: Harvard University Press, 1978), 139ff.; Popenoe, *War over the Family*, 95; Popenoe, *Life without Father*, 10–12, 172, 173–77; Blankenhorn, *Future of Marriage*, 103–4.

19 Thus it has been difficult to take Morgan or Engels seriously since the work of Westermarck and his successors, who show that the Marxist claims that there have been matriarchal societies or group marriages or about where the incest taboo comes from were almost wholly invented. See Westermarck, *History of Human Marriage*, vol. 1, chaps. 3, 8, 12; and Steven Goldberg, *Why Men Rule: A Theory of Male Dominance* (Peru, Ill.: Open Court, 1999).

20 Popenoe, *War over the Family*, 180. See also Popenoe, *Life without Father*,

4–5, 184–87; Blankenhorn, *Fatherless America*, 25; Wilson, *Marriage Problem*, 23, 30–32; and Fukuyama, *Great Disruption*, 121–22.

21 For Rousseau, as we have seen, however, women are the sexually aggressive ones since they can have sex several times a day, while men have to be aroused into having it and can only do it once a day (or so).

22 R. L. Trivers, "Parental Investment and Sexual Selection," in *Sexual Selection and the Descent of Man, 1871–1971*, ed. B. Campbell (Chicago: Aldine, 1972), 136–79, amplifies Darwin's theory of sexual selection, which notices that most female animals are more picky about their mates than are males. Trivers shows that females carry, feed, and protect the young, all of which require a great investment of time and energy. More interested in their young, females are choosier about their sexual partners, looking for signs of commitment to provide.

23 This is a distillation of Popenoe, *War over the Family*, 179–80; and *Life without Father*, 173–77. Men seem willing to invest in their own children, so paternity confidence is a decisive factor leading to paternal involvement.

24 Popenoe, *Life without Father*, 179 (emphasis omitted). Westermarck's conclusion in *History of Human Marriage*, 1:20, parallels Popenoe's: "We may conclude with absolute certainty that there were always intimate relations between a mother and her young child, since the causes of these relations most always have operated in a mammalian species, like man. . . . The family, consisting of a father, mother, and children, existed already in primeval times and probably among our pre-human ancestors, owing to the offspring's need for care and protection and to the economic obstacles in the way of a permanent living in hordes; but this conclusion has a less solid foundation than the former one, because the necessity of paternal care is not so certain as that of maternal care." See also Westermarck, *History of Human Marriage*, 1:37, 46, 68–69, 361. Also see Larry Arnhart, *Darwinian Natural Right* (New York: SUNY Press, 1998), 31; and Arnhart, *Darwinian Conservatism* (Charlottesville, Va.: Imprint Academic, 2005), 28–29. Arnhart suggests that parental care, sexual mating, and familial bonding are among the twenty natural (i.e., universally occurring) desires across human history. See also Sarah B. Hrdy, *Mothers and Others: The Evolutionary Origins of Mutual Understanding* (Cambridge, Mass.: Belknap, 2009), 161–71.

25 Popenoe, *Life without Father*, 143ff.; and Popenoe, *War over the*

Family, 176–78; Wilson, *On Human Nature*, 124–25; Hrdy, *Mothers and Others*, 38–45, 112–17.

26 Popenoe, *Life without Father*, 186; Blankenhorn, *Future of Marriage*, 33–37, 155–56; Rhoads, *Taking Sex Differences Seriously*, 195–202; Wilson, *On Human Nature*, 126–32.

27 Popenoe, *War over the Family*, 182–85. See also Wilson, *On Human Nature*, 132–34, 147–48.

28 Popenoe, *Life without Father*, 165.

29 Consider Hans Jonas, "Philosophical Aspects of Darwinism," in *The Phenomenon of Life* (New York: Harper & Row, 1966), 44–51; Wilson, *On Human Nature*, 125; Francis Fukuyama, *Our Posthuman Future* (New York: Picador, 2003), 152, 162.

30 Arnhart, *Darwinian Natural Right*, 103. See also James Q. Wilson, *The Moral Sense* (New York: Free Press, 1997), 158.

31 Arnhart, *Darwinian Natural Right*, 113, 95.

32 Consider Wilson, *On Human Nature*, 124: "The human egg is eighty-five thousand times larger than the human sperm. The consequences of this gametic dimorphism ramify throughout the biology and psychology of human sex. The most important immediate result is that the female places a greater investment in each of her sex cells."

33 Fukuyama, *Great Disruption*, 97; Arnhart, *Darwinian Natural Right*, 123–60.

34 Fukuyama, *Great Disruption*, 179. Also Wilson, *On Human Nature*, 124–25.

35 Recall William James' famous quip:

Hogamous, higamous
Man is polygamous
Higamous, hogamous
Woman monogamous.

36 Fukuyama, *Great Disruption*, 99. Consider also Hrdy, *Mothers and Others*.

37 Wilson, *Moral Sense*, 165.

38 Arnhart, *Darwinian Natural Right*, 135–36. See Carson Holloway, *The Right Darwin?* (Dallas, Tex.: Spence, 2008), 129ff., for an excellent discussion of this issue from which I have drawn.

39 See Rhoads, *Taking Sex Differences Seriously*, 27–28, 197–202; and Sax, *Why Gender Matters*, 11–38, for reviews of the scientific literature on these matters.

40 See Blankenhorn, *Future of Marriage*, 32–33; Wilson, *On Human Nature*, 139–41 ("Sexual love and the emotional satisfaction of family life can be reasonably postulated to be based on enabling mechanisms in the physiology of the brain that have been programmed to some extent through the genetic hardening of this compromise"); and Westermarck, *History of Human Marriage*, vol. 1, chaps. 1 and 2.

41 Popenoe, *Life without Father*, 168–70, summarizes the findings of this school of thought. See Rhoads, *Taking Sex Differences Seriously*, 141–43, 197–99, 202–4; and Sax, *Why Gender Matters*, 61–70.

42 Arnhart, *Darwinian Natural Right*, 121.

43 Rhoads, *Taking Sex Differences Seriously*, 196–97; Wilson, *On Human Nature*, 133–35; Arnhart, *Darwinian Natural Right*, 92–101, 97–98; Wilson, *Moral Sense*, 183–85.

44 Amnon Rubinstein, "Return of the Kibbutzim," *Jerusalem Post*, July 10, 2007.

45 Larry Arnhart begins his most arresting book with a most arresting comment: "Conservatives need Charles Darwin." *Darwinian Conservatism*, 1. See also Arnhart, "Friedrich Hayek's Darwinian Conservatism," in *Liberalism, Conservatism, and Hayek's Idea of Spontaneous Order*, ed. Louis Hunt and Peter M. McNamara (New York: Palgrave Macmillan, 2007), 127.

46 Friedrich Hayek, "The Use of Knowledge in Society," chap. 4 in *Individualism and Economic Order* (Chicago: University of Chicago Press, 1996), 85–88.

47 Hayek, *The Constitution of Liberty* (Chicago: University of Chicago Press, 1978), 61. See also Hayek, *The Fatal Conceit* (Chicago: University of Chicago Press, 1991), 63.

48 Hayek, *Fatal Conceit*, 137; also Hayek, *Fatal Conceit*, 57.

49 Hayek, *Fatal Conceit*, 51. I have developed this point in Yenor, "Spontaneous Order and the Problem of Religious Revolution," in Hunt and McNamara, *Liberalism, Conservatism*, 115–20.

50 Fukuyama, *Great Disruption*, 273–75.

51 Fukuyama, *Great Disruption*, 273.

52 See Morgan, *War*, 62–80.

53 Waite and Gallagher, *Case for Marriage*.

54 Wilson, *On Human Nature*, 208, 196. See also Hrdy, *Mothers and Others*, 290–94, who envisions a humanity with less capacity for

cooperative breeding and empathy than human beings have possessed heretofore.

55 Wilson, *On Human Nature*, 96–97. Notice also that Fukuyama follows up *The Great Disruption* with a book titled *Our Posthuman Future*. A discussion of the relationship between these two books can be found in Holloway, *Right Darwin*, 168–76.

56 Beauvoir, *Second Sex*, 36.

57 See especially David Sloan Wilson, *Darwin's Cathedral* (Chicago: University of Chicago Press, 2002).

Chapter 11

1 In *Evangelium Vitae* (*The Gospel of Life*), John Paul II contends that the crisis in modern thinking abets the modern "culture of death," a civilization that allows the "direct and voluntary killing of innocent human beings" through such actions as euthanasia and abortion. The culture of death and the crisis of the family both grow from the rotten tree of modern thinking, characterized, above all, by an eclipse of love. John Paul, *Evangelium Vitae* (papal encyclical, given in Rome on March 25, 1995), available at http://www.vatican.va/holy_father/john_paul_ii/encyclicals/documents/hf_jp-ii_enc_25031995_evangelium-vitae_en.html. See Carson Holloway, *The Way of Life* (Waco, Tex.: Baylor University Press, 2008), 7–30, 143–58, for a discussion of *Evangelium Vitae*.

2 John Paul, *Love and Responsibility*, 238.

3 See John Paul, *Familiaris Consortio* (apostolic exhortation, given in Rome on November 22, 1981), available at http://www.vatican.va/holy_father/john_paul_ii/apost_exhortations/documents/hf_jp-ii_exh_19811122_familiaris-consortio_en.html, §6 (a general statement listing indications that the marriage culture is in trouble), §20 (re: divorce), §§22–24 (re: the treatment of women), and §32 (re: contraception). Also see John Paul, *Letter to Families* (papal letter, given in Rome on February 2, 1994), available at http://www.vatican.va/holy_father/john_paul_ii/letters/documents/hf_jp-ii_let_02021994_families_en.html, §14 (re: free love), §19 (re: contraception), and §21 (re: abortion).

4 John Paul, *Letter to Families*, §19.

5 Consider, for instance, Hans Jonas, *The Gnostic Religion* (Boston: Beacon, 1971), 338–39; Leon R. Kass, *Toward a More Natural Science*

(New York: Free Press, 1985), 277; Leon R. Kass, *Life, Liberty and the Defense of Dignity* (New York: Encounter, 2002), 43–45, 286–87; Martin Heidegger, "The Question concerning Technology," in *Basic Writings*, ed. D. F. Krell (New York: HarperCollins, 1993), 318–28. See also Robert P. George, *The Clash of Orthodoxies* (Wilmington, Del.: ISI Books, 2001), 7–11, 34–37.

6 John Paul, *Letter to Families*, §19, §13. See Kenneth L. Schmitz, *At the Center of the Human Drama* (Washington, D.C.: Catholic University of America Press, 1993).

7 John Paul, *Love and Responsibility*, 57; see also John Paul, *Man and Woman He Created Them: A Theology of the Body* (Toronto: Pauline, 2006), sermon 59, para. 3; and John Paul, *Letter to Families*, §13. See also Kass, *Life, Liberty*, 281ff.

8 "Utilitarianism is a channel, so to speak, along which the lives of individuals and of collectives have tended to flow throughout the ages. In modern times, however, what we have to deal with is a conscious utilitarianism formulated from philosophical premises." John Paul, *Love and Responsibility*, 35.

9 George Weigel, *Witness to Hope* (New York: HarperCollins, 1999), 172–73, recalls how one priest, upon reading *Love and Responsibility*, told John Paul, "'Now you must write a book on the person.'"

10 John Paul, *Letter to Families*, §13.

11 John Paul, *Love and Responsibility*, 21–23. See also John Paul, *The Acting Person* (Heidelberg: Springer, 1979), 76–80.

12 John Paul, *Love and Responsibility*, 26–27. John Paul mentions a debt to Kant, or at least sees in Kant someone who corroborates John Paul's findings (27–28). "The person can never be considered a means to an end; above all never a means of 'pleasure.' The person is and must be nothing other than the end of every act. Only then does the action correspond to the true dignity of the person." John Paul, *Letter to Families*, §12.

13 John Paul, *Love and Responsibility*, 26–27.

14 John Paul, *Love and Responsibility*, 28.

15 For John Paul, the sexual relationship is the paradigm case of the temptation to treat persons as objects. See *Love and Responsibility*, 30, 38–39, 43.

16 Immanuel Kant, *The Metaphysics of Morals*, in *Gesammelte Schriften* (Berlin: Koniglick-Preussishe Akademie Der Wissenschaften, 1907), 6:277–78 (my translation).

17 John Paul, *Letter to Families*, §9.

18 John Paul, *Love and Responsibility*, 28–30, 66.

19 John Paul, *Love and Responsibility*, 37, 38–39.

20 John Paul, *Evaluation of the Possibility of Constructing a Christian Ethics on the Assumptions of Max Scheler's System of Philosophy* (Rome: Logos, 1980), 196. See also John Paul, "Address of John Paul II to a Delegation of the World Institute of Phenomenology of Hanover" (papal address, Hanover, N.H., March 22, 2003), available at http://www.vatican.va/holy_father/john_paul_ii/speeches/2003/march/documents/hf_jp-ii_spe_20030322_hanover_en.html.

21 John Paul, *Evaluation*, 109.

22 John Paul, *Love and Responsibility*, 43.

23 John Paul, *Love and Responsibility*, 52–53.

24 Viladrich, *Agony of Legal Marriage*, 128–37, contains a similar treatment of love.

25 John Paul, *Love and Responsibility*, 76–78.

26 John Paul, *Love and Responsibility*, 96. Consider also the formulation in John Paul, *Letter to Families*, §12: "Every man and every woman fully realizes himself or herself through the sincere gift of self."

27 John Paul, *Love and Responsibility*, 96, 87.

28 John Paul, *Love and Responsibility*, 229–30. See also John Paul, *Veritatis Splendor* (papal encyclical, given in Rome on August 6, 1993), available at http://www.vatican.va/holy_father/john_paul_ii/encyclicals/documents/hf_jp-ii_enc_06081993_veritatis-splendor_en.html, §50: "The natural law . . . does not allow for any division between freedom and nature. Indeed, these two realities are harmoniously bound together, and each is intimately linked to the other."

29 Durkheim, *DMC* 247–52. Consider the findings of social science in this respect. Regarding the unhealthy effects of divorce on children, see Popenoe, *Life without Father*, chaps. 1–2; Wilson, *Marriage Problem*, chap. 7; Hymowitz, *Marriage and Caste,* chaps. 5–7; and Fukuyama, *Great Disruption*, chaps. 2 and 6. Regarding how divorce violates the principle of self-interest rightly understood, see Waite and Gallagher, *Case for Marriage*, chaps. 3–6.

30 John Paul, "Address of John Paul II to the Prelate Auditors, Officials and Advocates of the Tribunal of the Roman Rota" (papal address, Rome, January 28, 2002), available at http://www.vatican.va/holy_father/john_paul_ii/speeches/2002/january/documents/hf_jp-ii_spe_20020128_roman-rota_en.htm, ¶8.

31 For Hegel, "marriage should be regarded as indissoluble *in itself*, for the end of marriage is the ethical end, which is so exalted that everything else appears powerless against it and subject to its authority. Marriage should not be disrupted by passion, for the latter is subordinate to it" (*PR* ¶163A). See also Hegel's account of the "subjective origin of marriage" in the "*particular inclination* of the two persons" and the "objective origin" of marriage in their willingness to form a single person in marriage (*PR* ¶162).

32 John Paul, *Love and Responsibility*, 215.

33 Hegel, *PR* ¶163, ¶l63A; also *PR* ¶176. In Matthew 19:8, Christ explains the actions of Moses in allowing for divorce in the law of the Israelites, but Christ immediately amends the Mosaic teaching when he contends that "in the beginning it was not so." It is also clear that Christ intends to show that marriage should be indissoluble—Hegel, in effect, puts the Pharisees' position into the mouth of Christ.

34 Cf. John Paul, "Address to the Roman Rota," ¶4; with Hegel, ¶*PR* 163, ¶163A.

35 Hegel, *PR* ¶176A.

36 He also mentions the case where husband and wife are psychologically and physiologically incompatible with one another and argues that such "a condition warrants separation 'from bed and table,' but cannot annul the fact that they are objectively united, and united in wedlock." John Paul, *Love and Responsibility*, 215.

37 John Paul, *Love and Responsibility*, 214.

38 Mary Ann Glendon, *Abortion and Divorce in Western Law* (Cambridge, Mass.: Harvard University Press, 1987), 63ff.

39 John Paul, *Love and Responsibility*, 213.

40 John Paul, *Letter to Families*, §19.

41 Hegel, *PR* ¶158A.

42 John Paul, *Love and Responsibility*, 81, 125–26, 129, 97; and John Paul, *Letter to Families*, §11. Both Hegel and John Paul use the concept of love to combat Kant's pitiful attempt to define marriage as a mutual ownership to things.

43 John Paul, *Familiaris Consortio*, §19, §18.

44 Consider Hegel, *PR* ¶258: "The state is the actuality of the substantial *will*, an actuality which it possesses in the particular *self-consciousness* when this has been raised to its universality; as such, it is the *rational* in and for itself. This substantial unity is an absolute and unmoved

end in itself, and in it, freedom enters into its highest right, just as this ultimate end possesses the highest right in relation to individuals, whose *highest duty* is to be members of the state."

45 Manent, *City of Man*, 159–60.

46 John Paul, *Love and Responsibility*, 135, 136.

47 John Paul, *Letter to Families*, para. 10. John Paul is referring to Augustine, *The Confessions* (book 1, chap. 1, para. 1).

48 Consider, for instance, John Paul, *Love and Responsibility*, 130.

49 John Paul, *Familiaris Consortio*, §23.

50 John Paul, *Familiaris Consortio*, §46, "The Charter of Rights."

51 John Paul, *Familiaris Consortio*, §23.

52 Consider William E. May, *Marriage: The Rock on Which the Family Is Built* (San Francisco: Ignatius, 1995), 59: "I do not mean to foreclose the possibility that in specific families the wife-mother may be the one who contributes most economically to the family. It may be that she has special talents and has acquired more marketably profitable capacities and could therefore more adequately meet the financial needs of the family than could the husband-fathers."

53 John Paul, *Love and Responsibility*, 132.

54 John Paul, *Love and Responsibility*, 111–14.

55 John Paul, *Theology of the Body*, sermon 21, para. 3 and 4.

56 John Paul, *Love and Responsibility*, 259.

57 John Paul, *Love and Responsibility*, 270–78.

58 John Paul, *Love and Responsibility*, 228.

59 Weigel, *Witness to Hope*, 206–10, argues that John Paul's position on birth control lies between the permissiveness of the majority report from the Papal Birth Control Commission, which would have approved birth control within the totality of marital experience, and Pope Paul's *Humanae Vitae*, which rejected artificial birth control. This middle position involved such hedging as discussed in the preceding paragraph, which seems to suggest sympathy with the majority report.

60 John Paul, *Familiaris Consortio*, §32.

61 John Paul, *Love and Responsibility*, 229, 230.

62 This is the central point in the work of George, *Clash of Orthodoxies*, 11, 77–80; and George, "What's Sex," 149–57. George writes, "Marriage is a two-in-one-flesh communion of persons that is consum-

mated and actualized by acts that are reproductive in type, whether or not they are reproductive in effect." *Clash of Orthodoxies*, 77.

63 Here the voices of social science and revelation are in harmony. Consider especially George Akerlof, Janet L. Yellen, and Michael L. Katz, "An Analysis of Out-of-Wedlock Childbearing in the United States," *Quarterly Journal of Economics* 111 (1996): 277–317; George Akerlof, "Men without Children," *Economic Journal* 108 (1998): 287–309; and Robert T. Michael, "Why Did the U.S. Divorce Rate Double within a Decade?" in *Research in Population Economics*, ed. T. Paul Schultz (Greenwich, Conn.: JAI Press, 1988).

64 Louis Janssens, "Considerations on *Humanae Vitae*," *Louvian Studies* 2 (1969): 249.

65 John Paul, *Love and Responsibility*, 82, 87–88, 99, 105, 107, 144, 124, 128, 136, 139.

Chapter 12

1 Longman, *Empty Cradle*, 34–36; Popenoe, *Disturbing the Nest*, 295–99.

2 Advocates of the family's end see just such a transfer of power and function from the family to the state. See especially Jan E. Dizard and Howard Gadlin, *Minimal Family* (Amherst: University of Massachusetts Press, 1992), who envisage a "shift in the locus of responsibility for well-being, one's own as well as that of others, from the family to the broader community" (201).

3 Locke, *2T* 83.

4 Consider the Law Commission of Canada, "Beyond Conjugality"; its American counterpart from the American Law Institute, *Law of Family Dissolution*; and *Goodridge v. Department of Public Health*, 798 N.E. 2nd 941 (2003), majority opinion, 5: "The exclusive and permanent commitment of the marriage partners to one another, not the begetting of children . . . is the sine qua non of civil marriage." It is difficult to ascertain what "exclusive" and "permanent" mean in this context.

5 Daniel Cere, "Redefining Marriage and Family: Trends in North American Jurisprudence," Family Law Project, Harvard University, 24. See also the collection of contemporary statements in Blankenhorn, *Future of Marriage*, 11–15.

6 Consider this as an application of Strauss, "What Is Political Philosophy?" 50.

7 Consider Goldscheider and Waite, *New Families*, 8–12, 31, 41, 53, 72ff., 83–84, and 202–5; and W. Bradford Wilcox, *Soft Patriarchs, New Men* (Chicago: University of Chicago Press, 2004), 7–15, 99–104.

8 Wilcox, *Soft Patriarchs*, 99–104, relates that, in contemporary society, religious practice correlates to greater paternal involvement in a child's life and higher marital satisfaction, though not a more egalitarian division of labor. In what he calls a brief excursus, Wilcox suggests that this might be because religious practice endows family life with collective purpose and transcendent significance. I would only add that this digression contains what I believe is the key insight: a unified self-image of marriage and family life drives its success.

9 Consider Plato's treatment of democracy in *The Republic*, 557b–563e, especially 559d–562a; and Hans Jonas, *The Imperative of Responsibility* (Chicago: University of Chicago Press, 1985), 94–110.

10 Consider Goldscheider and Waite, *New Families*, 111–23, 138–39; Wilcox, *Soft Patriarchs*, 146–50.

11 Consider the discussion of familialism, communitarian families, and the "institutional theory" of marriage in Wilcox, *Soft Patriarchs*, 49, 161–65, 174–76, 182–87.

12 Manent, *World beyond Politics*, 139.

13 Cf. the advocates of self-creation and transcendence, Mill, *OL* 261–62; Marx, *German Ideology*, 169; and Beauvoir, *Second Sex*, xxxv, 34, 60, 74, 624, with those developing an internal critique of this brand of autonomy: Myers, *Only Star and Compass*, 130–31 (plausibly imputing this view to Locke); Hegel, *PR* ¶5A, ¶15, ¶15A, ¶17, ¶17A; John Paul, *Love and Responsibility*, 119–20; John Paul, *Veritatis Splendor*, §32, §46; Jonas, *Imperative of Responsibility*, 125–26, 140–42; Joseph Cardinal Ratzinger, *Truth and Tolerance* (San Francisco: Ignatius, 2004), 242–49; Viladrich, *Agony of Legal Marriage*, 38–44.

14 Firestone, *Dialectic of Sex*, 126.

15 Popenoe, *Disturbing the Nest*, 302–4, 330–31; Berger, *Family in the Modern Age*, 33–37; Wilson, *Marriage Problem*, 92–105 (esp. 104); Wilcox, *Soft Patriarchs*, 22–23.

16 Contemporary scholars such as Philip Blumstein and Pepper Schwartz, *American Couples: Money, Work, Sex* (New York: Pocket Books, 1985); Stacey, *Name of the Family*; Goldscheider and Waite, *New Families*,

4–5 (and passim in discussion of "new families"); and McClain, *Place of Families*, 151ff., defend their vision of companionate marriage on the grounds of Mill and Russell and on the more radical grounds of Beauvoir and Friedan.

17 Wilcox, *Soft Patriarchs*, 161.

18 Waite and Gallagher, *Case for Marriage*, passim.

19 Wilcox, *Soft Patriarchs*, 176–80, 183–89, 208–12.

20 Carl Rogers, "The Implications of Client-Centered Therapy for Family Life," in *On Becoming a Person* (New York: Mariner Books, 1995), 328.

21 Hans Jonas seeks to define parenthood as the archetype of responsibility and responsibility as the most germane virtue of modern times. His effort, in my view, ignores the connection between sex and procreation and hence among love, marriage, and parenthood.

Bibliography

Akerlof, George. "Men without Children." *Economic Journal* 108 (1998): 287–309.

Akerlof, George, Janet L. Yellen, and Michael L. Katz. "An Analysis of Out-of-Wedlock Childbearing in the United States." *Quarterly Journal of Economics* 111 (1996): 277–317.

Amato, Paul, and Alan Booth. *A Generation at Risk: Growing Up in a Time of Family Upheaval*. Cambridge, Mass.: Harvard University Press, 1997.

American Law Institute. *Principles of the Law of Family Dissolution: Analysis and Recommendations*. Philadelphia: American Law Institute, 2002.

Annas, Julia. "Mill and the Subjection of Women." *Philosophy* 52 (1977): 179–94.

Aries, Philippe. *Centuries of Childhood*. London: Jonathan Cape, 1962.

Aristotle. *Nicomachean Ethics*. Translated by Martin Ostwald. New York: Macmillan, 1962.

———. *The Politics*. Translated by Carnes Lord. Chicago: University of Chicago Press, 1984.

Arnhart, Larry. *Darwinian Conservatism*. Charlottesville, Va.: Imprint Academic, 2005.

———. *Darwinian Natural Right*. New York: SUNY Press, 1998.

———. "Friedrich Hayek's Darwinian Conservatism." In Hunt and McNamara, *Liberalism, Conservatism*, 127–48.

Arp, Kristana. "Beauvoir's Concept of Bodily Alienation." In Simons, *Feminist Interpretations*, 161–78.

Augustine. *City of God*. In *Political Writings*, translated by Michael W. Tkacz and Douglas Kries. Indianapolis: Hackett, 1994.

———. *The Confessions*. Translated by Edward Pusey. New York: Modern Library, 1876.

Avineri, Schlomo. *Hegel's Theory of the Modern State*. Cambridge: Cambridge University Press, 1974.

———. *The Social and Political Thought of Karl Marx*. Cambridge: Cambridge University Press, 1970.

Bain, Alexander. *John Stuart Mill, A Criticism*. London: Longmans, 1882.

Barber, Benjamin. "Spirit's Phoenix and History's Owl." *Political Theory* 16 (1988): 5–28.

Beauvoir, Simone de. *The Second Sex*. Translated by H. M. Parshley. New York: Vintage, 1989.

Behnegar, Alice. "Women in Tocqueville's *Democracy in America*." In Velasquez, *Love and Friendship*, 339–76.

Benhabib, Seyla. "On Hegel, Women, and Irony." In *Feminist Interpretations of G. W. F. Hegel*, edited by Patricia Jagentowicz Mills, 25–44. University Park: Penn State University Press, 1996.

Berger, Brigitte. *The Family in the Modern Age: More Than a Lifestyle Choice*. New Brunswick, N.J.: Transaction, 2002.

Berger, Brigitte, and Peter Berger. *The War over the Family: Capturing the Middle Ground*. New York: Doubleday, 1983.

Bergoffen, Debra B. "Out from Under: Beauvoir's Philosophy of the Erotic." In Simons, *Feminist Interpretations*, 179–92.

Bernard, Jessie. *The Future of Marriage*. New York: Bantam, 1973.

Biskupic, Joan. "Ruth Bader Ginsburg: Feminist Justice." *Washington Post*, April 17, 1995.

Blackstone, William. *Commentaries on the Laws of England*. 4 vols. Chicago: University of Chicago Press, 1979.

Blankenhorn, David. *Fatherless America*. New York: HarperCollins, 1995.

———. *The Future of Marriage*. New York: Encounter, 2007.

Bloom, Allan. *The Closing of the American Mind*. New York: Simon & Schuster, 1987.

———. *Love & Friendship*. New York: Simon & Schuster, 1993.

Blum, Carol. *Rousseau and the Republic of Virtue*. Ithaca, N.Y.: Cornell University Press, 1989.

Blumstein, Philip, and Pepper Schwartz. *American Couples: Money, Work, Sex*. New York: Pocket Books, 1985.

Botting, Eileen Hunt. *Family Feuds*. New York: SUNY Press, 2006.

Brennan, Theresa, and Carole Pateman. "Mere Auxiliaries to the Commonwealth." In Hirschman and McClure, *Feminist Interpretations*, 51–73.

Browning, Don S., Bonnie J. Miller-McLemore, Pamela D. Couture, K. Brynolf Lyon, and Robert M. Franklin. *From Culture Wars to Common Ground*. 2nd ed. Louisville, Ky.: Westminster John Knox, 2000.

Buss, David. *The Evolution of Desire*. New York: Basic Books, 1975.

Butler, Judith. "Sex and Gender in Simone de Beauvoir's *Second Sex*." In "Simone de Beauvoir: Witness to a Century," edited by Helene Vivienne Wenzel. Special issue, *Yale French Studies* 72 (1986): 35–49.

Butler, Melissa. "Early Liberal Roots of Feminism: John Locke's Attack on Patriarchy." In Hirschman and McClure, *Feminist Interpretations*, 91–122.

Calvin, John. *Institutes of the Christian Religion*. Translated by Henry Beveridge. 2 vols. Grand Rapids: Eerdmans, 1957.

Capaldi, Nicholas. *John Stuart Mill: A Biography*. Cambridge: Cambridge University Press, 2004.

Carlson, Alan. *Conjugal America*. New Brunswick, N.J.: Transaction Publishers, 2007.

Cere, Daniel. "Redefining Marriage and Family: Trends in North American Jurisprudence." Family Law Project, Harvard University, 2003.

Cicero. *De Officiis*. Translated by Walter Miller. Loeb Classical Library. Cambridge, Mass.: Harvard University Press, 1913.

Comte, Auguste. "A Course in Positive Philosophy." In *The Essential Comte*, edited by Stanislav Andreski. London: Harper & Row, 1974.

———. *The Positive Philosophy of Auguste Comte*. Translated by Harriet Martineau. London: Calvin Blanchard, 1855.

———. *System of Positive Polity*. Translated by John Henry Bridges. 4 vols. London: Longmans, Green, 1875–1877.

Comte, Auguste, and John Stuart Mill. *The Correspondence of John Stuart Mill and Auguste Comte*. Edited and translated by Oscar Haac. New Brunswick, N.J.: Transaction, 1995.

Coole, Diana H. *Women in Political Theory*. 2nd ed. Boulder, Colo.: Lynne Rienner, 1993.

Coontz, Stephanie. *Marriage, a History: From Obedience to Intimacy, or How Love Conquered Marriage*. New York: Viking, 2005.

Degler, Carl N. *In Search of Human Nature*. Oxford: Oxford University Press, 1993.

Dizard, Jan E., and Howard Gadlin. *Minimal Family*. Amherst: University of Massachusetts Press, 1992.

Dobbs, Darrel. "Family Matters: Aristotle's Appreciation of Women and the Plural Structure of Society." *American Political Science Review* 90, no. 1 (1996): 74–89.

Draper, Hal. "Marx and Engels on Women's Liberation." *International Socialism* 40 (1970): 20–29.

Duncan, Graeme. *Marx and Mill.* Cambridge: Cambridge University Press, 1977.

Durkheim, Emile. "The Conjugal Family." In Traugott, *Durkheim on Institutional Analysis*, 229–39.

———. *The Division of Labor in Society*. New York: Free Press, 1997.

———. "Divorce by Mutual Consent." In Traugott, *Durkheim on Institutional Analysis*, 240–52.

———. "A Durkheim Fragment." *American Journal of Sociology* 70, no. 5 (1965): 527–36.

———. *Emile Durkheim: Contributions to "L'Annee Sociologique."* Edited by Yash Nandan. New York: Free Press, 1994.

———. "Introduction to the Sociology of the Family." In Traugott, *Durkheim on Institutional Analysis*, 205–28.

———. *Montesquieu and Rousseau: Forerunners of Sociology*. Ann Arbor: University of Michigan Press, 1960.

———. "Montesquieu's Contribution to the Rise of Social Science." In Durkheim, *Montesquieu and Rousseau*, 1–64.

———. *Moral Education*. New York: Free Press, 1973.

———. "Professional Ethics and Civic Morals." In *Readings from Emile Durkheim*, edited by Kenneth Thompson, 139–58. New York: Routledge, 1985.

———. "Review of Marianne Weber, *Ehefrau und Mutter in der Rechtsentwicklung*." In Traugott, *Durkheim on Institutional Analysis*, 139–44.

———. *Suicide*. New York: Free Press, 1997.

Eberstadt, Mary. *Home-Alone America*. New York: Penguin, 2004.

Ehrenreich, Barbara, Elizabeth Hess, and Gloria Jacobs. *Remaking Love: The Feminization of Sex*. Garden City, N.Y.: Anchor, 1987.

Eisenstein, Zillah. *The Radical Future of Liberal Feminism*. New York: Longmans, 1981.

Elshtain, Jean Bethke. *Public Man, Private Woman*. Princeton, N.J.: Princeton University Press, 1981.

Engels, Frederick. *The Origin of the Family, Private Property and the State*. Edited by Eleanor Burke Leacock. New York: International Publishers, 1972.

———. "Principles of Communism." In *The Communist Manifesto*, translated by Paul Sweezy. New York: Modern Reader Paperbacks, 1968.

Fermon, Nicole. *Domesticating Passions*. Middletown, Conn.: Wesleyan University Press, 1997.

Filmer, Robert. *Patriarcha and Other Writings*. Edited by Johann Sommerville. Cambridge: Cambridge University Press, 1991.

Fineman, Martha. *The Autonomy Myth*. London: New Press, 2005.

Firestone, Shulamith. *Dialectic of Sex*. New York: Bantam, 1970.

Foster, David. "Taming the Father: John Locke's Critique of Patriarchal Fatherhood." *Review of Politics* 56 (Fall 1994): 641–70.

Fox-Genovese, Elizabeth. *Marriage: The Dream That Refuses to Die*. Wilmington, Del.: ISI Books, 2008.

Freud, Sigmund. *Beyond the Pleasure Principle*. New York: Norton, 1990.

———. *Civilization and Its Discontents*. New York: Norton, 2005.

———. "'Civilized' Sexual Morality and Modern Nervous Illness." In Freud, *Complete Psychological Works*, 9:177–204.

———. "Future of an Illusion." In Freud, *Complete Psychological Works*, 21:5–58.

———. "Sexuality in the Aetiology of the Neuroses." In Freud, *Complete Psychological Works*, 3:259–85.

———. *The Standard Edition of the Complete Psychological Works of Sigmund Freud*. Edited by James Strachey. 24 vols. London: Hogarth, 1953–1974.

———. *Three Essays on the Theory of Sexuality*. New York: Basic Books, 2000.

———. *Totem and Taboo*. In Freud, *Complete Psychological Works*, 13:1–255.

Friedan, Betty. *The Feminine Mystique*. New York: Norton, 1997.

———. "Sex, Society, and the Female Dilemma: A Dialogue between Simone de Beauvoir and Betty Friedan." *Saturday Review*, June 14, 1975.

Fromm, Erich. *The Crisis of Psychoanalysis*. Greenwich, Conn.: Fawcett Premier, 1971.

Fukuyama, Francis. *The Great Disruption*. New York: Free Press, 1999.

———. *Our Posthuman Future*. New York: Picador, 2003.

Garrison, Marsha. "Marriage Matters." In Wilson, *Reconceiving the Family*, 305–30.

George, Robert P. *The Clash of Orthodoxies*. Wilmington, Del.: ISI Books, 2001.

———. "What's Sex Got to Do with It?" In *The Meaning of Marriage*, edited by Robert George and Jean Bethke Elshtain, 142–71. Dallas, Tex.: Spence, 2006.

Gilden, Hilail. "Mill's *On Liberty*." In *Ancients and Moderns*, edited by Joseph Cropsey, 288–303. New York: Basic Books, 1964.

Glendon, Mary Ann. *Abortion and Divorce in Western Law*. Cambridge, Mass.: Harvard University Press, 1987.

———. *The Transformation of Family Law*. Chicago: University of Chicago Press, 1989.

Goldberg, Steven. *Why Men Rule: A Theory of Male Dominance*. Peru, Ill.: Open Court, 1999.

Goldscheider, Frances K., and Linda J. Waite. *New Families, No Families?* Berkeley: University of California Press, 1993.

Goldstein, Leslie. "Mill, Marx, and Women's Liberation." *Journal of the History of Philosophy* 18, no. 3 (1980): 319–34.

Graff, E. G. *What Is Marriage For?* Boston: Beacon, 1999.

Gutman, Amy. *Democratic Education*. Princeton, N.J.: Princeton University Press, 1999.

Hamburger, Joseph. *John Stuart Mill on Liberty and Control*. Princeton, N.J.: Princeton University Press, 1999.

Hardimon, Michael O. *Hegel's Social Philosophy*. Cambridge: Cambridge University Press, 1994.

Hayek, Friedrich. *The Constitution of Liberty*. Chicago: University of Chicago Press, 1978.

———. *The Fatal Conceit*. Chicago: University of Chicago Press, 1991.

———. "The Use of Knowledge in Society." Chap. 4 in *Individualism and Economic Order*. Chicago: University of Chicago Press, 1996.

Hegel, G. W. F. *Elements of the Philosophy of Right*. Translated by Allen Wood. Cambridge: Cambridge University Press, 1991.

———. "Fragment on Love." In *Early Theological Writings*, translated by T. M. Knox, 302–8. Philadelphia: University of Pennsylvania Press, 1971.

———. *Philosophy of History*. New York: Dover, 1956.

Heidegger, Martin. "The Question concerning Technology." In *Basic Writings*, edited by D. F. Krell, 307–42. New York: HarperCollins, 1993.

Herodotus. *The Histories*. Translated by David Grene. Chicago: University of Chicago Press, 1987.

Himmelfarb, Gertrude. *On Liberty and Liberalism*. New York: Knopf, 1974.

Hirschman, Nancy J., and Kristie M. McClure, eds. *Feminist Interpretations of John Locke*. University Park: Penn State University Press, 2007.

Holloway, Carson. *The Right Darwin?* Dallas, Tex.: Spence, 2008.

———. *The Way of Life*. Waco, Tex.: Baylor University Press, 2008.

Hrdy, Sarah B. *Mothers and Others: The Evolutionary Origins of Mutual Understanding*. Cambridge, Mass.: Belknap, 2009.

Hume, David. *The History of England*. 6 vols. Indianapolis, Ind.: Liberty Fund, 1983.

———. "Of Polygamy and Divorce." In *Essays Moral, Political and Literary*, edited by Eugene Miller, 181–90. Indianapolis, Ind.: Liberty Fund, 1987.

Hunt, Louis, and Peter M. McNamara, eds. *Liberalism, Conservatism, and Hayek's Idea of Spontaneous Order*. New York: Palgrave Macmillan, 2007.

Hymowitz, Kay S. *Marriage and Caste in America*. Chicago: Ivan R. Dee, 2006.

Institute for American Values. "The Marriage Movement: A Statement of Principles." New York: Institute for American Values, 2000. http://www.americanvalues.org/pdfs/marriagemovement.pdf (accessed January 2010).

Janssens, Louis. "Considerations on *Humanae Vitae*." *Louvian Studies* 2 (1969): 231–53.

Jensen, Pamela. "Dangerous Liaisons." In Velasquez, *Love and Friendship*, 183–228.

John Paul II [Karol Wojtyla]. *The Acting Person*. Heidelberg: Springer, 1979.

———. "Address of John Paul II to a Delegation of the World Institute of Phenomenology of Hanover." Papal address, Hanover, N.H., March 22, 2003. Available at http://www.vatican.va/holy_father/john_paul_ii/speeches/2003/march/documents/hf_jp-ii_spe_20030322_hanover_en.html.

———. "Address of John Paul II to the Prelate Auditors, Officials and Advocates of the Tribunal of the Roman Rota." Papal address, Rome, January 28, 2002. Available at http://www.vatican.va/holy_father/john_paul_ii/speeches/2002/january/documents/hf_jp-ii_spe_20020128_roman-rota_en.html.

———. *Evaluation of the Possibility of Constructing a Christian Ethics on the Assumptions of Max Scheler's System of Philosophy*. Rome: Logos, 1980.

———. *Evangelium Vitae*. Papal encyclical, given in Rome on March 25, 1995. Available at http://www.vatican.va/holy_father/john_

paul_ii/encyclicals/documents/hf_jp-ii_enc_25031995_evangelium-vitae_en.html.

———. *Familiaris Consortio*. Apostolic exhortation, given in Rome on November 22, 1981. Available at http://www.vatican.va/holy_father/john_paul_ii/apost_exhortations/documents/hf_jp-ii_exh_19811122_familiaris-consortio_en.html.

———. *Letter to Families*. Papal letter, given in Rome on February 2, 1994. Available at http://www.vatican.va/holy_father/john_paul_ii/letters/documents/hf_jp-ii_let_02021994_families_en.html.

———. *Love and Responsibility*. San Francisco: Ignatius, 1981.

———. *Man and Woman He Created Them: A Theology of the Body*. Toronto: Pauline, 2006.

———. *Veritatis Splendor*. Papal encyclical, given in Rome on August 6, 1993. Available at http://www.vatican.va/holy_father/john_paul_ii/encyclicals/documents/hf_jp-ii_enc_06081993_veritatis-splendor_en.html.

Jonas, Hans. *The Gnostic Religion*. Boston: Beacon, 1971.

———. *The Imperative of Responsibility*. Chicago: University of Chicago Press, 1985.

———. "Philosophical Aspects of Darwinism." In *The Phenomenon of Life*, 38–63. New York: Harper & Row, 1966.

Kant, Immanuel. *The Metaphysics of Morals*, in *Gesammelte Schriften*, 6: 205–493. Berlin: Koniglick-Preussishe Akademie Der Wissenschaften, 1907.

Kass, Leon R. *Life, Liberty and the Defense of Dignity*. New York: Encounter, 2002.

———. *Toward a More Natural Science*. New York: Free Press, 1985.

Krause, Sharon. "Lady Liberty's Allure." *Philosophy and Social Criticism* 26, no. 1 (2000): 1–24.

Kremer, Mark. "Simone de Beauvoir's *The Second Sex*." In Velasquez, *Love and Friendship*, 479–500.

Krouse, Richard W. "Patriarchal Liberalism and Beyond: From John Stuart Mill to Harriet Taylor." In *The Family in Political Thought*, edited by Jean Bethke Elshtain, 145–72. Amherst: University of Massachusetts Press, 1982.

Lamanna, Mary Ann. *Emile Durkheim on the Family*. Thousand Oaks, Calif.: Sage, 2001.

Landes, Joan B. "Hegel's Conception of the Family." *Polity* 14 (1981): 5–28.

———. *Women and the Public Sphere in the Age of the French Revolution.* Ithaca, N.Y.: Cornell University Press, 1988.

Lasch, Christopher. *Haven in a Heartless World.* New York: Norton, 1995.

Laslett, Peter. *Family-Life and Illicit Love in Earlier Generations.* Cambridge: Cambridge University Press, 1977.

Law Commission of Canada. "Beyond Conjugality." 2001. http://www.samesexmarriage.ca/docs/beyond_conjugality.pdf (accessed February 2009).

Lawler, Peter Augustine. *Homeless and At Home in America.* South Bend, Ind.: St. Augustine's, 2007.

———. *Stuck with Virtue.* Wilmington, Del.: ISI Books, 2005.

Lecky, William Edward Hartpole. *History of European Morals.* 2 vols. New York: Appleton, 1869.

Lehmann, Jennifer M. *Durkheim and Women.* Lincoln: University of Nebraska Press, 1994.

———. "Durkheim's Theories of Deviance and Suicide: A Feminist Reconsideration." *American Journal of Sociology* 100 (1995): 904–30.

Locke, John. *Essay Concerning Human Understanding.* 2 vols. New York: Dover, 1959.

———. *Some Thoughts Concerning Education.* Edited by Ruth Grant. Indianapolis, Ind.: Hackett, 1996.

———. *Two Treatises of Government.* Edited by Peter Laslett. Cambridge: Cambridge University Press, 1960.

———. "Virtus." In *Political Writings*, edited by David Wootton, 240–41. Indianapolis, Ind.: Hackett, 2003.

Longman, Phillip. *The Empty Cradle.* New York: Basic Books, 2004.

Luther, Martin. "Explanation of the Fourth Commandment." In *Small Catechism.* St. Louis: Concordia Publishing House, 1943.

Machiavelli, Niccolo. *The Prince.* Translated by Harvey C. Mansfield Jr. Chicago: University of Chicago Press, 1985.

Manent, Pierre. *The City of Man.* Translated by Marc A. LePain. Princeton, N.J.: Princeton University Press, 2000.

———. *A World beyond Politics?* Translated by Marc LePain. Princeton, N.J.: Princeton University Press, 2006.

Mansbridge, Jane. *Why We Lost the ERA.* Chicago: University of Chicago Press, 1986.

Mansfield, Harvey C. *Manliness.* New Haven, Conn.: Yale University Press, 2006.

Marcuse, Herbert. *Eros and Civilization.* Boston: Beacon, 1965.

Marquardt, Elizabeth. *Between Two Worlds.* New York: Three Rivers, 2006.

Marx, Karl. *Capital.* Edited by Frederick Engels. New York: Modern Library, 1906.

———. *Early Writings.* New York: Penguin, 1992.

———. *Economic and Philosophic Manuscripts of 1844.* In Marx and Engels, *Collected Works*, 3:229–348.

———. *The German Ideology.* Amherst, N.Y.: Prometheus, 1998.

———. "On the Divorce Bill." In Marx and Engels, *Collected Works*, 1:307–10.

———. "On the Jewish Question." In Marx and Engels, *Collected Works*, 3:146–74.

———. *The Poverty of Philosophy.* In Marx and Engels, *Collected Works*, 6:105–212.

Marx, Karl, and Friedrich Engels. *Collected Works.* 50 vols. New York: International Publishers, 1975–2005.

———. *The Communist Manifesto.* Edited by Samuel H. Beer. Wheeling, Ill.: Harlan Davidson, 1955.

———. *The Holy Family.* Honolulu, Hawaii: University Press of the Pacific, 2002.

May, William E. *Marriage: The Rock on Which the Family Is Built.* San Francisco: Ignatius, 1995.

McClain, Linda. *The Place of Families.* Cambridge, Mass.: Harvard University Press, 2006.

McDonald, Forrest. *Novus Ordo Seclorum.* Lawrence: University Press of Kansas, 1986.

McLaren, Angus. "Contraception and Its Discontents: Sigmund Freud and Birth Control." *Journal of Social History* 12 (Summer 1979): 513–29.

Michael, Robert T. "Why Did the U.S. Divorce Rate Double within a Decade?" In *Research in Population Economics*, edited by T. Paul Schultz, 367–99. Greenwich, Conn.: JAI Press, 1988.

Mill, John Stuart. *The Collected Works of John Stuart Mill.* 33 vols. Toronto: University of Toronto Press, 1963–1991.

Montaigne. "Of Friendship." In *Complete Essays of Montaigne*, translated by Donald M. Frame, 135–44. Stanford: Stanford University Press, 1957.

Morgan, Patricia. *The War between the State and the Family*. New Brunswick, N.J.: Transaction, 2008.

Morgenstern, Mira. *Rousseau and the Politics of Ambiguity*. University Park: Penn State University Press, 1996.

Morse, Jennifer Roback. *Love and Economics*. Dallas, Tex.: Spence, 2001.

Myers, Peter C. *Only Star and Compass*. Lanham, Md.: Rowman & Littlefield, 1999.

Okin, Susan Moller. *Justice, Gender and the Family*. New York: Basic Books, 1991.

———. *Women in Western Political Theory*. Princeton, N.J.: Princeton University Press, 1979.

O'Neil, Nena, and George O'Neil. *Open Marriage*. New York: M. Evans, 1972.

Packe, Michael St. John. *The Life of John Stuart Mill*. New York: Capricorn, 1954.

Pangle, Thomas L. *The Spirit of Modern Republicanism*. Chicago: University of Chicago Press, 1990.

Parsons, Talcott. *Family Socialization and Interaction Process*. New York: Free Press, 1955.

———. *The Structure of Social Action*. New York: Free Press, 1970.

Pateman, Carole. *The Sexual Contract*. Stanford: Stanford University Press, 1988.

Pfeffer, Jacqueline L. "The Family in John Locke's Political Thought." *Polity* 33 (2001): 593–618.

Popenoe, David. *Disturbing the Nest*. New Brunswick, N.J.: Transaction, 1988.

———. *Life without Father: Compelling New Evidence That Fatherhood and Marriage Are Indispensable for the Good of Children and Society*. New York: Free Press, 1996.

———. *The War over the Family*. New Brunswick, N.J.: Transaction, 2008.

Pufendorf, Samuel. *On the Duty of Man and Citizen According to Natural Law*. Edited by James Tully. Translated by Michael Silverthorne. Cambridge: Cambridge University Press, 1991.

Ratzinger, Joseph Cardinal. *Truth and Tolerance*. San Francisco: Ignatius, 2004.

Rauch, Jonathan. *Gay Marriage: Why It Is Good for Gays, Good for Straights, and Good for America*. New York: Henry Holt and Company, 2004.

Rhoads, Steven E. *Taking Sex Differences Seriously*. New York: Encounter, 2004.

Richards, David A. J. *The Case for Gay Rights*. Lawrence: University Press of Kansas, 2005.

Rogers, Carl. *On Becoming a Person*. New York: Mariner Books, 1995.

Rougemont, Denis de. *Love in the Western World*. Princeton, N.J.: Princeton University Press, 1956.

Rousseau, Jean-Jacques. *Citizen of Geneva: Selections from the Letters of Jean-Jacques Rousseau*. Oxford: Oxford University Press, 1937.

———. *Discourse on Political Economy*. Translated by Judith R. Masters. New York: St. Martin's, 1978.

———. *Emile*. Translated by Allan Bloom. New York: Basic Books, 1979.

———. *Essay on the Origin of Languages*. Translated by John H. Moran. Chicago: University of Chicago Press, 1986.

———. *The First and Second Discourses*. Translated by Roger Masters and Judith Masters. New York: St. Martin's, 1969.

———. *On the Social Contract*. Translated by Judith R. Masters. New York: St. Martin's, 1978.

———. *Politics and the Arts: Letter to d'Alembert on the Theater*. Translated by Allan Bloom. Ithaca, N.Y.: Cornell University Press, 1968.

Rubinstein, Amnon. "Return of the Kibbutzim." *Jerusalem Post*, July 10, 2007.

Russell, Bertrand. *Marriage and Morals*. London: Allen & Unwin, 1929.

Sandel, Michael. *Democracy's Discontent*. Cambridge, Mass.: Harvard University Press, 1996.

Sax, Leonard. *Why Gender Matters*. New York: Doubleday, 2005.

Schmitz, Kenneth L. *At the Center of the Human Drama*. Washington, D.C.: Catholic University of America Press, 1993.

Schochet, Gordon. *The Authoritarian Family and Political Attitudes in 17th Century England*. New Brunswick, N.J.: Transaction, 1987.

———. *Patriarchalism in Political Thought*. New York: Basic Books, 1975.

Schwartz, Joel. *The Sexual Politics of Jean-Jacques Rousseau*. Chicago: University of Chicago Press, 1985.

Schwartz, Pepper. *Love Between Equals*. New York: Free Press, 1995.

Semmel, Bernard. *John Stuart Mill and the Practice of Virtue*. New Haven, Conn.: Yale University Press, 1984.

Shanley, Mary Lyndon. "Marital Slavery and Friendship." *Political Theory* 9 (1981): 229–47.

———. "Marriage Contract and Social Contract in Seventeenth Century Political Thought." In Hirschman and McClure, *Feminist Interpretations*, 17–38.

Simmons, Ernest J. *Leo Tolstoy*. London: John Lehman, 1949.

Simons, Margaret, ed. *Feminist Interpretations of Simone de Beauvoir*. University Park: Penn State University Press, 1995.

———. "*The Second Sex*: From Marxism to Radical Feminism." In Simons, *Feminist Interpretations*, 243–62.

Smith, Elizabeth S. "John Stuart Mill's *The Subjection of Women: A Reexamination*." *Polity* 34, no. 2 (2001): 181–203.

Smith, James. *Beyond Monogamy*. Baltimore: Johns Hopkins University Press, 1974.

Stacey, Judith. *In the Name of the Family: Rethinking the Family in a Postmodern Age*. Boston: Beacon, 1997.

Steinberger, Peter J. *Logic and Politics*. New Haven, Conn.: Yale University Press, 1988.

Stephen, James Fitzjames. *Liberty, Equality, Fraternity*. Edited by Stuart D. Warner. Indianapolis, Ind.: Liberty Fund, 1993.

Stone, Lawrence. *The Family, Sex and Marriage in England, 1500–1800*. New York: Harper & Row, 1977.

Strauss, Leo. "What Is Political Philosophy?" In *What Is Political Philosophy?* 9–55. Chicago: University of Chicago Press, 1988.

Sullivan, Andrew. *Virtually Normal: An Argument about Homosexuality*. New York: Vintage, 1996.

Tarcov, Nathan. *Locke's Education for Liberty*. Chicago: University of Chicago Press, 1989.

Taylor, Charles. *Hegel*. Cambridge: Cambridge University Press, 2008.

Tocqueville, Alexis de. *Democracy in America*. Translated by Harvey C. Mansfield Jr. and Delba Winthrop. Chicago: University of Chicago Press, 2000.

Traugott, Mark, ed. and trans. *Durkheim on Institutional Analysis*. Chicago: University of Chicago Press, 1985.

Trivers, R. L. "Parental Investment and Sexual Selection." In *Sexual Selection and the Descent of Man, 1871–1971*, edited by B. Campbell, 136–79. Chicago: Aldine, 1972.

Tubbs, David. *Freedom's Orphans*. Princeton, N.J.: Princeton University Press, 2007.

Urbinati, Nadia. "John Stuart Mill on Androgyny and Ideal Marriage." *Political Theory* 19, no. 4 (1991): 626–48.

Velasquez, Eduardo, ed. *Love and Friendship*. Lanham, Md.: Lexington, 2003.

———, ed. *Nature, Woman, and the Art of Politics*. Lanham, Md.: Rowman & Littlefield, 2000.

Velkley, Richard. "The Tension in the Beautiful: On Culture and Civilization in Rousseau and German Philosophy." In *The Legacy of Rousseau*, edited by Clifford Orwin and Nathan Tarcov, 65–86. Chicago: University of Chicago Press, 1997.

Viladrich, Pedro-Juan. *The Agony of Legal Marriage*. Pamplona: Servicio de Publicaciones de la Universidad de Navarra, 1990.

Waite, Linda, and Maggie Gallagher. *The Case for Marriage: Why Married People Are Happier, Healthier, and Better Off Financially*. New York: Broadway, 2000.

Wallerstein, Judith, Julia Lewis, and Sandra Blakeslee. *Unexpected Legacy of Divorce, A Landmark 25 Year Study*. New York: Hyperion, 2000.

Walzer, Michael. *Spheres of Justice*. New York: Basic Books, 1983.

Ward, Lee. "The Natural Rights Family." In Velasquez, *Nature, Woman*, 149–80.

Weigel, George. *Witness to Hope*. New York: HarperCollins, 1999.

Weiss, Penny, and Anne Harper. "Rousseau's Political Defense of the Sex-Roled Family." *Hypatia* 5 (1990): 90–109.

Westermarck, Edward. *History of Human Marriage*. 3 vols. New York: Allerton, 1922.

Whitehead, Barbara Defoe. *The Divorce Culture*. New York: Vintage, 1998.

Wilcox, W. Bradford. *Soft Patriarchs, New Men*. Chicago: University of Chicago Press, 2004.

———. *Why Marriage Matters*. 2nd ed. New York: Institute for American Values, 2005.

Wilson, David Sloan. *Darwin's Cathedral*. Chicago: University of Chicago Press, 2002.

Wilson, E. O. *On Human Nature*. Cambridge, Mass.: Harvard University Press, 1978.

Wilson, James Q. "Marriage, Evolution, and the Enlightenment." Lecture, American Enterprise Institute, May 3, 1999.

———. *The Marriage Problem: How Our Culture Has Weakened Families*. New York: HarperCollins, 2002.

———. *The Moral Sense*. New York: Free Press, 1997.

Wilson, Robin Fretwell, ed. *Reconceiving the Family*. Cambridge: Cambridge University Press, 2006.

Wingrove, Elizabeth Rose. *Rousseau's Republican Romance*. Princeton, N.J.: Princeton University Press, 2000.

Winkle, Deborah. "Convention and Constraint in the Education of Rousseau's Natural Woman." In Velasquez, *Nature, Woman*, 181–208.

Witte, John. *From Sacrament to Contract*. Louisville, Ky.: Westminster John Knox, 1997.

Wolfe, Alan. *One Nation, After All*. New York: Penguin, 1999.

Wolfe, Tom. *Hooking Up*. New York: Farrar, Straus, & Giroux, 2000.

Wolff, Robert Paul. "There's Nobody Here But Us Persons." In *Women and Philosophy*, edited by Carol C. Gould and Marx W. Wartofsky, 128–44. New York: Penguin, 1976.

Yenor, Scott E. "Spontaneous Order and the Problem of Religious Revolution." In Hunt and McNamara, *Liberalism, Conservatism*, 107–26.

Index